A SHORT HISTORY
OF THE WORLD

A SHORT HISTORY
OF THE WORLD

GEOFFREY BLAINEY

IVAN R. DEE

CHICAGO

A SHORT HISTORY OF THE WORLD. Copyright © 2000, 2002
by Geoffrey Blainey. Maps copyright © 2000 by Penguin Books Australia Ltd. All
rights reserved, including the right to reproduce this book or portions thereof in any
form. For information, address: Ivan R. Dee, Publisher, 1332 North Halsted Street,
Chicago 60622. Manufactured in the United States of America and printed on acid-
free paper.

First published by Penguin Books Australia Ltd., Victoria.

The paperback edition of this book carries the ISBN 1-56663-507-1.

Library of Congress Cataloging-in-Publication Data:
Blainey, Geoffrey.
    A short history of the world / Geoffrey Blainey.
        p. cm.
    Originally published: Ringwood, Vic.: Viking, 2000.
    ISBN 1-56663-421-0 (alk. paper)
    1. World history.   I. Title.

D23 .B48 2002
909—dc21   2001047623

CONTENTS

LIST OF MAPS

PREFACE

THIS IS an attempt to write a world history that is not too voluminous. I try to survey human history since the time when the first people left Africa to settle the globe: my survey ends in AD 2000. Inevitably, some large themes I investigated are described so fleetingly that they are like glimpses from the window of a passing train.

I resolved from the outset that I would pay attention to technology and skills, for they have done so much to shape the world. Certain skills that now seem primitive to us were initially a breakthrough for the human race. Likewise I gave much attention to the rise of the major religions, for they too are attempts to reshape the world. I looked also at geographical factors, for they often ordained what could not happen, what could not succeed. I gave some space to what people ate and how hard they worked in order to earn their daily bread. When the book was far advanced, I realized what must have once been obvious to everyone: the intense power of the moon, stars and the night sky on human experience and on the ways in which the universe was seen. Chapter Four, "The Dome of Night," and a section of the final chapter try to remedy that omission.

I found myself also looking at empires and the areas they covered. The size of the territory that one leader, or one state, can rule has grown progressively larger. For the first time in human history, world government of some sort is now possible: whether it is wise and whether it is wanted are other questions. Thus the shrinking of the world is one of the book's recurring themes. In 1966 I completed an Australian book called *The Tyranny of Distance*, and I find that some of the themes of that book are still in my mind when I try to look at the whole world.

A history of the world is not a substitute for an encyclopedia. I was conscious, from an early stage, of the danger of making the book too compressed, of trying to pack in too much. I began to realize that I was leading the readers on a long journey, parts of which had to be made with speed—otherwise the destination would never be reached. On the other hand, the journey occasionally had to be slowed down so that readers could look about them and savor a scene or milestone in the history of the human race. By design the book therefore is a mixture of fast movement and short periods of rest and meditation. Some of these pauses I wrote in advance, to ensure that they appeared at an appropriate place in the journey. Even though some of these leisurely episodes occupy perhaps more space than they deserve, they have their own value and symbolism. Among such episodes are the European man who died about 5,000 years ago and was recently found in the Alpine ice, still clothed and remarkably preserved; the way of life of the early Maoris of New Zealand; the influence of the Indian indigo plant on the color blue; the brides sacrificed in the rushing waters of the Yellow River in ancient China; Abraham Lincoln preparing to give his famous speech at Gettysburg; the strange death of the composer Tchaikovsky in tsarist Russia; and the signing of the peace on the deck of an American battleship in Tokyo harbor in 1945.

Europeans are mentioned little in some parts of the book. During the first dozen chapters, Europe rarely appears except as the home of the Greeks and the Romans. The continents of Africa, Asia and Asia Minor, and even the Americas, virtually dominate the story until it reaches the last 400 or 500 years when the European civilization has its turn at dominance. The United States and its very different kind of empire—what I call the "pale empire of ideas"—falls within the last few seconds of human history if measured by the ticking of a 60-minute clock.

One of the dilemmas was how much space to allot to the last 150 years. Such influential leaders as Garibaldi, Franklin Roosevelt, Winston Churchill, and Nasser surely deserve a mention; and such profound or symbolic events as the invention of anesthetics surely call for at least one paragraph; but they receive scant or no attention in this book. Such ideologies as Darwinism, socialism, fascism, and Keynesianism deserve elaboration, especially if the world of today is to be understood, but they receive inadequate attention. My relatively cramped treatment of the 20th century stems from a reluctance to permit that century to be as significant, indeed as self-important, as every century seems to those who live in it. When the history of the world is written in AD 2400, so many resounding events of our time will have receded in relevance or entered oblivion, just as many of the events that were momentous in Roman or Aztec times no longer raise our eyebrows. So this is the tightrope I have tried to walk.

The book's defects would have been larger but for the generous help and information I have received from many people. I especially thank Dr Jocelyn Chey of Sydney; Father Austin Cooper of the Catholic Theological College in Melbourne; Mr Raymond Flower of Sarnano, Italy; Dr Barry Jones, Peter Lawrence and Dr Malcolm Kennedy of Melbourne; Dr Glenn Mulligan and Dr Lotte Mulligan of La Trobe University; and Mr Kage-fumi Ueno, Japan's consul general in Melbourne. Katie Purvis of Penguin Books has been a fine editor. My indebtedness to others is expressed in the source notes at the back of the book.

I gained from visits to many museums and art galleries as well as libraries. I especially thank the Deutsches Museum in Munich, the Museum of Natural History and the Science Museum in London, the American Museum of Natural History in New York, and the libraries of the Melbourne, Ballarat, and La Trobe universities in Australia.

This book was first published in October 2000, in Australia. For subsequent printings I made minor corrections and alterations. The preface to this edition has also been altered for the benefit of American readers.

G. B.

Melbourne, October 2001

A SHORT HISTORY
OF THE WORLD

PART ONE

1

FROM AFRICA

THEY LIVED in Africa and, two million years ago, they were few. They were almost human beings, though they tended to be smaller than their descendants who now inhabit the world. They walked upright; they were also skilled climbers.

They ate mainly fruits, nuts, seeds and other food-plants but were beginning to eat meat. Their implements were primitive. If they tried to shape stone they did not carry the shaping very far. Probably they were capable of using a stick for defense or attack or even for digging—if a small rodent was hiding in a burrow. Whether they made simple shelters out of shrubs and sticks to ward off the cold winds in winter is not known. No doubt some lived in caves—if caves could be found—but such a permanent residence would have gravely restricted the mobility needed to find enough food, for their food must have varied according to the seasons. To live off the land called for long walks to the places where certain seeds or fruits could be found. Their diet was the result of a chain of discoveries, made over hundreds of thousands of years. A crucial discovery was whether a seemingly safe food-plant was poisonous. Scavenging for new foods in a time of drought and famine, some must have died or become seriously ill through poisoning.

Two million years ago these human beings—known as hominids—lived mainly in the lands now called Kenya, Tanzania and Ethiopia. If

Africa is divided into three horizontal zones, the human race occupied the middle or tropical zone. Probably much of it was grassland. Indeed, a change of climate one or two million years earlier, with grassland largely replacing forest in certain regions, might have encouraged these humans gradually to part company from their relatives—the apes—and spend more time on the ground.

They already had a long history, though they had no memory or record of it. We talk today of the vast span of time since the building of the pyramids in Egypt, but that span was merely a wink compared to the long history which the human race had already experienced. One early record has been uncovered in Tanzania. Two adults and a child were walking on top of volcanic ash softened by recent rain. Their footprints then were baked by the sun and slowly covered by layers of earth. The footprints, definitely human, are at least 3,600,000 years old. Even that is young in the history of the living world. The last of the dinosaurs were extinguished about 64,000,000 years ago.

In East Africa the early humans liked to camp on the shores of lakes and in sandy riverbeds or on the grassy plains: some of their remains have been found in such places. They were also able to adapt to cooler climates and in Ethiopia they preferred an open plateau at a height of 1,600 or 2,000 meters above sea level. In the evergreen forests of the uplands they were also at home. Their adaptability was impressive.

In the cutthroat contest to stay alive and to multiply, humans were usually successful. In their part of Africa they were far outnumbered by various species of large animals, some of them aggressive, but the humans flourished. Their population became too large for the resources of their area or perhaps a long drought drove them north. The evidence is strong that sometime around two million years ago they began to migrate farther north. The longest desert in the world—stretching from north-west Africa and past Arabia—may have temporarily blocked their way. The narrow land bridge between Africa and Asia Minor was easily crossed.

TREK INTO ASIA

They moved in small bands: they were explorers as well as settlers. In each unfamiliar region they had to adapt to new foods, and they had to watch for wild animals, venomous snakes and poisonous insects. The

4

people leading the way had one advantage. Those other stern opponents of territorial intruders, human beings, were not standing in their way.

It was more like a relay race than a trek. Possibly one group of maybe six or 12 moved a short distance and then settled down. Others came, leapfrogged them or drove them forward. The move across Asia might have taken 10,000 or 200,000 years. Mountain slopes had to be climbed, swamps traversed. Wide, fast, cold rivers had to be crossed. Did they cross them at fords in very dry seasons or cross them in the high country, before the streams became wide? Could the explorers swim? The answers are not known. At night in strange terrain, a shelter or a place of some security had to be selected. Without the aid of guard dogs, a watch had to be kept for wild animals hunting at night.

In the course of the slow and long migration—the first of many long migrations in the history of the human race—these people originating in the tropics moved into territory far colder than any which their ancestors had experienced. Presumably they stayed entirely in the milder parts of the temperate zone, whose climate and many of whose food-plants were familiar. During many phases, moreover, the climate became colder, and the ice sheets moved some distance to the south. Even southern Europe was long out of bounds to them.

Whether they could warm themselves by fires on cold nights is not certain. When a strike of lightning set fire to adjacent countryside they presumably collected the fire by lighting a stick and carrying the fire away. When the stick was almost burned and the fire faded, they could light another stick. Fire was so valuable that, once it was captured, it would be carefully tended. But fire could be extinguished through carelessness, or doused by heavy rain or lost through an absence of dry wood and kindling. While they possessed fire, they must have carried it on their travels as a precious possession, just as the early Australians travelled with fire. If it went out, they had to wait until another strike of lightning set fire to bush or they came across other humans who had kept their fire alight.

The ability to create fire, rather than borrow it already alight, came late in human history. Eventually humans could produce a flame through the friction and heat caused by rubbing dry wood against dry wood. Or they could strike a piece of pyrite or other suitable rock and thus make a spark. In both processes, some very dry kindling was required, as well as the art of gently blowing on the smoking kindling. Even the native Tasmanians, as observed early in the 19th century, carried fire sticks wherever they went and were despondent when the flames went out. It is far from certain that they could normally accomplish the laborious task of producing a spark that could light a fresh fire.

The skilled employing of fire—the result of many brainwaves and experiments during thousands of years—is one of the achievements of the human race. How ingeniously it was used can be seen in the way of life which survived in a few remote regions of Australia until the 20th century. On the flat cloudless plains of the outback the Aborigines lit small fires to send a smoke signal—it was a clever form of telegraph. Many explorers knew that they were being watched by Aborigines who, remaining out of sight, sent these smoke signals to one another. Aborigines used fire for cooking and warmth, and for smoking out game. Fire was the sole illuminant at night—except when a full moon gave them light for their ceremonial dances. Fire was used in manufacture—in hardening the digging sticks and shaping wood for spears. Fire was used to cremate the dead. It was used to burn a ceremonial pattern on the human skin. It was employed to drive snakes from long grass at a chosen camping site. It was an insect repellent. It was used by hunters to set fire to grass and so to drive animals in a certain direction, and fire was also used to burn the grass in a systematic mosaic at certain times of the year and so encourage new growth, when rains fell. So numerous were the eventual uses of fire that it was the most useful tool possessed by the human race until recent times.

Today humans possess weapons that make the claw and jaw of a wild animal seem pitiful. For a long period, however, it was the human race that was pitiful. Physically it was smaller and lighter than many of the animals living in the vicinity. It was also hopelessly outnumbered by individual herds of large animals. The entire human population of each region was small compared to that of other fighting species. In North America, still uninhabited, the bison ran in their millions. In Asia the big curved-horn mammoth, a species of elephant, must have far outnumbered the humans whom they occasionally saw nearby, while grazing.

The danger of attack from wild animals was high. Even in India in the 19th century, when villagers possessed organizing ability and metal weapons and other means of protecting themselves far superior to those possessed by the early humans, tigers were still a formidable threat. For that century, one estimate is that tigers ate some 300,000 Indians as well as several million animals on farms. Indian children were also vulnerable to attack by wolves. Even in 1996 in one Indian state, 33 children were fatally attacked by wolves. In the homeland of Africa the leopards and lions must have been feared by the humans. Obviously, the slow increase in human organizing capacity was a vital aid to self-defense, especially at night. Without that ability to cooperate against an enemy, the early humans venturing into new tropical areas might easily have been wiped out by beasts of prey. In a few places the advance guard, numbering less than a dozen, was perhaps wiped out.

About 1,800,000 years ago, the advance guard of this movement reached China and South-East Asia. They made their way, travelling on dry land, to Java where the bones of one of the early inhabitants have been found and minutely investigated. This was a period when the levels of the sea rose and fell many times, but Java and Sumatra usually formed a land extension of the Asian mainland.

So, by a long and slow roundabout route, these early humans had moved from the tropics of central and East Africa to the temperate zone of central Asia and then farther on to the tropics of South-East Asia. On a map their migration route formed a long unfinished loop.

Little is known about this long series of journeys by the human race, though much more will be uncovered by prehistorians and archaeologists in the next century. How much of Asia was occupied during the first million years is far from clear. Essentially people of the inland, these humans were probably late in settling along the coast and very late in mastering even shallow seas. Even on the African coast a mere 100,000 years ago, they did not fish. But on scattered beaches they were occasionally confronting the hazardous sea and embarking on it.

A recent excavation on an outer island in the Indonesian archipelago disclosed remains of human habitation dating back more than 800,000 years. The remains, discovered in the ancient bed of a lake at Mata Menge in the mountainous island of Flores, proved beyond any doubt that humans had learned to build water craft and to paddle them far out to sea: the sail itself lay far in the future. To reach the island of Flores, a brave easterly sea crossing was made from the nearest island. Even if the sea levels had been at their lowest, the distance crossed in a small boat or raft from the nearest island would have been at least 19 kilometers. Perhaps this was the longest sea voyage up to that time. It resembled the first journey to the moon in the 20th century, in the sense that it exceeded all previous voyages. Curiously it happened at about the time that Europe was first settled by humans.

Here and there can still be found glimmers of the daily life of these explorers and pioneer settlers. Near Beijing (Peking), at a camp site of humans, layers of ashes and charcoal were recently exposed by careful digging. Those camp fires had been dead for perhaps 400,000 years but they held the remains of a meal: the burned bone of a deer, and the shells taken from hackberry nuts.

The faces of those who sat in the light of the fire were distinctive. A long low ridge, commencing high in the forehead, ran along the top of the skull. Such was the shape of the jaws that the mouth protruded almost as far as the tip of the flattened nose. The ridge of the eyebrow was almost continuous rather than forming two distinct brows. The brow ridge in what was once called "Peking man" was so pronounced that it was almost like a tiny verandah or parapet above the eyes.

AN AWAKENING

In the space of several million years, humans had become more adaptable, more resourceful. The typical human brain was growing larger. Whereas it occupied about 500 cubic centimeters in the early humans, it occupied about 900 in the human species called Homo erectus which carried out this long migration. Somewhere between 500,000 and 200,000 years ago, the brain was again enlarged to a pronounced extent. This growth of the brain was one of the remarkable events in the history of biological change.

The brain's structure was also changing, and a "motor speech area" took shape. The larger brain seemed to be associated with increasing skill in using the hands and arms, and the slow rise of a spoken language. Such a substantial growth in the size of the brain in any species is a remarkable event. How it happened is largely a mystery. One possible cause is the eating of more and more meat. It is unlikely that the human race at this stage possessed either the weapons or the organizing ability to kill wild animals of any size and feast on their meat. Possibly the meals of meat came from increasing bravery in scavenging the carcasses of recently dead animals, while the main pack or herd was grazing not far away, or from a growing skill in hunting the smaller animals which posed no danger but were not easily caught. It is feasible that in the course of time the fatty acids in the meat improved the brain and its functioning. In turn, that advantage enabled humans to devise better ways of hunting animals and so to increase their intake of meat. All this is speculation.

The spoken language was acquiring more words and more precision. The fine arts were emerging. The fine arts and the act of communicating by speech both rely on the use of symbols, whether those detected by the ear or the eye. The ability to invent symbols and to recognize them was one result of the slow improvements in the brain. Perhaps a development in the human voice box was also an aid to expressing these symbols in sound. Some scholars argue that human speech began as a social activity, a way of bringing up the young, after which it was slowly extended to such other activities as the gathering of food or the organizing of a defense against a human or animal enemy.

Despite the advances in studying the mind in the last half-century, the brain and human speech are still far from explored. One medical specialist has suggested that in an intricate activity such as speech, "the interaction of the parts of the brain will not resemble those of an orderly machine but will more resemble a crazy quilt." Whatever its origins, language is the greatest of all inventions.

Some 60,000 years ago came signs of a human awakening. Prehistorians and archaeologists, looking back, have pieced together the evidence for a slow-moving succession of changes which in the next 30,000 years merited such descriptions as a "Great Leap Forward" or a "Cultural Explosion." There is dispute about who did the leaping and exploding. Possibly the changes were the work of a new human group that emerged in Africa and then emigrated to Asia and Europe, where they coexisted with the Neanderthals, a species that later vanished. What is clear is the existence of human creativity on many fronts.

The speech of the hundreds of generations of people who were alive during the Awakening is silent and lost, but some of their arts and crafts survive, either in fragments or intact. The arts blossomed in Europe during that long glacial phase which began about 75,000 years ago. Persistent evidence suggests that many humans expected to renew their existence in an afterlife. The journey to that new life required artistic offerings, accessories or indications of one's status, and the chosen items were arranged in the grave, either on the body or alongside it. The new reverence was visible in the burial of a child in Uzbekistan in central Asia some 70,000 years ago. In the shallow grave was placed an offering of curved goat-horns. In Sunghir in Russia about 28,000 years ago a man of some 60 years of age was buried, his body adorned with more than 2,000 pieces of ivory and other ornaments. To reach the age of 60 was to be almost venerable, for most adults died younger. On the "old" man's forearms and biceps were arranged polished bracelets made of mammoth ivory.

In another grave was buried, alongside a male, an adolescent girl. She was dressed in a bead cap, and perhaps in a cloak of which the only trace is the ivory pin that fastened it near the throat. Her body was covered with more than 5,000 beads and other adorning snippets. Alongside her were placed decorated antlers and ivory disks. The long time spent by friends or the whole tribe in making these decorations, and the care with which they were arranged in the grave, was a sign that death was as important as life.

At many times the people of this nomadic world must have felt an acute uncertainty. They were at the mercy of the seasons, for they hoarded no grains, nuts or other foods with which to face the first phase of a famine. Most of their sheltering places were flimsy. In some regions they lived side by side with tigers, lions, bears, panthers, elephants and other animals of formidable strength or ferocity. Death often arrived suddenly and mysteriously. They sought certainty and consolation. They began to construct religions and to make objects of devotion and homage as well as depictions of the world around them.

In southwestern France, ivory was collected and cut into suitable pieces and carved in imitation of seashells. In the concealed Chauvet Cave, discovered in France as recently as 1994, are vivid depictions of lions, horses, reindeer and rhinoceroses, each of which was skillfully painted some 30,000 years ago. In southern Germany the tusk of a mammoth was selected and cut into lengths, then one suitable piece was carved into the likeness of a man's body capped with a lion's head.

The same manual skill which appears in the small statues or the rock paintings was at work in the shaping of stone. Little pieces of stone shaped into spear points, blades and other piercing and cutting instruments—superior to most of those formerly used—were produced in their hundreds of thousands in any one year. Bones were also shaped into tools, including needles. That versatile weapon the spear-thrower came into play. Indirectly it so extended the arm of the thrower that maybe some spears could cover 100 meters.

The techniques of hunting were slowly improved. Instead of pursuing only small animals, the hunters tried to attack larger ones. Elephants were hunted in Germany, and at Lehringen the bones of a butchered elephant were dug up in modern times: a wooden spear was still lodged in its bones. In southeastern France the leopard was hunted for its hide and meat. In Italy the wild boar was pursued.

An improved organizing ability seemed to come with the improved weapons. The weapons and the skill in human cooperation were part of the same mental awakening. Herds of animals were hunted and trapped, or driven to their death over a precipice, where they provided an extravagant feast of meat. On the shores of the Black Sea large herds of bison were killed in one place. In the Pyrenees Mountains in France at least 108 bison were killed on one site. It is now customary to observe that human beings at that time lived in harmony with their environment and did not kill needlessly and recklessly, but the observation has to be treated cautiously due to inconclusive evidence.

In northern Europe the hunt was aided by the emerging of a prairie-like grassland covering a vast area. There the wild game multiplied far more than if the land had remained forest. Huge herds of animals migrated south or north, according to the season, and the hunters knew their route and awaited them. The mammoth and rhinoceros and red deer, along with birds, were hunted. In the cold dry winters of this period the Arctic fox and the hare were trapped, and their skin and fur provided warm clothing. In the warm summers around the lower Rhineland, humans hunted mainly the horse, which was much smaller than the present riding horse. All hunting was done on foot.

In Europe and Asia, wherever the supply of food was favorable, camps and villages were more permanent than probably ever before. Houses were usually built on slopes that gave protection from the icy winds. A small circular excavation provided a flat space for the floor made of slate, and wooden posts held up the roof which was covered with the hides of horses and other animals. From the fireplace in the middle of the one large room the smoke drifted up to a small hole in the roof. Many groups had one house for the winter and another for the summer. It was a paradise for meat eaters, and for a time game was so plentiful and hunting methods so improved that hunters did not have to move far from their permanent camp to hunt with success. In cold weather—and the cold of winter was intense—the air supplied natural refrigeration for their meat.

When the climate became colder and wetter, the returning forest re-clothed much of the old European prairie. The herds of wild animals were thinned, perhaps as much by the new vegetation as by the success of the new hunting methods. The bow and arrow, a vital invention, was used more often by the hunters. Some of the larger species of animals were in danger of extinction, but eventually that danger point was passed.

Throughout the world, people lived a seminomadic life. Small groups of people, perhaps rarely numbering as many as 20, each occupied a large territory. In the course of a year they moved systematically from place to place, carrying virtually no possessions and making use of the variety of foods that came into season: a grain ripening here, a root crop growing there, a nest of bird's eggs available here, a nut ripening there. So long as the population was small and the natural resources were large the people lived in relative abundance. If a site offered food for several weeks they settled down.

Sometimes several groups might come together each year at a place with prolific food, but large gatherings must have been a rarity. In the entire world it is possible that at no time before, say, 20,000 BC did as many as 500 people ever assemble together in one place. Even then their assembly was temporary. As they hoarded no food and kept no livestock they could not feed a large gathering for very long. In some parts of the world, however, plant and animal foods and sea-fish were so plentiful that a small group could settle in one place for a considerable part of the year.

A group or tribe of people that was often on the move could not cope with those who were too sick and weak to walk. Even twin babies were a burden, and one was probably killed. Old people who could no longer walk were left behind to die. A mobile society had no alternative. Its advantage was that, so long as the population remained relatively small, it had access to a wide variety of foods and meats for most of the year. Materially, this was not the most miserable period in human history,

THE BLACK COLUMBUS

Each morning, as the sun first rose in eastern Asia, people could be seen stirring themselves—putting wood on the fire, breastfeeding children, setting out to gather nuts or catch wild animals, scraping the inside of an animal skin to turn it into clothing, or chipping away at a rock to shape it into a tool. The same scenes could probably be witnessed at tens of thousands of places as the sun's early rays moved west across Asia and then across Europe to the Atlantic. Similar scenes of early-morning activity could be seen in Africa, where humans occupied an increasingly large area.

About 100,000 years ago the area occupied by the human race was extensive, but a vast part of the globe still remained empty of people. The animals of the Americas had never heard a human voice or seen a spear. In Australia and New Guinea, which formed one continent, there were no human footprints. Islands far out to sea were inaccessible to the human race. In the Pacific Ocean most of those islands which now are inhabited were unknown to human beings: Hawaii and Easter Island, Tahiti and Samoa, Tonga and Fiji and the large islands of New Zealand were not inhabited. In the Indian Ocean the large and relatively warm island of Madagascar knew no camp fires and on the remote volcanic islands of Mauritius and Réunion the strange flightless bird, the dodo, was not disturbed by human beings. In the Atlantic Ocean, north of the equator, the Azores and Madeira were uninhabited. Greenland and Iceland were covered by ice. The birds of the islands of the West Indies were completely safe from human hunters.

The human race, in effect, was confined to one landmass. The combined area of the empty lands was huge. In total area, the lands which were habitable but empty were the equal of Asia, the Sahara Desert and North Africa, all added together.

From South-East Asia and the string of islands in the Indonesian archipelago a succession of voyages of discovery was now being made. Humans were undertaking a second long migration, and its unknown terminus was Australia and New Guinea. Between the nearest shores of South-East Asia, which then included Java, and the nearest coastline of New Guinea–Australia were some eight barriers of sea. Most were short gaps or straits, with the opposite shore visible from the point of setting out. The widest gap was about 80 kilometers. Pioneering people on rafts or in tiny canoes occasionally ventured across from one island to the next—so long as one shore was visible from the other. Their progress depended on the currents and their own paddling, with a little help from the wind. But if the wind blew too strongly, their flimsy vessel would be swamped, and all aboard would be drowned.

The crossing of this mosaic of seas and islands standing between Asia in the west and New Guinea–Australia in the east was spread over thousands of years. On some occasions it was halted, perhaps for as long as 10,000 years. One island would be discovered and settled, and then another boat or raft would find by accident or intention yet another island. Through this zone of frequent earthquakes the sporadic procession moved forward on land and sea. Finally, without any idea of the significance of the discovery, the human race came ashore in New Guinea–Australia. There was no reason to think that a continent had been discovered. It was assumed to be yet another tropical island, like those left behind. Where the discoverer waded ashore was near the present New Guinea or to the northwest of the present Australia. The site has long since vanished. It is deep beneath the sea and far from the present coastline. The date is not known but was almost certainly more than 52,000 years ago.

The new continent was a surprise, a puzzle and sometimes a terror. No dangerous animals existed but many of the snakes and a few of the spiders were highly venomous. To receive a bite on the bare foot or arm from a brown snake or tiger snake or many others was usually a quick injection of death. Giant kangaroos, now extinct, and several other large marsupials were watched nervously—until it was realized that they did not readily attack humans.

The newcomers explored the continent, every estuary, every mountain, every plain and desert. Much of the center of Australia was probably not as parched as it is today, and they settled permanently and flourished, their population multiplying, in some places that are now largely uninhabited. Walking overland to Tasmania, they cooked in riverbank caves in what was then the tundra but is now the rainforest. More than 20,000 years ago these new inhabitants of southern and western Tasmania were the most southerly inhabitants of the globe. Measured by normal land and sea routes, they were living further away from central Africa than any human had ever lived. It was a testimony to the adaptability of humans that they had originated in the tropics, had moved north and then east, and were now halfway to the South Pole.

The other end of the elongated continent, more than 3,000 kilometers to the north, was the springboard for another short burst of exploration. In small watercraft the voyage was made from New Guinea to the large islands not far to the northeast. By 35,000 BC the islands of New Britain and New Ireland were settled. The navigators, becoming bolder and more experienced, penetrated the dangerous barrier of more than

150 kilometers of sea which protected the virgin tropical island of Buka. It too was colonized. Farther to the east, across the wide Pacific, was a chain of uninhabited islands stretching most of the way to South America. The discovery and settling of these islands, some 30,000 years later, would await the coming of a new breed of navigators, the Polynesians.

In the latter phase of this slow movement of peoples, originating in Africa and extending far, the growth of language was one of the triumphs. Dialects and languages multiplied. Even in a large region where everybody, in the era of initial settlement, might have spoken alike, languages diverged. Groups lived in relative isolation from one another, and so their languages evolved. There must have been several thousand different languages when a geographical event began which, permanently separating so many peoples from each other, multiplied even further their languages.

2

WHEN THE SEAS WERE RISING

IN 20,000 BC the human race was virtually confined to one massive continent. Europe and Africa, Asia and America were not then separated by seas, and this one landmass was the scene of nearly all human activity. Australia and New Guinea together formed the second inhabited landmass but it held less than 5 per cent of the world's population. There was another curious facet of this population: it was confined almost entirely to tropical and temperate zones. The cold areas of the world were largely uninhabited.

At this time temperatures everywhere were much colder than they are today. Glaciers were active and extensive even in the far south of Australia, while in the Northern Hemisphere a vast area was covered by ice for most of the year. Finland, Sweden and even most of Ireland—it was not an island—were wastelands. In the high country of central Europe an area far larger than Switzerland was overlaid with permanent ice. Some of the present sea resorts in western Europe, where now crowds of people bathe along the beaches on summer days, were a bleak sight, with ice floating in the water even at the height of summer. Most of the present sea resorts were far from the sea.

North America was mainly a land of ice. Nearly all of the present Canada lay under compacted snow. A huge expanse of what is now the United States—an expanse supporting maybe half of its present population—lay under almost permanent ice. Parts of Central America, which in the 20th century have seen no snow, experienced frequent falls. On the high, western side of South America snow covered a vast area even in summer.

In a majority of the inhabited regions of the world the heat of summer was milder and the patterns of rainfall and evaporation were different from those of today. For human beings as a whole, however, this climate offered one advantage. Dry land spread over vast tracts of territory which now lie under the sea. In the temperate and tropical zones of Asia and Africa, perhaps one-quarter of the population lived in wide river valleys and on grassy plains and gentle slopes which were later covered by ocean. In North America the present St Lawrence estuary was washed by no sea. In what is now the capacious Gulf of Carpentaria in northern Australia, countless kangaroos grazed, and at night the fires of a myriad camp sites burned on hard ground that is now the open sea.

As the oceans were at such a low level, a man could walk from southern England to France and keep on walking—if the people along his route so allowed him—all the way to Java. A strong and fit Javanese, at high risk to life, could walk by a most indirect and northerly route to north Asia, and cross by a land bridge to unexplored Alaska. At that period Java was not an island but part of Asia.

Places that are now the world's busy seaports lay on dry land or on the banks of rivers that were far from the open sea. At that time the sites of Panama and San Francisco, New York and Rio de Janeiro could not be reached by ship. Rotterdam and Odessa lay far from the sea. People lived near Shanghai and Calcutta, Singapore and Sydney, but had never seen the sea. It was too far away.

Many now-strategic sea straits, which are busy day and night with passing tankers and bulk carriers, were simply corridors of grassland or forest. The Dardanelles and the Bosporus, the straits of Gibraltar and Malacca, Sunda Strait and Torres Strait were only a few of the now-busy seaways which did not exist.

Certain of today's seas and many of the large gulfs did not exist or their shapes were quite different. The Black Sea was a deep lake with no outlet to the Mediterranean. It was in effect a miniature Caspian Sea. The Baltic Sea did not empty into the North Sea. In fact it was rather a cluster of lakes, some of which were deep. On the northern plains of Germany it was not easy to tell which was lake and which was marsh and grassland, for it must have been covered by ice for nearly the whole year. Such large arms of the sea as today's Persian Gulf consisted of land. Even much of the South China Sea was dry land with a large sea in the middle.

About 15,000 BC a remarkable change began, ever so slowly. The summers and winters became just a trifle warmer. Glaciers retreated a little. Old people, whose memory served as the public library, must have remarked to the young that some kinds of spring flowers and trees seemed to be in bud a little earlier than was usual. They must have been puzzled that certain animals and birds were more plentiful than in the past, and that half a hundred other changes in nature seemed to be taking place. Perhaps a rhinoceros appeared in a region where previously that creature was unknown. Perhaps reindeer became scarce in regions which they had once dominated.

The melting of the ice was rapid between about 12,000 BC and 9000 BC. In many parts of the habitable globe the change in climate must have been remarkable even in one long lifetime. Those people living on the seashores noticed one other change: the sea was rising. It was rising even before the climate became noticeably warmer.

Many villagers near the sea feared that their houses would be swamped one day. Some lived to see that day. Nobody understood the cause of this strange happening, though they would have had their own explanations. They had no means of knowing that vast areas of ice at both ends of the world were slowly melting, and that the melting ice was raising the level of the seas.

At previous times in human history the seas had risen and then retreated, but this rising of the seas was persistent, eventually flooding vast areas of low-lying coastline in every habitable continent. Occasionally the rise of the seas became slower, and there were even pauses, but then the rise continued. An uncountable number of human camping places and villages, shrines and rock quarries, and even caves and lookouts, vanished beneath the seas. Dry plains on which people had hunted for what seemed eternity slowly became salty marshes. There, for a century or two, seabirds could be hunted instead of the four-legged animals, until at last the marsh became a permanent arm of the sea. In this momentous era, new islands were formed. England and Ireland were separated from Europe, Sri Lanka was parted from India, the Philippines were cut off from Asia and slowly converted into a chain of islands, while Taiwan was severed from eastern Asia.

Small groups of people who had lived and roamed together for centuries found their territory cut in two or three by the rising seas. Eventually the separated parts of land were far apart, and even a crossing by boat became too dangerous to be attempted. Some tribes who had lived side by side and intermarried and shared rituals were now permanently apart, separated by wide seas. Others lived on new islands within sight of each other but their contacts now were few. A voyage by canoe and raft had replaced the long walk on land.

The temperatures slowly rose. Highlands in central Europe, the Americas and Asia had been too bleak even in summer but now were open for human settlement or for the seasonal coming of grazing animals. Country close to the polar regions lost its cap of ice and became attractive in summertime, providing pastures and hunting grounds. Vast lakes were formed by the melting of ice.

With the changing climate came alterations in the flow of big rivers. In Africa, in about 10,000 BC, the water of Lake Victoria began to run into the Nile, and for the first time the Nile became the longest river in the world. In eastern and southern Asia the speeding-up of the flow of the great rivers must have had profound effects. Most of the long Asian rivers depended on the melting of ice in the high mountains of central Asia, and as the summer climate warmed, the flow of some rivers must have been substantially increased by the melt. The flood of silt that came floating along the Ganges, the Yellow and other rivers was partly a result of the increased volume of ice-cold water. These plains, topped with silt, were to be the early cradles of what is called civilization.

New combinations of rain and sun and winds harmed some regions and favored others. Some areas with low rainfall became semidesert. On the other hand, people poured into the southern half of Africa. For a time North Africa also became attractive to human settlers. In some of the arid country in about 7000 BC, three times as much rain fell as now falls in a typical year. Lakes and marshes dotted the Sahara. People could walk across vast tracts of the region and see nothing but grasslands or park-like expanses where countless trees offered shade. The population of North Africa must have increased rapidly during the more favored centuries. Then a dryness came and, sometime after 3000 BC, people began to flee from the ever-widening deserts to moister territories.

The rising of the seas was almost completed by 8000 BC. Curiously, the change to warmer temperatures and longer summers continued a lit-

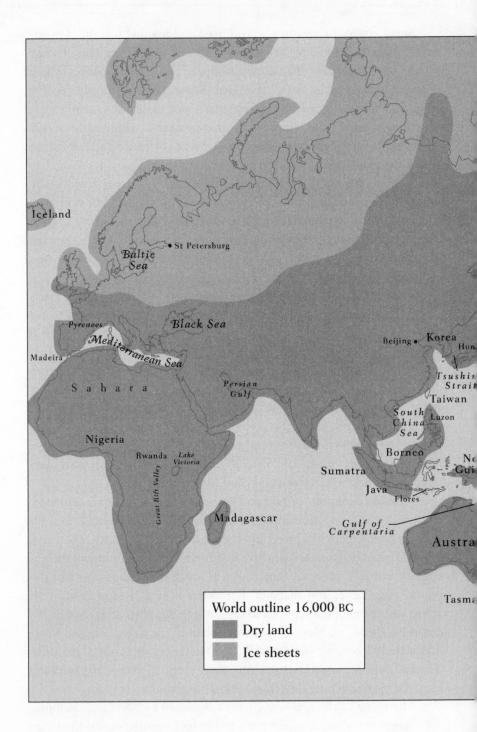

Iceland

Baltic
Sea

• St Petersburg

Black Sea

Pyrenees

Mediterranean Sea

Madeira

S a h a r a

Persian
Gulf

Beijing • Korea

Hon

Tsushi
Strai

Taiwan

South
China
Sea

Luzon

Nigeria

Rwanda   *Lake*
          Victoria

Great Rift Valley

Borneo

Sumatra

Ne
Gui

Java

Flores

Madagascar

Gulf of
Carpentaria

Austra

World outline 16,000 BC

Dry land

Ice sheets

Tasma

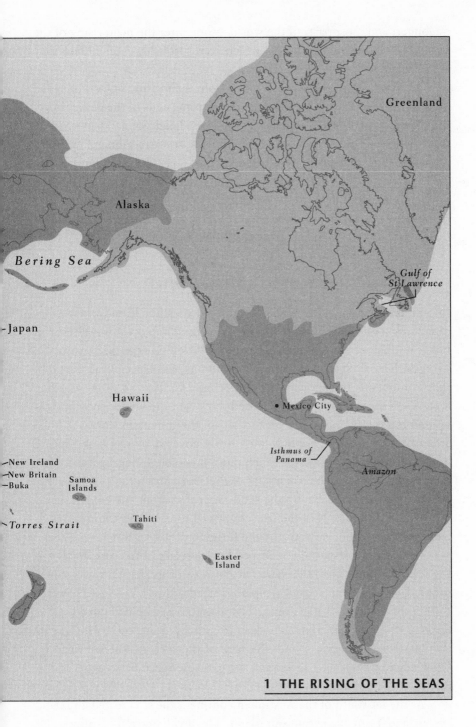

Greenland

Alaska

Bering Sea

Gulf of
St Lawrence

–Japan

Hawaii

• Mexico City

–New Ireland
–New Britain
–Buka

Samoa
Islands

Isthmus of
Panama

Amazon

~Torres Strait

Tahiti

Easter
Island

1 THE RISING OF THE SEAS

tle longer; and most parts of the world—soon after the main rising of the seas—experienced temperatures which were probably higher than they are today.

The vast volume of seawater came from the melting of ice which had long lain in glaciers and ice sheets at the extreme ends of the globe. In all, the seas had risen by as much as 140 meters: a height of 400 feet or more is a common assessment. This was the most extraordinary event in human history during the last 100,000 years—far more influential than the invention of the steam engine, the discovery of bacteria, the landing on the moon and indeed all the combined events of the 20th century. The rising seas, in ways that cannot always be traced, were to spur a transformation in human life and an explosion of population.

ISOLATED SOUTH LANDS

In South-East Asia, as the seas rose, the old coastline in most places became unrecognizable. It ceased to be a coastline. No coast was altered as much as that of the continent combining New Guinea and Australia. Tropical New Guinea, with its high mountains, was especially affected. In those mountains the snowline in winter used to descend as far as 3,600 meters. As the temperatures increased, however, the winter snowline retreated more than 1,000 meters further up the mountain slopes. A huge area of the bleak high country was slowly covered by trees; and in the highlands the climate became much more favorable for agriculture. New Guinea did not lose from the rising of the seas: the land it lost under the sea was compensated for by the land recovered from the cold snow or chill winds. As the level of the seas continued to rise, New Guinea was finally separated from Australia by the forming of Torres Strait.

Australia was especially reshaped by the rising of the seas, for it was the flattest of continents. Maybe one-seventh of its dry land was slowly submerged while the coastal people watched, quite powerless. Towards the end of this remarkable event, Australian tribes who had once lived as far as 500 kilometers from the ocean eventually heard on stormy nights an unfamiliar and eerie sound, the roar of the surf. People who had no knowledge of boats and navigation were, in the space of 10 generations, turned into apprentice seafarers.

At the far south of the Australian continent the sea created an inland wedge, and Tasmania became an island. The dividing strait became wider and stormier, and the people on the island were marooned. It was to become perhaps the longest-known segregation in human history. Indeed the features of the Tasmanians were much altered during the long isolation. They became frizzy-haired and tended to be smaller than the Aborigines from whom they were descended. Probably the influence of a small genetic pool, at the time when the seas cut them off, followed by thousands of years of isolation, allowed certain physical facets to become dominant. When their isolation was virtually ended late in the 18th century, on the eve of the American and French revolutions, and they were seen again by other members of the human race, they seemed decidedly African in appearance, though in their recent ancestry they were not African.

Mainland Australia, unlike Tasmania, was not completely isolated. A stepping stone of islands linked it to New Guinea; and from time to time the two peoples separated by the narrow sea engaged in trade. But in effect the narrow strait, for reasons that are not clear, served as a deep ditch or barrier for thousands of years. On the New Guinea side emerged a way of life based on large gardens, the hoarding of food, a much higher density of population, and a different political and social organization. On the other side the Australians remained gatherers and hunters, staying in small nomadic groups and living systematically off the land. There can be little doubt that if the seas had not risen, and if Australia and New Guinea had remained part of the same continent with links along a wide front, Australia's later history would have been more in tune with New Guinea's. When the isolation was finally broken by the landing of the British at Sydney in AD 1788, the shock and dislocation for the Australians, their way of life being so different, was acute.

THE LOST AMERICAS

The continent of America had not long been discovered by the human race when the seas began to rise. The first humans probably crossed the gap between Siberia and Alaska sometime before 22,000 BC. The two continents were joined by a cold corridor of land, and in summer the crossing cannot have been difficult. Indeed it is possible that hunters and their families simply crossed the corridor in pursuit of game, found the other side more attractive and decided to stay. In effect they were the discoverers of a new continent, and entitled to a special place in history, but—so far as they knew—they were just doing their normal day's work. Various waves of people probably crossed the corridor and moved down the west coast towards warmer Mexico. Their presence in Mexico in about 22,000 BC can be verified by the precious pieces of shaped obsidian rock that they left in campsites.

Large animals roamed the grassland, making it a hunter's paradise. Giant bison, mammoths, mastodon, horses and camels ranged across the landscape, and did not know that skilled hunters were arriving. Small game such as rabbits and deer could also be caught in their millions, and new food-plants grew in abundance. When winter approached, the new inhabitants had access to more fur and skins than they could possibly wear.

The population of America increased. Many excavations of human camp sites point to a quicker spread of settlement in about 11,000 BC. The isthmus of Panama was crossed, South America was entered, and few barriers impeded the southward movement of peoples until the permanent ice in the far south came into sight.

Then the rising seas—without warning—began to split America from the world. In about 10,000 BC the land corridor from Asia to Alaska—the only gateway to the Americas—was cut by the rising seas. The Bering Strait was formed. For a time the sea in the new strait was frozen and the ice could be walked over. Even that crossing place was perilous when the climate became warmer. Virtually all contact between the Americas and the outside world ceased, and maybe for another 10,000 years the silence continued. Migratory birds moved between the two continents, but the people lived in isolation. Eventually the inhabitants of America had no knowledge of the place of their origins.

The rising seas, at first sight, did not affect the Americas as much as they affected Australia. Whereas most of Australia was flat and low-lying, with an abnormal area consisting of coastal lowlands which were flooded by the rising seas, the Americas possessed less land that was vulnerable. Indeed the northern half gained by the changing climate, for dry land emerged from the huge sheet of ice which had covered all of Canada and extended into New England and across to the southern border of Wisconsin. With the melting of the ice, and the slow uplifting of land which had been suppressed by the sheer weight of ice, numerous large lakes were formed and Niagara Falls emerged. In total, the new land in North

America that was reclaimed from ice was larger than the coastal rim that was slowly lost to the rising seas.

In South America the only large area inundated was in the southeast, where a vast region of lowland off the present Argentine coast was flooded. In compensation the ice sheets of southern Chile were slowly melted. In the whole of South America the area reclaimed from ice was perhaps as large as the land lost to the rising seas.

In their prolonged isolation from Asia, the Americas did not stagnate. Humans quickly penetrated every part that was habitable. Slowly the people branched into a variety of ways of life: Inuit hunters in the icy north, gatherer-hunters roaming the cold far south, a variety of peoples combining hunting and farming in various parts of North and South America, while some tribes lived on the abundance of salmon—and the labor of slaves—along the Fraser and Columbia rivers in the northwest. By 2000 BC the Americas possessed a diversity of economies and cultures.

In the late 20th century the idea arose that somehow the rain forest of the Amazon, being isolated and impenetrable, had largely escaped the interference of the human race. With the quickening respect for nature in many quarters of the western world, the rainforest of the Amazon is often marvelled at. Here is primitive nature in all its vulnerable glory: a huge green basin drained by a silent majestic river. Even the Amazon, however, is now known to have had its own remarkable human history during that long period when the Americas were cut off from Europe and Asia. The earliest pottery in the whole of the Americas was made, not in Central and North America, but in the tropical rainforest of the Amazon basin before 5000 BC. There is even evidence that maize, the wonder cereal, was first domesticated by gardeners in this region.

On the lower reaches of the Amazon and its tributaries riverside villages flourished, long ago. The silt that came with the mud-heavy water was deposited as a dark carpet on the riverside gardens, and year after year lush crops could be grown, for the soil remained fertile. Here were straggling villages with chieftains' houses and temples, large storehouses of food, manufacturers of pottery and textiles, and as many as 2,500 people. In many villages the wooden houses formed a long and almost unbroken avenue along the riverbanks. In the delta near the Atlantic Ocean were other villages, perched on mounds consisting of earth which had been moved in massive quantities by human muscle. And in the distant uplands, with poorer soil and no fertilizing floods, lay a wide scattering of smaller villages consisting of pole-and-thatch houses: villages abandoned when the soil was exhausted.

In the 16th century of the Christian era, Europeans were to venture up the wide Amazon for the first time. Destroying some villages, driving away or enslaving the inhabitants of others, and unknowingly spreading their fatal diseases far into the uplands, the incoming Portuguese saw this old way of life crumble in the space of years. The forest closed ranks where once stood clearings and rich gardens, and floods swept away or buried the debris of the villages, including their thousands of broken pots. Slowly arose the idea, in Europe and North America, that this primeval forest had always been there, little changed until this latest era of fast forest destruction. Curiously, the biological diversity in this region is usually the most impressive not in the untouched rain forest, but in those areas which were cultivated by the pioneering Amazonian gardeners and now are camouflaged by new growth.

JAPAN MAROONED

Like the Americas, Japan was also thrust into a prolonged isolation. Its human history was much longer than that of the Americas. It had been settled for tens of thousands of years before the seas began to rise. One of the coldest of the world's inhabited regions, its snowy peaks had for long looked down on vast areas of woodland. Alongside the badgers, hares and wild boar were tigers, panthers, brown bears and bison, a species of elephant and other large animals, though their numbers were diminishing. The subalpine forest came closer to the plains, and parts of the low-lying ground were a bleak tundra.

As the seas began to rise they cut off Japan's settled, southern areas and converted them into islands. The Tsushima Strait, separating Japan from Korea, was soon formed, but there remained a land connection, further north, with Siberia. For a time Japan was probably a long appendage extending in a southerly direction from Siberia.

When at last Japan was completely isolated, its population was tiny, numbering fewer than 30,000. Most people must have lived on the coast or close to it, and the sea gave them fish, and low-lying valleys and plains gave them wild vegetables in summer. Small groups of people moved about to make best use of the seasons. Prolific seasons were rejoiced in; but lean years were bound to arrive.

For the Japanese in what they call the Jomon period, the expectation of life was low as it was for most peoples. To live for 45 years was unusual, and to reach 70 was a miracle. The bones of a Yokohama man, excavated in 1949, were studied by an X ray which disclosed that as a child he was sometimes starving. His teeth, like those of so many nomadic people, were eroded, and the lower molars on one side of his mouth were almost level with the top of the gum. The grinding down of the teeth was accelerated by the practice of cooking meat on hot stones or on an open fire resting on sand, and so a mouthful of meat was often sprinkled with grit.

Already the Japanese made handsome pottery on the large island of Kyushu. One piece, dated at 10,500 BC, is probably older than any pottery in China and perhaps in the whole world. Even older pottery has recently been found. The early pots, probably made by women, were round at the bottom and had to be eased into soft soil so that they could stand upright. Later the flat bottom became normal. Small pots could be used as drinking cups, and larger pots could store liquid, or heat those grasses and ferns which were edible only after they had been steamed. Originally a dull brown, the pots later appeared in orange, salmon and brighter colors and often carried distinctive patterns made by the fingernails and fingertips of the potter. In the course of thousands of years their design became as ornate as the pots of Egyptian, Greek and Chinese civilizations, of which Japan in its remoteness could have no knowledge.

Pots were heavy and fragile and were not likely to be carried by a seminomadic people. Nor were they likely to be made and used by a people who were constantly on the move. The presence of pots suggests that the people stayed in one place for some months at a time, and then moved to new areas where other food could be found. At the appropriate season they returned to the old site.

By about 5000 BC, some of the Japanese huts or houses were impressive, measured by the standards of most regions of the globe. A pit was dug, and the walls of the small house of about 4 meters square stood partly in the pit and partly above the surface of the ground. Vertical poles held up the roof of thatched grass and reeds. Within easy talking distance of one another might stand four or five houses which, in all, sheltered maybe 15 people. On cold nights the heat of people's bodies huddled together must have provided much of the warmth, for the fireplace was located outside the house; though in a later era a fireplace was constructed inside. Small dogs were kept, perhaps for hunting and also for companionship. Occasionally, near the site of the houses, small clay figures have been excavated displaying breasts and buttocks that are unduly inflated. Possibly they were sacred statues which protected a woman when she was giving birth.

Already the Japanese in certain districts were hoarding food. Many groups lived for part of the year near the forests, where a large quantity of nuts could be gathered, part of which was eaten and part hoarded. September, October and November were the months for gathering nuts, the chestnuts falling first. While chestnuts were less nutritious than walnuts, they were more easily preserved on layers of leaves placed in the storage pits near or inside the houses. In contrast, the acorns which fell from the deciduous oak trees required slow treatment in running water to remove the tannic acid. Reduced to fine flour by the action of grinding stones, the acorns were highly palatable. The task of pounding and grinding acorns—and kneading clay for the making of pots—fell largely on the women. The constant exercise had the curious effect of lengthening their collarbones.

Tribes with access to plentiful acorns acquired some of the characteristics of a farming society. Eventually some Japanese were transplanting seedlings of the chestnut tree and thus forming nut orchards. Possibly this was at the time when the notion of gardening arrived from southern China, for Japan's isolation was being eased by the inventing of small deep-sea vessels. On the lowlands taro and yams were sometimes planted by about 3000 BC. With increased ingenuity in producing food, Japan's population in 2000 BC possibly exceeded 200,000, making it one of the most densely populated parts of the world. By present standards, however, Japan was a sparsely peopled wilderness.

Meanwhile the hunters developed fine equipment. Their bows and arrows were probably their own invention, and the arrows with their sharp tip of stone could fell an animal standing more than 50 meters away. The sharp point was made deadly by its coating of poison, extracted from a certain root.

In particular months the sea yielded plenty of fish. It was not salted or smoked and set aside, a hoard for the lean season, but was eaten while fresh. Shellfish were also gathered in large quantities, and on the shores of the east coast arose long middens or rubbish mounds consisting solely of clam shells discarded at the moment they were eaten. One mound extends for 175 meters. An inspection of the ring marks on a typical shell reveals that two of every three clams were picked from the rocks in springtime. By about 2000 BC the coastal Japanese were fishing in long dugout wooden canoes, with a kind of outrigger that provided stability in choppy seas.

While Japan was largely cut off from Asia by the rising seas, it remained relatively receptive to what was new. When at last, in the one or two millenniums before Christ, the isolation was reduced, and small boats occasionally crossed the seas from Korea and China, the Japanese often adopted the ideas that came in the boats. One sign of their adventurous spirit was the growing of rice in wet fields, in the new east Asian manner, about 300 BC. The Japanese were reentering a world which had been transformed, in their absence, by the farming of cereals.

THE PARADOX OF ISOLATION

For thousands of years the people living in the territories of what are now Japan and the United States were largely or entirely cut off from the outside world. Their experience was unusual. It would seem that they could have been permanently impaired by this long isolation, at the very time when Europe and Asia were changing rapidly. And yet today these two once-marooned lands are the world's great financial powers.

Perhaps this paradox has an explanation. Geographical isolation, at one time or another, was an acute problem for all peoples. But in the last 150 years, geographical isolation has become a mixed blessing and sometimes an asset. In a shrinking world, ideas and goods and people can cross with ease a sea barrier that was impenetrable 10,000 years ago. But the sea is still a barrier for invading armies. For Japan and the United States the sea barrier ceased to be a disadvantage and became a major strength. It largely saved them from invasion. Facilitating a policy of deliberate isolationism, the sea made them reluctant to become entangled in costly wars fought far from home.

Europe has been weakened again and again by wars fought on its soil and seas in the last 150 years. It has always revived, but the extent of its revival and global influence has been impaired by its own divisions. In contrast, in the United States during that time, only one war has been fought on its soil—a civil war and not a war against invaders. If the United States in 1800 had been situated in Europe it probably would never have been able to rise to its ultimate power. It would never have succeeded in a policy of isolationism. Likewise, Japan's main islands, facing a desperate military situation during the final months of the Second World War, were not invaded even then. Indeed, recognizing the sheer difficulty of invading Japan, the United States in 1945 had little alternative but to drop the first atomic bombs in the hope of frightening the Japanese into surrendering. In essence, the geographical factors which had penalized and isolated Japan and North America after the rising of the seas were an advantage in certain situations.

Proximity and isolation have long been powerful determinants of history. The dynamic ideas of human history have come more often from the play of proximity. The ideas which were reshaping human life in most lands, just when the Americas and Japan and Australia were largely living in isolation, arose at a crossroads of the world. The new dynamo, 10,000 years ago, was a corridor of land between the Mediterranean Sea and the Persian Gulf: a corridor where Asia, Africa and Europe met.

3

THE FIRST GREEN REVOLUTION

IN Syria and Palestine, soon after the seas had reached their new high water, a minor revolution seemed to be taking place. Unlike the better-known industrial revolution it was incredibly slow, and the force of its impact would not be felt for thousands of years. But human life was on a course from which there was no retreat.

The village of Jericho was a showcase of the revolution by about 8000 BC. Consisting of little mud-brick houses, it grew wheat and barley on tiny patches of garden. These cereals, originally growing wild, were selected for cultivation because the grains were large compared to those of other wild cereals; and a large grain was more easily collected and ground down into a rough wholemeal flour. The villagers must have prepared the ground, selected a firm kind of seed which did not shatter once it ripened, and sown the seed in a more concentrated way than nature did. The grain, harvested with stone knives or scythes, was stored in the village. Today half of the world's calories come from a small variety of cereals, the first of which were cultivated by these villagers of the Middle East.

Meanwhile other villagers in the region continued to depend on wild grains and wild animals. In the Taurus Mountains in Turkey in about 6600 BC stood the village of Suberde, with its roofed huts. Their mud-brick walls and plastered floors provided comfort in a cold winter.

Nearby were clay-lined pits for the storing of the wild grain which periodically was ground into a wholemeal flour. For meat the village depended on the hunting of sheep which swarmed over the hillsides. Later wild cattle and red deer became more common, judging by bones found in the refuse heaps.

At first the people of Jericho and similar villages possessed no domesticated animals. Much of their meat still came from wild gazelle and other beasts and birds which they diligently hunted. But within about 500 years of first taming wheat and barley and certain peas and pulses, they were keeping goats and sheep in small herds, presumably near the village. Here was yet another hoard of food: indeed a herd is a hoard. Evidence suggests that the early species of animals were first domesticated in a different part of the Middle East—sheep on the borders of the present Turkey and Iraq, goats in the mountains of Iran, and cattle on the Anatolian plateau. Sheep and goats were especially gregarious and so were more easily tamed: to tame one was to tame many. Mostly the younger male animals were killed for meat, the females being kept for breeding. The animals themselves were small, for the concept of careful breeding was in its infancy.

The people who first domesticated sheep and goats and cattle and kept them together in flocks and herds were not likely to be the same as those who began to domesticate plants. To grow wheat or tame the first goat required at least a dozen sharp-eyed observations, each one coming from a different man or woman. It is probable that men, being normally the hunters, were the domesticators of animals, and that women domesticated the early cereals. The cereals and the livestock did not initially coexist in harmony. Early gardeners did not want animals grazing near their young crops and eating them or trampling them down.

On the little farms and gardens the daily work had to follow a timetable more rigid than in nomadic days. If it was the time for weeding or for digging or for sowing the seed, the opportunity had to be seized—or it might be lost. The new way of life called for a discipline and a succession of duties that contrasted with the freedom of the gatherers and hunters. Thus the early farmers or gardeners probably had to build and renew wooden fences in order to protect their young crops. Otherwise wild deer, pigs, rabbits and other herbivorous animals would poach by day, and certainly by night, and eat the growing shoots or dig for the growing tubers. By day the gardeners had to guard freshly sown seed against birds, which multiplied when the grain was ripening. Today in parts of South-East Asia the watchers sit in huts to guard the ripening. The domesticating of plants and animals was a two-way process.

It is far from certain why this double breakthrough should have come in the same corner of the Mediterranean, but that region did offer advantages. Its countryside possessed two wild cereals which yielded very large grains. It was also inhabited by sheep and goats, which, being small and gregarious, were more easily tamed than most of the world's large animals. But these lucky advantages in themselves are not enough to explain change. In the history of the world, opportunities and luck have been relatively plentiful but the people who grasped them have been rare.

Other factors had molded the beginnings of this new way of life. The rising seas drowning coastal land had driven people inland, where, as a result, a mingling took place of peoples, ideas and habits. Furthermore the climate was becoming warmer, thus making certain plants and animals more prolific. Cereals, certainly, grew over a wider area than hitherto. The big animals, traditionally a vital source of food, were becoming fewer; and that provided an incentive to tame wild animals.

For long periods the pioneering tribes who were setting up gardens and keeping flocks had to coexist with nomadic peoples. To live side by side imposed a strain. In times of near-famine the hungry nomads were tempted to raid the neighboring villages which kept a store of grain and a flock of animals. The villagers in turn fortified themselves and kept constant guard. One advantage of the farming villages was that their population multiplied more quickly than that of the nomads. With larger numbers and better organizing—to farm was to organize—they were usually a match for the nomads in any fight. So they made punitive raids on nomadic groups or forced them to adopt versions of the new way of life.

The future lay with the new farmers and flock-keepers. To have access to the granary in a time of starvation was to own an asset such as no tribe in the nomadic era could possess. During a drought the village which possessed a store of grains and a flock of sheep or goats could survive longer.

The people might own the sheep but the sheep in a sense owned the people, virtually enchaining them. Therefore, the traditional way of life—the scavenging and foraging and the joys of the successful hunt— still carried an appeal. It also provided food, especially in spring. Several

33

thousand years after the origins of farming, many villages relied more on hunting and gathering food in swamps, forests and plains than they did on the new output of cereals, milk and meat.

The spread of this new way of life along the shores of the Mediterranean was slow. By 7000 BC, crops were grown, and sheep and goats were feeding under the close watch of their owners in Greece and Serbia and in the short Italian valleys sloping down to the Adriatic Sea. At times the revolution was spread by migrating peoples: somewhere in the world there were always people on the move.

To reach islands out of sight of the Mediterranean was a difficult adventure. Few wooden ships were capable of travelling far out to sea. By 6000 BC, however, ships were venturing to the western Mediterranean islands of Corsica and Sardinia. At the Greek island of Melos the strategic rock obsidian was being mined and shipped to the mainland. Obsidian served as an early version of steel, being ideal for manufacturing primitive knives, thin scraping instruments and sharp spear-points. As the shipbuilder's kit of tools and skills was enlarged, ships became larger. Many centuries later the Greek long ships, with their rows of oars, were constructed with bronze tools and possibly bolts made of bronze. Twenty meters long, their wooden prows rose high, like the neck of a seafaring monster.

Soon sheep and goats were herded and crops harvested in southern Ukraine and the plains of Hungary. In southeastern Spain and the north German plain the new farmers were at work. By 5400 BC the farmers with their digging sticks were in western Scotland and Ulster. By 3000 BC in Scandinavia, patches of crops and herds and flocks could be seen.

At least 2,000 years separated the first farms in Greece from the first farms near the Baltic. In marvelling at such a slow spread of farms and flocks across Europe, one obstacle should be remembered. Dense or spaced forest covered 80 per cent of Europe. To fell much of that forest with stone axes—the iron axe was unknown—and a million little fires called for patience and sweat. To forage was easier.

The new way of life advanced towards the Persian Gulf, and to the southern shores of the Caspian Sea and the Black Sea. Another 2,000 years went by before it made the short step from Syria to the mouth of the River Nile. Farming did not begin along the Nile until about 4300 BC. Why the valley of the Nile, so suited to agriculture, did not quickly take to farming is a puzzle.

Meanwhile, cattle had been driven by their herders into many parts of North Africa, ranging from Egypt and Libya to Algeria. Even the plateau of the Sahara region, being moister then, was attractive for cattle in lush seasons. Soon they were grazing on the far side of the Sahara, in what is now the Republic of Niger. The movement of livestock into Africa then lost momentum; and cattle, goats and sheep did not reach Zambia until about 1000 BC. They were still unknown in the southern third of Africa.

While Africa largely imported its first domesticated animals and crops, it domesticated the ass—a beast of burden—and the small guinea fowl, which was to be a favorite dish on the tables of ancient Egypt and later of Rome. The first domestic cats were African, and later they became dutiful guardians of the grain storages which were so attractive to mice. Africans were the first to domesticate and grow millet, which was usually viewed as an inferior grain. They were the first to grow sorghum and its luxuriant heads of grain, along with wild rice and yams. From Africa came palm oil. From China came a different kind of rice and millet, as well as a cluster of other domesticated food-plants.

Everywhere the tilling of the soil began in the most primitive way. The main digging tool was a wooden stick with its end sharpened and then made harder by fire. The fire-hardened stick must have been one of the vital inventions in the history of the human race—more important than the tractor—and it served gardeners in many parts of the world for thousands of years. Later came spades drawn by a rope, with one man pulling the rope and the other guiding the spade so that it cut a shallow furrow in which could be sprinkled the seed. This kind of two-man plough, with a cutting edge of wood or stone, was used in places as far apart as Iran and Korea. As early as 4000 BC the sturdy little oxen or bullocks were drawing the wooden plough in the Balkans, and that enabled the cultivating of heavy soil which had been too hard for the wooden digging stick held in the hand. The move from digging stick to the heavier plough was usually a move from women to men.

To sow the seed called for experiments. It is easy to assume that early farmers carried a woven bag full of seed, sprinkling it with a wide movement of the hand as they walked over the freshly dug soil; but in many places that way of scattering seed was unknown. In some African regions, women dug thousands of holes with a digging stick or hoe, or even with the quick stab of a toe in soft soil, and dropped a few grains of millet in each hole. Others filled their mouth with grain and spat it out, a few grains at a time, after each hole was dug. In some parts of southern Africa the grain was actually sprinkled on the grass and soil before the simple ploughing took place.

Greece, not long after 3000 BC, developed a distinctive kind of farming centered on the olive tree and the grapevine. On the steep slopes which hitherto had been fit only for sheep and goats, the vineyards and olive groves increased the yearly calories available to a village by as much as 40 per cent. At harvest time, wooden flails were used to knock the olives from the branches, and the olives were then soaked in a vat filled with hot water before the oil was removed with the aid of hard pressing. Olive oil was used not only for cooking but to fill lamps and clean the body. A vat was also used for trampling with bare feet the grapes brought down from the vineyards on the hills. The grape juice, having fermented into wine, was poured into a heavy pottery jar. Wine and olive oil altered the diet in the eastern Mediterranean.

The harvest involved heavier and more disciplined work than the old nomadic life. After the heads of grain were harvested and brought to the farmhouse or barn, they had to dry outside in the sun and then be threshed or beaten by both women and men, a strenuous and dusty process which sorted the heavier grain from the lighter chaff. The grain was now ready for use; but about one-third of it had to be set aside as the seed to be sown in the following year. This was the social security for the coming winter. Most farmers stored their eating grain in rounded pits dug in earth, chalk or clay and fitted with a floor of stone, wood or dry sand. The top of the pit was sealed with stones or clay in order to prevent mice or rats from stealing the grain and to prevent mould from growing on the grain in the humid pit.

If the winter proved harsh, villagers were tempted by their hunger to eat the seed grain preserved for planting in the early spring. Perhaps the children were crying out for food. Perhaps the mother was breastfeeding and hungry. Perhaps the older sons, exhausted after their day's work, wanted nourishment on a bitterly cold evening. Only a few steps away the precious seed grain was in sight, and could so easily be ground down and cooked and eaten. To eat part of the seed grain was to devour, like unthinking wolves, the future. Fortunately those who depended much on the olive and the wine-grape partly escaped this dilemma, for they did not have to preserve part of their produce each year as "seed."

Whereas every nomad had once spent the main part of each day gathering and hunting food, the new order fostered such specialists as brickmakers, house builders, bakers, brewers, potters, weavers, makers of garments, soldiers, shoemakers, tailors, keepers of granaries, diggers of irrigation ditches, and of course farmers and shepherds. Perhaps 90 of every 100 people in a region were still engaged in the growing of food and foraging for food and allied tasks, but the other 10 people took up a variety of specialist callings. The new specialists lived in villages, and the larger villages grew into towns. The town and the city were impossibilities before the development of farming.

The capacity of a district to feed people was being multiplied three or six or even more times by more efficient use of soil and grasslands, minerals and fisheries: a set of achievements beyond the skills of nomadic peoples. The population of the world, hitherto tiny, increased dramatically. Perhaps only 10 million people had lived in the whole world at the time of the first experiments in the farming of crops and the keeping of flocks. Then the world's population would have fitted with ease into the present Mexico City, with space to spare. But by 2000 BC the population of the world was probably approaching 90 million. Two thousand years later, at the time of Christ, it was close to 300 million.

At times the expanding population was cut back by epidemics. The nomads, without knowing it, had possessed advantages in health. Being on the move they left their sewage behind. Wearing few or no clothes in tropical climates they were more exposed to germ-killing sunlight. Owning no animals, they were a target for fewer diseases. In contrast, in the new order the crowding of people into towns increased the risk of infection. Human sewage in a town could infect the drinking water. The collecting of animal and perhaps human manure by hand and the practice of using it to fertilize the fields—a practice which was probably common by 3000 BC—was not yet seen as spreading infection.

While the new way of life provided more food and so increased the population of the world, it fostered viruses which periodically cut back the population. The daily handling of the newly domesticated livestock probably exposed people to diseases which hitherto were confined to those animals. One form of tuberculosis came with milk from cows and goats. Measles and smallpox were transferred from cattle to the people who herded them, milked them and ate their flesh. One form of malaria probably came from birds. Influenza came from pigs and ducks.

THE HUMAN SACRIFICE

A new form of political organization was emerging. Whereas in nomadic societies the power had been shared mainly by the older men, the new farming order was increasingly controlled by a small elite of rulers or by a chieftain who was usually male. While defending his town and farmland, the chieftain repaid his enemies for old slights or wounds. He captured some and enslaved them. Whereas a nomadic people rarely had a use for slaves, a sedentary ruler could employ slaves or forced labor in making irrigation canals, temples, fortifications and other projects. The new rulers could collect taxes in the form of grain, meat or other goods whereas the lands of the nomads had been tax-free zones. The official granary where the taxes were stored was an early form of the state treasury.

The new rulers ordained priests, or nationalized existing priests. The priests in turn gave legitimacy and moral support to the rulers. While religion itself was an ancient ally of the human race, full-time priests and priestesses were a novelty. They helped to bring down the rains that ended the drought; they paved the way for a plentiful harvest; they helped to defeat enemies in war; and they probably provided a feeling of inner peace for those who might otherwise have felt troubled.

By 3500 BC many of the rural villages and small towns of Europe and the Middle East were building religious monuments of impressive size. Several of the stones which were hauled or laboriously rolled to a sacred site and arranged there weighed as much as 300 tons. These dolmens, menhirs and other monuments extended from Malta and Spain and Portugal all the way to the southern coast of Sweden and to the west of Ireland. Maybe 600 such avenues or circles of stone stood in Britain and the west of France, where the stone chambers of Brittany were as awe-inspiring, in their day, as the dominating pyramids of Egypt were to be. England's Stonehenge, now a sight for tourists, was a later project, its main circle of stones being erected in about 2000 BC.

Stonehenge and similar structures were so arranged that the summer and winter solstices could be predicted and celebrated. They provided a calendar for farmers, whose tasks were dictated by the cycle of seasons. Usually standing in fertile farming districts, they were also the setting of dances, processions and those human sacrifices made in order to increase the fertility of both women and crops. Sometimes the stones honored dead ancestors.

In some parts of the world—especially in tropical regions which relied on yams and other root crops—it was assumed that the fertility of crops and the fertility of women were somehow linked. Some roots and tubers were seen as originating from the actual body of a goddess who had died. She had to be worshipped or the annual harvest might be lean.

The new religions reflected a sense of wonder at the universe and its workings and also the fears and hopes felt towards the immense powers of nature. Nature had to be worshipped and placated. The population of a region could be decimated by a hailstorm that flattened or bruised crops, diseases that killed livestock, a plague of insects or fungus that attacked the harvest, a spring which passed without rain, the decline of wild game because of disease or drought, and an unexpected flood. The ritual sacrificing of the lives of humans and animals seemed vital. To ensure a fertile soil, or a prolific annual harvest, gifts might be offered to the gods. The greatest gift was the sacrifice of a human life. That sacrifice might open the gate through which abundance could flow.

The Danes, who were late to adopt agriculture, clung to the belief that the new agriculture required blessings from the goddess of fertility. Her help was vital, for the Danish summer was short. If it was unexpectedly late or cool, only the goddess of fertility could rescue them. Human lives were the price she demanded. To sacrifice even three human lives for the sake of a fine harvest was cheap compared to the dozens of slow deaths likely in the shadow of a lean harvest.

Many of the Danes who were ritually sacrificed were buried in the bogs that covered much of Jutland. The acid in the bogs had the effect of embalming the bodies. It so happened that centuries later the bogs provided the peat which kept alight the fires in cottages; and those laborers who dug up the peat occasionally found ancient bodies, astonishingly preserved. Thus in 1946 was found a man killed in the first century before Christ. A hemp rope of three strands was around his neck, indicating that he had been hanged or strangled. The skin on his face, black and leather-like, carried a thin beard of red stubble. Remarkably, when he was moved, one eye slipped half-open, revealing an eyeball which was yellowy-white in color with a black iris. In his stomach were found the grains of the cereals and weeds he had recently consumed, probably in the form of a gruel. Two sheepskin capes and a piece of woven cloth lay beside him. The same bogs also yielded long-dead women who had been buried face down with a coarse woollen blanket laid over them.

The sacrifices seem brutal; but it is not certain whether the victims themselves felt despondent and frightened. They possibly imagined that, in death, their spirit would fly at once to a land of plenty. Close to the remains of one buried child were found four large and 12 small wings which had been cut from jackdaws and crows. On these wings the spirit of the child would fly away to the land of the blessed.

THE PUZZLE OF NEW GUINEA AND
THE AMERICAS

The highlands of New Guinea were so remote that they were little explored by Europeans until the 20th century. In another sense they were not remote but one of the pivots of the green revolution. As early as 7000 BC, when agriculture had not yet reached Europe, New Guineans cultivated various yams and other root crops, the shade-loving taro, the sugarcane and the native banana. Drains dug by hand improved the soil and aided this simple form of farming. That the idea of gardening came to New Guinea from South-East Asia is unlikely but not impossible.

In New Guinea the trees were cut with stone axes, the cutter using the short, sharp blows typical of the tomahawk rather than the long-handled swings of the modern axe. Eventually the wood and undergrowth were burned, a surrounding fence was built, and edible roots were planted with fresh fire-ashes serving as nutrient. Weeding was a vital task, and performed usually by women. After a couple of crops the soil was temporarily exhausted, and some distance away a new patch was reclaimed arduously from the forest. It was pioneering, with an abundance of muscle and stamina and sweat. This shifting form of cultivation, sometimes called "slash and burn," was still a source of food for maybe 200 million people in various parts of the tropics during the last quarter of the 20th century. Wasteful in the use of land, it required large tracts of forest, of which only a fraction was tilled and planted in any year.

While making this breakthrough, New Guinea did not keep pace with the Middle East. A prime reason is that it could not cultivate cereals. Not one of its wild grasses carries the large seeds naturally favored by early farmers elsewhere. Hard grains such as the wheat and barley of the Middle East could be safely stored for much longer than the root crops and produce from New Guinea's gardens; and it was the existence of large hoards and granaries of cereals that indirectly fostered the kind of specialized society that slowly developed in the Middle East but not in New Guinea. Likewise, China had the advantage of possessing rice, another hard grain which could be stored for long periods. New Guinea, therefore, did not require big granaries and so it did not require bookkeeping and writing and counting and accounting.

New Guinea also lacked animals that could be domesticated. So the combined step of domesticating both plants and animals, a step made easily in the Middle East and China, was impossible in New Guinea. The absence of large animals that could be hunted also led to a deficiency in proteins. This deficiency was aggravated because the staple diet of root crops was lacking in proteins compared to a diet of cereals. It is possible that cannibalism in New Guinea was partly the result of a craving for protein.

The Americas, like New Guinea, developed their own gardens. Plants such as squash and cotton and chili peppers were being cultivated in Mexico by the year 6000 BC, and later emerged maize and beans. On the east coast of what is now the United States, gardens appeared in about 2500 BC. In due time, agriculture became the basis of the American civilizations which the Spanish eventually discovered.

The prevailing view is that American agriculture and its distinctive civilizations arose largely in isolation. It is widely assumed that the rising of the seas permanently isolated the new settlers who crossed from northern Asia to the Americas; but the possibility of a recurring cultural influence from eastern Asia, Africa or Europe cannot be eliminated entirely. Perhaps a new wave of settlers occasionally reached the American continent.

A few pieces of evidence favor the theory that Asia and the Americas remained in contact. Thus the Chinese melanotic chicken, with its black bones and dark meat, existed in the Americas, where it was treated in the same way as it was in China, being sacrificed for magic and healing but shunned at mealtimes. Did this chicken arrive later from China in the boats of second-wave colonists? Likewise, a few scholars argue that the distinctive Mayan calendar of tropical America probably came from Taxila in the present Pakistan, and that four of the 20 names given to the days of that calendar were borrowed directly from Hindu deities.

The flow of ideas and plants and animals across the Pacific was perhaps in both directions, and there is evidence—not conclusive—that more than 1,000 years ago the American peanut plant found its way to coastal China and that American cotton found its way to India. In the 21st century more evidence will be unearthed on this tantalizing question.

Nonetheless, one farming region arose earlier than the others and was more dynamic in its effects. The Middle East was like a fire which, once blazing, gave out more and more light.

OVEN, KILN AND FURNACE

Hand-shaped pots—whether baked by the sun or by a red-hot fire—were a vital part of the new way of life. Whereas nomadic people moving frequently had no use for pots, people living in the same place for much of the year gained enormously from the invention of pottery. In the western world it is now difficult to comprehend why pots once were all-important, so little are they used except for ornament. Today the substitutes for pottery are numerous, including containers made of plastic and wood and cardboard, bags made of many materials, vessels of steel and glass, wooden barrels, aluminum saucepans and copper jugs. But visitors in recent times to Tanzania, Lesotho, Uganda, Nigeria, Sudan, Zambia and other parts of Africa could see how indispensable pottery was for the whole way of living. Pots were especially valuable for lighting and cooking, and efficient in using fuel. There were pottery lamps, or bowls in which candles stood upright. Large pots, some of which were equipped with lids and handles, held water and beer inside a house. An unglazed pot was favored as a receptacle, for it seemed to keep water cool. In the Cameroon grasslands huge pots were used for the making of palm wine while others held kola nuts. Nigerians played pottery drums at funerals. The Tutsi in Rwanda used large black pots for the burning of grass or leaves in order to fumigate a house. Some pots were so heavy that when full of liquid they could not be lifted by two men. Women were the potters in some regions: they ran what was then the main manufacturing industry.

A sedentary society skilled in making pots was able to move towards a new menu of food and drink. It was far, far more likely than nomads to brew fermented drinks, for heavy pots were needed in which to store them. A society owning pots was able to make yeast and then employ the yeast in baking bread in a pottery oven. A society which boiled its meat in pots rather than heated it on an open fire or hot rocks was, curiously, more likely to crave salt. Indeed, salt was the first food to become a regular item of trade in the Middle East and Asia.

The potter was the stepparent of the metallurgist. Potters and their clay were to be the forerunners of the metalworkers and their ores. While the making of pottery under intense heat did not lead automatically to the smelting of metallic ores, it served as a vital step. How to make the best use of fuel, how to increase the heat by a blast of fresh air, how to handle the burning sides of the pots, how long to allow them to cool— answers to these problems served as guides and pointers to the treating of metallic ores with an intense heat.

One of the momentous days in the history of the world was when almost-pure metal was first extracted, with the aid of a very hot fire, from lumps of hard and rich copper-bearing rock. The earliest furnaces and workshops for smelting copper have been unearthed at Timna in southern Israel, in sight of the bare mountains of Jordan. The furnace, first operated around 4200 BC, was a little hole in the ground, oval in shape and scooped to the depth of maybe an adult's hand. To prevent too much of the heat from escaping, a simple wedge of rock was placed flat over the fire like a loose lid. It was a backyard enterprise. Even to say that is to exaggerate its scale.

In its slowness the melting process was like a bakehouse making bread at the rate of a small loaf every two hours. In the homemade furnace the separation of the copper from the waste slag was not perfect, and most of the copper was extracted by hand in the form of small pellets. Bit by bit more was learned about the process of smelting. A pioneering metallurgist who returned to the smelter at Timna after 1,000 years would probably have been surprised to see the improvements, though in our eyes they might seem to be merely a slow procession of tiny steps.

The smelting of copper eventually led to the discovery of how to make bronze. Possibly it was an accident, but only an alert mind is capable of seeing the significance of what arrives by accident. Bronze was made by fusing 90 per cent pure copper with 10 per cent tin; the resultant alloy was tougher than copper and easier to cast into shapes. By about 3500 BC, bronze was being made by the metal smiths in the city-states of Mesopotamia. Where they found the tin, an essential ingredient, remains uncertain. The Middle East is rich in copper and poor in tin, but it is now known that the surface of the ground in areas such as Egypt's eastern desert held small patches of alluvial tin. Bronze weapons and knives at first were so expensive that they were rarely owned by ordinary people.

A LOST ALPINE SHEPHERD

Miraculously, a person of this era of copper was recently glimpsed in the flesh. The body of one man—the flesh still on the bones—was discovered about 5,000 years after he set out on a risky walk in the Tyrolean Alps, near the present borders of Austria and Italy. He was crossing a mountain gap which at 3,200 meters was higher than the highest roads across those mountains today. The season was probably autumn, and he was warmly clad. His head was covered by a cap consisting of many pieces of fur sewn together. His shoulders were protected from snow and cold wind by an outer cape neatly woven from reeds or strong grass. His coat, of deerskin, must have kept part of his body warm as he walked, but it is not certain whether the coat had sleeves. Certainly his legs were clad in leather leggings, while his feet were covered by calfskin shoes. A variety of animals, their skins and fur, had contributed to making him warm; but as the day went on he must have felt the cold.

He might well have been a mountain shepherd, bringing his flock down to the low country or searching for a lost sheep. That he was making a long rather than a short journey is suggested by the equipment he carried: an axe with a copper blade, a knife with a cutting edge made of flint and a handle of wood, a quiver with 14 broken or used arrows, and a half-completed bow with which to shoot arrows. To assist in bearing the weight of his load he wore a backpack constructed of light wood and animal skins. Of importance to a mountain man, in an area where fuel and kindling were not easily found for the fires so necessary on cold nights, he carried an ingenious birch-bark container capable of holding the embers of a past fire so that he could light his own without undue trouble.

He vanished in the snow. Perhaps, when his return home was long overdue, friends or family searched for him. He could easily be identified, for his skin displayed several small tattoos and his prized copper axe must have been familiar to friends. The search ceased, and the blanket of ice covered him, century after century. Only in AD 1991 did the melting of the ice expose his body.

4

THE DOME OF NIGHT

IN big and brilliantly lit cities—the headquarters of today's world—the power of the night sky can hardly be appreciated, for the sky is dulled by the city lights. Moreover, new explanations of human events, both secular and religious, have largely superseded explanations based on the stars and moon and sun. But for most of the years of human experience, whether recorded or unrecorded history, the night sky possessed a splendor and a magic. And when the first civilizations arose, the "heavenly objects" increasingly possessed a powerful symbolism.

THE MYSTERY OF LIGHTNING AND
THE SHOOTING STAR

In nomadic tribes and in farming villages, deep fear was stirred by meteorological events. In Tasmania numerous Aborigines were frightened by severe storms. "Heavy rain during the night," wrote a white observer in 1831, "accompanied by loud peals of thunder and vivid flashes of lightning, at which the natives evinced considerable fear." On the following evening the sight of "an electric spark" in the dark sky inspired calls of dismay. Perhaps the thought of being struck by lightning heightened the fear. Glancing nervously at a tree which had been shivered by lightning, they refused—like rural Germans on the other side of the world—to touch the exposed wood. They feared that it would make them ill. For storms and other frightening events they offered their own remedies. In the face of a rushing wind and the fireworks of a storm they tried to set fire to a tree or two in the belief that the wind would be silenced.

The night sky was the domed roof during all those years when people largely slept under the stars. Children were taught to observe the regular marching of the stars across the night sky. On rare occasions, they saw the dark sky crossed by swift-moving lights. Some lights were shooting stars and visible for only a second or two, and others showed an arresting tail of fire. The nomadic hunters and gatherers were remarkably observant of the night sky, and so they possibly learned by observation that shooting stars were more frequent at certain times of the year than others. Such stars were twice as numerous in the early hours of the morning as in the first hours of night. As for comets and fireballs, they must have been watched with fear and joy. When a strange happening was visible, the night sky was believed to be speaking.

All over the world, people devoted mental activity to the comets and stars. Few events were more exciting to them than the sight of a burning meteor falling in the night. Most of the meteors disintegrated while falling, and most which reached the globe fell into the ocean, but a few hit the earth. A meteorite is a meteor that reaches its destination, usually in the form of a black piece of rock; and such rocks, seemingly falling from the home of the gods, were treated with wonder when they were found. Smooth and often strangely pocked, giving the impression that they had come from a hot furnace, these fragments were widely regarded as sacred.

One meteorite that fell on the plateau of Phrygia in Asia Minor was taken to the shrine where Cybele, the mother of the gods, was worshipped. Century after century the dark stone itself was so venerated as a bringer of good fortune that in about 204 BC it was taken to Rome and housed. In Mexico the precious stone of the pyramid of Cholula, and in Syria the stone worshipped at Ermesa, were probably meteorites. In Mecca, in the holy building, was a sacred stone said to have fallen from the heavens. It was worshipped by Arabian tribes and by Mohammed himself. The practice of viewing a meteorite as sacred was so widespread that in the 18th century the leading natural scientists in France concluded, a little rashly, that meteorites were simply objects of superstition and that only a credulous person could believe that these stones had actually fallen from the sky.

The idea that a meteorite or shooting star was a message from the gods seemed to be confirmed by its noisiness—as well as its incandescent brilliance—when it plunged to earth. It sounded to some like the rumbling of thunder. To others, in the era of steam, it sounded like a train roaring past. In some societies a falling star was viewed as fortunate and in others as evil. In Central Australia a shooting star was an evil spirit, and songs were chanted and amulets worn in order to ward off its influence. Tasmanians shrieked at the sight of a falling star.

The nomadic people who lived under the stars, and the settled people who lived under the cloudless skies of the first civilizations in the Middle East, had every reason to observe the night sky. On a moonless night the sky was a wonderful tapestry set out above them. It also altered from hour to hour, and the pattern of alterations was observed and talked about. When the early British settlers first saw the Tasmanian Aborigines, long marooned from the outside world, and hastily concluded that they had little knowledge of any science, they did not realize how carefully these half-naked people had mapped and named the night sky. Likewise, 1,000 kilometers to the north, the people inhabiting the plains of New South Wales had constructed their own different map of the night sky, in which the Pleiades were the bees' nest, the Southern Cross was the tea-tree, and two stars near Scorpio were known as the green parrots. In the dryness of Central Australia, where no permanent river existed, some Aboriginal groups saw the Milky Way as a wide river flowing across the sky. In the eyes of many peoples, powerful creatures lived in the sky. To some, a dark gap in the Milky Way was the home of a demon.

The early civilizations flourishing along the rivers Tigris and Euphrates were to continue the enthroning of the stars. Skilled in astronomy, their people could predict many of the movements of major planets and clusters of stars, and in turn believed that these movements enabled them to predict human events. The Babylonians even learned how to predict an eclipse of the moon long before the eclipse occurred.

The stars were studied and observed all the way from Mesopotamia to China and the Andes. Thus the Pleiades—a procession of a few hundred stars, seven being highly visible—were watched closely at certain times of the year in towns and lonely cottages which lay thousands of kilometers apart. For early farmers in Africa and Europe the appearance of the Pleiades, rising at about dawn in the springtime, marked the start of the agricultural year. This was the signal to prepare the ground and sow the seed. In Central America the Maya probably used the Pleiades as a clock, and its exact position in the sky marked the successive stages of the night. In midwinter in the big Inca city of Cuzco, the appearance, just after sunset, of the Pleiades was eagerly waited for. It marked the commencement of the year.

The rise of astrology, and the study of the possible influence of the stars and planets on human events, is now dismissed in intellectual circles as make-believe, but there was a tentative logic in this intellectual discipline that was to attract some of the best minds in the early civilizations in China and the Middle East. If the sun could shape summer and winter, and the moon could determine the high tides and shape the calendar, why could these powerful forces not also shape human destinies? This question intrigued scholars for thousands of years. Physicians were also taken with it, and until the 20th century those persons suffering from mental illness were called lunatics, meaning that their sickness was influenced by the moon.

The moon, small or large, was usually a commanding presence. The largest object in the night sky, rising and setting some 50 minutes later on each successive day, it moved majestically. A new moon was invisible, for it marched in step with the sun across the day sky. In contrast the full moon could be seen throughout the night. Alive and powerful and personal, the moon was a female to some peoples and a male to others. It was a symbol of life and death, and was said to determine when the rains would fall. It was believed to influence the growth of vegetation; and for thousands of years it was a rural rule that farmers always should plant during the new moon. At a later time, in India and Iran and Greece, it was believed that people after death journeyed to the moon. The cycles of the moon were to constitute the first calendars, after the art of astronomy appeared.

When the universal religions of Judaism, Christianity and Islam arose, they selected the new moon or the full moon for holy days. Long before there was a calendar engraved on stone or in the minds of priests, the moon's visible act of rising and setting, its waxing and waning, was closely observed by people in hundreds of thousands of campsites. An eclipse of the moon or the sun was a momentous event. The moon's eclipse—it passed through the earth's shadow—was the more frequent event, and a startling spectacle to mere mortals on earth.

The sky, like the earth, was seemingly inhabited. It had such height and space that it was usually seen as the home of Supreme Beings. Because mountains climbed towards the sky they were often venerated as sacred. In China and Japan stand sacred mountains which even today retain some of that veneration. As the sky was the home of the gods, whatever fell from the sky, whatever reverberated in the sky, might have divine associations.

The Arrernte of central Australia believed that their creators had once walked the earth but now lived in a paradise in the sky. They were immortal and their wives were eternally young: "they are women whose breasts remain firm and round forever." At night the people down below, lying on the ground and about to fall asleep, could look up and see the great ones. They could gain reassurance from their presence above, though they could never share in their paradise.

"I HAVE DREAMED A DREAM"

Night was the time when people had dreams—jubilant, terrifying, peaceful, familiar or strange. Night was seen as a mysterious realm by a variety of tribes, and humans were admitted to that realm while they slept. The dream was the evidence of their visit. In northern Canada the native peoples near Hudson Bay believed that, when they were asleep, their soul slipped away from their body and temporarily entered another world. In central Australia the Arrernte believed that each person had two souls; and that during sleep the second soul actually left the body. They understood that their own dreams were really themselves seeing the simultaneous activities of that second soul, taking place outside the body. The dream was almost an eerie form of television. If a terrible event happened to the soul which had left the body, the terror was instantly conveyed to the person who was asleep and dreaming.

In Luzon in the Philippines, the Tjan people did not try to awaken those who were fast asleep. While they slept, their soul was absent from their body. In ancient Greece it was believed that those who were dreaming were especially susceptible to outside influences. A sick woman who fell asleep in a sacred place, and began to dream, came under the spell of powerful spiritual forces which might heal her as she slept.

Dreams were often seen as messages from the gods, delivered while the recipient of the message was asleep. A function of the priesthood was to interpret dreams, especially those of rulers. In the Old Testament the capacity of dreams to foretell events was confidently affirmed. Thus the ruler of Egypt was perplexed by a strange dream: "I have dreamed a dream, and there is none that can interpret it." On advice he sent for Joseph, an unshaven prisoner, and asked whether he could explain why, in his recent and vivid dream, seven fat cows emerged from the river and grazed in the lush reed-beds, and then came seven skinny cows who consumed the fat cows. Joseph replied that God had ordained that seven years of wonderful harvests and lush cow pastures would be followed by seven years of famine; "and the famine shall consume the land." In due course the famine came. Written tablets or guides setting out the meaning of dreams were compiled in Egypt perhaps as early as 1786 BC, and in the city of Nineveh about 1,000 years later.

Tens of thousands of years before the rise of priests and soothsayers, vivid dreams must have been recounted with awe. The importance of the dream was a reflection of the importance of night, when dreams took place. In a simple camp, in a nomadic society, the presence of night and the intensity of the darkness was almost overpowering. Today, a huge brilliantly lit city almost overpowers the night.

In the modern era the dream quietly changed its meaning. Dreams ceased to be interpreted simply as forward-looking. The psychologist Sigmund Freud saw a dream not as a glimpse of the future but as a mirror of the personality and past of the dreamer.

It is impossible to say when human beings first read a meaning into the moon, sun, stars and comets. It is impossible even to tell how those views were altered during the long period when humans did not live in permanent settlements. And yet the night sky and the night were vital in molding their religions and their sense of who they were. To ignore the night and the night sky because they are recorded so sparsely and fleetingly would be to neglect a vital and tantalizing part of human history.

THE HIDDEN MONUMENTS

Nomads built no grand monuments, no pyramids and lofty columns of stone, no temples and no lighthouses. They were incapable of hewing heavy blocks of stone and carrying them far, but in a sense they did not require monuments. A monument is a proclamation of what is important; but to the people living 15,000 years ago the sky and earth were crowded with monuments, some visible only to those with trained eyes.

For some nomadic societies the sky was a monument created by their own ancestral beings. Their land was created in the same way. Every hill and rocky ridge, every detail of the landscape, had been created by these beings when they first lived on earth. In the eyes of the early Australians, the hills, cliffs, animals and everything vital in their own tribal territory were virtually sacred monuments to their ancestral beings, and the original act of creation had to be periodically repeated through the religious rituals, ceremonies and dances left behind by those creators. Thus the living people maintained their contact with those who long ago had created this life-giving landscape and skyscape.

It was typical of early religions to be absorbed in the beginnings—in how people and their world were created. This absorption in creation was also the essence of their religious rituals. They feared that this world might vanish unless they constantly renewed it with their ceremonies. Whereas the later religions such as Judaism, Christianity and Islam were to view the human story differently, seeing not only a beginning but also a definite end to human history, the early religions saw the possibility of eternity for earth and sky—so long as humans carried out the duties entrusted to them. Many of the early tribes took comfort from the fact that the night sky, in which their ancestral creators dwelt, would be there forever.

It is jumping ahead of this story but it should be said: the later religions, while they formally contradicted the influence of astrology, were also profoundly affected by the night sky. The Jewish calendar was based on the moon; and the commencement of the religious year was determined by the juxtaposition of two distinct events—the sight of the ears appearing on the crops of barley and the first sight of the crescent new moon. Buddha was born at a special point in the cycle of the moon, while a bright guiding star was said to pinpoint where Jesus was being born. In Hinduism and Jainism one of the sacred events is a festival of lamps, and it takes place on the full-moon day of a certain month. The holiest day in the Christian calendar is determined by the moon. In Islam the calendar is still based on the moon; and Ramadan—the month of fasting—officially begins at the moment when the new moon is visible to the naked eye. Chinese civilization honored the moon and stars. Even the first universities, rising in the Middle Ages, gave emphasis to astrology. To be a professor of astrology in one of these universities, or to be the consulting astrologer to a Christian king or a general in the 12th century, was to possess real power. It was Copernicus who, four centuries later, was to shoot astrology from the academic sky—but not from the people's sky, where it remains powerful.

5

CITIES OF THE VALLEYS

IF A tireless traveller had lived in the Middle East in 4000 BC, and had performed the unusual—perhaps impossible—feat of journeying over-land all the way from the shores of the Black Sea to the upper Nile, they would have found no breathtaking monument. They would have found no city. They would have found no temple of learning and no royal palace of luxury. If, some 1,500 years later, their footsteps had been retraced by another traveller, grand sights would have been relatively common. They would have existed, however, mostly along the big rivers of the region. In the rise of civilization, four impressive rivers in this corner of the world and several great rivers in other remote lands were central.

The big rivers of the Middle East crossed dry plains whose soil was enriched each year by floods. Tens of millions of tons of silt were carried downstream and spread thinly on top of the exhausted ground like a new layer of fertilizer. Likewise in the dry seasons canals carried water from the rivers to irrigate the parched farmlands. On the floodplains more people could be fed within a small area, and bigger towns could be nour-ished, than almost anywhere else in the world at that time. In an era when land transport was primitive, the wide river was also the superhighway, along which boats could cheaply carry grain and building stones to dis-tant parts of the kingdom.

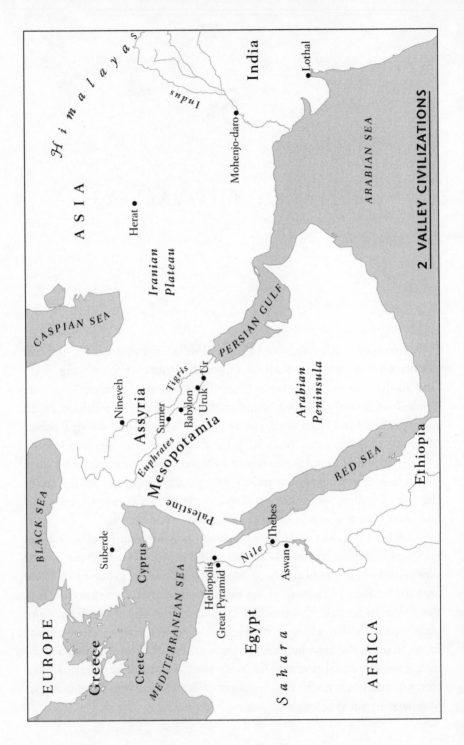

Lothal

India

Mohenjo-daro

Indus

Himalayas

ARABIAN SEA

ASIA

Herat

2 VALLEY CIVILIZATIONS

Iranian
Plateau

CASPIAN SEA

PERSIAN GULF

Nineveh

Tigris

Ur

Assyria

Sumer

Babylon

Uruk

Arabian
Peninsula

Euphrates

Mesopotamia

RED SEA

BLACK SEA

Palestine

Ethiopia

Suberde

Nile

Thebes

Cyprus

Heliopolis

Aswan

EUROPE

Great Pyramid

Greece

Crete

Egypt

MEDITERRANEAN SEA

Sahara

AFRICA

THE VIEW FROM THE PYRAMID

The banks of the Nile nursed Egypt's civilization. The river threaded its way along a narrow valley, which near Aswan in upper Egypt was only 2 kilometers wide. The sand of the desert actually trickled into the river here and there. Further downstream the valley was often 30 or more kilometers in width, while in the delta the mosaic of rich low-lying land and river channels was over 200 kilometers wide. At floodtime the delta countryside, the main source of Egyptian wealth, became a sweeping lake which lapped the edges of the permanent villages perched on their low mounds. Indeed the delta villages were known as "islands." The earth, freshly top-dressed with new soil carried down by the flood, was ready for another harvest of barley and wheat after the floodwaters subsided.

The river was not always a wonderful asset. If the flood was too high or flowed too fast, all kinds of earthen levy banks and water channels were destroyed. Moreover the water did not flow effortlessly to the higher fields. As farming became more developed, people or roped animals had to be employed to lift the water in buckets or baskets from a lower to a higher level.

The prosperity of Egypt depended on the annual fertilizing flood. In the years of a bumper harvest, the temples and other granaries were filled with grain. In some years, heavy rain did not fall in equatorial Africa and Ethiopia; and along the lower Nile everyone waited with increasing anxiety for the flood that did not arrive. Then crops failed along stretches of the valley, the temples were slowly emptied of old grain, and famine set in.

Egypt began as a chain of city-states spaced along the Nile. They were ruled by eight separate kings. Eight, however, was too many. Some in their decadence were too weak to defend their territory, and some were the unknowing puppets of the priests of Heliopolis. In 3165 BC, Menes united the country, proclaimed himself pharaoh, tamed the priesthood and became the god-king. Only he had a spark of divinity, a piece of God within him; and when he died he ascended into heaven, while on earth his name was worshipped forever. In the eyes of some, the pharaoh and his dynasty carried the seeds of the religious ideas that sprouted and blossomed, many centuries later, in the Middle East. Egypt's religious writings were to influence passages in the Psalms and other books of the Jewish scripture.

Egypt had a long line of powerful monarchs, impressive cities, a vigorous religious and economic life, granaries jammed with grain in the years of prolific harvests, and royal tombs in which rich treasures lay in permanent darkness. Here lived army generals, bureaucrats and priests who showed considerable powers of organizing and of record-keeping. Their picture script, an early form of writing, served as a method of communication along the river.

Here were architects setting out their fine schemes, and builders capable of implementing the plans in massive stone, and thousands of artists working in precious metals, copper, wood, textiles and precious stones. Here were designers of canals for transport and irrigation, one canal even linking the Nile and the Red Sea. Here lived scientists who increased the knowledge of the moon and stars and devised the pioneering calendar dividing the year into 365 days. Here paraded influential priests who formulated a view of the afterlife in which princesses continued to be honored as princesses, while even commoners might have a taste of eternity. The king, being a god hiding inside a human body, merited a tomb to match.

The annual flooding of the Nile was not taken for granted. Everywhere, even amidst the oases in the desert, costly temples were built in honor of the divine ruler, without whose blessing there could be no "annual rise of the Nile." In return, tribute or taxation was paid to the temple in the form of barley and wheat or even land. Eventually the temples owned about one-third of all the arable land along the Nile. In most years of the 12th century BC the temple Medinet Habu—only one of hundreds of temples—received enough grain to feed from 3,600 to 4,800 adults. Each prosperous year was almost regarded as a miracle, the result of successful intercessions by the king and his priests.

The tall reeds waving in the wind were a familiar sight in parts of Egypt—and also Mesopotamia—where the rivers overflowed into marshes or fanned across a delta. A host of laborers gathered the reeds for the thatching of houses. The sharp end of the reed also served as the pen or stylus with which pictures and syllables were cut in damp tablets of clay. Ultimately clay was challenged by another writing material from the rivers. The papyrus plant grew in the marshes of the Nile—or, as the Book of Job expressed it, "Can papyrus grow where there is no marsh?" As early as 2700 BC, clever Egyptians were converting papyrus into a thick form of paper or parchment, ready to receive markings from the reed pen. Paper, which is almost the essence of a bureaucracy, was Egypt's own invention.

Perhaps the Egyptians were the first people to treat dogs and cats as pets. Cats were depicted on tombs; in death their bodies were mummified in readiness for the afterlife; and they were mourned by families, who showed their grief by shaving off their own eyebrows. As early as 2000 BC the greyhound was also kept, especially to participate in the sport of hunting the hare.

In other pleasures and pastimes, Egypt pointed the way. The earliest garden of which there is detailed knowledge—the plan may be seen in the New York Public Library—was created at the city of Thebes in about 1400 BC. The garden was dissected by walls which gave privacy, avenues of trees which conferred shade, and four oblong ponds in which water-fowl splashed. The walled gardens and the displays of shade and water were adopted by Islam, two millenniums later, and carried far from the hot lands of the Middle East to the courtyard of the Alhambra in Spain and even to central Asia.

In medicine the Egyptians probably led the known world. Magic and knowledge were mixed: a potent mix in the mind of the believer. Much of the knowledge of human bodies came from the custom of preparing them to be mummified. In anatomy, surgery and pharmaceuticals the Egyptians had their triumphs, and possibly they were the first to use bandages and splints. In their cures they used the fat of such creatures as mice and snakes, as well as herbs and vegetables, each ingredient being carefully weighed or measured. The Greek classic by Homer, *The Odyssey*, referred to Egypt's physicians as the best, and by that time their medical reputation for skill and flair and bravado was close to 2,000 years old.

In 2600 BC the Egyptians were the first known bakers of a modern style of yeast bread. In shape, their loaf of bread was more like a flat omelette than the taller loaf which was eaten in Greek times. A baking stove, with a firebox at the bottom and an oven at the top, was their invention.

The flood plain of the Nile normally produced a surplus of food which not only fed those who worked the fields but also that one-tenth of the population who lived in the cities and served the monarch and his attendants and priests. It was this surplus of food, this small overflow of wealth, that enabled a succession of the kings to plan some 80 pyramids as royal tombs.

As the country along the Nile was fringed only by low foothills or escarpments, the pyramids could attain a dominance impossible in a mountainous landscape. The first pyramid was built about 2700 BC. The Great Pyramid, 200 years later, was designed to be 146 meters high, or equal to the height of a modern 50-storey skyscraper. It called for the efforts of some 100,000 workers, including slaves and those farmers who were idle when the annual floods were at their height. Heavy blocks of limestone and granite had to be cut in the quarries and transported to the site without the aid of wheeled vehicles or pulleys. Maybe 2,300,000 blocks of stone were cut, moved and fitted one on top of the other to form this lofty pyramid. It was the most remarkable structure so far built in the world. That it was built by a kingdom with a total population barely exceeding one million is even more remarkable. Egypt's population was to rise, and in the time of the New Kingdom some 1,500 years later it reached maybe three or four million.

Egypt, more than any other of the river civilizations, enjoyed long periods of stability. Its continuity in language and culture was remarkable. Its monarchy lasted for some 3,000 years—one of the most durable institutions in recorded history. While Egypt's defects were conspicuous, so too were its virtues.

Egypt's continuity came partly from geography. It was guarded by desert on both flanks and so was not easily invaded, though occasionally Libyan armies advanced to the western edge of the Nile delta. Protected by the desert and the relative military weakness of its neighbors, and sustained by the mighty river, Egypt was able to build grandly and leave behind stately reminders of its glory.

WHERE THE WHEEL FIRST TURNED

A rival civilization flourished in Mesopotamia. There, the world's first known state, with its accompanying secular and religious bureaucracy, arose in about 3700 BC. The state occupied a warm plain between two rivers, the Tigris and the Euphrates. Indeed, it was a creature of the fertile valley.

Fed by melting snow in the mountains of Turkey, the twin rivers had covered about two-thirds of their journey to the sea before they reached the edge of the plain, and were close to the sea when they finally merged. They occasionally changed course or were filled with silt, but for centuries they were used by small boats or by rafts made of skins, which carried much-needed timber down from the wooded hinterland. The lower valleys of the twin rivers were prolific when planted with barley and wheat. Whereas in most other regions the farmers were digging with sharpened sticks and simple spades, here they actually ploughed the ground, thus enabling a large area to be cultivated by a small number of servants. Part of the barley was fermented into beer, possibly the first beer in the world.

In the south of Mesopotamia, known as Sumer, fine cities arose on the banks of the rivers and canals. Several of the Sumerian cities were in sight of each other. In about the year 3000 BC, 18 cities were flourishing in an area no larger than the present Republic of Ireland. Uruk, standing in the present Iraq, was said to hold as many as 50,000 people, all of whom were fed by the farmlands close by. The cities tended to be the capital of a small surrounding territory or state, but warfare reduced the number of states. To be conquered was a common experience for the peoples of southern Mesopotamia.

In these cities the temple was as vital as the cathedral was to be in Europe more than 3,000 years later. The priests with their rituals, sacrifices and prayers called on the rain-bringing winds to blow from the right direction and shower the parched ground. The priests also pleaded, when their prayers were answered too readily, for the floods to subside. They proclaimed the wonder of the universe too.

Whether these cities of Mesopotamia were more inventive than Egypt is a question not easily answered. Almost certainly the solid wooden wheel was invented here. One cart with solid wheels could, if drawn by an ox, exceed the carrying capacity of a short procession of men. Later the devising of a light wheel, with radiating spokes, transformed peacetime transport and also led to the extensive use of horse-drawn chariots in warfare. The wheeled vehicle, in war or peace, was especially suited to the plains.

The arts of writing and reading arose at one of these cities in about 3400 BC, though Egypt is also a contender for this honor. The early writing took the form of pictures. These writing-pictures were drawn with a sharp instrument on damp clay, which was then allowed to dry and harden. An orchard was depicted as two trees in a tub. A container of grain was symbolized by an ear of barley. The head of an ox, accompanied by the numeral 3, signified 3 oxen. One of the purposes of writing was to record the foodstuffs and textiles carried into the temples, which also served as storehouses.

A more sophisticated form of writing can be seen in the tablets written about 600 years later and collected from the ruins of the city of Ur, near the shores of the Persian Gulf. The new writing recorded syllables from the spoken language. Ur's move to the syllable has been called "the most important advance in the history of writing"; and this same advance possibly occurred quite independently in Mesopotamia, Egypt and China. It was followed later in slow and subtle stages by the invention of the letters of the alphabet. The act of writing was thus broken down, like the links of an iron chain, into its smallest components.

The art of counting also made headway. The more advanced of the river-cities devised two distinct numeral systems, one using 60 and the other using 10 as its base. The 10s or decimal method ultimately won; but the 60s method had a more lasting victory. As a result of the calculations of the mathematicians of Babylon, the 60 survives in the 60 minutes that constitute each hour.

These cities were often extravagant in their willingness to sacrifice human lives. While Egypt was building fine pyramids in honor of its dead kings, the city of Ur celebrated royal deaths in its own way. Excavations reveal that, around the year 2600 BC, a spacious tomb was prepared for a dead monarch. Servants, musicians and guards were also chosen to be buried with him. These victims—perhaps they saw themselves rather as the privileged ones—were so numerous that, on the day of the burial, they had to be assembled like a small regiment. After drinking poison from a bowl—so that their death would not be lingering—the male and female sacrifices were shown to their allotted place in the tomb. Dressed in scarlet coats with short sleeves, the 64 women wore long banana-shaped earrings, headbands ornate with gold leaves, or necklaces consisting of handsome beads made from precious minerals. These ornamental minerals had been carried long distances: the orange-colored cornelian came all the way from India and the lapis lazuli from Afghanistan.

In these lands of the twin rivers, the rival cities and empires fought for the right to exist. Eventually the empires close to the Persian Gulf were superseded by those whose home was in the foothills. One empire of the hills was the Assyrian. Its name echoes in the modern nation of Syria, but its heartland lay in the present Iraq; and its first capital city,

Assur, stood on the fertile plains of the winding Tigris River. Rather late in the course of a long history the Assyrians were vigorous enough to capture their rival, Babylon, and bold enough to attempt the conquest of Egypt. The most powerful empire in the western world, its rule extended to within a few days' horseback-ride of both the Caspian Sea and the Persian Gulf.

Members of the royal family were enthusiastic hunters, either in the wild or in the game parks and zoological gardens kept for their pleasure. The king himself rode to the hunt in a chariot drawn by three horses, each wearing blinkers to prevent it from being distracted as it ran. The driver stood in an unroofed cabin and a hunter or two stood beside him, ready to fire arrows. When a chariot horse was allowed to graze in the long grass, it wore on its neck a small bell—occasionally found in excavations—so that the metallic sound would denote its whereabouts.

The Mesopotamian lion, which was smaller than the African lion, was the target of countless hunts. It is easy to guess why this species of lion became extinct. A baked tablet surviving from 1100 BC records that one royal hunter while on foot killed a total of 120 lions. When he was hunting from the relative safety of the chariot he killed another 800 lions. Occasionally there were diversions, and it is proudly recorded that he killed 10 elephants and four wild bulls. Presumably the elephants also became scarce.

In Assyria the sciences—especially astronomy—and the visual arts flourished, along with engineering. Here the masters of irrigation designed canals to carry water across the plains to large cities and so create a green carpet of irrigated fields. Fine palaces and temples stood in their cities. In the art of warfare they were not backward.

Early glassmakers worked here in about 1500 BC. For centuries they made glass vessels by surrounding with molten liquid a smooth core which was later removed, leaving behind the shaped glass. In the British Museum the delicate Sargon vase, of light green, still responds to different lights. Whether it was created in Assyria or made its way there through trade or conquest is not known. Glass was only for the rich.

The fine murals of Assyria were carved from gypsum. It is rather a let-down to learn that such works of art were fashioned from what is known today as the raw material of plaster of paris. Nonetheless in many of the murals the carved faces of long-dead Assyrians are visually still alive. Here is the flabby face of a eunuch and the alert, watchful face of a hunter. Certain of the faces combine a quiet dignity with a hooked, parrot-like nose.

The climate of the irrigated plains can be glimpsed in the murals. The summer sun beats down on the hard ground, and the king himself is shaded by a large umbrella. War, often present, is also carved in vivid detail. In or about 878 BC, three men are depicted fleeing from a city which has probably been captured. Dressed in long robes, they jump into the Euphrates River where one is swimming while the others hug a lifebuoy to their chests. Like a long pillow, the lifebuoy consists of the skin of an animal, inflated with air. As the hands of the refugees are clutching the inflated lifebuoy, and as much of their breath is expended in blowing air into it, they can only stay afloat by swimming with their legs. Whether they reached the opposite shore will never be known.

The houses, meadows and orchards of Nineveh, the most impressive of Assyria's capital cities, were supplied with water flowing down a canal from mountain ranges. As the canal had to cross a valley, a bridge of five pointed arches was designed to carry it. Teams probably made up of thousands of prisoners of war were assembled, and they began to quarry chunks of limestone and neatly shape them into heavy blocks. Two million stones were cut and carted to the site of the long bridge or aqueduct. If this bridge of about 700 BC had lasted until the railway age it would have allowed three trains to run side by side, such was its width.

On the wide plains where two large rivers wandered, various cities were born during a period of 2,000 years. They left behind oblong tablets of clay on which were recorded lists of their kings and the earliest dictionaries. They left behind tiny sunbaked or fire-kilned barrels, with writing circling the barrel, one line on top of the other. The script is impressively neat, straight lines having been lightly ruled on the wet clay to guide the writing.

How eagerly many of these messages, in tiny handwriting, must have been read. Here is a tablet from an astronomer or astrologer warning the king that the approach at sunrise of a crescent moon is a special warning for his soldiers fighting far from home. Here in burned clay, baked in 667 BC, is a prediction that an eclipse of the moon will occur. The Assyrians believed that movements in the sky profoundly affected human events. Even the activities of thieves were so affected.

The rival empire ruled from Babylon was no less advanced in astronomy. Its calendar was based on the moon, the moon god being in charge of the night just as the sun god was in charge of the day and all its events. Of these competing gods the moon was the more powerful. A new moon was believed to be a boat in which the moon god travelled in a slow and stately way across the expanse of the night sky. That same crescent moon was to be revived many centuries later by the new religion of Islam.

The moon determined the calendar. The new moon marked the start of the month. Ultimately Babylonian astronomers could predict to the minute when the new moon would be seen on the horizon. The prediction was important because the calendar month formally began not at midnight, but at the moment when the tip of the new moon peeped above the horizon. In Babylon's calendar, 12 lunar months equalled 354 days, thus giving each year a shortage of 11-and-a-quarter days. The shortage was solved by adding a 13th month to the calendar in every third year.

Many people did not necessarily glory in these river-valley civilizations. Slavery was widespread. In Assyria the foreign-born slaves, usually captives of war, had no rights. On the other hand local inhabitants who were enslaved as punishment for their unpaid debts retained certain rights. They could also marry a free person. Assyrian wives were treated like property, and had social contact only with females or with male relatives. Babylon was slightly more sympathetic to women.

A FORETASTE OF EROSION

Bold steps in the advancement of knowledge had been made on these wide river valleys and their uplands, sometimes called the Fertile Crescent. Eventually these wide valleys knew decay. Rise and decline are normal processes in human history. Here the bruised environment also hastened the decline.

The miracle is that some of the green farmland on the lower Euphrates and the Tigris lasted so long. In their hilly hinterland, more and more trees were felled for firewood and for building materials. Meanwhile the topsoil eroded, the valleys became silted, and the rivers tended to overflow their banks.

On parts of the plains the constant irrigating of the soil, and the destruction of the trees with their deep network of roots, forced the underlying salt to creep towards the surface. Freshwater ponds became salty. It was observed that the crops of wheat—unlike those of barley—could not tolerate salt in the soil, and that in some regions wheat became a rarity. The plains were a foretaste of what would eventually happen in the irrigated zones in numerous arid lands extending from Australia to California. In the dozen or more centuries after 2000 BC the population of certain regions in Mesopotamia slowly declined.

These city-states, so mighty in their day, were also weakened by periodic wars. With their bows and spears and javelins, they turned warfare into an art form. Many of the soldiers also carried slings—maybe as long as their arm—and used them to hurl stones at an enemy upwards of 100 meters away. To protect themselves they wore caps coming down to the top of the ears and a light armor on the upper part of the body.

The Assyrians became masters of another weapon: this powerful weapon was called terror. When they finally entered a city which had refused its opportunity to surrender peacefully, they would murder, torture and mutilate people on a large scale as a warning to other cities. To be defeated in war was a painful experience in nearly all the early civilizations, but it was especially painful for those defeated by Assyria. And yet Assyria could also be constructive. It moved large numbers of rebellious or defeated peoples to a distant region, there to cultivate the soil or build monuments and public works.

Energy and ingenuity were wasted in fighting. Later rulers realized that the powerful rivers could be converted into destructive weapons, like a wave of bombers in a later millennium. The Assyrians marched from Nineveh and punished their enemies by breaking the walls of dams and canals and by diverting torrents of water against low-lying cities, thus undermining their foundations. About 700 BC the King of Assyria decided to let loose this "water bomb" on the rival city of Babylon. As he recalled with maybe a hint of vengeance in his voice: "I completely blotted it out with water-floods and made it like a meadow."

Babylon rebuilt itself. Converting the reedy meadow into city streets again, it awaited its opportunity for revenge. It gathered allies from the Medes and the Scythians who were so skilled with horses. In 612 BC the allies began a three-month siege of the enemy city of Nineveh. Surrounded by moats and walls, the noble city was almost impregnable. But it could not resist a sudden surge of water if the Babylonians broke the nearby dams. The walls were finally knocked down, probably by a man-made torrent. The Assyrian king was killed. His city was ransacked. The library, crammed with clay writing tablets, was wrecked. But many of the tablets in their shades of pink and brown and ochre do survive, revealing snatches of history from the last era of a long-lived empire.

A WELL-SCRUBBED CITY OF THE INDUS

Egypt and Mesopotamia had been flourishing for 1,000 years when another valley civilization emerged not far to the east. The wide Indus valley was watered by rivers that tumbled out of the snowy Himalayas and glided down to the Arabian Sea. Nearly all of the valley lay outside the tropic zone. While the Indus River eventually gave India its name, most of it now lies inside the Republic of Pakistan.

The Indus valley was generously endowed by nature. Jungle originally grew along its fertile riverbanks, and when cleared away, revealed a rich soil. The river was wonderful for agriculture, for the annual floods, larger than those of the Nile, inundated the low-lying areas from about June to September. Each year they spread a layer of life-giving silt. The evidence suggests that the monsoon came further inland and that the climate was unusually moist by today's standards. So extensive was the flow of muddy water that today some of the sites of this civilization are covered by 10 meters of silt. So soft was the soil that it was possible to sow wheat not by hand but by trampling down the seed with feet or toes.

Farmers were at work in the valley as early as 6000 BC. From time to time they were invaded by people who, coming from the present Iran, had seen or heard of one or other of the valley civilizations. They began to create a distinctive Indus civilization. Emerging by about 2500 BC, it was to flourish for seven or more centuries. Covering an area perhaps five times the size of Great Britain, and ruled by priest-kings, it gave rise to large cities. One city, Mohenjo-Daro, possibly held 40,000 people and was therefore one of the world's largest cities. Dominated by a citadel at one end and laid out in rectangular streets, it was well drained and amply provided with freshwater. Even the private houses were fitted with a brick-paved bath.

Skilled in the arts, the people of the Indus cities left behind images of their daily life. Many of the inhabitants so depicted were of a tall distinctive build with a big, domed head and a very broad nose. The women wore a kind of miniskirt with a belt around the waist and nothing above. They liked to see their own face in copper mirrors, to shape their hair into a bun with the aid of a comb made of ivory, and to decorate their lips or eyes with a red pigment. At night, lamps or candles consisting of vegetable oil lit up their houses.

Wheat and barley in several varieties, field peas, sesame and mustard seed were grown. The fruits included dates and watermelon. It is likely that sugarcane and cotton were first cultivated here, later spreading to the Middle East and eventually to the Americas. That two notable crops should come from the Indus was a measure of its importance.

Amongst the animals grazing along the valley were pigs, sheep, goats, camels, asses and humped cattle. Some of the animals were used for transport, and bullock carts carried a canopy to provide shade for passengers. Cats and dogs were kept, and the egg-laying hen was possibly domesticated here. Pottery was mass-produced, and toys made for children included imitation cattle that nodded their heads. On the coast were busy ports with sophisticated traders writing in a distinctive script and using an advanced system of weights and measures. They handled a variety of products from Mesopotamia and the shores of the Red Sea, including grain, wool textiles, silver and tin.

One of the marvels of the Indus civilization, excavated in modern times, was an artificial dock joined by canal to the sea. The dock was at Lothal, a town of, say, 3,000 people, which was much closer to the present Mumbai (Bombay) than to the mouth of the Indus. A basin with brick walls nearly 5 meters high, the dock was shaped like a corridor, extended more than 200 meters, and could hold large seagoing vessels.

The river and its annual floods served as the artery of this civilization but the arteries must have become clogged. More and more forest was removed by the farmers, and then isolated trees were cut down to provide wood for the kilns that baked the mudbricks. The floods eroded some areas and filled others with silt. The big towns had to sit themselves on mounds in order to escape the floods which, as the valley silted, rose higher and higher. The city of Mohenjo-Daro was rebuilt about nine times, often after floods damaged or endangered it. How far the interplay of farmers and the environment hastened the decline of the civilization is not clear.

The life of the Indus, as a center of power, was much shorter than that of the Nile or the rivers of Mesopotamia. By about 1800 BC, long before the arrival of the new techniques of working in bronze and iron, its cities were beginning to decline. The climate was becoming drier. More significantly, the valley was penetrated by the Aryan invaders who for centuries had been increasing their domain in northwestern India.

The creating of large villages and the domesticating of plants and animals had been a vital step in the history of the human race. The early valley civilizations formed another step. Sitting in the silt-rich valleys of the Middle East and the Indus, they borrowed from each other and sometimes stimulated each other. A clear geographical advantage, apart from the river and the silt, was that the flanks of each civilization were partly protected by desert, thus providing a defense against attackers. The climate of the river valleys was another asset, for they could grow cereals which in turn were especially easy to preserve for long periods. The effective hoarding of grain was vital if cities—far larger than the world had yet known—were to survive. That the other civilization of Asia arose in the warm silt valleys in China is further evidence of the influence of the big snow-fed rivers on human history.

6

AMAZING SEA

No stretch of salt water exerted such a pervasive influence on the rise of today's world as the Mediterranean. Without that sea and its peculiar qualities and unusual position, the world's political, economic, cultural and social life would have veered in another direction.

In an age when the sea—so long as it was calm—was cheaper and swifter than land for the carrying of cargo and passengers, the Mediterranean offered advantages. It extended from the Atlantic Ocean in the west almost to two inlets of the Indian Ocean in the east: the protruding Red Sea and the Persian Gulf. The long arm of the Mediterranean, the Black Sea, stretched towards the interior of Asia. Two shorter arms, flanking the Italian peninsula, extended almost to the foothills of the snow-clad European Alps.

This sea united Africa and Europe and Asia. A maritime freeway, it linked diverse regions that each produced something different—copper and tin, gold and silver and lead, wine and olive oil, grain, timber, livestock, dyestuffs, cloth, weapons, spices, obsidian and other luxuries. It was a swift conduit for ideas and religious faiths. If Asia or Africa had themselves possessed a sea as large and central, the history of those continents would have been profoundly different. In essence this sea was a strategic lake, with the crowning advantage that, at the Strait of Gibraltar, its narrow throat opened into the wide ocean.

WITH FOUR WINDS IN YOUR HAND

The Mediterranean, being almost surrounded by land, could be astonishingly smooth for long periods. On some days it was a flat mirror, and in summer it was relatively free from storms. Here the large rowing boats known as galleys were in favor, partly because of the absence of wind at certain times of the year. In calm weather, oars were the only motive power. Most galleys were able to row close to the coast for almost the whole of their voyage; and whenever the sky looked ominous they could creep into one of the hundreds of natural harbors that dotted the coast. The oars enabled galleys to enter narrow harbors which, if the wind were blowing from the wrong direction, were too risky for a sailing ship to approach.

When storms did arise, and whitecapped waves pounded the pebbly beaches, galleys could be sunk in the space of minutes. Whole fleets could vanish, with few sailors surviving. In 480 BC, when the Persians were attacking Athens, the outcome of the war was partly determined by a rising wind which dashed Persian ships against the rocky Greek coast. Century after century, famous lives were to be influenced by these occasional Mediterranean storms. In 1833 John Henry Newman, sailing from Sicily to France, was so affected by a storm that he wrote a hymn which became famous, "Lead, kindly Light."

The hazards of the Mediterranean were part of the Greek and Roman legends. On the rocks waited the Sirens, whose haunting voices lured sailors to their death. At the narrow entrance to one strait stood two sea monsters: Scylla barked like a dog while Charybdis, three times each day, sucked down the seawater in a huge gulp and blew it up again. In all, the bones of hundreds of thousands of sailors and passengers probably rest on the bed of this sea. But that formidable total is only a fraction of the lives that would have been lost if the sea and its shores had been less friendly. It was a friendly sea with wild moments.

The Mediterranean was blessed by another gift. It experienced no heavy rising and falling of the tides. The level of its water changed little during the course of 24 hours, and so ships could tie up to piers and docks and be unloaded with relative ease. In only a few shallow ports did ships have to wait for high tide before they could enter or leave. The city of Venice, with canals instead of streets, was only practicable because the tidal range was low.

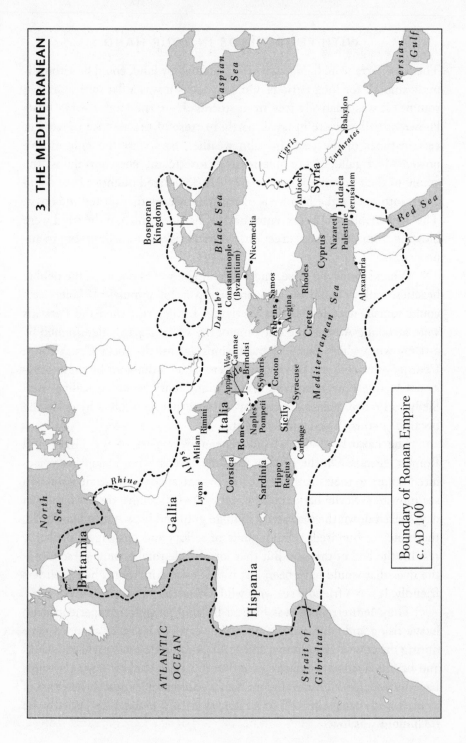

3 THE MEDITERRANEAN

Boundary of Roman Empire
c. AD 100

The advantages of this long attenuated sea, and its deep gulfs, meant that a strong military power could command a large area. In turn, the Phoenicians, Greeks, Carthaginians and Romans made use of it. Here, too, the wonderful invention the sail was first seen. The earliest record of a sail is a decoration on a vase made in Egypt about 3100 BC. The sail is square and resembles a big blackboard on an easel, and no doubt was employed in a ship sailing along the busy River Nile. Leather or skins might well have been used for the early sails, but by 2000 BC they were being replaced by linen which was woven from the strong fibers of the flax plant. A sure supply of flax was to remain an ingredient of naval power until the age of the steamship.

The hoisting of sails on masts, and the more skilled use of ropes, went arm in arm with an improved knowledge of the winds. By the time of the poet Homer, the Greeks knew much about the winds and their prevailing directions; indeed a knowledge of the winds and stars was virtually the only compass when at sea. Thus sailors far out to sea on a dark night could ascertain their bearings partly by noting the direction from which the wet, cold and blustery wind came. Known as the Zephuros, the source of that wind usually signified the west. Similarly the north lay in the direction from which came the Boreas, the dry and cold wind.

The most common of the early compasses was really a diagram which, carried in the mind, signified the directions from which came each of the distinctive winds. Gods were in charge of each wind. A version of this idea was accepted by early Christians partly because John the Divine was recorded as saying, in the Book of Revelation: "I saw four angels standing on the four corners of the earth, holding the four winds of the earth." The angels temporarily prevented the wind from churning up the sea.

The galleys carried a sail. When the wind was blowing from a favorable quarter, a square sail was raised; but if the wind was only light the crew plied the oars. Eventually small galleys gave way to large galleys, which were especially favored for fighting at sea. Oarsmen were now stationed on two decks instead of one. Later the trireme had three decks and maybe 170 oarsmen. Those oarsmen seated on the upper deck had to ply very long oars so that the blades could reach the water far below.

Much is now known about the seaworthiness of the ancient Athenian triremes or three-decker galleys of the fifth century BC because a replica was built for the Greek navy as recently as 1987 and experimented with at sea by a full crew. The modern oarsmen soon found that they needed overhead protection from the hot sun, and even then they perspired heavily while rowing and felt a need to drink on average 1 liter of water an hour. Exhaustion soon set in, as it must have in ancient days. Therefore the oarsmen realized that Greek three-decker galleys must normally have been rowed at a steady rather than a fast pace—unless a battle was about to take place.

The combination of sails and oars enabled ships to attain a speed which the sails alone or the oars alone would not have achieved. Thus a light tailwind enabled the galley, when fully manned, to increase its speed from 4 to 6 knots. Sometimes a powerful wind pushed the ship up to 10 knots and the oars were not even needed. If sails were raised on two masts, the ship sometimes heeled over so far that use of the oars was impossible.

In Athens the naval galleys relied more on the effort of free men, but the galleys which carried cargo relied more on slaves. On any calm day, tens of thousands of slaves must have been at work at the rowing benches of ships owned by Greek cities and colonies. Their ankles carried fetters which prevented them from leaving their position beside the oar. If their ship suddenly went down during a battle or storm, they had little hope of escape.

The Mediterranean, especially its northern shores, was to become the center of power and creativity. Its rising influence was aided by the landsmen's slowly increasing mastery of ships and by another slow-moving event: the advent of cheap iron.

Iron items had long been a luxury. Early iron did not come from the rocks, where it was abundant, but as a rare gift from the skies. For long the meteorite provided the only kind of iron in use. Being heavenly in origin it was often set aside for sacred rituals. Eventually, iron ore was detected in the rock; the heavier and richer pockets were mined in a primitive way, and attempts were made to separate the iron from the barren materials permeating it. Copper smelting offered guidance. In about 1500 BC, unknown but brilliant metallurgists learned to smelt iron ore by raising the temperature of the furnace to more than 1,500 degrees Celsius, which was 400 higher than the temperature required for the smelting of copper ore. Quickly iron from the earth became cheaper than iron that dropped from the sky.

Nonetheless, metallic iron was still so expensive that most Europeans did not even own one fragment of this metal that was capable of transforming the ploughing of the ground and the axing of trees. It was sparingly used in Palestine, Cyprus and Syria and virtually unknown elsewhere. By 900 BC, however, iron tools were frequently used in the eastern Mediterranean.

Iron still carried sacred and magical associations. The act of going into the darkness below the surface of the earth to mine the ore was vested in mystery. The process of smelting useless lumps of rock into valuable lumps of pure iron was also hailed as magical. The smelterer and blacksmith were the makers of miracles. High was their prestige. In the eyes of Homer metallurgy was probably the king of the crafts. In his *Iliad*, even the stars shining in the heavens were the handiwork of the god Hephaestus, whose working tools were the anvil and bellows.

By about 1000 BC iron was challenging bronze in central Greece as a precious metal to be buried with the dead. Two centuries later, iron wares and weapons were widely used along the Aegean. Though wood remained more important, even for the making of work tools, iron's special strength and sharpness were changing warfare, agriculture and some of the crafts.

THE BRIGHT LIGHT OF ATHENS

Every few centuries in relatively modern times there have been brief periods of vitality which, long after they are over, seem to stand like a light along a lonely coast. These eras have usually been confined to a small part of the world, though their light might shine far around. The Greeks lit such a light. Day and night it burned on the high headlands overlooking many stretches of sea, and for centuries it could be seen from afar.

The Greek colonists spread wide. Today on the Black Sea, tourists in the coastal pleasure boats in the Russian harbor of Sukhumi are told that they pass over rippled sand covering the ruins of an ancient Greek city. In southern Italy one can walk along marshy ground and imagine, beneath the river silt, the banquet houses of Sybaris, a Greek city celebrated for its sensuality.

By the sixth century BC the Greek colonists occupied a strip of coastline in southern France and Spain. Their cities were sprinkled along the coasts of southern Italy, Sicily and North Africa, the islands of Crete and Cyprus, as well as a long belt of what is now the coast of Turkey. These cities were small, but most were bubbling with vitality. Part of their vitality was reflected in vigorous quarrels with one another. If they had combined instead of clashed, they would have conquered most of the western world.

Athens emerged as the most impressive of the Greek city-states. Its territory of dry hills, known as Attica, was no larger than the present urban area of greater Los Angeles. Its total population rarely exceeded 300,000, and yet it was the most influential pocket of territory the world had so far seen. After it was burned or looted by Persian invaders in 480 BC, the Athenians fought back and trounced the enemy. Defeat and humiliation gave them opportunity and incentive. Bold dreams were set in stone. The Athenians built a parallel set of walls from their city to the port about 7 kilometers away, thus providing a defended roadway along which imported grain and other supplies could be rushed to the city in time of war. In the heart of Athens, on the rocky knoll of the Acropolis, they built in white marble a temple that became a glory of the western world. The Parthenon, begun in about 447 BC and completed in less than 10 years, housed the elegant statue of the goddess Athena, carved by Phidias and adorned with gold and ivory. Other temples on this sacred hill guarded graven images of various gods.

These temples on the Acropolis survived long after Athens ceased to be a powerful city. The Parthenon served centuries later as a Christian church and then as an Islamic mosque before it was damaged heavily by shots fired from the Venetian artillery in 1687. It is ironic that one of the world's treasures should have been mutilated by soldiers coming from the city of Venice, which itself is one of the world's treasures. The sculptor's metallic chisel and the barrel of a gun are often the work of the same hands.

Now revered as secular art treasures, the buildings adorning the Acropolis were in effect the predecessors of Christian basilicas and Gothic cathedrals. In the course of each summer, worshippers climbed the steep hill three times in order to honor the goddess Athena. The first time was during the cleansing festival, in celebration of her birth, and the last was the festival honoring the four-yearly athletic games sponsored by the city. The middle or grain-threshing festival highlighted the power of the gods in those long eras when life and death depended on the state of the weather. Performed in midsummer on a night of the full moon, the threshing festival formally initiated that symbolic event of the rural year, the first threshing of newly harvested grain in the farming valley west of the city. Athena made the west wind blow, and the thousands of farm laborers who threw the grain into the air trusted that the wind would continue to blow away the husks and so clean the fresh grain.

The city, with its increasing population, eventually had to import from the Black Sea much of the grain from which its bread was baked. But the threshing festival survived; and each year, in the light of the moon, the procession—with the priestesses prominent—set out from the Acropolis to perform the blessing of the first wheat-threshing.

Athens and a few other city-republics of Greece led a bright flowering in the history of art. Learning from the Egyptians, the Greek artists gained too from their own exciting and confident intellectual climate. Possibly the finest period was between 520 and 420 BC, when grace and fluency marked so many of their buildings, paintings and sculptures.

The expansion of trade called for something less clumsy and cumbersome than the bartering of one set of commodities for another. In 670 BC the Greek island of Aegina was perhaps the first to mint coins. Made of silver, they were recognizable because their face had the imprint of the sea tortoise. Money eased the trading of goods, for a merchant accepted money when there was no trade item he desired.

Objects as small as the nail of the little finger, as well as stately temples, displayed the skills of the working artists of Greece. Two tiny scaraboids, carved from rock crystal late in the sixth century, can be seen in the Getty Museum in California. One depicts a horse swishing its tail while being led by a young man. Another is a tiny ring, almost the color of a ripe red currant, depicting a naked youth scraping oil, dirt and sweat from his leg with a curved blade. Whether they were imported gemstones or luminous pieces of brown amber collected on the shores of the Baltic, the Greek necklaces, amulets, brooches and tiny statues were carved with flair.

In the art of luxurious living the elite of the Greek cities, especially in Sicily and southern Italy, were perfectionists too. Delicacies came from afar. Fresh fish, including such small species as the sea squirt, were a familiar sight and smell in the markets. Poultry was introduced from India about 600 BC, but the popular bird of the Greek farmyard was the little quail.

For slaves and poorer citizens the main foods were wheat, barley, beans, and the acorns that fell to the ground. Beef was a rarity. At times even olive oil—used as "butter" on bread and oil for cooking—was almost too expensive for the average household, and indeed most olives grown near Athens were crushed, squeezed and then shipped as oil in large pottery jars to faraway ports. For the poor a drink of wine—and it was always diluted with water—was not a daily pleasure. In contrast, the richer Greeks set out to seek and savor the best; and the later invention of retsina wine was not the accidental result of keeping wine in pinewood casks but yet another product of the quest for novelty.

THE WRESTLER OF CROTON

The Greeks were the first people to become obsessed by an activity so characteristic of the present era: competitive sports. Their Olympic Games, open only to citizens of the network of the Greek world, became a red-letter event every fourth year. Usually said to have commenced in 776 BC, they were a minor carnival at first. Whether competing as runners, throwers, wrestlers or chariot-drivers, the Greek athletes originally wore clothes but eventually nearly all preferred to be naked in the thronged arena.

A few ambitious cities recruited athletes and paid them handsomely if they won. Professionalism quietly permeated a festival which was later hailed as the heart of amateurism by those Europeans who revived the Olympic Games in AD 1896. A Greek city named Croton, at the foot of southern Italy, displayed the modern desire to win whatever the cost. Rich and large—to walk around its walls was a journey of perhaps two hours—Croton was able to entice athletes from other cities. In the hundred years beginning in 588 BC, the runners of Croton were victorious again and again.

The athlete Milo brought more glory to Croton by winning the Olympic wrestling six times in succession. His massive shoulders were strong enough to carry a live ox around the stadium; and his stomach, it was reported with perhaps a dash of exaggeration, was capacious enough to hold all the meat of that ox. Once he devoured an ox in a single day. When he walked through his city, breathing the evening air, his presence must have been the focus of more civic pride than was aroused by the presence of another of that city's immortals, the eminent mathematician Pythagoras.

Envy and rivalry weakened the Greek cities. It is sometimes predicted that international sport will become a happy substitute for international war, but the experience of the cities of Croton and Sybaris, which were Greek-speaking rivals standing by the Gulf of Tarentum, casts doubt on this prediction. Sybaris, jealous of Croton's prowess in athletics, set up its own sporting carnival in about 512 BC. Croton was not impressed. Ultimately it despatched to Sybaris an army under the command of none other than Milo the wrestler. Greek fought Greek, with blood spilling on the temple floors and the grassy arena. The city of sensuality was virtually destroyed. Croton, in contrast, continued to send its muscular athletes in ships to Olympia, in the confidence that some would bring home the laurel wreaths of victory.

The Greek city-states learned to excel in the sport of popular politics. Experimenting in democracy, they carried it further than perhaps any other early society. In Athens the property owners, assembling almost every week, made speeches and gave instructions to those who were briefly in power above them. Nobody was long in power. Even the influential council—consisting of 500 men, all over the age of 30—was always in flux. Its members were chosen by lot or lottery, and no member could serve for a lifelong total of more than two years. Above the council sat another group, one of whose members was selected—again by lottery—to preside formally over the city and its hinterland. His term of office was astonishingly brief. He ruled simply from sunset to the next day's sunset. In effect the assembly of citizens leased out its power in tiny morsels to the higher officials and then summoned back those morsels and inspected them.

How could a small state, often engaged in war, be effectively governed in this way? The chief of the armed forces was partly exempt from the short-term rule. In the fifth century, at the height of Athens' democracy, the military chief was personally elected, not chosen by lot. The position rotated regularly from one general to the next until the time of Pericles, who was elected for 15 years in a row.

Greek democracy was vulnerable in time of crisis or war. It was slow to make decisions and, like most democracies in modern times, reluctant to impose the necessary taxes. Aristotle, one of the remarkable Greek minds, detected the virtues and failings of this rare mode of government. He regretted that if too many of the poorer property owners attended the assembly, their clamour for subsidies to be paid to themselves might milk the country dry. In his opinion, "the poor are always receiving and always wanting more and more." And yet he supported the idea that all who held land should share in the right to govern their country and the duty to pay taxes. In his eyes, however, the smaller farmers should not serve as magistrates—they would be tempted by bribes—nor as heads of state, for they lacked experience.

In Athens public decisions were made directly by the people and not at arms length, as is now the practice in every mass democracy. But the democracy of Athens, like the roadway running from the city to the port of Piraeus, was hemmed in by walls. Only those classified formally as citizens were eligible to speak and vote; and after the year 451 BC, an Athenian citizen who married a foreign woman thereby deprived any of their ensuing children of the right of voting. The poor did not vote. Women and the numerous slaves did not vote. Only owners of property could vote, but many farmers were too poor or lived too far from Athens to be able to halt work and attend the vociferous debates.

Aristotle's ideal was a nation, small in population and area, where all voters knew, by sight or by reputation, everybody else of importance. Such voters could assess the moral character and other qualifications of those seeking high administrative and judicial offices. Significantly, the rebirth of democracy more than 2,000 years later owed much to observers such as Aristotle, who wrote down their assessment of what was one of the extraordinary experiments in the history of the world up to that time.

The Athenians believed in democracy, though not in equality. In their opinion, people were born unequal and never would be equal. In a fighting speech in 330 BC, the orator Demosthenes directed disdain against a rival orator, Aeschines, accusing him of coming from a humble background: "As a boy you were reared in abject poverty, waiting with your father in his school, grinding the ink, sponging the benches, sweeping the room, doing the duty of a menial rather than a freeborn man." It was as if one's humble past could never be forgiven.

An ability to speak grippingly—whether as a storyteller or poet, prophet or persuader—had been prized by a thousand different tribal and illiterate societies over the space of countless years. The Greeks called it oratory and converted it into an art form. Oratory was also a tool of power, because the open-air assemblies of rowdy and moody voters, sometimes numbering 6,000, could be swayed by a magnetic speaker.

The celebrated orator of the ancient world was Demosthenes. The son of a manufacturer of swords, he tried when young to turn his own tongue into a sword. Frail in physique, not suited to the gymnastic and other sports favored by young Greeks, he concentrated on law and on the art of delivering speeches. His early attempts to speak must have been embarrassing. He stammered at first, but exposing himself to the self-made obstacle of holding pebbles in his mouth, he learned to speak each word slowly and firmly. Sometimes he stood before a mirror and watched his mouth, eyes and expression at work, for orators had to be actors too.

Plutarch the historian records that the fledgling orator once shaved the hair from half of his head, thus deterring him from walking in the city and compelling him instead to concentrate on improving his speaking. Demosthenes, not very convivial, was known derisively as the "water drinker." When at about the age of 30 he first spoke in the assembly, he was mannered, slightly effeminate and bereft of humor. He was almost laughed down.

In time, listeners came to marvel at his wide vocabulary, melodious sentences and clever arguments. Many of his finest speeches were patriotic pleas for Athens to prepare its navy and army against potential enemies. He lived to see one of those enemies, Alexander the Great of Macedonia, conquer more territory than any known commander in the world had previously conquered, and even keep Athens under his heel. Macedonia had hitherto been seen as a backwoods country. Therefore its military victory was as humiliating to Athens as a victory by Mexico over the United States would, today, be humiliating to Washington. To be subjected by people believed to be second-rate was a shock to proud Athens.

Demosthenes was in peril in Athens in 322 BC, after a rival orator led the cry that he be put to death. He escaped, only to be caught by Macedonian soldiers. His only sword—the art of persuasion—was blunt in the face of iron swords. He took poison. The palmy era of Greek democracy was almost over.

Masters of debate, the Greek cities dotting the Mediterranean shores were also masters of violence when a need arose or was imagined. While Athens was listening to the honeyed tongues of orators, Greeks in Sicily were slaughtering and torturing one another. Agathocles, ruler of the powerful city-state of Syracuse, killed 4,000 in one day. The Romans were to improve on that record.

These remarkable Greek harbor-cities, even after the death of democracy, buzzed with intellectual energy. Today, many discerning scholars suggest that Plato of Athens was the most gifted of all philosophers, while Aristotle is revered in what is now called political science. In architecture and the arts the Greek cities, while indebted to Egypt, laid new paths. In medicine, a doctor on the small island of Kos was foremost in the western world; and his name lives on in the Hippocratic oath—the ethical vow of modern medicine. In physics, ethics, linguistics, biology, logic and mathematics, the finest of the Greek thinkers and investigators were like a succession of lights flashing in the darkness. History, stemming from a Greek word, was another field in which the Greeks were pathfinders. Their vitality and genius also went into theatre, sports and democratic politics, as well as difficult abstract ideas.

Engineering was another of the Greeks' strengths. On the island of Samos in the sixth century BC a tunnel was driven 1 kilometer through a high limestone hill in order to tap a supply of freshwater. At about the same time, Greek stonemasons were the first to use the claw chisel, so useful in working marble. Their builders were possibly the first to use a crane to lift materials to rising walls, but slaves were preferred to the new crane.

Overall the Greeks excelled more in science than in technology. Even their most ingenious weapons called for physical labor on a massive scale. During the siege of Rhodes in 304 BC, a portable tower and stone-thrower, running on wheels, was built to aid the attack, but several thousand men were required to haul it into place. In Athens and its rural hinterland, one-quarter—and at times one-half—of the workforce consisted of slaves brought from what are now Turkey, Bulgaria, Romania and Ukraine. The work of these slaves even underwrote the democracy, for small landholders were able to afford the time to attend the assembly only because slaves could look after their households, flocks, olive groves and vineyards.

One vital aid to manual work does appear to have originated near Athens. During the building of a shrine at Eleusis in about 333 BC a strange contraption was noticed by visitors. Instead of the laborers carrying bricks and other materials in a handheld stretcher, they were pushing a wheelbarrow. A simple and clever idea, it saved muscle power, as most home gardeners would eventually affirm. In regions where slaves were plentiful, however, this labor-saving idea did not spread widely. It was the

Christians participating in the second crusade who, about AD 1150, brought the wheelbarrow to western Europe.

THE CITY BY THE LIGHTHOUSE

Alexander the Great conquered terrain as far away as India and central Asia, but he spread urban Greek ways rather than rural Macedonian culture. A new city in Egypt, named Alexandria in his honor, was to become the chief inheritor of the Athenian tradition. Founded in 331 BC—eight years before the death of its namesake—the rising city was soon to be ruled by one of Alexander's generals, who crowned himself as Ptolemy I of Egypt. The body of Alexander himself was carried there and entombed in magnificence.

The city, designed to be the new Athens of North Africa, became the intellectual dynamo of the western world. A remarkable library and museum were built. Brilliant Greek scholars such as Euclid arrived to pursue their thinking; medical research was advanced by the anatomist Herophilus, who dissected the human brain and eye in the year 285 BC; and a quarter-century later a famous medical school was born. Jews came to the city in numbers to trade, and Jewish scholars accompanied them and translated their Old Testament from Hebrew into Greek. It was known as the Septuagint, for it was the work of more than 70 translators.

Alexandria was sympathetic to practical and impractical scientists. Hero of Alexandria, a pioneer in the science of optics, also devised a fire-engine, the first slot machine, and a screw press which was valuable in squeezing more wine from grapes and more oil from olives. Ctesibius, the son of a barber, devised a forced pump and a toothed wheel; and his water clock became a rival to the sundial, which, utterly dependent on the rays of the sun, was useless at night. If there had been Nobel prizes for science, medicine and literature in that epoch, Alexandria would have been the home of more prize-winners than any other city. And yet all this ingenuity did not transform the daily work of a civilization in which the slave served as the all-purpose machine. Alexandria and other Greek cities were probably capable of making many of the steps which constituted, just over 2,000 years later, the industrial revolution; but they had no need for an industrial revolution.

Alexandria was built where the River Nile, almost reaching the sea, flowed through a delta of ever-changing channels. Opposite the city, only 1 kilometer across the water, lay the elongated island of Pharos which partly protected the port. A narrow causeway—its ruins can still be seen—was built from the city to the island of Pharos, thus protecting the harbor from rough seas. On the island was commenced one of the marvels of the world, the Pharos lighthouse.

The lighthouse was of unusual design—square at the base, octagonal in the middle, and circular at the top where, each night, was lit a brilliant fire. As Alexandria possessed no prominent hill which could serve as a landmark to ships standing out to sea, and as the shoreline of that coast was low and barely visible, the lighthouse served as a warning pillar by day and a bright light at night. It was also a sculpture gallery, decorated with large statues of gods, kings and queens.

Completed in about 280 BC, almost at the same time as that other seaport marvel, the Colossus of Rhodes, the lighthouse was eventually acclaimed as one of the noblest sights of Egypt: as astonishing as the pyramids but more useful. The light itself, burning at a height equal to the top of a modern skyscraper of 25 storeys, could be seen far out to sea. With the passing centuries, however, the lighthouse became dilapidated. In medieval times it was shaken by two earthquakes, and its upper stones and statues were toppled. In 1962, the Egyptian navy would rescue from the adjacent sea the fallen statue of Isis, whose feet had been amputated by the fall. The statue, when in place, must have stood as tall as a building of four storeys, and yet it was a dwarf compared to the lighthouse itself.

The lighthouse was the symbol of the power of the conquerors. Native-born Egyptians, in contrast, were consigned by the new rulers to the shadows. They had to surrender their big rural estates to the Greek-Macedonian elites and were left only with small plots, many of which lay beyond the reach of the annual life-renewing flood. In the new order the native Egyptians stood so far below the Greeks that they were almost invisible.

The Hellenistic rulers kept the Egyptians firmly on the bottom rung of the ladder. For an Egyptian to adopt a Greek name required formal permission. The disdain of the Greek-Macedonian towards the native Egyptian was said by some to be the most pronounced antipathy in the ancient world. Curiously, it was more honorable for a Greek to marry his own sister than to marry a member of any one of the numerous races which settled in cosmopolitan Alexandria. In this custom they were largely imitating royal Egyptians, who had often preferred to marry their own flesh and blood. It was the practice for the monarch to marry his sister; and 10 of the 15 Ptolemy rulers did so. The censuses of Egypt about the time of Christ reveal that in Greek-Macedonian families, perhaps one in six marriages was between brother and sister. No record survives of a Greek woman marrying an Egyptian man and bearing his children. A rigid way of maintaining Greek purity and caste, it also ensured that rich land did not leave the family. Presumably the biological effects of the in-marrying were not disastrous.

For nearly 300 years the Greek-Macedonian monarchs did not even learn the local language; and Queen Cleopatra, the last of that long succession, was probably the first to speak it. Alexandria's official name proclaimed the aloofness of the immigrant Greeks. Wishing that this city be not seen as an integral part of Egypt, they officially called it "Alexandria Beside Egypt."

The powerful Hellenic civilization, now centered on Alexandria as well as the old Greek heartland of Europe and Asia Minor, was not lacking in self-esteem. It was often imitated. More than 2,000 years later the map of the world, including lands never known to the Greeks, was sprinkled with Greek echoes and reminders. In the United States the early capital city, Philadelphia, carried a Greek name. In upper New York State arose Syracuse, Ithaca and a cluster of towns with names honoring ancient Greece. In Australia in the 1850s, the gold diggers setting out from Melbourne to the new goldfields passed two mountains, Mount Macedon and Mount Alexander.

Greek names moved easily from Macedonia's hills to the cold as well as the hot places of the New World. An archipelago in Alaska and an island opposite Antarctica both carry the name of Alexander. In the 19th century the three largest empires in the world were for long periods presided over by monarchs bearing Greek names: Queen Alexandrina Victoria of England, Alexander II of Russia, and Louis Philippe of France.

Perhaps the most powerful influence exerted by Hellenistic civilization was on the Roman Empire. The Romans, especially after 200 BC, happily imitated much that was Greek. They admired the literature, theatre, food, politics, visual arts, oratory and much of the style and culture that had first flourished and taken shape in Athens. This process of imitation has been likened to the worldwide imitation of America in popular culture today.

Athens was pervasive and persuasive in ways which were almost impossible to predict. It had long passed its political prime when it became the quiet teacher of the Romans.

7

LORD OF THE YELLOW, KING OF THE GANGES

A HIGHWAY of grassland ran nearly all the way—interrupted sometimes by mountains and lakes—from central Europe to eastern Asia. It ran from the banks of the River Danube to the forests of Manchuria. Measured from coast to coast, the grass highway ran almost from the Adriatic Sea to the Yellow Sea. The land along that wide corridor embraced poor soil and rich; and in southern Russia, where the soil was rich and the climate more gentle, it was called the steppe. Here, soon after the year 2000 BC, people were beginning to make an important conquest. They were taming or domesticating the horse, which hitherto had been simply hunted for meat.

Not as tall as today's typical pony, these small native horses were an asset. When trained, they were loyal and intelligent allies. When they lost their rider they could find their way home. They supplied milk for infants and so enabled mothers to cease breastfeeding a baby at an earlier age. In turn the gap between pregnancies became shorter, and so the population of the steppes was likely to increase more rapidly. The horse could provide meat, especially in winter when food was scarce; and its dung, when dry, served as a fuel on those grassy steppes where trees were few. Thanks to the horse, the sparsely settled grasslands eventually supported more people than before: perhaps too many.

Many centuries later, especially after 700 BC, the riders learned how to become cavalry and to ride horses into war. Riding long distances, they could take an enemy by surprise or retreat swiftly when necessary. About 500 BC the invention of the stirrup—in effect a metal footrest suspended by a leather strap—enabled riders to stand up on a fast-moving horse and use their full strength to thrust a spear at an opposing foot soldier.

The Sarmatians, a steppe people who moved from central Asia towards fertile lands and richer plunder in the west, were inventive. They probably first devised the metal stirrup and they also used metal armor to protect the rider and part of the horse. They enlisted young women as riders in time of war; and it is said that these women were not permitted to marry until they had killed one of the enemy. When they were felled in a battle, they were formally buried with their lance and sword by their side. In about 200 BC, these mounted warriors controlled much of southern Russia, and their surprise attacks frightened people in the outlying provinces of the Roman Empire. Raids on the agricultural districts at the Chinese and European ends of the steppes were much feared. Some of the turning points in European and Chinese history were to be shaped by these swift invasions.

Horses made up for the lack of people when the raiders of the steppes had to face a more numerous enemy. One warhorse might often be worth 10 foot soldiers fighting on the opposite side. In response to this fast-moving aggressor from the steppes, Assyria and other large agricultural states had to breed their own horses in order to defend themselves against the fast armed riders of the steppes. These states preferred strong horses which could pull a chariot in which rode a driver and a bowman who shot the arrows. There was one hitch in this plan. These larger warhorses required feed previously grown for human mouths, and so competed with human beings for the produce of fertile land. In contrast the riders of the steppes had access to half a continent of grass. In due course they were to raid the heart of China.

BIRD'S EYE ON CHINA

Around the year 1500 BC, China lagged some way behind the Fertile Crescent in political organization, in the art of producing metals, in writing, and probably in agriculture and astronomy. But as makers of pottery in kilns, China and Japan were well advanced. These fire-based skills paved the way for advances in metallurgy. The casting of bronze became a Chinese speciality, and their hunting chariots were decorated with bronze, almost like the chrome on large postwar American cars. Then a few Chinese began to make cast iron, and by 400 BC they were learning to specialize in the manufacture of ploughshares—the strong cutting edge that turned over the soil. The production of the high heat needed in the furnace was achieved by a blast coming from sophisticated double-cylinder bellows. Some of the bellows were later driven by power derived from water rushing down narrow streams.

In the 500 or more years before the start of the first Christian millennium, the Chinese were, for a time, the most inventive of the peoples for whom early records survive. In metallurgy they were kings. In handling water for irrigation they devised new methods. In mathematics and astronomy they sought new knowledge. With looms they made silk for fine garments. They grew hemp and, like the Egyptians half a world away, turned it into a fiber from which most of their coarse ordinary clothes were woven. They became skilled in haulage and transport, using wheelbarrows pushed by humans, carts and ploughs pulled by oxen, and carriages drawn by horses. Their early examples of glazed pottery and carved jade were admired by later generations of craftspeople.

The rulers of the larger states inside China lived in luxury and helped themselves to a generous share of the wealth produced by the toiling peasants and artisans. While many Chinese owned their own small lot of land, they had to devote part of their time to the needs of their ruler, either in building public works or fighting in local wars. In death the rulers also helped themselves to the peasants. When a king died, as many as 40 people might be entombed with him. In earlier centuries they were buried in the belief that they could serve him in the afterlife with the help of some of the thousands of jade and bronze items that were buried with them, but later the workers who constructed the elaborate tombs were buried so that they could not disclose to others the secret of how to enter the carefully locked burial chambers and steal the treasures.

China consisted of a galaxy of more than 100 small independent states; but between about 700 and 464 BC, most of these were eliminated, largely as a result of warfare. Seven major kingdoms now ruled most of China. In the following three centuries, known as the time of the Warring States, the elimination race continued. New techniques of warfare were adopted, and chariots were replaced as the dynamic weapon-carrier by soldiers riding horses and firing arrows from powerful crossbows. The succession of wars reduced the number of kingdoms to two and then to one. By 221 BC, China was united.

The strongest influence on the training of the new Chinese bureaucracy was Confucius. He was a scholar of a kind more likely to be found in Athens than perhaps in any other state along the Mediterranean. More a secular than a spiritual thinker, he saw no urgent need for a religion, for he was relatively optimistic about human nature. He came to the view that the good life was more important than any afterlife. He mainly called for good conduct and good citizenship, self-knowledge and self-cultivation.

Born in 551 BC in the heartland of China, in a minor principality near the Yellow River, he belonged to a poor and moldy wing of the aristocracy. Initially he held rural posts such as managing a horse stable and keeping records for a granary: the kind of minor tasks that ambitious young people now recite in their curriculum vitae in the hope of persuading future employers that they have not been idle. Eventually Confucius became a full-time teacher, a profession which was not then important. He was a radical in the vital sense that he espoused learning at a time when its status was low, but otherwise he was conservative.

He believed that the nobility should govern, wisely and humanely. He believed in a hierarchy rather than equality. He tended to believe in the old rather than the new; and he thought that the ancestors had much to teach the present. He praised courtesy and loyalty, humility and kindness. Once, in answer to a question about the kind of person he was, he charmingly described himself in the third person: "he is the sort of man who forgets to eat when he engages himself in vigorous pursuit of learning, who is so full of joy that he forgets his worries, and who does not notice that old age is coming on."

He died at the age of 73, having created no church or institution. But his ideas lived on, being reinterpreted by different generations. Students had to learn his precepts by heart if they hoped to enter the Chinese bureaucracy. That it was probably the best bureaucracy in the world, century after century, was a tribute to his ideals of conscientious service. No other secular thinker who is influential today has exercised that influence for a total of 2,500 years. It is a measure of the power of ideas as distinct from masonry that Confucius has outlived the Great Wall.

A rival philosophy known as Taoism emerged during the lifetime of Confucius. Later it became a religion dear to Chinese peasants, but in 500 BC it was more a view of the present world with no concept of the afterlife. The celebrated exponent of early Taoism was a wise librarian called Zi Erh who was later revered as the Old Philosopher. His creed opposed an interfering government, resented taxation and disapproved of war, and so it was not likely during that warring period to become an official cult. Taoism admired the passive, likening it to water which was seemingly weak but was able to sweep away heavy obstacles. It revered landscape, believing that the stones, trees and mountains spoke like a religious spirit to those willing to listen. This veneration for landscape was almost a hallmark of Chinese culture until the coming of communism, more than 2,000 years later.

THE GREAT WALL

China had remarkable linguistic and cultural unity, but its political unity was precarious. In addition to the internal divisions, attacks came from outside. China was much closer to those grasslands which nurtured the riders so skilled in fighting, and it was to suffer even more than Europe from their invasions. Significantly, a great wall to defend the Roman Empire from the inland invaders was never built, but China at an early stage had to plan such a wall in order to keep in check its enemies living in the dry and sparsely peopled lands to the northwest.

The Great Wall of China was completed in 214 BC, though in another sense it was never completed because it always had to be extended or enlarged. A few decades later, at the other end of Asia, there were said to be seven wonders of the world, all being in Asia Minor or the eastern Mediterranean, but China possessed what might have been acclaimed as *the* wonder of the world, if only the Greeks and Romans had inspected it.

The Great Wall reflected the organizing ability of the rulers and the stamina and strength of the hundreds of thousands of laborers who were compulsorily assigned to national tasks. They had less reason than their rulers to admire the wall. They had been taken far from home, perhaps never to see their families again, in order to work long hours in the brickyards and quarries that served the wall. They soon learned that the country near the wall was rugged and that here and there the steep landscape defied the engineers. At one point the wall had to make a long detour to avoid the big bend of the Yellow River (Huang He).

It was really a continuous network of walls, built in stages and varying in strength, and sections of the original walls were flimsy brush fences—warning signs rather than solid obstacles. While the main wall was designed to keep out the armed riders of the interior, some of the loops or extensions were actually built to fend off local enemies who might emerge inside the wall. In total the wall and its loops extended for 6,300 kilometers. If a similar wall had been built across the widest part of Australia, from east to west, it would have been no longer than the Great Wall of China.

In times of danger the Chinese armies guarding the wall must have been huge by the standards of the time. They had to be huge, for they had to occupy an entire defensive system embracing 40,000 lookout towers either built into the wall or standing alone on strategic or high ground. To keep a constant watch, day and night, from most of the towers, when an invader was expected, would have called for tens of thousands of eyes. In addition the wall required a big number of soldiers whose main task was to fight rather than watch.

After it was united in about 200 BC, China mostly retained its unity. It usually consisted of one or two states, whereas Europe—except in the Romans' heyday—possessed a multitude of states. To be united was the best form of defense for China. Culturally and ethnically its land had unusual unity by European standards. There was one dominant ethnic group, the Han Chinese, who far outnumbered all the minorities added together. The empire also gained cultural unity from the Chinese script, which was used throughout the land. As it was not primarily a phonetic script it could be read even by people whose dialect or language was different.

In the long term, another factor helped to promote China's political unity. Whereas Europe was dissected by large intrusive seas and long peninsulas, China's coastline was more regular in shape. Many European states could be independent for long periods because they were islands or peninsulas, and so the sea defended them. The sea in all its unpredictability does offer a defense against enemies sailing in what are unfamiliar waters. Very often, in the history of Britain and Greece, for example, invasions were thwarted by storms. A strait offers a stronger natural defense than does a land border.

If China's coastlines had been marked by deep peninsulas and large islands, it might have supported more states, and they might have retained their independence. Significantly, offshore Taiwan, though far inferior to communist China in its military and economic strength, celebrated 50 years of independence in 1999.

The Chinese population was comparable to that of Europe. In the six centuries between 300 BC and AD 300 it is doubtful whether the population of Europe surpassed that of China for more than a few years. On the other hand, a comparison of Europe and China is tinged with unreality. Europe at that time was an artificial entity. The more populous shores of North Africa and the crowded cities and rural valleys of the present Palestine and Syria and Turkey, though technically outside Europe, were then much more part of a Europe which had the Mediterranean Sea as its pivot. Likewise, the territorial borders of China have slid backwards and forwards.

The spread of China's population had little relation to its present spread. Most people lived in the north. The climate on the northern plains then was especially favorable to agriculture. Spring arrived earlier than it arrives today. The house-swallow returned a few weeks earlier than is its custom today. The long-awaited song of the cuckoo was heard earlier. The peach tree, spiritual in its appeal to the Chinese, burst earlier into blossom; and summers were longer.

FROM THE SEA OF STARS
TO THE PLAIN OF FLOODS

Most of the Chinese lived in the basin of the mighty Yellow River. At that time it was the Nile of China but less tameable than the Nile. This second largest of the country's rivers arose in western China, not far from the source of its rival, the Yangtze or Long River (Chang); and its first journey was on a high plateau, the name of which in the Chinese language means "the Sea of Stars." The Yellow River tumbled, glided and rippled for days before it approached the lowlands of China. Unable to make up its mind where to go, it flowed north and then for about 800 kilometers it flowed south—as if it had no intention of ever turning east and flowing to the China Sea. Those who fly over this wayward part of the river can see it far below, a brown streak in the gorges, with forests on one side and parched terraced farms on the other, and no bridge to link the two riverbanks.

Once the trees were more numerous than they are today. As the population of China increased, the felling of trees for firewood or for the making of charcoal led to massive erosion in the hill country. The silted Yellow River became a torrent of thick brown soup. The people of China had no means of knowing that this river was the leading silt-carrier of the world, besides which the Amazon and the Nile were poor relations.

To stand at the ferry wharf on the loess plain near Jinan (Tsinan) and watch the same river today, even when it is in half-flood, is to see a monster. Thick with brownish-yellow sediment, forming itself into strange clockwise whirlpools, its current is so fast that it sucks down and swallows many people who accidentally fall in.

The sediment which it carried made a new bed for the river. A layer of mud 1 meter high was deposited on the bed in a typical century. With almost every new flood the channel was too shallow for the volume of water, and it overflowed onto the plain. A wonderful source of fertile top-dressing and irrigation water for the people living in rural congestion near its banks, it was also a wrecker of villages and a drowner of thousands of people even during the century when Confucius lived nearby.

The river was so vital but so tempestuous that it had to be wooed by a human sacrifice. In the 400s BC it was the annual custom to placate the invisible Lord of the Yellow River by giving him a human present. A pretty girl was dressed as a bride and placed on a wooden raft shaped like a marriage bed. The marriage bed was pushed into the rushing river where soon the bride slipped from sight.

To tame the river called for ingenuity and the conscripting of an army of laborers to build and rebuild the embankments and training walls. In 109 BC the emperor erected a pavilion to honor all the people who plugged holes in the dykes and so saved villages from the raging waters. In each decade the bed of the river continued to rise, and therefore the artificial embankments had to be raised even higher. In many places the bottom of the river was well above the level of the surrounding plain. It is a measure of the might and flexibility of the Yellow River that in different centuries it has rushed into the sea either to the north or the south of the mountainous Shandong (Shantung) Peninsula. This change of direction was the equivalent of the Nile changing course so sharply that it ran into the Indian Ocean rather than into the Mediterranean.

Whereas the Nile was confined to a narrow plain, the Yellow River refused to be confined. Its valley was possibly the most densely settled place in the world during the five centuries before the time of Christ. The constructing of its earthen banks and training walls was perhaps a mightier project than the Great Wall, and a candidate for the title of the greatest engineering work the world had seen up to that time.

Even in 500 BC, a time when the Greek port-cities and the Persian empire were both flourishing, a line of large towns prospered along the valley of the Yellow River. Its valley or plain was the hub of China and held well over half of the population: the movement of people to the Yangtze in central China and to the warm south commenced later.

As the production of millet and rice became more efficient, and as irrigation channels were dug, the farms could support larger cities. A few were defended by long walls made of rammed earth. One wall was a massive 36 meters in width at the base and extended so far that it encircled a small city. The moving of the earth to construct these walls would have occupied some 12,000 people for about 10 years, and they in turn would have been fed by a procession of carts carrying grain. Along the Yellow River several cities grew to a size which must have impressed all travellers who passed though their gates. The new capital city of Loyang (now Luoyang), commenced in AD 25, held a population of close to half a million: perhaps only Rome was larger.

The population of China apparently was then passing through one of its periods of fast growth. A census conducted in the years AD 1 and 2 counted 59,595,000 people living in China. Perhaps another million had been overlooked by the census-takers. The census was remarkable less for the large population it actually counted than for the fact that the government was so much in control of its territories and so well served by bureaucrats that it could actually organize this complicated and far-flung operation in note-taking and counting.

China had some of the characteristics of the Roman Empire, and the marching army was as important for China as for the Romans. Spaced along the Chinese highways were hundreds of official rest houses, with beds and places for washing, and feed and stables for the horses. Along the highways came couriers on horseback, carrying secret despatches written on thin strips of wood and enclosed in bamboo tubes which were then locked, so providing maximum security. At well-spaced points along the roads stood beacons, which in times of emergency could transmit simple signals of smoke to the next beacon, which was then set alight. In 74 BC the news of the death of the emperor was relayed some 1,300 kilometers in the space of 30 hours, largely by the smoke rising from the beacons.

Riches and poverty stood side by side, in countryside and city. A wedding or funeral for a rich rural family was a time for heavy spending, and even the slaves and concubines of the rich would at times be dressed in the finest silks and deerskin slippers and ornamented with amber, pearl and jade. For the mass of Chinese, daily life was a struggle, except in years of wonderful harvests. Such years, however, tended to lead to an increase of population, which accentuated the agony when the next famine arrived. The Chinese chroniclers, about 2,000 years ago, often recorded bad news: a flood, a plague of locusts, drought, and the cattle epidemic of the year AD 76. In some years, hundreds of thousands of peasants took to the roads and begged or searched for work, while others would sell wife and children to pay off debts.

There was one source of hope. China was rather like the United States in the 19th century, when an abundance of unused forest and marsh could be taken up for farming, thus serving as a safety valve for the press of population. In southern China, the vast areas of forest, scattered woodland and semitropical river flats supported few people. But hundreds of thousands of northern Chinese peasants were migrating south in search of land. Rice was being planted as the main crop of the south and it was heavy in its demand for water. Here, too, the tea bush was first cultivated, giving China a commodity which, more than 1,000 years later, was to outshine silk in the eyes of Europe. Not until about AD 1200 did the population living in the drainage area of the Yangtze and in the new south exceed that of the old north, and even then their superiority over northern China was temporary.

Korea and Japan lay in the shadow of China and its new ideas and techniques, but flashes of light shone in their direction. The new metallurgy arrived, and iron began to replace stone in the heads of axes and in the sharp edges of the sickles which reaped the grain. A new kind of pottery was made with a potter's wheel and placed in an oven to be fired at a high temperature. Earlier than 500 BC, a new food-crop, rice, crossed from China to Korea and Japan and began to transform daily meals. In Japan, which consisted of many states rather than one, short-grained rice was grown on the hills and in wet paddy fields constructed with heavy labor in the valleys and marshes. As the climate was humid, and rice could easily deteriorate while being stored, the freshly harvested grains were dried and even toasted before being placed in tall, well-aired storehouses resting on stout wooden posts.

THE ISLAND OF INDIA

In Asia at this time the only potential rival to China was India. In fact they were too far apart to be real rivals. They knew little of each other. The fact that both were in Asia meant nothing to them. Asia was a European concept in geography; and for long the concept was unknown to the more learned of the Chinese, who thought China was too pivotal to be part of any other geographical unit.

India, unlike China, was virtually an island. Cut off from most of Asia by the Himalaya Mountains, which ran east for almost 2,500 kilometers, India could be approached more easily from the northwest. There the mountain passes encouraged traffic. India lay closer to the civilizations of the Middle East and Greece than to the heartland of China; and the exact position of the mountain passes increased the likelihood that its links would favor the Mediterranean world. India's main language was of the Indo-European family, not of the Chinese. Its invaders arrived more from the direction of Europe. Its external trade, whether by sea or land, also favored that direction.

The isolation created by the world's highest barrier of mountains helped to give a unity to India. In the last 2,500 years, despite its many divisions, India has usually possessed a stronger sense of unity than Europe or the Middle East.

Of the countries in the tropics and the temperate zones of the world, India holds a larger area of ice than any other. It also embraces a very large area of hot country. Fortunately the high mountains, with their melting snow and ice, sent a flow of water to the parched plains in summer. The melting water from the high mountains helped to make up for the deficiencies and irregularities in the rainfall, which came mostly with the southwest monsoon from the Indian Ocean. While some regions received plentiful rain in the average year, many others received inadequate rain and could not even rely on that amount.

Those areas of unreliable rain carried big populations of tillers of the soil. When the monsoons brought little rain, famine set in. Until long railways and irrigation canals were built in modern times—and by 1900 India was possibly the most irrigated of lands—famine could be deadly. This was the mystery of India: an ability to support a huge population and a parallel ability to starve them.

The Ganges River was a child of these whitecapped mountains. It normally ran for the whole year, carrying water across a huge plain. After 1000 BC, the Ganges replaced the Indus as the populous part of the Indian subcontinent. Cities multiplied along the valley, and the farms had to multiply in order to feed the cities. By 400 BC, India probably held 30 million people. In the whole world, only northern China could surpass this press of people.

At this time it is probable that China and India between them held one-third of the world's people, perhaps more. The silt-strewn plains and the snow-fed rivers were the secret of their capacity to support such large populations. Recent research based on the monitoring of the flowing sediment suspended in the main rivers of the world produced several statistics which, transferred for the first time from hydraulic engineering to history, are highly illuminating for both India and China. These nations possess the great silt-carrying rivers of the world. The Yellow River carries in a typical year a suspended load of about 2,100 million tons of soil, far more than any other river in the world. Second is the Ganges with about 1,600 million tons. About half of the silt of these rivers is deposited at the delta and the river estuaries, though much comes to rest in farms and irrigation channels. In contrast the Amazon, which discharges more water than any other river in the world, carries only 400 million tons of sediment a year. These mighty, muddy rivers of India and China are unparalleled. Without their vast volume of silt, the population of China and India would have been much lower.

Whereas China's special talent at this time was in technology, India's was in religion. Hinduism, which arrived with the Indo-European migrants, held its high priests or brahmans in almost godlike esteem. It was a flexible religion, given to producing branches and offshoots. Its devotees ranged from rich priests and lonely threadbare wanderers to crowds who combined newer Hinduism with their old idols. The religion was never static. At an early stage it sacrificed animals on important occasions while later it tended to sanctify most living things. It ranged from a belief in many specialist gods to a belief in the supreme god, Brahma.

Hindus believed that every creature had a soul and that after death it migrated to a new body. The idea now is seen as essentially belonging to Indian religions but it was found at one time in many places, including intellectual circles in Athens. There, the philosopher Plato, in his book *Republic*, depicted Orpheus becoming a swan. Devoted Hindus also had the faith that any person, with the aid of good conduct and sheer devotion, could escape from earthly pain and commune with the gods.

A human being could be reborn into a variety of insect or animal species. Therefore cows and goats, mites and insects had to be treated with respect. Why the cow, alone of the meat-providing animals, was especially venerated in India is a puzzle. Certainly cows served a vital function by breeding the oxen or bullocks which pulled the plough; and by 1000 BC, some Indian farmers employed as many as 24 oxen to draw their ploughs. But the cow and oxen were useful in many other lands and were not venerated there.

Hinduism did not depend on its followers assembling in large numbers in a temple: its wooden temples were not assembly halls but statements of faith. The creed was full of rules for daily life and eternal life. It also came to emphasize the recycling of lives. This idea implanted some hope, while blessing the miseries of the status quo. The consolation for living in poverty and being humble in status was that one's life, if lived virtuously, might be rewarded at death by the passing of the soul into a worthier being. On the other hand, the dead person's soul might pass, on returning to earth, into a lesser animal. While this doctrine does not appear to have been vital to early Hinduism and is barely touched upon in the collection of 1,028 hymns known as the Rig-Veda, it slowly became important.

The Hindu religion, as the centuries passed by, accentuated the caste system. All Indians were assigned a caste or station. In theory a person could not marry outside the assigned caste, work outside it or rise beyond it. At first it was as much a theory as a practice, and many people married outside their caste and, without suffering social stigma, took on an occupation which did not belong to their caste. Thus a man for whom the craft of potter was the ordained occupation might begin, like his father, as a potter and eventually become a basketmaker and then a cook: these occupations belonged to other castes. In the course of time, however, the castes tended to become more rigid.

It is remarkable that India became a democracy in modern times, because the long-lasting Hindu civilization at first sight was innately hostile to the ideas that all adults should have an equal vote, irrespective of their caste, and that all adults should be able to share in the social mobility which was part of the democratic spirit. But to graft exotic new trees onto old, when there seemed little hope of success, and to watch them grow vigorously, is not a rare experience in human institutions.

THE PRODIGAL SON BECOMES THE BUDDHA

In the 6th century BC, Hinduism, tolerant of diversity, gave birth to new religions. It gave rise to Jainism and to the more influential Buddhism. Siddhartha Gautama, the founder of Buddhism, had similarities to Christ. Born at the time of the full moon, his arrival was greeted not by three wise men but by one. A wise hermit came down from the Himalayas and expressed his regrets that he would not live long enough to hear the words of the prophet into which this much-blessed baby would surely grow. Nor did the mother live: she died when her boy was a week old.

Gautama's father was a Nepalese prince living near the border of India, in the steamy lowlands which are one source of the River Ganges. He owned three palaces where Gautama, when older, enjoyed the entertainment provided. Showing no early sign of that sense of duty which he later preached, he was constantly entertained by female musicians; and when the music stopped he was further entertained. He supped at the fleshpots, a kind of prodigal son. He married his cousin and they had one son; but this brought no sense of responsibility to Gautama.

Then, to the surprise of his friends, he sought salvation. He left home at night, on horseback, and his life changed forever. Following that strong Indian tradition of asceticism he tried to punish his body, eventually losing so much weight that his ribs protruded "like rafters" in a shed. After enduring much pain and spending time in the wilderness, he found the light. He became "the Enlightened One" or the Buddha.

Henceforth, Buddha pursued holiness. He thought it was essential to annihilate the self: the ultimate goal was *nirvana*, an ideal condition in which he would virtually extinguish himself. Pursuing the goal of quiet self-extinction, he was rewarded with inexpressible happiness.

The hot and sweaty city of Varanasi (Benares), standing where the River Ganges changed its direction in a great sweeping crescent, was to become the inaugural holy place of Buddhism, and the goal of pilgrimages from far away. It was near Varanasi, in the Deer Park of Sarnath, that Buddha preached his doctrine for the first time.

He won the admiration of many of the poor, for he did not accept the Hindu idea of caste. He also attracted the rich, who established, in cities and towns along the Ganges, Buddhist monasteries for those men who wished to perfect themselves. He set up a religious order for women, and his aunt was the first to enter the nunnery. Spending part of each year in a monastery, he also walked over large areas of northern India, his disciples with him. The emergence, centuries later, of monastic institutions amongst some of the early Christians in Egypt and Syria was possibly one sign of his wide influence.

In the dry season the Buddha moved about, begging for food and teaching the word. Those who gave him food felt that they shared in some of his holiness. Like Francis of Assisi, who was to tame a wild wolf in central Italy during the Christian era, Buddha succeeded in taming, with his calm presence, a mad elephant. An empathy with nature, and the curbing of the violent by nonviolent methods, was part of his creed. His teachings were later summed up by the Indian politician Mahatma Gandhi in the words: "Life is not a bundle of enjoyments, but a bundle of duties."

At this time the dynamic parts of the globe were India, the eastern Mediterranean and China. Far apart, they had few links with each other; and yet each was simultaneously living in a seedtime. In the 480s BC, Buddha in old age was preaching his word along the Ganges, Confucius was writing down his precepts in northern China, and the Athenians, having just defeated the Persians at the Battle of Marathon, were cultivating those arts and that democracy on which their fame was to rest.

Buddha died in about 486 BC, when he was close to 80 years of age. His death was widely mourned in the region but his creed did not seem likely to win converts far from the banks of the Ganges. A little more than two centuries after his death, his creed received a lucky break. It so happened that King Asoka became the first ruler to govern nearly all of a land which in Buddha's lifetime had been fragmented into many kingdoms. With the aid of his huge army, consisting of some half a million foot soldiers, 30,000 horsemen and 9,000 elephant-riders, King Asoka tightened his control of nearly all of India except the southern triangle.

Ruling from a city on the Ganges, this powerful king—perhaps the most powerful in the world—could be remarkably benign. In the 250s BC he built hospitals—at the same time as the distant city of Alexandria was building its medical school—and he favored the educating of women. Tolerant towards religions, he eventually became a devout Buddhist and even erected shrines to honor the ashes of Buddha. At a time when Buddhism might otherwise have been pushed aside by the central and versatile creed of Hinduism, the king quietly spread its religious message. A king with absolute power is the most persuasive of all missionaries, in the short term.

With the king's help, Buddhism won a foothold in Ceylon (Sri Lanka) in about the year 250 BC. According to tradition the spirit of Buddhism crossed the narrow strait by air, landed on a hill and promptly embraced and converted the King of Ceylon. The day would come when Buddhism would virtually die in its homeland but hold the loyalties of hundreds of millions living in lands beyond India.

At first it was Hinduism which attracted foreigners. Renewing itself from time to time, it spread along the coast of South-East Asia and to a cluster of islands. The delta of the Mekong River became the seat of the empire of Funan, a strong Hindu kingdom which often controlled the sea route between India and China. The phase of strong Hindu influence in South-East Asia lasted for centuries, and then, almost everywhere, the Hindu gods retreated. The small island of Bali, far from the mouth of the Ganges, remains a lonely Hindu outpost.

In the history of the world's religions, northern India rivals the Middle East as the most fertile birthplace. Curiously the Indian religions made little headway to the west. Their recruiting grounds lay to the east. Buddhism proved to be the most successful recruiter, and its victories were to be won in lands where India had possessed virtually no cultural or commercial influence during Buddha's own lifetime.

8

THE RISE OF ROME

ROME was built, its historians and legend-makers liked to proclaim, on the seven hills. Not all the hills, however, were peopled when Rome was young. The town was too small to require such space. Past the walled town ran the Tiber River, flowing at last into the Mediterranean less than 40 kilometers away. Sometimes yellow with mud washed down from the steep hills after heavy rain, the river was used by small boats carrying cargo to and from the river mouth.

At first a monarch ruled the town and the small territory nearby, but in 509 BC the landed families were victorious and their republic was to last nearly five centuries. The Romans initially could not control the tribes to the south, and in 458 BC they had to recall a former politician from his work at the plough in order to save the embattled republic. Rome lacked the political experience of the older Greek cities, and four years after the crisis it sent a deputation of three to study the enlightened laws of Athens.

The small city of Rome was still struggling to survive. In 390 BC it was besieged for seven months by an army of Gauls who finally entered and half-wrecked the city. Rome did not yet command even half of the Italian peninsula. In 300 BC it did not even control Milan and the site of Venice, which was not yet a village. Rome ruled none of the islands of the western Mediterranean, virtually all of which were in the rival sphere of influence of Carthage, the powerful city on the coast of North Africa. There was no building in Rome or even in Italy that could be compared with the new lighthouse at Alexandria in Egypt, and no academy of learning along the Tiber could hold a candle to even the minor meeting places of the laureates in some of the Hellenic cities.

Rome's talent was in producing generals and soldiers, admirals and sailors. These fighting men, having subdued the neighboring Sabines, Etruscans and the Piceni, began to challenge the land and sea empire based on Carthage. By 240 BC the Romans controlled the rich island of Sicily, once part of Greek civilization. In the following year they captured the Carthaginian island of Sardinia. But then Hannibal, the great general of Carthage, seemed likely for a time to crush Rome, for he led a victorious army through Spain and over the French Alps and far into Italy. His forces were finally defeated on the Adriatic coast of Italy in 207 BC. It was the Romans who now extended their overseas empire, easily penetrating Carthage's domain in North Africa. From these new possessions in North Africa and Sicily came a procession of ships whose cargoes of grain were needed to feed the expanding city of Rome.

For the Greeks the sea was a natural highway but the Romans built their own highways. In 312 BC Roman engineers began to build the first of their arteries, the Appian Way, which ran all the way from Rome to the southern port of Tarentum, on the inner heel of Italy. Soon that highway was extended to the back of the heel—the Adriatic port of Brindisi where today can be seen the ancient stone column celebrating that feat of engineering. Ultimately, well-built Roman roads extended along much of the coast of North Africa, around much of the northern coast of the Mediterranean, and to the remote rivers the Danube and Euphrates. They were not mere roads. Where they survive they are still known as "Roman roads," as if they are a distinct species, which indeed they are. Surveyed with an eye to the shortest route, cutting through hills, and crossing marshes on stone or earthen causeways, they were described by the English novelist Thomas Hardy as like a parting line in a head of hair—thin and straight.

It is usual to envisage the network of Roman roads as they were in their heyday. For several hundred years, however, some of the main rivers intersecting the roads had no bridges and so people, horses, oxen and mules crossed them on a barge or punt. Horace the poet describes an episode at a river crossing along the road from Rome to Brindisi:

And there began a wild brawl;
With slaves and ferry men, short and tall.

All night long, in calm weather, traffic quietly moved on the seas as well as the roads, with the Roman captain steering his ship by the stars so familiar to him. Even war galleys, when the need arose, rowed their way through the night, with the sails dyed black so that they could barely be noticed.

The Roman roads for their time were more remarkable than the superhighways built in Europe for the motor era. Fast couriers could travel along the roads and, as in China, feel certain that, unless floods or snow intervened, their horsedrawn vehicle would adhere to its timetable. In many parts of the Roman Empire a message sent by road arrived long before a message sent by sea. Along the Roman roads went fast horsemen, tramping soldiers, merchants, slaves and babes in arms.

The Roman bridge was a work of art, though the Romans had gifted predecessors in the building of roads and bridges. The Persians had built trunk roads and long bridges. An arched bridge was built in Mesopotamia before 3000 BC; and the pontoon bridge—a brainwave of an idea for the crossing of narrow straits—was tried before 500 BC. A line of boats laid side by side, the pontoon served as a row of stepping blocks along which the Persian army could cross calm water.

To see a Roman bridge still bearing traffic is to feel a sense of awe. The engineer, the people who quarried the stone and the stonemasons who built the bridge have long been silent but their bridge stands in all its strength and elegance. The Roman bridge at Rimini, within sound of the Adriatic Sea, consists of dressed blocks of whitish limestone, with shells and the remains of a fish or two still embedded in the white stone. Built about the year 5 BC, it consists of five barrel or semicircular arches beneath which a river, now shrunken, briskly flowed in floodtime. The bridge was used by Roman carts and travellers on foot, by the prancing horses of the army, by women and men on their way to make offerings to the reigning gods in shrines and temples, by small herds of cattle and geese travelling to market, and by dawdling children. Even today the bridge is a one-direction crossing, used by Italian cars and motor scooters, and enhanced by a ledge on which pedestrians can walk with a narrow margin of safety.

INSIDE THE MARBLE CITY

All roads did lead to Rome, and it grew to an almost unmanageable size. It was probably the first city in the world—though China too had large cities—to support a population approaching one million. It was the goal for drifters and the destitute with nowhere else to go, for those who wanted work and excitement, and for the fiercely ambitious who wanted the top chance. Rome's stonepaved streets were crowded with wheeled traffic and people, local and foreign, some pouring in from Italian farmlands and others arriving as prisoners from the latest war. The growing city relied on aqueducts; and the long arched bridges conveyed from the foothills the continuous flow of water that filled the public baths and the water pots and jugs in countless homes, and flushed away the sewage. The public baths were almost the town halls of Roman civilization. Some were huge marble halls with numerous lesser rooms and many baths, both hot and cold. Places for gossip and pleasure, they multiplied. The city of Rome alone held about 800 public baths.

Stately and even pompous buildings were erected for public purposes. The Colosseum, which was opened in AD 80, held about 50,000 spectators, far more than had assembled in the smaller Greek stadiums. Here was a foretaste of the four-yearly spectacles of the modern era, the World Cup in football and the revived Olympic Games.

To build and rebuild Rome called for a mountain of marble, which was brought from afar. Earlier, marble had been denounced by Roman leaders as a luxury, and a reminder of the declining Greek cities and civilization. Accordingly, when the Roman orator Crassus grafted six columns of shining white marble onto his house on the Palatine in 92 BC his display did not win admiration. Soon marble came into favor; and Emperor Augustus boasted that he remembered a Rome built of brick but now he ruled a Rome crowned with marble.

The building stones came in massive blocks from many ports. Whiter marble came from Mount Hymettus near Athens as well as from newer quarries opened at Carrara, on the coast to the north of Rome. A marble bearing distinctive layers of white and pale green was quarried on the Greek island of Euboea and loaded laboriously aboard wooden sailing ships. A vast tonnage of yellow marble from North Africa was widely used in columns and the more ornate pavements of Rome. An oriental alabaster or "onyx" was quarried near the River Nile and a similar stone came from Arabia. Red basalt came from Egypt and green from Greece, so that Rome began to resemble an outdoor museum of Mediterranean geology. The work of building was aided by the Roman invention of hydraulic cement, which set the stones more firmly than did the old lime-based cement.

Many of the ships which carried stone and timber and grain to Rome were larger than any built in the western world in the following thousand or more years. They could be longer than 50 meters and as wide as 15 meters, making them appear rather tubby or even ungainly by present standards of design. A fleet of ships, almost like today's bulk carriers, was especially built for the carrying of building stone. These large Roman ships relied on the wind instead of oars. Their task was to carry cargoes cheaply rather than quickly, but occasionally they made fast passages. One cargo ship is reported to have sailed from the Italian port of Naples to the Egyptian port of Alexandria in a mere nine days. More remarkable was the Roman ship which sailed from Alexandria to Marseilles, in the face of adverse winds, in a mere 30 days.

If European sailors at the time of Columbus had chanced to be shown the wreck of a big wooden Roman ship, uncovered by shifting sands, they would have been surprised by her length. Columbus's flagship, *Santa Maria*, was only about 30 meters in length, much smaller than those Roman ships which had been engaged in carrying grain or building stones from Egypt. Even the eye-opening steamship of 1843, the *Great Britain*, with her one funnel and six masts, was to be no wider and not quite twice as long as the big Roman cargo ships sailing the seas 2,000 years previously.

While the Romans could build nothing to match the lighthouse of Pharos at the entrance to the artificial harbor of Alexandria, they lit beacons on hilltops overlooking dangerous places on the sea lanes. At night, small woodfires were burned on the top of high headlands or were kept alight in newly built lighthouses. By AD 100 the best lighthouses were equipped with oil lamps or large candles with a surround of glass or strips of animal horn to reflect the light. Three centuries later the Romans operated about 30 prominent lighthouses, including those at Dover and Boulogne on opposite sides of the narrow English Channel and that tall lighthouse at La Coruña which the Spanish have since restored. If a deep-sea sailor on a clear night climbed a mast 5 or 6 meters above the surface of the sea he could see the warning light, shining 30 kilometers away.

Some 1,600 Roman shipwrecks have already been discovered on the seabed of the Mediterranean but that is only two or three for each busy year of Rome's long heyday. The wrecks would have been far more frequent but for these simple night beacons. Eventually the Romans devised a sensible method of insuring their ships against loss at sea.

Roman writers left for future generations a detailed picture of daily life and its fun, anguish, pleasure and pain. We can almost taste the meals of the common people: the coarse bread, the "fresh hand-pressed cheese, and green figs of the second crop," and of course that tiny but popular fish, the whitebait. We can walk around Roman farms, thanks to the poetry of Virgil, and hear advice on how to farm. Thus the seventh day of the moon was considered lucky for roping and taming wild cattle, and in summer the hay of a parched meadow should best be cut after dark: a haymaking rule which was often followed in Italy even in living memory. As for the signs of rain, so welcome when young crops grew on dry soil, Virgil believed that a bright farm girl could tell when rain was about to break a short drought. Spinning wool in the farmhouse by the light of the oil lamp, she would notice that the light itself would sputter or that a trace of mould would become visible on the wick: signs, in Roman eyes, of the approach of rain.

Through the writings of the Roman historian Livy, the battlefield at Cannae in the south of Italy is vividly before us in 216 BC. In the early light the armies were ready for battle, the sun shining from the side so that neither army was looking into the sun, and a wind out of Africa throwing dust straight into the face of the Roman forces. Their enemy, the mighty Carthaginians, arranged at least 10,000 horsemen in readiness for battle as well as soldiers from Gaul, naked "from the navel up," men from Majorca and Minorca armed with slings and stones, and Spaniards wearing linen tunics of dazzling white with borders of crimson—as if they were in a fashion parade rather than on a battlefield. Carthage won that battle: the Roman dead could be counted in the thousands. For a time the city of Rome seemed on the verge of defeat. But instead, 70 years later, the Romans laid waste the African city of Carthage; and Rome alone stood supreme in the western Mediterranean.

The republic of Rome, as it expanded, had to fight many little wars as well as major wars. In the remote provinces an armed opponent could burn Rome's whiskers and even cut off its ears. Mithridates, the young ruler of Pontus, a kingdom on the Turkish shores of the Black Sea, was often singeing Rome's beard. A wonderful all-rounder, he was said to speak more languages than he had fingers and toes. Physically strong, he was bouncing with energy, quick to learn, and possessing that kind of intelligence of which cunning is a keen component.

For about 30 years, on and off, he was at war with several of Rome's finest generals. At his best he virtually drove them from their own province in Asia Minor. Towards the end, in his last stronghold at the mouth of the Sea of Azov, he suffered mutinies. Even his son turned against him. In 64 BC he resolved to commit suicide and commanded one of his mercenaries, a soldier from distant Gaul, to kill him. In the long history of republican Rome there were many Mithridates but nearly all were ultimately defeated: a tribute to Rome's military skills. The Roman victors of these battles fought far from home did not always accept the humbler role awaiting them when they returned in triumph to Rome.

The mighty city, like the parent village which had once nestled on the banks of the Tiber, kept one eye fixed on the skies. Its rulers believed that the heavens ordained what would happen in politics. In the republic of Rome the two consuls who shared power were permitted to hold that highest of offices for only one year, and they formally began their year by watching the sky at twilight: they felt reassured if there was a flash of lightning, but only if it was on their left side. They believed that the gods brought success if they were honored at the right time by the sacrificing of cattle and other animals. Roman cities also supported astrologers, fortune tellers and magicians. Some were an early version of today's grief counsellors, while others pretended to be long-range forecasters of the weather.

As Rome expanded, more foreign gods were adopted or attuned for Roman needs. From Egypt was to come the mother god, Isis, who was believed to rule the cosmos. From Persia was to come Mithras, the Iranian god of the sun, who quietly penetrated the Roman army and found his way to army camps in places as far apart as the rivers Euphrates and Rhine. From Palestine was to come Christianity, which was first seen as a worthy rival to astrology by some Romans, who consulted their favorite fortune teller to see which was the best day of the week for becoming a Christian.

Looking back on Rome's success, it is all too easy to conclude that its victories were preordained. It is almost as if Rome arose with consummate certainty from the seven hills, gaining such a height that seemingly it could not be challenged. But in almost every phase of Rome's history there were crises. Thus in the last century of the pre-Christian age came severe setbacks. In 86 BC many members of patrician families—once so powerful—were massacred by their rivals. In the following decade Spartacus the slave led a rebellion, attracting rural slaves to his banner in their tens of thousands. When he was finally defeated in Italy in 71 BC, some 6,000 of his followers were captured and crucified along the Appian Way. In the following decade pirates were so persistent that a campaign was launched to drive them from the sea lanes near Italy.

Civilizing strands were intertwined with the violent strands. Even in slavery there could be civility and compassion. Early in the second century AD the son of a slave died; and the slaveowners commissioned the carving of the dead boy's head from a block of marble, adding this simple message in Latin:

> To the dearest Martial,
> A slave child,
> Who lived two years, ten months, and eight days.

The child wears an innocent look, with his long elegant ears, short mouth, neatly clipped hair raked halfway down the forehead and—just above the right ear—an Egyptian good-luck charm. The insignia did not denote that the child was living in Egypt, which was then a Roman colony. Rome's was a cosmopolitan empire, and ideas and religions and fashions flowed with ease across the Mediterranean and along its coasts, just as ideas and objects at present flow with ease: indeed the child's head can be seen today in a museum in Los Angeles.

Rome began as a republic in which a small number of families shared power. Later the electorate of citizens living in Italy and entitled to vote was increased to hundreds of thousands: in the end they numbered more than one million. Of course it was pointless for Rome to imitate Greek democracy and the public meetings of citizens voting on the spot; and so the secret ballot was the Roman alternative. For several centuries Rome ran a form of representative government which virtually every leader in Europe, 300 years ago, would have condemned, by their own standards, as dangerously democratic. The heads of state were elected. No politician or general could hold the reins of power for long. Much of the decision-making rested with the representative assemblies.

Rome's distant and ever-expanding empire was not easily governed.

Success imposed penalties. The cost of maintaining and enlarging the huge extent of territory was heavy. Where could new taxes be found? Citizen armies could no longer carry the brunt of the military service and so mercenaries and even slaves were recruited, and some were likely to be loyal more to their general than to Rome. Even the generals fighting on far frontiers were not easily kept in check. They needed some independence in order to fight successfully, but if they were too victorious and too popular with the Roman public they were indirectly a challenge to those civic leaders holding power in Rome.

The more thoughtful of the Roman citizens were not certain that their swelling empire would outlast their children's lifetime. In 45 BC, a year of political turmoil, the Roman governor in Athens hinted at this uncertainty when he wrote in the hope of consoling an Italian friend, the celebrated Cicero, whose daughter Tullia had unexpectedly died. The governor felt that her death was his tragedy too, but how, he wondered, could he comfort her father? He offered this slight consolation. He confided that he had just sailed back to Athens from the Asian coast, and from the deck of the ship had seen the sites of Corinth and Piraeus, which once were famous. But now he could see only tumbled stones and spreading ruins. He mused to himself how fragile was every empire, every family.

Eighteen years later the perpetual tension in Rome seemed to find a solution. To people proud of their republic an emperor was unthinkable, but the unthinkable was now thought aloud. Augustus became the emperor, while contending that he was simply first citizen of the old republic. He held military control and he held a firm hand on the senate. Slowly the Roman emperor became all-powerful in life and venerated as a god in death. Each emperor now named his own successor.

The transition from republic to monarchy, while drastic, breathed new stability into the Roman Empire. It continued to expand and to hold on to what it had won. As the citizens no longer voted for or against those wishing to lead the empire, citizenship could safely be extended. The climax came in AD 212, when all free men could become Roman citizens, enjoy the protection of the remarkable and evolving system of Roman law, and pretend to enjoy that other privilege of citizens: the right to pay taxes to an empire which was often short of revenue. Rome was such an incredibly successful empire, its political history and its modes of government were so well recorded, that when London became another Rome in the 18th century, its political and cultural leaders were to be obsessed with Roman history. And its grand houses and gardens were filled with objects carried home from Rome, just as American grand houses in the 20th century would be filled with objects carried home from Europe.

ALONG THE SILK ROUTE

Between the two major civilizations of the world, those of Rome and China, lay a wide geographical gap. The land route between western China and the nearest ports of the Black Sea was, even before the time of Christ, the longest in the world. It crossed mountains and plateaus, stony plains and salty deserts, fast streams and gorges, and immense pastures. The route was more like a relay race than a procession, for the goods being exchanged were handed from merchant to merchant, from bazaar to bazaar, and so they made their slow way across the continent in carts or on the backs of horses and camels moving in long convoys.

The ultimate price of these goods travelling across Asia was heavily increased by the profits taken, and the taxes and tributes demanded, along the way. To cut out half a dozen middlemen, European merchants would occasionally despatch a brave agent halfway to China to act as expediter and negotiator. As early as 300 BC, Greek merchants could be seen in the market of Samarkand in central Asia.

The main cargo carried from the east was silk. To the Romans the Chinese were "the Seres," the people of silk. Few presents gave more delight to a rich Roman matron than the Chinese silk which arrived in tiny quantities after the hazardous journey across Asia.

The rich of Rome and Alexandria craved silk garments, and for long China was the only supplier of them. The humble silkworms, feeding on the leaves cut from millions of Chinese mulberry trees, lived for only 45 days; but during a short life each worm produced a cocoon of slender strands which, unravelled, might run to 900 meters. The thin strands were woven into a thread from which the silk was manufactured by hand in many Chinese towns.

A roll of silk was a magical textile. Light in weight, capable of being stretched without breaking, easily dyed with bright colors such as Tyrian purple, and soft when rubbed against human flesh, silk was prized by the few Romans who had a chance to touch it or wear it. Being expensive, it was not worn by the average person in China; and being far more expensive by the time it reached the Mediterranean it was regarded as a high luxury when landed in Rome.

As the silkworm was a living spinning machine of tireless energy, it was certain to be captured by merchants from other nations. Eventually silkworms were smuggled to India, where silk fabric, not of the highest quality, was produced. About AD 550, two Persian monks visiting China succeeded in concealing live silkworms in the hollows of their bamboo canes. With their precious contraband they set out on the long journey home. The smuggled worms themselves did not reach Persia because the journey took more than 45 days. But they laid eggs along the way, and so their descendants reached Persia where they multiplied. Silkworms eventually reached Sicily and France, but the skills of the Chinese spinners and weavers remained at home. China continued to manufacture the superior silk.

China's economic life was so advanced and so versatile that it wanted little from the west. China was pleased to acquire small amounts of the fine glass which was made in Lebanon and Egypt and carried along the trade route across Asia: a fragile cargo to be perched on the swaying back of camels. China also accepted occasional parcels of wool and other cloth. As its silk flowed in the opposite direction in large quantities, it liked to be paid in precious metals. So much gold and silver travelled east to China that its loss was seen by some scholars as accelerating the economic decline of the Roman Empire.

Along the silk route, into the setting sun, came not only silk but other items valued highly in the west. Such prized medicines as preserved rhubarb and cinnamon bark came from China. Even more important were seeds and living plants. China was a botanical garden from which the outside world, century after century, borrowed seeds and cuttings. The Chinese were probably the first to cultivate the peach tree and pear tree, which eventually reached India about the second century after Christ. These fruit trees finally found their way to southern Europe by way of Persia: indeed the peach's botanical name is *Prunus persica*.

It was in China that the orange was first cultivated, bringing wealth to the owners of orchards. The orange tree was valued not only as a source of fruit but also for its wood, which was often selected for making the bows that shot the arrows. Just before the time of Christ the first Chinese oranges and lemons reached the Middle East, having come part of the way in ships using the route from India to the Red Sea. An orange is clearly depicted in a mosaic at the town of Pompeii, which was buried by volcanic ash in AD 79. The oranges eaten in that doomed city were considered to be sour, the sweeter orange not arriving from China for another millennium and a half.

The botanical exchanges between east and west went in both directions. In this two-way exchange across Asia the seeds of a variety of fruits, vegetables and flowers travelled to China and were welcomed as novelties. The grape came from the west, and the watermelon even now is known as *xigua* or the western melon.

The Chinese and Romans held one view in common. Each of their peoples believed that their own civilization was superior to any other. While China possessed an extent of territory that vied with Rome's, its emperor did not hold sway over as many languages, cultures and peoples as did the Roman emperor.

At the time of Christ, Roman ships were in command of nearly every major port in the Mediterranean. Wherever the Greek sea-cities had prospered, whether in Sicily or Egypt, the emperor was now in control. The tramp of Roman soldiers, the systematic splash of the oars of the galleys, could be heard from the eastern to the western shores of the Mediterranean and even beyond the Strait of Gibraltar—a region into which Greek influence had never extended. Roman coins were the currency along the west coast of the Atlantic from Spain to Brittany, and north as far as the sandhills and salt marshes along the coast of what is now Holland.

The north of Morocco was firmly in Rome's control by the year AD 40. Three years later, parts of distant Britain fell to the Roman legions and the elephants that went with them. In the following decade Roman soldiers were pressing far into Armenia. In the 70s the lowlands of Scotland and the borders of Wales were conquered. Early in the new century Rome ruled the lands that are now Hungary and Romania. Even the sites of the ancient river civilizations, near the Persian Gulf, fell into Roman hands.

Rome's rule extended from the Black Sea to the north of England. Roman regiments were quartered as far down the River Rhine as the town of Cologne where that stately river was crossed by a Roman bridge. Likewise the Danube River in the present Hungary was crossed by a Roman bridge whose stone piers and semicircular wooden arches were designed by the notable builder Apollodorus of Damascus.

These outlying cities, harbors, garrison towns and provinces were important to Rome. Outposts, they protected the inner empire. They also contributed food, soldiers, slaves, raw materials and, not least, they provided revenue. From time to time they also brought vexation to the Roman rulers. One source of vexation was a new creed that would outlive the Roman armies.

9

ISRAEL AND THE ANOINTED ONE

THE COAST of the present Israel was fringed with sand dunes and not welcoming to a strange ship. It was meagre in those inlets and natural harbors where a ship could anchor. Indeed the city of Jerusalem, compared to most of the other famous cities of the Mediterranean, lacked easy access to a natural harbor. The Hebrews—or Israelites or Jews—originally owned flocks rather than ships, for they were people of the pastures and not the sea. Lebanon, to the north, possessed the natural harbors; and there the Phoenicians traded and flourished, their boats rocking in the sheltered waters of Tyre, Sidon and other ports which were bustling when Rome was only a village.

Whereas the port of Tyre was founded so that it could trade with strangers, the site of Jerusalem was chosen because it could keep out strangers. It was ironic that this armed citadel was to become the most famous of the world's holy cities. Jerusalem sat on a mountain ridge with steep slopes, and so was not easily conquered by an enemy. Another advantage was that it possessed a natural supply of water—an inexhaustible spring that enabled the town to withstand a siege. In its contacts and attitudes Jerusalem looked more towards the desert than to the sea. This stony desert, extending far to the east, offered a few oases to refresh the merchant travelling some 900 kilometers towards the meandering rivers of Mesopotamia.

The word Hebrew signified a wanderer, or one who "crossed over." For most of their history—and they probably originated from the head-waters of the Persian Gulf or the nearby deserts—the Hebrews had no secure home. These wandering people knew times of prosperity, when their flocks and tents occupied fine pastures, but they also remembered times of humiliation, captivity and exile.

Enslaved in Egypt, they eventually escaped with their leader Moses towards a land they believed God had promised them, the present Israel. According to one version of their history, preserved in scripture, they were almost trapped by their pursuers on the western edge of the Red Sea. Then suddenly the sea parted, allowing them to proceed. The event seems miraculous; but perhaps it was not. For the early name of the Red Sea was the reed sea or the marshy sea, and in many places it was shallow. Such is the shape of the shore that unusual tides can occur. Indeed in 1993 a team of oceanographers observed that when a wild wind has blown at about 70 kilometers an hour for about 10 continuous hours, the sea virtually recedes. It is conceivable that the Hebrews, with the Egyptians not far behind, crossed the sea on such a freakish day. Then the sea rose, drowning the pursuing Egyptians.

Around 1000 BC, the Hebrews under King David had their years of glory, for he captured Jerusalem. His son and successor, King Solomon, built the magnificent temple atop the city's hill; and in that building of al-most unparalleled splendor, his people worshipped God, who had guided them to this promised land.

The surviving record of the formal opening of the temple may well be a blend of myth and reality, but it must have been a wonderful day. In-side the majestic stone temple were carvings of palm trees overlaid with gold, and tall cherubim carved in olive wood, their wings spreading so wide that those who saw them could only marvel. The Hebrew Bible or Old Testament describes how on this memorable day King Solomon spread his hands towards heaven and promised his people that when they confessed their sins their voices would be heard. Their prayers would be answered if armies of enemies besieged their towns, or "if there is famine in the land, if there is pestilence or blight or mildew or locust or caterpil-lar." The emphasis on the hazards of nature was understandable. Grow-ing grapes, olives and grain in the dry and stony hills of Israel, they needed God's protection.

After the death of King Solomon, in about 935 BC, his kingdom was divided into two states, Israel and Judah. It is from Judah that the Jews take their name. Eventually these two pocket-sized states became too weak to fend off ambitious outsiders. In 587 BC soldiers of the New Babylonian empire looted and destroyed the noble temple at Jerusalem and the Jewish leaders went into exile for nearly a century. On returning home, they lived under a succession of foreign rulers: the Persians, Alexander the Great, and the Greek-speaking Seleucids. For much of this time the spiritual life of the Jews blossomed. As the Judean royal family was not permitted to return home, the high priest in Jerusalem became the focus of spiritual and national unity. The temple in Jerusalem was rebuilt; and the Day of Atonement and other festivals of the rich religious calendar were honored. Prophets were heeded, scholars of theology were encouraged, and the idea took root of spiritual survival beyond the grave.

THE TEN COMMANDMENTS AND
100 LESSER RULES

The Jewish God was all-powerful and everlasting. Known as YHWH, or "The Eternal One," his name was rarely spoken, such was the awe and majesty surrounding him. He was eventually to be called "Jehovah" by the Protestant reformers 2,000 years later. Jehovah protected the Jews on condition that they obeyed his precepts, his commandments.

The first of the Ten Commandments proclaimed that there was only one god in the whole world. At a time when the typical religion had many gods—the temples of the Middle East were crowded with gods for each season and each purpose—the Jewish religion was unusual. Its members were instructed to bow down before no other god. Their God threatened to punish those people who were disloyal, even their children and grandchildren and great-grandchildren, but rewarded the loyal by showing "steadfast love to the thousands of generations of those who love Me and keep my commandments."

The Ten Commandments instructed the Jews how to conduct their lives. An underlying rule was that they must respect their neighbors and show them sympathy. They were commanded to honor their parents. They must not kill, they must not commit adultery. They must not tell lies about their neighbor, and not even think of stealing the neighbor's ox and ass. It will be observed that the ox and ass, but not the sheep, were so mentioned. Vital as beasts of burden and high in price, the ox and ass were widely used for ploughing the fields and for carrying and hauling heavy loads.

The rigid practice of Jews was to work only six days in each week and to worship and rest on the seventh day, which, according to their reckoning, was Saturday. One of the first wide-ranging laws of social welfare in the world, the Sabbath day of rest extended not only to householders but also to their servants, female and male. More than 20 centuries later the most advanced of the world's social democracies were to introduce, for many employees, a working day limited to eight hours; but that recent experiment in social welfare was less significant than the six-day working week religiously adhered to by these children of Israel.

The Jews were more obsessed with their own history than any other people the world had known. They busily recorded their trials and tribulations, their defeats as well as their victories. But their profound sense of themselves and their destiny ran up against one obstinate fact. During several long spans of time they seemed to be almost perpetual losers. Their own sacred writings proclaimed they were people of destiny, but century after century their actual history seemed to suggest that they might be doomed to lose. Their own religion, however, was capable of converting adversity into a virtue.

They believed that as a people they knew where they had come from and where they were destined to go, so long as they honored and obeyed God. They believed, with humility more than arrogance, that they were God's chosen people. They possessed an acute sense of their place in history: they knew that they possessed a future. In the 20th century their bewilderment that they should be the main victims of the Holocaust was partly a sign of their agony but it was also a mirror of their persistent faith in their own destiny.

Along with their sense of history was an emphasis on fairness and ethical behavior in daily life. At times they were almost overwhelmed by rules and guideposts. There were detailed rules governing diet and cleanliness and defining Jewishness. The penis had to be circumcised as a sign of the covenant or contract between the Jewish people and their God. Intricate rules demanded that the orphan and widow be fed and that compensation be paid to those who had been wronged. For example, if a slaveowner knocked out the tooth or eye of his slave, then freedom was the right of that slave, as compensation.

Rules governed the behavior of Jews in their crowded farmlands.

Thus a farmer who set fire to thorns, only to see the fire burning out of hand and spreading to a neighbor's wheat field or threshing yard, was obliged to "make full restitution." If an ox gored a woman to death, the ox itself had to be stoned to death. As for those who broke a commandment or a lesser rule, prescribed fines—a ram here and two pigeons there—had to be paid to the priest.

One virtue which the Jews valued highly was what they called wisdom. A book read aloud in synagogues was the *Wisdom of Solomon*. Written down on a papyrus scroll long after Solomon's death, it taught that wisdom came from obeying the countless rules of the all-wise God. "The fear of the Eternal is the beginning of wisdom," it affirmed.

Constantly probing the nature and mission of human beings, and absorbed in every facet of religion, the Jewish spiritual leaders were to become as influential as those Europeans who, in the scientific and industrial revolutions some 2,000 years later, immersed themselves in the task of mastering the material world. But if a history of the world had been written in 200 BC, the Jews would not have merited many sentences. So far they had been no more influential than hundreds of other states and monarchies, peoples and tribes, in Africa and Asia, Europe and the Americas.

THE ROMANS GOVERN JUDEA

Israel, after centuries of vicissitudes and few victories, experienced a miracle in the second century BC. It enjoyed 80 years of near-independence. The miracle did not last, and Rome's ever-expanding empire arrived in 63 BC. Curiously, the people of Israel were to leave their mark on the final phase of the Roman Empire almost as much as the Roman Empire was to leave its mark on Israel.

Rome initially tolerated Judaism as one of the official religions within its domain. Jewish soldiers serving in Roman armies were permitted to observe the Sabbath. Emigrating Jews, scattered far and wide along the Mediterranean, were privileged to enjoy the commercial opportunities provided by the Roman Empire. But many of the Jews still living in their own homeland became wary of Roman rule. Towards Rome the priests were divided. Some even permitted the Roman governor to appoint or dismiss the high priest. At the other extreme were a few itinerant prophets and preachers who spoke on behalf of the land which had been promised to them by Jehovah. It was their intuition that Jehovah would intervene and save his favored people. Jesus was foremost amongst these prophets.

Jesus was born in about 6 BC, according to the Gregorian calendar used today in the West. Growing up in a village that was tucked away in the hills, he followed his father's trade as a carpenter or builder. A skilled trade, it probably earned an income well above that of most workers in Palestine. At a time when few people could read and write, he also possessed the advantage of literacy. Moreover some evidence suggests that his trade allowed him to travel: not only did he make the wooden yokes and ploughs much used by farmers but possibly he also worked on big building projects away from home.

His intellect, imagination, sensitivity and ability to argue made him stand out. Imbibing the intensely religious and political atmosphere of Israel, then under Roman occupation, he mastered the teachings of the Old Testament. He was especially inspired by the urgent preaching of John the Baptist, a wandering preacher who shunned all the outward comforts of the cities and showed his distaste for comfort by eating the simplest foods and dressing in a coat made from the hide of a camel. His message to all who listened was "Repent." His symbolic gesture was to baptize, or to immerse in water, those who deeply repented their sins. Jesus was eventually baptized by John in the waters of the River Jordan.

In his early thirties Jesus put down his hammer, saw and chisel and left his village—he had no wife—and took up the same calling as John the Baptist. He began to preach and teach in villages, in the countryside and even in synagogues. He could now reason and preach and persuade with what can safely be called genius. The sick were brought to him; and to everybody's astonishment he seemed to heal them with a touch of his hand or a quietly confident command.

That such an extraordinary young man should come from a rural village caused no surprise. Indeed he was known simply as the Nazarene, meaning a native of the village of Nazareth. Later he would be called the Christ, meaning in Greek "the anointed one." Today he might well be called a faith healer.

For Jesus to claim to be in touch with God's will, and to prophesy that God would return to reward and to punish, was part of a long Jewish tradition. Every educated adult in Israel knew the names of maybe a dozen prophets of old, whether Isaiah or Jeremiah or Amos, whose prophecies were recorded in the Old Testament and read aloud in the synagogues. Many of these prophets had been freelance preachers, tied to no organization and no synagogue, and not connected to the bureaucracy of the priesthood. Many were poets as well as moralists. Jesus joined that tradition. His sayings flew on golden wings.

His preaching could be mysterious but was also down to earth. He would tell a simple story about daily life, fix to it a moral message and conclude with a plea for his wayside listeners to adopt his new way of thinking. Indeed his preaching and his parables have left behind a wonderful record of daily life. He spoke about the hiring of laborers to work in a vineyard at a penny a day, and told of the vineyard owner who was perplexed that his fig tree yielded no fruit, or discussed, in passing, the sensible way to bottle the new season's wine: "Neither do men put new wine into old bottles," he said. No doubt his rural listeners nodded in agreement.

Jesus once likened his preachings to the sowing of grains of wheat in a newly ploughed field:

> Behold, a sower went forth to sow;
> And when he sowed, some seeds fell by the wayside,
>   and the fowls came and devoured them up:
> Some fell upon stony places where they had not much earth . . .

He went on to say that some seeds fell amongst young thorns and were choked, but some fell on fertile ground and grew, and so the original grain was multiplied. In a similar way his own message would spread, he explained. His message in essence was that people should give love in this world—give and give and give again—and duly be rewarded in the next world with eternal joy.

People craved to hear his message, but the only mass medium available was simple word of mouth. Huge crowds assembled when it was announced that he would preach and heal. He must have been a fine orator with a distinct voice that could float to the most distant member of the crowd, but in the course of a hectic month his voice would reach only a fraction of the people of Israel. As he needed the help of other men to preach in all those villages that could not be fitted into his busy timetable, he gathered full-time volunteers or disciples. The first were fishermen from a nearby lake. Soon there were 12 disciples, gripped by his magnetism. Even more disciples were needed. As he explained with his homely rural reminders: "The harvest truly is plenteous but the laborers are few." He showed every sign of being a homespun prophet, but in the eyes of many of his followers he was not homespun but fashioned by God himself.

Jesus displayed a deep feeling for the underdog: for those who were poor, those who were reviled, those who were sick, and those who mourned. The poor especially respected him. He seemed to uphold the old Jewish values and the authority of the Old Testament, but he also had a revolutionary streak. He announced that the day would come when "the last shall be first" and the humble would be the most powerful. This was not reassuring news for those holding positions of civil and religious power in Jerusalem. He implied that their power was temporary: God would descend and reign on earth.

Such a dramatic event had profound implications for Roman rule. As Rome collected taxes systematically in all its outlying provinces—its empire was primarily an efficient taxing machine for the ultimate benefit of Rome—it would not welcome a bush preacher who implied that the day was soon coming when there would be no more taxes. It could see only danger in a homespun religious leader who daringly announced that the might of Rome would count for nothing in the presence of the all-powerful Jehovah. Nor did all Jewish religious leaders think highly of a rising rival who might undermine their authority.

The main Jewish sects and synagogues were not sure how to regard this prophet. Some felt threatened by his swelling influence on the crowds. Some were understandably alarmed because he disputed the rigidity of their teaching and their cementlike adherence to the hundreds of ancient Jewish rules and rituals. That he would take the fight into their synagogues and challenge their moral credentials was an additional threat. He was not frightened by rebukes. Thus, when he was accused by religious leaders of doing tasks which were not permitted on the Sabbath day, he enquired whether they themselves would always uphold the letter of the law: "What man shall there be among you, that shall have one sheep, and if it fall into a pit on the Sabbath day, will he not lay hold on it and lift it out?" Surely, he argued, a sensible farmer would break the strict rules of his religion in order to save his valuable sheep, on which his family relied for wool, milk, and ultimately for meat.

Jesus probably saw himself as an orthodox Jew trying to rescue a spirit which was sometimes drowned by the rigid rules covering the Sabbath and a hundred other occasions and activities. In politics and culture, in religion and sport, the clash between those who call for more and more rules and those who rely on the free spirit is age-old and never-ending. In the Jewish religion it was a fertile source of conflict, and Jesus inflamed that conflict. He was also looked upon by the Roman rulers as potentially subversive.

His life as a preacher and healer was to be short. In about AD 30, when still in his thirties, he sensed that he was in peril. Indeed he virtually beckoned his enemies to lay their hands on him. He resolved to come to Jerusalem with his followers at a holy time of the year. There, one evening, he celebrated a last supper with his disciples and, in their presence, foretold his own death. Arrested at the demand of his numerous enemies, he was tried for blasphemy in a Jewish court and then sentenced by the Roman rulers to die by a humiliating procedure from which Roman citizens were exempted. He was flogged and then his body was nailed to a tall cross-shaped structure of timber, with two common criminals placed on smaller but similar crosses on each side of him. A placard written in three languages—Latin and Greek and Hebrew—proclaimed what was viewed as his dangerous pretension: "Jesus of Nazareth, King of the Jews." He died slowly, in acute pain.

It is said that an eclipse of the sun then occurred, as if the heavens knew that an event of magnitude was taking place. That afternoon he was taken from the cross and buried by loyal friends. On the third day his body disappeared from its grave. In the following days his disciples believed that they had briefly glimpsed or heard him, here and there, in Jerusalem and Emmaus and Galilee. They were convinced beyond a flutter of doubt that he had ascended to heaven: that he was the son of God, to whose presence he had now returned.

Nothing did more to make his whole life seem momentous than the ascent into heaven. There, it was said, he would wait until the day of judgment when he would appear on earth again to punish the wicked and reward the good.

While the possibility of the resurrection of the human body was not a theme of mainstream Jewish religion, the idea appears briefly in the Old Testament. It began to attract many followers just when Christ was preaching and healing. News of his resurrection therefore brought elation and a sense of triumph to his small circle of loyal disciples and many members of those large crowds who, having heard him preach, respected or admired him. But these supporters were largely unorganized. Moreover, many must have been cowed by the way in which Jesus had been publicly humiliated and killed.

10

AFTER CHRIST

IF Christ's message was to stay alive, it could do so only with the help of the Jews. They were a scattered people, mostly living far from their homeland and thus offering a network through which the Christian message could spread.

At the end of that period now known as BC or "Before Christ," most of the Jews had never set eyes on the land of their ancestors. Many Jewish families, having gone into exile as captives, became part of their new land. Other Jews went as traders or soldiers to distant ports and lived there, generation after generation. A census conducted by the Romans in AD 48 indicated that seven million Jews lived in the vast Roman Empire. Maybe as many as 9 per cent of the empire's population was Jewish—a proportion of Jews higher than that inhabiting Europe on the eve of the Second World War. Another five million Jews lived in parts of Asia Minor and Africa that lay beyond the empire. As political conditions deteriorated in Palestine, and as more and more Jews decided to leave, the city of Babylon became the dynamic center of Jewish culture and the home of spirited Jewish theologians.

Jewish synagogues could be found all the way from Sicily to the Black Sea, southern Arabia and Ethiopia The synagogues in Rome alone served about 50,000 Jews. In many of the remote Jewish settlements the synagogue remained the hub of social life, with a library and perhaps a hospice. At Sardis in Asia Minor the synagogue, in its length, must have resembled a town hall or concert hall in a modern city. Visitors to the port of Alexandria marvelled at the basilica synagogue and its double colonnade. These faraway synagogues were often a testimony to the generosity of congregations, many of whose members donated one-tenth of their annual income.

The Jewish religion, though initially for the Jews, had long ago widened its appeal. Many gentiles or non-Jews attended a synagogue and accepted its ethical code and its view of the world, though did not necessarily submit to the minor surgery and major ritual of circumcision. In many synagogues in the eastern parts of the Roman Empire during the first century BC, the Hebrew language was superseded. The congregation prayed in Greek and heard the scriptures read aloud in Greek.

The chain of synagogues along the Mediterranean and in the interior of Asia Minor became an early forum for the spread of Christ's teachings. St Paul was the first notable convert. He had not spoken with Christ or heard him preach, and at first he opposed his cult following, seeing it as a danger to mainstream Jewish religion. Paul's attitude was transformed, however, by a mystical experience on the Damascus road. He became an ardent Christian missionary. Some 14 years after the death of Christ, he began to reshape the infant church. As a preacher and theologian for Jews and non-Jews he possessed unusual qualities. He felt at home in a synagogue: his parents were Jewish and he himself had once trained to be a rabbi. He held Roman citizenship, which gave him a passport to official circles; and he spoke Greek, the tongue of the cultured.

While the early converts to Christianity were mainly Jews, others were equally attracted. Soon, many people who had no connection with a synagogue heard the Christian message and began to meet together in private houses or public rooms. The question of who could become a Christian was increasingly debated within the new congregations. Many Jewish Christians objected to outsiders, for they saw Christianity as simply a branch of their own religion. Accordingly, they insisted that a new convert should be circumcised before becoming a Christian. It was in the city of Antioch that this dilemma was first debated with vigor.

Some centuries later there were five chief cities in Christendom, and four of them are still famous—Jerusalem, Rome, Alexandria and Istanbul (Constantinople). The fifth of the major Christian cities was Antioch. It has so fallen from fame and is so little known outside southern Turkey that it merits a digression. Antioch is now called Antakya, a small and sleepy city of dark alleyways with only a scattering of broken or dislodged monumental stones to point to its heyday. At one time it was the most influential Christian city in the world, the home of St Paul and the residence of St Luke, the local doctor who wrote one of the four gospels narrating the life of Christ. In this city the small groups of converts were first given the name "Christian."

Those who approached ancient Antioch from the Mediterranean Sea landed at the mouth of the Orontes River and went by road or boat upstream some 30 kilometers. In the time of St Paul the noble city had fine buildings and aqueducts. The Roman emperors intended it to be their main city in the eastern Mediterranean, preferring it to the more remote Alexandria, and eventually Antioch's population was to exceed a quarter of a million, of whom one-fourth could be fitted in the huge Roman stadium or amphitheatre. Steep hills and mountain torrents, one of which was known as the "donkey-drowner," made the city appear to be a civilized haven sitting in the wilderness; and the wild aspect was enlarged by the fact that the city sat on an earthquake zone. Antioch was to be a goal for Christian pilgrims coming from as far away as Spain, and the training place of priests who then went to the hazardous ends of the known world. England was one of those ends, and the seventh archbishop of Canterbury, Theodore of Tarsus, learned his theology in Antioch.

In Antioch, a decade or two after the death of Christ, the question of who should be allowed to be a full member of the Christian church was resolved in favor of the internationalists rather than the Jews. Everyone who came in a state of repentance could become a Christian. This inevitably led to a widening rift between the synagogues and the new Christian churches. Each competed for the same worshippers, whether Jew or gentile. While many of the Christian congregations consisted exclusively of Jews, more and more of the new congregations attracted people from all races and backgrounds. St Paul emphasized this all-welcoming strand when he wrote his powerful letter to the Galatians: "There is neither Jew nor Greek, there is neither slave nor free, there is neither male nor female, for you are all one in Christ Jesus."

In the first century after the crucifixion of Christ his followers lived mostly in the towns rather than the villages and countryside. Women probably were the majority of Christians. Those who clung to the church in these difficult years had to be brave. The emperors in Rome occasionally turned against the Christians, and Emperor Nero Claudius blamed them for the famous fire in Rome in AD 64. In a kind of match of the day, many Christians were gored to death by wild beasts in the presence of a crowd of spectators.

In their inward tussles on the question of how far to follow and how to deviate from the rules of the synagogue, the early Christians were not sure whether to obey or discard the strict Jewish rules on food. Many of the early Christian converts no doubt followed the Jewish prohibitions on pork, shellfish and other foods. Paul himself, though Jewish, was more relaxed towards food. In response to the argument that some foods were innately unclean, he decreed that "nothing is unclean in itself." Paul was seen by numerous Jews as a traitor to their faith. He was harried and persecuted by them.

Ultimately most of the early Christians, knowing that Christ's last supper in the presence of his disciples was a momentous event, adopted a positive attitude to food. As wine was part of the last supper, it was enthroned along with bread in the special ceremony known as the sacrament or Eucharist. To eat a meal together became the symbolic custom at early church services. As Christians were inclined to see their creed as embracing all peoples—the Jewish religion being more the creed of one people—they saw merit in abandoning the restrictive Jewish rules on food.

Those who had known Christ became the first leaders of the church and of course they were Jewish. Peter, once a fisherman, was the senior disciple after the death of Christ; and he is said to have led the early church in Rome. At times it was an underground movement and persecuted by the Roman authorities. Eventually native-born Italians came to the fore. Linus, said to be a native of Tuscany, was the bishop of Rome, or the pope, not long after Nero's persecution of the Christians.

In Rome itself and in far-flung cities of the Roman Empire, mobs—with Jews sometimes taking part—rampaged against Christians. At the French town of Lyons in AD 177, many Christians were killed, including Pothinus the bishop. The list of martyrs grew long. As it was rare for Christians to form a majority of the population in any city or large town in the empire, they depended on the toleration accorded them by others. They would have been more tolerated if they had been less assertive. At times they did not publicly respect the statues and shrines of the popular pagan gods of the Roman Empire, and they did not pay sufficient homage to those Roman emperors who increasingly saw themselves as godlike. Being a tiny minority in a vast empire they could not afford to be too different, and yet their religious beliefs were profoundly different to those of most people with whom they rubbed shoulders in the markets and streets.

Christianity became like a shoe in the hands of a hundred shoemakers, taking on many shapes by the year AD 300. While its forms of worship within the Roman Empire were still conducted mainly in Greek, Latin was its language of worship in North Africa. From province to province the expanding church differed in its beliefs and rituals. A merchant and his wife who transferred from a congregation in Asia Minor to one in Italy might blink when they first saw their new pastor perform the rituals or explain his theology.

SUNDAYS, SALT AND SCRIPTURES

The present form of Christianity, the observances and holy days, emerged slowly. Sunday at first was not necessarily the Lord's day. The Jews had honored Saturday as their day and at first the Christians tended to honor that day as the heart of their week. St Paul began to accord the place of honor to Sunday, that being the day of Christ's resurrection. When Emperor Constantine became a Christian and made the Roman Empire conform to his new faith, his law of 321 declared Sunday to be the day of worship in the city but not in the countryside. There the cows and goats had to be milked, the harvest brought in and the ground ploughed, irrespective of the day.

Easter soon became the special time in the calendar of Christians, but its exact date was not easily chosen. Along the coasts of Asia Minor, the early heart of Christendom, Easter Day was not at first on a Sunday. Eventually it was almost agreed that each year the Easter Day was to be celebrated on a Sunday, at or near the full moon, but which full moon? For years Christian theologians argued about the day when Easter should ideally fall. Their disagreement was strident in 387. In that year, in Gaul, Easter Sunday was celebrated on 18 March, in Italy it dawned exactly one month later, and in Alexandria it was even later, being celebrated on 25 April. In the seventh century one region of England was celebrating Palm Sunday on the same day that another part was celebrating Easter. The unity of Christendom was often precarious.

Many of the special days in the Christian year were latecomers to the church's calendar of holy days. For three centuries the early churches around the shores of the Mediterranean did not celebrate Christ's birthday; and when they did decide to celebrate it many churches chose the month of May. Eventually the Christians sensibly seized upon the popular festivals which had long been set aside to mark the shortest day of the year in the Northern Hemisphere. Thus in Rome, 17 December had been celebrated as the pagan day of merrymaking known as Saturnalia, but that day of rejoicing was eventually commandeered by the Christians and moved to 25 December, where it was proclaimed as the birthday of Christ. Even when Rome definitely decided to celebrate the present Christmas Day, the Christians in Jerusalem adhered instead to 6 January.

On marriage and kinship, Christianity slowly reached a new view. It eschewed the preference, common in parts of Europe, for men and women to marry other members of their extended family or clan rather than those who were not related to them. In the fourth century it banned marriage between cousins. The aim, seemingly, was to break up the clannish and extended families and so make their loyalty to Christ stand higher than loyalty to their family. In like spirit, with the same suspicion of the tightly bonded family circle, the church followed the Greek and Roman civic custom of allowing easy divorces.

To make the pilgrimage to see the holy sites was to be a burning desire of most Christians but it was not a conspicuous desire during the first centuries. The desire grew during the time of St Helena, who was the daughter of an innkeeper and the mother of Emperor Constantine. A convert, she became sober in her mode of dressing and exemplary in her frequent visiting of the poor and prisoners. In the 320s she made the pilgrimage to Jerusalem, where she tried to retrace the footsteps of Christ. She was said during her visit to have discovered the buried remains of the true cross—one of the most prized of Christian relics—so her pilgrimage to the Holy Land was doubly blessed in the eyes of the devout.

In the light of the rivalry between the leading bishops of the Christian church and the rivalry between the cities they represented, it was not easy to agree on which was the holiest place. Some bishops were not eager to preach the virtues of a pilgrimage to Jerusalem. Too much extolling of its sacred sites might make that city a rival to their own bishopric in prestige and sanctity. It was not until 125 years after St Helena's celebrated pilgrimage that Jerusalem became the regular home of a bishop. Hitherto it had been presided over by the Bishop of Caesarea, a harbor-city which has long since vanished.

Like Christ's birthday, the special day set apart for Mary, the mother of Christ, was slow to find its place in the Christian calendar. In 431 the Council of Ephesus gave Mary an honored role; and her own day, 25 March, increasingly became known as Lady Day. As the cult of Mary grew, a minor cult developed around her own mother, Anne or Hannah; and a day called "the conception of St Anne" was eventually honored in the Italian city of Naples. For hundreds of years Mary was given more veneration in the eastern than in the western churches.

Christianity, a borrower as well as an initiator, slowly adapted some of its rituals from the everyday life of the Romans. For example, when a Roman baby reached its eighth day, a few grains of salt were placed on the tiny lips in the faith that the salt would drive away the demons who might otherwise harm the child. When the early Christian church was baptizing new followers, it blessed a small morsel of salt and, in imitation of the Roman custom, gave it to the baptized ones. At a later time salt was added to the holy water. This was in keeping with the teaching of Jesus who, knowing how sparing in the use of salt were the poorer people, selected salt as a symbol for the precious and the rare. When he went into the mountains he had told his disciples: "Ye are the salt of the earth."

What was the sacred word? Even that question aroused argument amongst Christians. The New Testament did not quickly take precedence over other sacred writings. When the early generations of Christians met together they did not read from that Bible which now sits in a place of honor in most churches. Reared initially in the traditions of the synagogue, they used its liturgy for their divine service and read extensively from the Jewish Old Testament. The reading aloud of Christian as distinct from Jewish scriptures was not widespread until about AD 150. One obstacle posed by the early writings about Christ, and his life and message, was that the writings were too numerous. Athanasius, who became Bishop of Alexandria in 328, was active in promoting those hard decisions which eventually reduced the numerous competing books of the New Testament down to the four gospels and, in addition, the writings of St Paul and Revelation. In contrast the Syriac Christian church long preferred the version of the New Testament produced by that way-out Syrian heretic Tatian, who converted the four separate and often contradictory gospels into his own continuous narrative. He believed that it was easier to teach his streamlined version of Christ's story than four separate ones.

In many of the places where large numbers of Christians assembled, they sparked debates amongst themselves. They argued because each brought differing assumptions and values from various parts of the Roman Empire. They argued because Christ sometimes spoke in parables and did not quite make his meaning clear to those who heard his message secondhand. They argued because they relied on those who, after Christ's death, wrote down his teachings and offered conflicting accounts of the same sermon or miracle. And sometimes Christians argued with each other because they each read into Christ's words what they themselves wished to read. And yet a thread of unity was unmistakable. Travellers usually felt at home, at least in spirit, when they entered a Christian church far from home.

St Augustine—his real name was Aurelius Augustinus—found himself being encircled by some of these controversies. Born in the present Algeria in AD 353, his hometown lay 70 kilometers south of the ancient port of Hippo, which is now called Annaba and is today a busy loader of iron ore and phosphate rock into deep-sea ships. Like so many of the church's gifted theologians, Augustine was not brought up as a Christian. He taught rhetoric and philosophy in Carthage and Rome without initially taking a Christian view. To the dismay of his mother, who was a Christian, he was an agnostic and then for nine years a Manichean worshipper. Mani, the founder of this Persian religion, combined the new Christianity with other eastern cults. His numerous followers, including Augustine, prayed seven times each day, fasted on a Sunday, and believed that after the final day of judgment the terrestrial globe would burn for a total of 1,468 years. Clearly the followers of Mani liked to be precise on those religious matters which, to members of various other creeds, were shrouded in uncertainty.

Augustine, finally lured from Mani's creed, was baptized a Christian in the Italian city of Milan. Back in his native North Africa nine years later, he became the bishop of Hippo. He made that city celebrated in the eyes of Christians by the way he successfully defended mainstream religion against various heresies and by propagating evangelical views which were again to become influential in the days of Luther and Calvin. For a time, however, all his work seemed to be in vain. In 431, one year after his death, the city of Hippo was destroyed by the Vandals. Rebuilt and repaired it was later occupied by Islam, whose fine mosque was partly constructed with stone scavenged from the ruins of the city in which Augustine had defended the faith.

For at least four centuries Christianity was like hot metal being poured from furnaces into molds of varied shapes. Sometimes a furnace almost exploded or the fire was put out. Often the furnaces were remodelled and many times they were enlarged. The molds were changed again and again, so that the early followers of Christ, if they had come alive again, would not have quite recognized many of the beliefs and rituals of the church which they had helped to found. They would also have been mystified by another fact: the end of the world—so imminent in their eyes and such an urgent spur to their deep beliefs—still lay in the future.

ROME VERSUS THE EAST

Meanwhile, the city of Rome was ceasing to be the heart of the vast empire. The empire's armies, and their procession of famous generals, were replacing the old institutions of Rome as the hub of power. Moreover that city was situated too far towards the western end of an empire whose real wealth and balance of population lay at the opposite end of the Mediterranean Sea. Accordingly in the year 285 the empire was divided for administrative ease into two: a Western Empire ruled from Milan, and the main or Eastern Empire ruled from the city of Nicomedia: it lay on the Sea of Marmara, about 100 kilometers east of the present city of Istanbul.

Today Nicomedia, known as Izmit, lacks the sheen of marble and the music of imperial processions; but in the year 303 it was more powerful than Rome. It blossomed with grand buildings. The emperor, Diocletian, wearing cloth made of gold and a pearl diadem, resided here. Almost everywhere, piles of newly quarried and cut marble caught the eye. But not many of the blocks of marble were used in the building of Christian temples, for that creed was suddenly turned upon by Emperor Diocletian. The cathedral at Nicomedia was burned down. In the empire Christian books were burned in their thousands and many congregations were closed and their land and buildings confiscated.

In history many vital events are shaped by underlying forces, movements and factors, but occasionally one person almost alone changes the direction of the world. A boy who lived in the city of Nicomedia in its proudest years, when the battalions of stonemasons were almost tumbling over one another, was to be such a shaper of great events. Constantine was the son of an army officer who was to rise swiftly to become the emperor of the western half of the empire. When Emperor Constantine was killed in battle at York in England in 306, the son, barely into his twenties, was acclaimed by the army as his father's successor. Constantine proved to be a fine general. To the surprise of many, he was intensely sympathetic to Christianity. In France six years later, he was converted. In his military campaigns he henceforth carried a portable chapel which his servants could quickly install inside a tent, thus enabling divine service to be held for him and his comrades at a few minutes' notice. He was not formally baptized as a Christian, however, until shortly before his death.

Constantine believed that Christianity was intrinsically suited to be his ally. It did not wish to take over the state, having been long accustomed to a humbler role. It did not readily take up arms, even when in a desperate plight. Tending to be internationalist, it did not display the ardent nationalist strand sometimes visible in Judaism. It could fit neatly into a multiracial empire. By treating all peoples as equal, Christianity seemed well suited to an empire which consisted of Greeks, Jews, Persians, Slavs, Germans, Iberians, Romans, Egyptians, northwest Africans and many others. Its only blemish was that it did not always pay respect to the emperor and his claims to divinity. But once Constantine became a Christian, even that blemish was automatically erased.

In the history of Christianity no single event since the crucifixion of its founder was as influential as the change of heart of the young Emperor Constantine in the year AD 312. He offered civic toleration to Christians. He restored properties that had been confiscated from them. With his mother he began to build grand churches, one of them as far away as Jerusalem. Until then the Christians, conscious that their church buildings might be confiscated by a contrary emperor, had built on a humble scale. An early result of Constantine's change of heart was the erecting of grand Christian churches, modelled not on Roman temples but on the oblong Roman assembly halls used as courts and markets.

Hitherto, Christians had constituted probably no more than one in 12 of the inhabitants of the vast Roman Empire, but now—suddenly seated in a privileged position alongside the emperor—their adherents quickly multiplied. For the first time more people within the empire attended Christian worship on Sunday than attended the synagogue on

Saturday. Roman soldiers on the march found themselves attending Christian services organized for their instruction. City residents who might have once sneered at Christians found themselves wondering whether in the new religious climate they might gain secular favors or promotion if they were seen attending a Christian place of worship.

In contrast the synagogues, which sometimes had been in favor with Roman rulers, were now despised. In less than a century Jews lost the right, unless they changed their religion, to marry Christians. They lost the right to serve in the army. They could not seek converts for their religion. Here and there mobs destroyed synagogues. Even Palestine was to experience such attacks. The Jewish religion was now an outcast. The godfather of Christianity was in effect declared to be illegitimate. Without doubt, in the earlier era, some Jews in some cities had tried to harm Christians, turning the Roman authorities against them. But now the boot was on the other foot and used more frequently and more ruthlessly.

Constantine was hardly an orthodox Christian—he arranged that his own son be put to death—but he did not deviate from his belief that God was on his side. There was only one religion in his eyes, and those who did not subscribe to it were a threat to the empire. He became more fervent in his faith and took part in religious controversies as best he could. Imagining that he himself was really the 13th apostle, he nursed in his last years a longing to be baptized in the holy waters of the distant River Jordan where Jesus himself had been baptized. Constantine died in 337, and was buried in the baby city of Constantinople which he had planned. The heyday of Rome had clearly passed, and it had lost its supremacy to this new city of the east.

Neither empire, east or west, was in full control. The fighters advancing from the steppes were increasingly capable of victory. The Huns, who were probably Turkish in speech, first reached the River Don in Ukraine in 370. That was dangerously close to the Roman frontiers. Eighteen years later they were camped close to the Mediterranean. Rome, accustomed to these raids by everchanging "barbarians," had a long history of successes against them; but now it was incapable of repelling them. While Constantinople was easily defended, Rome became vulnerable.

Enemies coming from the far interior had no trouble entering Italy and even approaching Rome. The famous city was invaded, looted and half-destroyed in 410 and again in 455. People fled the city which for so long had been the mecca for migrants. Rome declined with sobering speed; and a century later it perhaps held no more than 50,000 people.

The Roman civilization was mighty, but how mighty? It inherited much from Greece and was not as imaginative as Greece. Perhaps Rome should have been far more creative, given its huge population and the longer period of its ascendancy. Rome was more skilled in warfare than the Greeks and more successful in imposing the first vital ingredient of a civilization: law and order. Rome set up the vast free-trade zone or common market, and for a long period it maintained on its frontiers a relative peace, measured by the warlike standards of human history. The Romans shaped what is still called Roman law, the legal system adopted by most peoples of Europe and South America. They devised fair methods of solving civil disputes. They were probably the world's finest engineers up to that time, building impressive aqueducts that provided a safe supply of water for cities, and constructing highways which lasted for centuries.

The Romans left behind a superb literature. They handed on Latin, which remained Europe's shared language for close to 2,000 years. Even at the beginning of the 20th century, Latin remained the language of prayer and ritual for the world's main Christian denomination and a second language within European lands. Furthermore, Latin is alive and eloquent through the Romance languages, of which Spanish, French, Portuguese and Italian have the most speakers. The Latin-based languages dominate Central and South America, the existence of which was unknown to the Romans. Even in eastern Europe, the Romanian language uses a grammar based on Latin. Above all, the last phase of Roman history gave the official blessing to Christianity. Here was a launching pad more powerful than that available to any other major religion in the world's history.

Rome was influential during so many centuries that its time of vitality in one field coincided with slumber or sleepiness in another. Literature was flourishing before the time of triumph in architecture and sculpture. Public participation in government and civic spirit were high in earlier times, but the triumph of Roman law came five or six centuries later. Military security was highest in the middle period, and material comfort was highest at a later period. A long-lived republic, it was eventually ruled by emperors, half of whom died violently. It is really the history of many societies one after the other, all centered on Rome.

Such a mighty state, powerful for so long and described by many of its own wise and reflective writers, was bound to remain a sign in the sky for future generations. Indeed in the 18th century many Europeans saw Rome—before the emperors became tyrants—as providing the formula for their own nation's political maturing. They admired its civic virtues and the sense of honor of many of its earlier leaders. Europeans, long after Rome's decline, gave praise freely to its willingness to fight with ideas as well as swords. They also tried to learn moral lessons from its collapse. Many later observers were inclined to agree with the historian Livy, who, at work when Rome was still mighty, saw the sober writing on the wall. He believed that greed, self-indulgence and the collapse of the old morality and of the civic virtues were undermining what his ancestors had created.

Why did the Roman Empire decline? It is one of the fascinating questions of history and open to a combination of answers, ranging from lead poisoning in Rome itself and soil exhaustion in the countryside to the rise of Christianity. The Huns and other outside raiders were significant, but their raids were successful partly because they were meeting weaker resistance. The empire largely decayed from within. Almost certainly the more important question—and just as elusive—is why the empire lasted so long. Rise and decline form the normal pattern of human institutions. It is easier to rise than to remain on top.

How remarkable that a city which by 200 BC was becoming the most powerful of the states along the Mediterranean should still be dominating western civilization more than five centuries later. The sheer length of its dominance can be assessed more easily if transposed to a modern chronology. It is the equivalent of a nation which was dominant in most of Europe during the heyday of Columbus and still supreme in the presidency of Clinton and Castro.

THE RIVAL

Constantinople was a new city arising within the old city of Byzantium. Founded by Greek colonists in the eighth century before Christ, the old town had sometimes been captured by enemies and sometimes ransacked, but it was always rebuilt. It stood on a superb triangle of land with the sea washing two sides. Commanding a vital trade route and the only entrance to the Black Sea, its position was symbolic as well as strategic, for it was on the very edge of Europe and within a short rowing distance of Asia.

To enlarge the living and building space of this new city, outer walls were built at some distance from the previous walls, and later the perimeter of these walls went out even further, such was the city's swift growth. Thick walls were needed, for the city was to be besieged nine times between the years 600 and 1100. Meanwhile it became a marvel of the western world—only China possessed larger cities. Visitors expressed their wonder at the large marble doors of the private palaces, the fine statues confiscated from other cities, the triumphal columns erected in honor of the emperors, and the long two-storey aqueduct on which freshwater was borne aloft.

Constantinople was the first city so designed as to provide prominent sites for Christian churches. Soon the churches were numerous. Visitors especially wished to pray in one of the noblest buildings in the world, the Hagia Sofia or "Divine Wisdom." Its dome was rebuilt after the earthquake of 559 and the church was to be converted nearly a millennium later into a mosque capped by minarets, but the tiers of arched windows and the soaring dome and the sense of space are still breathtaking.

A bishop or patriarch was consecrated in the new city, and soon his spiritual status rivalled that of the pope of Rome. As Constantinople held the palace of the Roman emperor, that heightened its bishop's status. Already the rival bishops were tugging the church, century after century, in slightly different directions, for the cultures and peoples of Asia Minor were far apart from those of Italy. Even in language the western and eastern churches were separate. Greek was the language of the eastern church, and Latin of the church of Rome. As the two cities were separated by a voyage which could occupy up to a month when seas were rough or the winds unkind, they did not always keep in touch. Moreover Constantinople now held more than 500,000 people, whereas Rome, at the mercy of the incoming barbarians, had so dwindled that it held no more than one-tenth of that population.

The two bishops might reassure each other that they were brothers, sharing the body and blood of Christ; but the eastern church let it be quietly known that it was the senior church and that in Italy and France and Spain resided "the bishops of darkness." Surely the east was the king. Did not Christ himself come from the east? Did not the sun rise in the east? Were not four of the five traditional Christian cities, each with its independent patriarch, founded in the east?

In their ways of worship and belief the two churches, eastern and western, also drifted apart over matters which seemed to be minor. But any universal creed that is alive and vigorous will be quick to argue about matters which bystanders see as insignificant. These are not minor matters if they are an integral part of worship. Thus many monks and priests in the eastern church saw a special place for icons or small pictures which, painted on flat boards, depicted Christ or Mary, saints or angels. On the other hand, many priests, especially in the west, protested at this practice. They argued that to worship icons, to pray to them and to seek miracles through them, was a form of worship which the Old Testament specifically forbade. Such arguments flew to and fro across the Mediterranean.

The rise of Islam—pursued in the next chapter—was to sharpen the differences between the eastern and western churches. The eastern church had to face, more than did Rome, the competition from the Muslims. Leo III, who in 717 became the emperor in Constantinople, concluded that his church's obsession with icons was an obstacle to the conversion of Muslims and Jews to Christianity. As Islam and Israel strongly opposed the worship of idols, their adherents might be more willing to worship in Christian churches if all icons of Christ were banned. Nine years later, Leo issued to the eastern church the unpopular order to destroy all the icons.

While Rome disliked an excessive love of icons, it also disapproved of their destruction. More than six decades after the edict to destroy icons, the bishops from east and west came together at the Council of Nicaea in 787 and found a compromise. Icons would be restored to the churches in the east, where they could be venerated but not given the same fullness of worship as would be offered to God. It seemed a sensible decision. Sixty years later, however, icons were triumphant in the east. The split with Rome became so deep in 1054 that it was now "The Great Schism."

In the eastern church the simple worshippers would reverently touch and lovingly kiss an icon depicting Christ or one of the apostles and martyrs. The icons, it was said, were really "books for the illiterate." However, they raised the danger that a peasant woman or a simple fisherman would eventually worship the icon itself rather than what it stood for.

In the course of many centuries the western and eastern churches, or the Catholic and the Orthodox, would grow apart in their theology as well as their organization. Thus the Catholics, but not their rivals, believed in purgatory—a halfway house on the path to heaven where the more deserving of the dead received such punishment as they merited. In Orthodox churches the division between the layman and the priest was not as sharp as in Catholic churches, and moreover a married man could be ordained as a priest. In their congregations laymen could even preach, but Catholics were allowed no such privilege. In that sense the Orthodox churches had close resemblances to the Protestants who were to arise in northern Europe.

So Christianity slowly lost its unity—if ever it possessed real unity, for it had long been a decentralized religion. But diversity, in the long term, was perhaps one of its strengths. Christianity was adaptable. Easily understood but adaptable to different cultures, it brought hope—and sometimes fear—to hundreds of millions of people. Its new rival, Islam, showed those same qualities.

11

THE SIGN OF THE CRESCENT

ISLAM is often a puzzle. The West tends to cloud its origins in mystery. It is assumed that Islam, arising out of the land of camels and nomadic pastoralists, must be a mirror of the ideas of a simple people for whom anything larger than a tent was an unfamiliar sight. In fact Islam arose less from the desert than from walled towns. It arose less from the herders and shepherds than from merchants who were in weekly contact with the outside world. It arose less from the red windblown sands and the arid loneliness of the interior than from towns shadowed by rugged bony mountains and standing close to the sea, or towns in the center of irrigated oases. Some of the towns of Arabia were busy ports, and many Arabians piloted a seagoing ship with as much ease as others guided a caravan of camels. They traded with India and East Africa by sea and with Asia Minor by land.

Mecca, which became the birthplace of Islam, was situated just over 60 kilometers from the Red Sea. It relied on long-distance commerce, for it stood astride the overland route which ran from the more fertile southwest of Arabia across the desert to the Mediterranean Sea. This route, served by strings of load-carrying camels, was a vital stage in one of the trade routes linking lands as far apart as India and Italy. Two of southern Arabia's traded products were the expensive myrrh and frankincense, which were used to make incense, perfume, embalming fluids, and the anointing oils used by Jewish priests. It could well be that the valuable gifts of myrrh and frankincense presented to the baby Jesus had actually been carried by camels along this desert trade route traversing the birthplace of Mecca. On the eve of the founding of Islam this overland route was flourishing, perhaps because it was a safe alternative during the long wars between Persia and Byzantium.

Mohammed, the founder of Islam, was born in Mecca in AD 570. When he was young he lost both his father and mother. Arabs, being seafarers of the desert, sometimes sent their boys or young men as apprentices with the camel-caravans that traded in far-off cities; and Mohammed went in one such caravan. At night the orphan boy learned to identify many of the stars in the brilliant night sky, and to know the hour when the moon would rise above the desert edge: the new moon would be a symbol of his faith.

Mohammed was highly intelligent and impressed his rich employer, a widow. They married when she was 40 and he was 25. She bore him two boys, who died as infants, and four daughters. It is curious to contemplate that the founder of a religion now singled out for its subjection of women owed so much to a woman. Mohammed probably could not have launched a new religion but for her financial backing at a time when he was buffeted by opponents.

He grew up when Arabia was weak and politically fragmented. It was largely controlled by intruders, of which Byzantium and Persia and Abyssinia were the strongest. Arabia was close to the major civilizations but did not necessarily gain from them nor feel at home with them. In religion it had large numbers of Jews and Christians, but in the interior and in many of the towns most of its people were pagans who worshipped moon gods or local deities. For them Mecca was a holy place and those who could afford the journey visited it as pilgrims. In Mecca, at the shrine called Ka'ba, they reverently approached the black stone which, perhaps a thousand years previously, had fallen to earth as a meteorite. Seven times they kissed it.

Mohammed as a trader and courier travelled to distant cities where he learned much about the ideas of that outside world. He inhaled ideas from Judaism and Christianity—not in one deep breath but in many short breaths. In 610 he experienced an intense religious awakening during which he received the message that there was only one god—an idea not supported by the tribal religions of his land.

Mohammed felt that he was filled with the spirit of God. He preached his ideas with fervor: he was a powerful persuader. He made enemies too. When he began to criticize the pagan pilgrims who idolized the black sacred stone at Mecca, he was bound to make enemies. Mecca was a pilgrims' town as well as a trading town, and its economic life depended on religious tourism as well as trade. Many who came as pilgrims stayed on to trade for a few days. For Mohammed to criticize idolatry and the worship of the black stone was rather like today's mayor of Venice calling for a ban on the entry of tourists.

In the politics of the town of Mecca, Mohammed was connected to some families of substance and influence but he was not in the elite circle. He found his ardent converts amongst the poorer merchants and their servants, amongst strangers, and amongst people tending livestock. He soon fell out with the rich merchants who largely ruled the town. As his influence as a prophet grew, they saw him as a threat.

Mohammed knew that his prospects in Mecca were limp. In 622, after making careful plans, he fled across the coastal mountains and dry watercourses to Medina, a town less than 400 kilometers to the north. Standing amidst a large oasis of date palms and fields of irrigated cereals, it became his home. The day of his arrival, 24 September 622, was to become the first day in the new Islamic calendar. In Medina he became the secular and spiritual ruler. Whereas the early Christians had been, generation after generation, a minority possessing no political power, Islam was soon the dominant religion in its chosen town and district and the possessor of all political power.

Medina had a considerable colony of Jews, some of whom were farmers or dealers in edible dates, and at first they were sympathetic to Mohammed, seeing him as a religious teacher following their own tradition and accepting much of the Old Testament. But he was not a Jew and his treatment of their creed was individualistic. His teachings and rituals, more than his handling of regional rivalries, perturbed many of them. One sign of the parting of the ways was visible in February 624. Hitherto Mohammed and his followers, when engaged in their daily prayers, were accustomed to face in the direction of Jerusalem. Now they turned towards Mecca.

HOLY WAR

Mohammed quietly declared war on Mecca's main merchants. He sent out forces to raid their richly laden processions of camels that passed nearby on their way to and from distant towns. In 626 he planned to attack a caravan said to consist of 1,000 camels. Though Mecca learned of the plan and applied superior forces, it suffered a surprising defeat. Mecca, the larger and richer town, should have been capable of trouncing Medina; but Mohammed was a skilled general, many of his troops were enthusiasts, and he increased his military strength by making alliances with nomadic tribes, several of which were Christian. In the year 630 he captured Mecca with ease.

His creed took shape with speed and precision. Its rules were simple. The believers had to pray five times daily, facing Mecca as they prayed: the first man to call the muezzin or summons for prayer was to be a black man. The holy day was Friday, which marked out the Mohammedans from the Jews with their worship on a Saturday and the Christians with their Sunday. Devout believers had to try to make a pilgrimage to Mecca once in their life. They had to give generously to the poor. And they had to fast between daylight and sunset in the lunar month called Ramadan. The fasting rule now seems strict, but at that time most Christians also fasted during the 40 days of the season leading up to Easter. Other rules protected worshippers of Islam from moral danger, though women were more protected than men. Women wore veils in public so that their face could not be glimpsed. On the other hand, richer men could each take four wives, and Mohammed himself in his last years also slept with Māriya, a Coptic concubine.

Alcohol and other stimulants were forbidden by the new religion; but the prohibition cannot have been too comprehensive, because the evergreen bush that produced one of the world's most popular stimulants, coffee, was to be first farmed in southern Arabia in the 15th century. Many worshippers were said to chew coffee beans quietly during the long services in the mosque on Friday. Coffee was soon banned by the Orthodox leaders, thus permitting more of the crop to be exported to European coffee houses at a time when Arabia was the world's sole supplier.

Several of these Islamic principles reveal much about the early aims of Mohammed. He must have initially envisaged Islam as only a religion of the Middle East: in itself that was a highly ambitious goal. If a worldwide creed had been envisaged at the start, the idea of a pilgrimage to Mecca would not have been a central tenet. After all, how could a convert living in eastern Asia, in an age when only the rich could travel, be expected to make a pilgrimage to Mecca? Few peasants in central Asia could expect to save the money for such a long and often dangerous journey. Nonetheless the pilgrimage remained a core principle even after the religion spread further and further from Arabia.

The early emphasis on the pilgrimage reflects not only the early role of heathen Mecca but also the fact that so many Arabs were travellers. During the course of the year they moved a considerable distance with their flocks and herds in search of pastures or anything edible. Likewise, in the towns of Arabia long-distance commerce was a mainstay. To travel and to trade were almost the same. Mohammed himself was much travelled by the standards of the time.

Islam retained, perhaps more than any other of the world's five powerful religions, a strand of the ancient pagan religions. It reflected a sense of the power of nature. It retained a sense of wonder at the universe and the heavens; and indeed the moon held a more distinctive place in Islam than in the other main religions. The crescent moon was often a symbol of Islam and today appears on the flags of many Islamic nations. The Islamic calendar was based on moon rather than sun; and that is why the feast of Ramadan moves on and on, and never stays for long in the same month. Perhaps the moon also had a special place in the imagination of people living in or close to desert. At night the clouds rarely hid the moon, and on a typical night the moon was the main spectacle in the night sky.

Mohammed's preachings were to be brought together in the one book, the Koran, which was written in Arabic. Poetic and often inspiring, simple and emphatic, it was the Bible of the new religion. It was far shorter than the Old Testament of the Jews and a little longer than the New Testament of the Christians, running to a total of 78,000 words, or 77,934 words to be exact. It painted the joys of the heaven waiting for true believers. It preached the omnipotence of God. It told how God from time to time sent down to earth such prophets as Adam and Jesus and finally the last and greatest of the prophets, Mohammed. But Mohammed was not as central to his creed as was Jesus to Christianity. He did not see himself as the son of God. He was simply the messenger and the recorder for God's word, and the prophet too.

Men and women, he emphasized, were worthless unless they surrendered their will to Allah. Indeed, the word "Islam" means "submission"
or "surrender." He preached, in the manner of the Christians, that a day
of judgment would come and that all must so order their daily life that
they would not be judged unfavorably by God and thereafter be punished
in hell with all its terrors. Everyone who heard the Koran read aloud was
familiar with the portents of that final day on earth when the wicked and
the just would be rewarded:

> When the sun is overthrown,
> And the stars fall from the sky
> And the hills are flattened,
> And the camels big with young are abandoned.

When Mohammed captured Mecca in 630 he was well on the way to unifying the long-divided Arabia. He died two years later and was buried at
Medina. A mosque arose over his grave, and as a place of pilgrimage it is
second only to Mecca.

An English clergyman and scholar, W.R. Inge, once summed up the
special place in history achieved by small populations. "The nations
which have put mankind and posterity most in their debt," he wrote,
"have been small states—Israel, Athens, Florence, Elizabethan England."
He was a committed Christian: otherwise he might have added Mohammed's little city of Medina to his list.

Mohammed was not yet seen as the savior of surrounding countries.
But his armies grew in size and began to win victory after victory far from
home. Many Arabs joined the armies for secular reasons but accepted the
religion as part of their loyalty. Islam also offered hope. From about 590
to 640, most of Arabia experienced extreme drought. To visit more fertile
lands as part of a conquering army, and to survive the bloody battles, was
to win food, excitement and sometimes treasure.

The early victories of Islam were resounding. The enemies abroad
began to fall just as easily as those at home. The city of Damascus was
captured in 635 and Jerusalem a year later. Many Christians hoped that
the loss of Jerusalem to the new and militant religion would only be temporary; but this holy city of Christianity was to be held by Islam for about
1,100 of the following 1,300 years. One of the minor results of the First
World War was that Jerusalem was recaptured from Islam. This victory
in Jerusalem by the British allies of the industrial era would have been

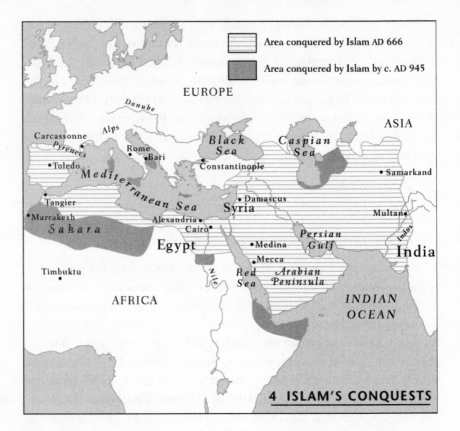

| | Area conquered by Islam AD 666 |
| | Area conquered by Islam by c. AD 945 |

4 ISLAM'S CONQUESTS

hailed more jubilantly if it had occurred in an earlier and more spiritual century and been achieved by the medieval crusaders and their swords.

Soon after winning most of the Holy Land, the Arabs invaded Egypt. Their attack seemed overconfident. Only 4,000 Arabs took part in the first prong of the invasion but they held their own until another 6,000 arrived to provide momentum. The invaders captured Alexandria in 641 and forced that famous city to eat humble pie when they founded Cairo as the new city of Islam on the banks of the Nile.

In capturing Egypt and Syria the Arab soldiers were actually welcomed by many of the inhabitants who had long resented the previous rulers. Likewise, in moving west the Islamic armies gained from the vacuum left by the collapse of the Western Roman Empire. For the invaders these were favorable conditions; but to make full use of them required armies that were led capably, high in their morale and skilled in using horses.

Less than 20 years after the death of Mohammed, his religion and his sword ruled from the fringes of Afghanistan in the east to Tripoli in the west, a distance of some 5,000 kilometers. The loud call to prayer could be heard on the shores of the Mediterranean, the Black Sea and the Caspian Sea, the Persian Gulf and the Red Sea. The spearheads of Islam continued to probe in all directions. They soon reached the Strait of Gibraltar, at the gateway to the Atlantic. Far to the east they reached the mouth of the River Indus, on the Indian Ocean. The towns of Multan in the present Pakistan and Samarkand in central Asia were taken in 712; and one year later, far to the west, Seville in Spain was held by Islam.

Periods of slow advance and even slight retreat were followed by surges into virgin territory. The word of the Koran was spread by sea as well as land, for the new religion was aided at times by powerful navies. In the ninth century nearly all the large islands in the Mediterranean became Islamic citadels—even Sicily and Sardinia, Malta and Crete. For a time the south coast of France and the heel of Italy were Islamic. Far into the Sahara desert rode the conquerors. Even the western frontier of China seemed in their grasp. Late in the 10th century the message penetrated far into India, and eventually the skyline of the northwest and the Ganges valley—but rarely the south—was dotted with mosques. The spread of the creed into the islands of Indonesia and the Malay Peninsula was slower, and in the year 1200 nobody in full command of the facts could have predicted what eventually came to pass: that Indonesia would be the most populous Islamic nation in the world.

Amidst almost continual triumph, one devastating blow fell on the heart of Islam. In the year 930, Mecca was entered not by the faithful but by invaders who carried away the black sacred stone to Bahrain, where it rested in exile for several decades.

Islam was not a centralized empire on the Roman pattern, but everywhere its adherents worshipped the same God and revered the same book. Moreover Arabic was its unifying language in much the same way as Latin or Greek had been for a large part of the Roman Empire. Given the communications and arms of the time, Islam's empire was too extensive to be ruled from one central city. But its creation was an extraordinary achievement and, seen in its context, dwarfed even the remarkable spread of communist rule in the first half of the 20th century.

During the fast spread of Islam, the Jews were less disconcerted than were the Christians. In some cities the Jews welcomed the arrival of Islam in place of the Christian rule based on Constantinople. Byzantium had often been more hostile than was Rome to the Jewish religion. When the Islamic invaders reached Spain they were often hailed by the Jews as liberators. And when some eight centuries later the Jews were expelled from Spain and Portugal, Christianity now being dominant, Jews in their tens of thousands made their way to Islamic cities in North Africa and Asia Minor. Jews and Christians were usually both treated by Islam as second-class citizens, and were normally forced to pay high taxes, but Jews found it comforting to be treated as second-class instead of third-class citizens.

TRIUMPH IN AFRICA

Penetrating into Africa, Islam extended beyond the outer reaches of the Roman Empire. It quickly crossed the Red Sea to the shore opposite Arabia, while the prophet himself was still alive. At the same time it penetrated but did not dominate the Christian kingdom of Nubia, which held the territory on both sides of the upper Nile. As early as the eighth century, ports in East Africa resounded with the call to prayer from the little mosques. South of the Sahara desert a long band of dry territory extending to the Atlantic Ocean received its first Islamic merchants in the eighth century. Archaeologists working in a caravan town in southern Mauritania have recently uncovered glazed pottery carried from Islamic Tunisia sometime before AD 900.

The Koran was spread in Africa mainly by persuasion and example. In most of the ports and inland trading towns it won initial converts from only a fraction of the citizens. In many towns the new faith was first reflected in the building of a small mosque and in the architecture of those houses which enclosed a courtyard so that the women could wear no veil and enjoy privacy. Little mosques were replaced in time by ones that could hold a large congregation. In the present northern Kenya, on the shores of the Indian Ocean, the first mosque at a trading port was built between 750 and 780. Only 25 worshippers could fit inside this wooden rectangle. It was replaced by a succession of new mosques, mostly larger, the crowning one being built of coral stone in about the year 1000.

The people of the desert with their herds of camels and their moving camps were more sympathetic than the farmers of the fertile land to the new religion. The desert nomads found that the religion could not only give their life a new meaning but fit neatly into their wandering ways. In

Islam a group did not necessarily need a permanent mosque for its Friday services and it did not need access to a priest even for a burial. For wanderers a religion requiring no priest and no church was highly practical.

The diffusion of the new religion and way of life was conducted through an alien language. Arabic was the only language of worship for Islam. No translations of the Koran were provided for the speakers of any native African tongue. Converts learned by heart the key passages of the Koran, understanding them as best they could while reciting them with fervor. With the religion came new taboos on food. African villages which voted a roast pig as a meal to remember soon abandoned this delight; and some villages where home-brewed beer was a pleasure abandoned it forever. With the religion came a host of commercial contacts from which African traders gained, for Islamic traders did business at open-air markets as far apart as Mombasa, Canton and Timbuktu.

Islam proclaimed the kinship of all peoples, but the idea did not extend fully to slaves. Islamic traders escorted female and male slaves on long journeys to the point of sale, though they rarely enslaved people of their own faith. Many of the slaves who, centuries later, were shipped to the Americas belonged to lands where Islam had long been a force; but relatively few of those slaves were fervently Islamic. So in the American plantations, Islam did not gain a firm footing, leaving the ground clear for Christianity.

12

THE WILD GEESE CROSS
THE MOUNTAINS

CHINA was far more an importer than an exporter of religions. The new religions travelled on the silk route across Asia but not in the same direction as the silk. Rarely in the history of the world did the one road carry in the same direction, in quick succession, such a long procession of missionaries of new religions. Thus, Syrian monks and missionaries carried east the version of Christianity shaped in Persia, which was known as Nestorianism. They built their temples in western China but won few converts. In the Chinese city of Xi'an (Sian), the terminus of the silk road, is a handsome slab of stone which records the Nestorian advent. Larger than a single bed, it is inscribed in Chinese and a language which for long was a puzzle but is now identified as Syriac. The slab records that a Nestorian Christian missionary arrived in China in the year 635. From Persia, a few decades later, came the followers of Mani, who won converts amongst the Uigur people in Mongolia. Zoroastrians from Persia also came along the silk road and received for a time the blessing of the Chinese government.

Jewish merchants travelled along the grass highway, and in the Chinese city of Kaifeng set up their own synagogue. It was flourishing as late as AD 1163, long after the Christian churches in western China had vanished. It was rebuilt four times in the following 500 years. By that time its small band of adherents must have lost all personal contact with the land so vividly described in the Old Testament. In their synagogues they presumably read in Hebrew—a language which they were in danger of completely losing through their long isolation.

Islam came along the silk route, travelling with caravans and armies. Half the road was in Islamic control by the early 700s, when even the walled city of Tashkent was an Islamic stronghold. Some Muslims in their caravans traded all the way to western China, where they eventually had more success than Christians, Jews or miscellaneous Persian sects in winning converts.

It was the Buddhists who, coming out of India, penetrated the furthest into China. They actually led this cavalcade of religions. A few walked up the valleys of the Ganges and Irrawaddy rivers and then passed through high country and so to the border of China. Others possibly went to China by sea. Many walked north of India and took the route through a pass in the Hindu Kush, at a height of 4,000 meters, and so on to Bactria where they joined the silk route.

At first Buddhism did not expand dramatically. It was long confined to India and Sri Lanka. Then in India's northwest, centuries after the death of the Buddha, the creed recycled itself. Known as the Great Vehicle or Mahayana version of Buddhism, it was more saleable abroad and gave Buddhism a missionary appeal. It increased the prospects of ordinary people finding salvation through devotion to Buddha.

The creed did not expand in eastern Asia until the time when the young creed of Christianity began to expand in Asia Minor. Indeed the first Christian possibly reached India at about the same time as the first Buddhist reached the river-cities of China. By AD 65 Buddhism had won a tiny foothold in China. It was so different to the prevailing Confucianism in its attitudes, so revolutionary in its belief in the reincarnation of human beings in another body at the instant of their death, that the two creeds seemed unlikely to coexist. But the Indian creed sat down quietly, as a rule, alongside the older doctrines of Confucianism and Taoism. In the following three centuries, millions of Chinese were happy to accept the precepts taught by Buddhist monks as well as those handed down by Confucianism and the popular Taoism. Many Chinese peasants gladly worshipped in new temples as well as old, even on the same day. It was as if Buddhism were simply the new, expanding department in the religious supermarket of China.

Early Buddhists in India did not wish to move mountains: they mostly accepted the mountains. In China the new version of Buddhism was more activist. Buddhist missionaries harnessed the energy of millions of people. At their new monasteries the Buddhist monks used slaves—slavery was an accepted institution in China as in India—to clear away forests and cultivate new soil. The monks' willingness to teach the rudiments of reading to the villagers, and even their inclination to act as pawnbrokers and banks, altered social and economic life in many regions.

Buddhism not only generated economic energy but also inspired contemplation and mysticism. Under the combined influence of Buddhism and Taoism, both of which were sympathetic to nature, Chinese nature-poets emerged. Hsieh Ling-Yun, an aristocratic playboy and bureaucrat who was virtually sent into exile in AD 422, settled down on his rural estate, almost surrounded by rivers, about 500 kilometers from Nanjing. A student of Buddhism, he now had time to ponder problems in theology. He also began to absorb the spirit of the countryside as he climbed the rock faces in his special walking boots. Meanwhile a small regiment of laborers did the work on the estate and he watched as they collected riverside rushes and wove them into ropes, knocked the chestnuts from tall trees, cut firewood and dry grass, made "mountain-fresh" wine from wild fruits, or drained a lake to expose rich soil to the plough.

He lived in turbulent times but wrote mostly verses about the silence of the forest and the scentless orchids and the rivers roaring by. Far away, the city of Rome was about to fall to invaders, and in his own China there was fighting and turmoil, but he was absorbed in the clouds, the wind, the colored blossoms, the cutting of a track through the wild bamboo, or a night spent in open air in high mountains. Alternating between melancholy and jubilation, he spelled out his moods in verse. That his poetry was revered in China some 1,400 years before Wordsworth and the nature-poets became famous in England was a sign that many Chinese already viewed the landscape as a kind of mystical temple. Into that mood Buddhism fitted with ease.

The devout Buddhists erected grand monuments, especially during the seventh and eighth centuries. Along the wide rippling river at Luoshan (Lo-shan), opposite dangerous rapids, one comes across a gargantuan statue of the Buddha, carved in the red face of the cliff and standing 71 meters in height, or as tall as a 20-storey building. The carving, begun in 685, was probably intended to be the largest in the known world. Seen from the river on a day of autumn mist, it resembles the face of a huge pilot, ready to guide the riverboats.

On top of the cliff in the early 1980s the Luoshan temple still attracted a few elderly worshippers, with bells ringing, drum and cymbals sounding, incense wafting, and a few ancient monks chanting and bowing before a likeness of the fat-bellied, big-eared Buddha.

In the western city of Xi'an can still be seen the tall octagonal tower sometimes known as the Big Wild Goose Pagoda: in early Chinese poetry the migration of the wild geese was treated as an auspicious sign. The pagoda was completed in AD 704 but an earlier temple on the same site had been built to guard the precious scriptures brought from India by the early Chinese monk Xuan Zang. European traders arriving in Xi'an for the first time must have mentally compared the pagoda with some of the noble triumphal columns which had survived from the Roman Empire: in height and ornamentation the Big Wild Goose Pagoda was the more impressive.

In China the largest of the Buddhist pagodas displayed that same soaring quality as the later Gothic cathedrals would exhibit in western Europe. It was as if the builders had delicately raised one umbrella, and then unfurled another smaller umbrella and placed it on top, and so, floor after floor, the tower rose, reaching a height of 11 or even 13 storeys. In fact some pagodas were built from the top down, a wooden frame having first been constructed. The interlocking beams used to support the tall building were a Chinese invention. To worshippers walking home from a day in the rice fields, a tapering pagoda must have been an inspiring sight.

The creed made more headway in China than any other outside creed, and the Buddha was the most influential teacher of the Chinese for an unbroken period extending for about 800 years. He was not always in favor but his influence was enduring. The last of the Chinese emperors, early in the 20th century, was a follower of the Tibetan branch of Buddhism.

BUDDHISM ON THE MARCH

During its first millennium as a religion, Buddhism extended further from its birthplace than did Christianity in a similar span of time. Buddhism reached lower Burma before AD 300, and Java and Korea before 400. By the 600s one of the kings of Sumatra was a Buddhist and the town of Palembang, a center of Chinese trade, was much influenced by Buddhists coming from both China and India.

Japan, not yet a united country, was almost like blotting paper in the way it absorbed a variety of Chinese influences, including architecture, painting, poetry, law and religion, but it was also quick to modify them when appropriate. Buddhism became dynamic in Japan at the very time when Islam was dynamic on the far side of Asia. By the end of the seventh century Japan was becoming a Buddhist land.

Nara, a new capital city built in imitation of Chinese cities, became virtually a city devoted to Buddha. Emperor Shomū was already sympathetic to the religion when in 737 his country was hit by an epidemic. The smallpox proved to be more devastating for the Japanese than the Black Death was to be for the Europeans. The emperor, turning for comfort and guidance to the Enlightened One, ordered the construction of a magnificent bronze statue, the Great Buddha of Nara, which, after many failures during the process of casting, still stands upright.

The emperor instructed every province to build a monastery and a nunnery. Temples spread to every corner of the land. In 749, after surrendering his throne to his daughter, the emperor himself became a priest. But the local Shinto shrines did not easily surrender their domain to Buddha, even when the emperor pointed the way. They were built in honor of the kami, the spirits who lived in mountains or rivers, on moon and sun, and in rain and wind and thunder, and were believed to control the rain, so vital for all living things. The kami were sometimes viewed as the souls of dead ancestors who during the winter retired to the lonely hills and then appeared in warmer weather to guard the villages and the people. By AD 800 the two creeds were becoming allies, and Shinto shrines even carried echoes of Buddhism in their architecture.

In eastern Asia, Buddhism depended, like any imported religion, on royal approval. In China, Japan and Korea that approval was sometimes withdrawn and then it was renewed. In the ninth century in China, Buddhists, who for long had been the favored ones, were often persecuted. A century later the Japanese city of Kyoto, which was now the royal capital, permitted no land in its gridlike streets to be set aside for Buddhist temples. Later the temples were permitted. In Korea the creed flourished in the 14th century, but after General Yi won power in 1393 the tide turned, and huge landholdings of the monasteries were redistributed. And yet the Buddhists remained tenacious even in adversity, and occasionally they became the favorites again. Thus in northern China in 1219 the invading Mongols exempted the Buddhists and other religious groups from paying the taxes demanded of other peoples.

Here and there in eastern Asia the Buddhists established huge monasteries, some with as many as 7,000 members and nearly all serving as dispensers of charity and resting places for travellers. The Buddha inspired such monumental buildings as the temple built in sombre stone in the early 800s at Borobudur near the south coast of Java, and the temple built at Angkor in Cambodia in the early 1100s. He inspired a religious devotion which he himself would probably have disowned; and his relics became prized possessions. In Burma the capital city is dominated by the gold dome of the temple Shwedagon; and worshippers climb the steps to the top terrace where they are close to the holiest of relics—a cluster of eight hairs from the head of the Buddha.

For centuries Buddhism was like a flock of wild geese that soared out of India and, landing safely in almost every part of eastern Asia, flourished and multiplied. The stone statues carved in the Buddha's honor took on the faces of the peoples who erected them: he was prone to facial surgery. In central Thailand the statues show him with the typical square face, wide nose, wide mouth and thick lips of the Khmer. In northern Thailand the stone statues portray a narrow aquiline nose, round small chin and curved smaller lips. A religious prophet, to be successful, had to wear travelling clothes and change his garments when entering a new region.

The spread of the major religions towards eastern Asia owed much to the overland routes, but a sea route also carried missionaries. Just as the land route was endangered by robbers on the plains and by snow across the mountain passes, so the ships were exposed to danger from pirates and sudden storms. Nonetheless Islamic traders began to make themselves at home in various ports of southern China. In 758, Persian and Arab traders were bold enough to set fire to parts of Canton (now Guangzhou).

The sea lane between Arabia and the remote islands far to the east was Islam's transmission line. Merchants brought their creeds along with their trading goods. Just when the dominance of Buddhism throughout the eastern half of Asia seemed inevitable, Islam made a successful assault. It moved into the Malay Peninsula and captured most of the Indonesian islands: an early sign of Islam's presence in the Indonesian archipelago is a tombstone found in eastern Java and carved in about the year 1082. Islam swept through the southerly part of the Philippines. The combined success of Buddhism and Islam in eastern Asia, in places so far from home, was a sign of how the world was shrinking appreciably even before the Europeans discovered their own sea lanes to the outside world.

THE TRIUMPHANT THREE

The three crusading universal religions, capable of converting a diversity of lands and peoples, had been born during a special phase of human history. Buddha, Christ and Mohammed arose in a period spanning a little more than 1,000 years. The first creed—Buddhism—appeared in about the fifth century before Christ and the last—Islam—emerged in the seventh century after Christ. Since then no new version of a universal religion has achieved wide success.

These world religions reflected a transition from a belief that God was predominantly a symbol of fear to a conviction that love was divine. They embodied a heightened sense of humanity. None of these religions was ever likely to be the monopoly of one race. Admittedly, Judaism was in part a universal religion, being itself the parent of two of the far-spreading religions, but in most periods it did not actively seek converts.

Buddhism, Christianity and Islam stemmed from a new state of thinking and feeling. Their spirit transcended small neighborhoods. Their spread to many lands reflected the growing importance of trade in much of Europe, Asia and North Africa. Mercantile cities and the merchants who traded between cities were initially more likely than the countryside to welcome the new religions. These creeds emphasized trust at a time when the merchants in strange lands needed a climate of trust in which contracts and word-of-mouth agreements could be honored. The early followers of Buddha were often merchants. Mohammed too was a merchant. Christianity was first disseminated far from its homeland by Jews, many of whom were merchants in strange lands. Though Christ drove the money merchants out of the temple in Jerusalem, it was because they were in the wrong place rather than because they pursued an unworthy occupation. Many of his sympathetic parables about the daily dilemmas of the farmer and shepherd suggest that he was not hostile to business enterprise. As a carpenter or the son of a carpenter, he knew the mercantile world.

The three religions, while unique, shared half-patterns. It was Jesus who regretted that a prophet was "without honor" in his own country. It was true: a prophet was more likely to be honored when he came from afar and his message could be hailed as exotic and exciting. Every influential religion prized the mysterious; and a message arriving from afar was laced with mystery. Buddha, Jesus Christ and Mohammed won their long-term successes far from their homeland. Perhaps in the same way many of the earlier religions were compelling because they centered on the moon and stars, which were also far away.

The ultimate success of these religions in new lands owed most to the devout and the selfless who were willing to give their lives, or lose their lives, for the sake of the cause. Whether a religion spreads to a new land also depends on whether the ruler is eager to welcome it. The universal religions especially appealed to emperors trying to govern peoples lacking social cohesion. Buddhism and Christianity, which were still struggling after several centuries of faithful preaching, owed much of their subsequent success to the conversion of two mighty emperors, Asoka of India and Constantine of Rome. A king of a large domain was likely to welcome a religion which made his subjects feel content with their simple and sometimes harsh daily life.

By the year 900 the three universal religions had penetrated, between them, most of the known world. Only the American continent, southern Africa, New Guinea, Australia and very remote islands were beyond their reach. Of these three religions, the youngest was perhaps the most vigorous; and with the aid of Arab traders Islam was tapping a vast area of South-East Asia. On the other hand, the oldest of the religions, Buddhism, was influencing the largest number of lives because of its strength in populous China, Korea, Japan and Indochina. Though it had almost exhausted its influence in its Indian homelands, it was still tapping new regions.

Christianity was now the least lively of the three. It held parts of northeastern Africa and Asia Minor but won few converts in Asia proper.

In Europe it was dominant nearly all the way from Ireland to Greece but had lost ground to Islam along the Mediterranean and had failed to penetrate the cold north. St Anskar, a French-born missionary who died in 865, had failed to convert Sweden and Denmark. Other evangelists had made little headway in Russia.

Every major religion relied much on the support of strong secular rulers; but the rulers of Christian Europe were not as powerful as they had been in the era of the Roman Empire. A major religion also relied, for expansion opportunities, on those of its adherents who were merchants and, trading far from home, spread the word or prepared the way for missionaries. In the year 900, however, the Christian merchants of Europe were hemmed in by Islam on one side and by the unknown Atlantic Ocean on another. In contrast, the Arab merchants, shipowners and missionaries had increasing access to South-East Asia, where some of Islam's striking successes lay ahead.

If there had been, in the year 900, a few wise observers with wide knowledge of the known world, and if they had been asked which of the major religions seemed to hold the future in its hands, they would not have pointed to Christianity. It was mainly anchored to the stagnating civilization of Europe; and yet, almost miraculously, its prospects were to be transformed six centuries later.

13

TOWARDS POLYNESIA

THE WORLD was still partitioned into hundreds of tiny worlds that were almost self-contained. While Europe and China each formed large worlds, with traffic flowing between them, Africa and the Americas and Australasia consisted of numerous small and isolated worlds: there, a small group typically had little or no direct contact with people living only 1,000 kilometers away. In parts of the globe a gap of that width, especially if it was a sea-gap, was really a chasm.

At times the chasm was leaped over, and such leaps had vital consequences for the human race. In the whole of human history there have been only three important leaps across the oceans in order to settle major uninhabited lands. One was the migration, more than 50,000 years ago, from Asia to New Guinea and Australia. Another was the migration from Asia to Alaska more than 20,000 years ago, followed by the slow settling of the whole American continent. The third, in very recent times, was the migration of Polynesian peoples to a long ribbon of uninhabited islands in the Pacific and Indian oceans. It is a mark of how recent this migration was that it took place in the Christian era, though the migrants themselves had not heard the name of Christ.

The Polynesians' voyages across the ocean to new lands were amongst the most remarkable migrations in human history. Some of their voyages were more courageous than that which Christopher Columbus was to make across the Atlantic in 1492. Indeed there is a strange similarity between the procession of Polynesian navigators and the voyages of Columbus. The one left China in search of new lands. The other left Europe in search of China.

The slow migration to the islands began in tropical and wooded southern China. Maybe it was in about 4000 BC that adventurous settlers began to cross the straits to the rugged island of Taiwan. Many seafarers must have died while attempting such a dangerous voyage. Once ashore they established their way of life, presumably as farmers and as fishers. They made their own stone tools; they knew how to make the kind of pottery then commonly used in China; and they probably kept pigs, chickens and dogs. That they were skilled in sailing goes without question. Their chosen vessel, at least by the time they approached the central Pacific many centuries later, was the outrigger canoe. With a hull in the middle, and logs arranged parallel to the hull and roped tightly to it, these outriggers stabilized the vessel in rough seas.

Their succession of voyages went slowly east, in fits and starts, from island to island. In the following thousand years these seafaring peoples reached the islands of the Philippines, patches of which they cleared for gardening. Further voyages carried their descendants to Borneo, Sulawesi and Timor, to Sumatra and Java, all of which were in the process of being settled by the year 2000 BC. Some voyagers doubled back and settled parts of the Malay Peninsula and a strip of coast in Vietnam. Many of these settlements were on new islands but some were in areas which had long been settled. There the existing inhabitants were either defeated in war, reduced by new diseases, driven into the less favorable hills or simply absorbed into the ranks of the invading peoples.

In explaining such a persistent outward movement of peoples it is tempting to offer simple explanations. Perhaps they were reacting to overpopulation, perhaps they were occasionally driven to seek new homes by volcanoes, earthquakes, typhoons or other natural disasters. No single explanation is sufficient. A variety of factors propelled these Chinese-like people, just as many influences drove the first European settlers to North America. Being seafarers, they probably shunned the thought of living in the hills, far from the sea, and instead sought other bays and coastal valleys where they could both fish and grow their crops. In any locality the number of underpopulated bays and beaches was limited, and so the incentive to emigrate to a new island or coastline was frequent.

The voyages of these people crammed in their sailing canoes followed a kind of logic. Venturing in an easterly direction they were likely to discover islands, settled or unsettled, with a tropical climate and a vegetation like that which they had just left behind. In the early phase of migration the winds were also favorable. The monsoons, based on the region's proximity to the big landmass of Asia and its seasonal cooling and warming, enabled the seafarers to travel south or north or east or west, so long as they were content to remain relatively close to the equator. Geography smiled on them. It had arranged islands to the east, thousands of them, like a path of stepping stones. Many could be seen from high hills by the naked eye, while others were found only by a blind voyage. As success came again and again to those sailors who set out for the east, this must have spurred others. Their gods, they must have thought, were guiding and piloting them. Those who were let down by the gods were drowned far out to sea or spent their last days on a rocky islet, craving freshwater.

The slow route of equatorial migration reached the long-inhabited island of New Guinea, occupying a few coastal fringes about 1600 BC, and then entered a region of tropical islands where no human beings lived. By 1200 BC the brown sails of their boats were in harbor-villages of New Caledonia, Tonga, Fiji, the Solomon Islands and Samoa. By AD 500, their boats were seen around Hawaii and Easter Island. In distance travelled along an east–west line—the combined total of voyage after voyage made generation after generation—it was the equivalent of a journey on land from Europe to China, spread over more than 4,000 years. Later these navigators doubled back and discovered the remote islands of New Zealand.

Along a line of islands that formed a kind of Milky Way across the Pacific, these sailors left behind eloquent evidence of their origins. Even today, all the way from isolated parts of the mountains of Taiwan to Easter Island and Pitcairn Island in the east, the Austronesian family of languages survives. When in Tahiti in 1770, the English navigator James Cook—who rediscovered many of these long-settled islands—invited aboard his exploring ship *Endeavour* a Polynesian priest and navigator named Tupaia, he made a shrewd decision. Thenceforth he carried with him his interpreter. Sailing far to the west, Cook eventually reached isolated New Zealand. There, in an explosive situation, Tupaia was able to call out a message to armed Maori men. Cook noted to his surprise that the Maoris "perfectly understood him." The Maori people had not met an outside Polynesian for hundreds of years, perhaps even for 1,000 years, but the ancestral language still united them.

Cook marvelled at the magnificence of the Polynesians' oceangoing canoes. Undoubtedly those he saw were superior to the small canoes which, several thousand years earlier, had set out from southern China and Taiwan; but they were probably the same kind of vessel in which Polynesian sailors had discovered the isolated islands around Tahiti. One ship, carefully measured, was found to be as long as Cook's own *Endeavour*. Most of the canoes had one outrigger, used a very tall oblong sail of brown matting, could beat to windward, and were capable of sailing 200 kilometers in the course of a day and a night if winds and currents were kind. Their appearance was striking, and from the deck the sail rose dramatically like a little skyscraper.

Polynesian sailors knew much about winds and currents and stars. Alert for signs of unseen lands, they watched the passing clouds—a certain cloud sometimes denoted land—and the pattern of the waves, the winds, or the sudden appearance overhead of seabirds. Skilled men like Tupaia carried in their mind a picture of hundreds of islands and their position, and by word of mouth he presented to Captain Cook a more or less accurate map of sea and islands spanning a longitude of 5,000 kilometers. These sailors could not perform miracles; many set out and were not heard of again, and many failed to find new islands.

For the Polynesians to find volcanic Easter Island was a special triumph. It was merely a dot in the ocean, 1,600 kilometers from the nearest inhabited land. Once heavily timbered, it was so deforested by the new settlers that in the end its imposing landmarks were not old trees but stone statues, about 600 in all. One statue—never completed—was 20 meters high. In language and society the Easter Islanders were Polynesian; but their statues and their script suggest an additional ancestry or influence.

The Easter Islanders sometimes inscribed pieces of wood with a script, whereas the Polynesians elsewhere were not literate. The existence of a form of writing on Easter Island is therefore a puzzle. It gives some support to the theory that the island was also settled from South America, the nearest landmass. A voyage of 3,600 kilometers from Chile by seafarers is feasible.

On several of these islands settled by the Polynesians the standard of living was high—indeed higher than that of most Europeans. The handsome breadfruit tree was a special boon, for it could bear fruit for as long as half a century, producing annually up to 150 edible fruit, each of which was heavier than a large pineapple. Joseph Banks, the British botanist who sailed with Cook, expressed his wonder at the tree. He argued that a peasant toiling on European soil for most of the year produced less than a Tahitian who simply planted "four breadfruit trees, a work which cannot last more than an hour." He thought this prolific tree—and the coconut palm with its fruit and milk and textile fibers—gave the people so much food and so much leisure that making love was their "Chief Occupation." His romanticized opinion held a core of truth. It was the attractions of the breadfruit which in 1787 motivated the voyage of Captain Bligh to Tahiti in the English ship *Bounty* in the hope of carrying hundreds of potted young trees to the West Indies as a potential food for the slaves in the sugar plantations. His voyage ended in mutiny.

The Polynesians ranged from tribes living uneasily one with another to strong monarchies governing many islands. Hawaii, with perhaps 200,000 or more people, was largely a monarchy by the time of the arrival of the first Europeans. Some of these Polynesian monarchs, like their counterparts in western Europe, believed they were of divine descent.

DETOUR TO AFRICA

During this long chain of migration other explorers reached the large uninhabited island of Madagascar. Lying off the east coast of Africa, it was too far away to be visible to ships hugging the coast of that continent. The Mozambique Channel, which separates the island from Africa, was 800 kilometers wide in most places and not easily crossed by small craft. On the other side of Madagascar the ocean was infinitely wider, and ran—with the sea often forming itself into a long swell—all the way to Australia. To the northeast of Madagascar the unbroken sea stretched to the Indonesian archipelago, some 5,000 kilometers away. From Indonesian islands the first settlers of Madagascar almost certainly came. Even today their language, Malagasy, belongs to the Malayo-Polynesian group. The language spoken today in Madagascar has more affinity with speech in faraway Tahiti than with speech in adjacent Africa. Indeed the closest of the existing languages is that still spoken in a valley in Borneo.

The first voyage to Madagascar took place when the city of Rome was in fast decline, in about AD 400. It was made just when, almost half a world to the east, other Polynesians were first settling on Easter Island. The voyage to Madagascar was aided by the northeast monsoon. It is likely that those who set sail in flimsy outrigger canoes had East Africa in mind, having heard about it from Arab and other traders who called at Indonesian ports. It is even possible that the discoverers landed first in East Africa, though it is more likely that they first reached the east coast of Madagascar, with its coral reefs protecting sandy beaches and those narrow fertile valleys along which the silt-swollen rivers rush down to the sea.

Most of the island was covered with tropical evergreen forest. Rainfall—except in the southwest—was high. The immigrants, using their simple methods of hacking down and burning the forest, exposed patches of fertile soil where they could grow food. They came prepared. They planted their own Asian yam and the plantain. They brought another remarkable gift, the true banana, to this part of the world. Africa itself grew a native banana, the *ensete*, which produced no edible fruit though its taproot and starchy stem were eaten. Ultimately the Asian yam and banana crossed the channel to East Africa, where they enriched the people's diet.

To stand on the palm-dotted beach in Madagascar and see the waves of the Indian Ocean lazily breaking on the coral reefs is to envisage the brown matting sails coming slowly into view, a small Indonesian boat or two bobbing on the ocean swell. Everyone on those approaching boats must have eagerly or anxiously viewed the surf frothing just ahead, and the jungle in the hilly background; and they must have wondered if they could reach land before their boats were broken by the surf and reef.

Madagascar and New Zealand were the last two sizeable areas of habitable land to be discovered and settled by the human race. Perhaps Madagascar was the more important of the two, for in area it was more than twice as large as New Zealand. Triumphs in the history of human seafaring, both were part of a saga of discovery and migration which was virtually completed by AD 1000.

LAND OF THE MOA

From the sea the fortified villages of the early Maoris must have been easily visible. Some occupied narrow headlands and so were surrounded on three sides by the sea—their first line of defense. The steep and often perpendicular climb from the beach or the sea rocks to the fort was the second line of defense. The third and even higher line of defense was a well-constructed fence with stout posts sunk into the ground at regular intervals and between the posts a line of tall wooden pickets. The picket fence went right around the fortified village or *pa*. Those attackers who managed to climb the fence or break down a section then had to climb perhaps 3 meters until they reached another fence and maybe, after a further climb, yet another fence. The village inside the fort consisted of several level terraces, one on top of the other, and so invaders had to climb and climb and be the target for attack as they climbed. While they climbed, their hands were not free to use their own weapons.

On the upper levels of the village were wooden houses of residence with here and there a storehouse. The storehouses were on platforms so that rats could not steal the food: an occasional pit covered by a low roof also served as a store for vegetables. The houses themselves with their sloping thatched roofs had no walls and let in the sea breeze. In the event of a surprise attack these fortified villages formed a fine defense but they were incapable of withstanding a siege, for as a rule they had no wells, springs or sure supplies of permanent freshwater. Even firewood had to be carried from afar.

The forts must have been an impressive sight, being the result of heavy labor in digging and moving rock and soil, and in cutting timber in a nearby forest and carrying it by hand or shoulder to the site and then up the slopes. In time the forts were abandoned and new ones built. On the North Island, the home of the *pa*, the sites of about 5,000 forts have been identified. The terraces have eroded and the palisades have tumbled down and rotted away and the bush and creepers and grasses have reclaimed the site, but from a distance the outline of a fort—like a small open cut with its series of benches or terraces—can sometimes be seen.

A wide radius of countryside was needed to support each tribe or village with food. Gardens were dug with a long wooden stick rather like a crowbar in shape, the topsoil was heaped into neat rows with a wooden spade and the raised soil was planted with vegetable tubers. Kumara was the most valued of these vegetables. Like a very long yam or sweet potato, slightly nobbly with an outer skin of reddish-pink, the kumara was planted on a day dictated by the phase of the moon. When the crop was ready it was collected in baskets woven from flax, and carried up to the village for storage in stone-lined pits.

As these root crops plucked much of the fertility from the soil, a second and third crop on the same site were less prolific. So new ground was cleared of trees, any stones were laboriously removed to one side, and another garden was dug and planted. Usually the garden patch selected was on a well-drained slope facing the sun. Often gravel was added to lighten the soil, and brushwood was burned to provide ash as fertilizer. It was the women who planted the tubers and weeded the gardens.

For the early settlers one prize was waiting. Meat was in unbelievable abundance. On the South and North islands the tall moa bird, able to run swiftly but unable to fly, was easily caught or trapped by the hunting Maoris. Growing to a height of about 3 meters, with powerful thighs for running but with a head that could not easily damage human hunters, the moa resembled a genial pack animal. Its back was so straight and long that if it had been tamed it could have carried four or more little children sitting in a row.

The moa lacked aggression. It had lived too long in a land where, once it was fully grown, it faced no powerful enemies. It did not even have to face snakes. The only potential enemy was the long-winged New Zealand eagle. With its wings spanning more than 3 meters it was probably the king of the world's surviving species of eagles. One of its sources of food was the moa chick.

The Maoris themselves hunted the moa with such vigor that by AD 1400 or 1500 the species was almost extinct. The long-winged eagles that preyed on the moa chicks were also doomed. They were no longer to be seen soaring in flight when the first European settlers arrived.

Having extinguished, in the space of maybe 500 years, the tall moa, the early New Zealanders concentrated on pigeons and smaller birds. In the autumn, when trees were covered with edible berries, the hunters built makeshift platforms to which they would tie the legs of a captured bird which served as their decoy. Other birds came down to eat the ripe berries, not knowing that under the platform or the leafy branch was concealed a Maori with his hand grasping an upright spear-pole perhaps 6 or 8 meters long, with a point of wood or bone. Once the bird had roosted, the pole was thrust upward, its sharp point impaling the bird.

A Maori tribe could launch, from the same bay, as many as 70 small wooden canoes when the seas were not too rough. The men often fished with a line and a sharp bone hook, even catching that noble and too-inquisitive a seabird, the albatross, by trailing a line behind the paddling canoe. Sometimes a large handmade net—shaped like a diamond and up to 1 kilometer long—was trailed behind the canoes, yielding 1,000 or more fish on fortunate days. The fish, when dried in the sun, could be stored for months.

Possessing no pottery, the Maoris used the outer shell of the large gourd that in summer grew from vines trailing along the roof of their houses or across the planted gardens. They had no herds and no pigs, their only domesticated animal being the dog. Stone had to serve instead of metal, and was shaped or manufactured with artisan skills that were probably as fine as those required by metalworkers. Sources of toolmaking stone were found, and specimens of stone were quarried and then carried long distances on foot and by canoe to those regions which lacked suitable stone. An island off Marlborough Sound yielded a deposit of argillite, a hardened form of mudstone, and from it were shaped efficient adzes. Larger than the head of a modern steel pick, they were heavy enough to brain a human opponent as well as a fur seal.

The art of shaping stone so that the cutting edge was sharp—dangerously sharp—called for the finding of special grinding-stones. On the beach in the Bay of Plenty stood flattish rocks of yellow sandstone that proved ideal for grinding pieces of other rock into axes and other sharp instruments. One rock was capacious enough to sleep three or four children side by side. It served as a hand-driven grinding machine decade after decade. Year after year, as hundreds of pieces of hard stone were ground into shape, long grooves appeared in the yellow sandstone rock as a result of the thrusting motion by the hand of the Maori artisans. In the end the grinding-rock, though hard, resembled a flat mound of butter into which the blades of dozens of knives had been inserted horizontally and then plucked out, leaving a crisscross of deep grooves. One of the large Maori grinding-stones, transported from the beach to the floor of the museum in Auckland, draws clusters of admirers.

Most Europeans who saw the Polynesians, when their way of life was suddenly about to change, were impressed by their courage. Young women calmly accepted the pain caused by the tattooing of parts of their bare body: "their contempt of pain at so early an age, we could not but admire," wrote a British onlooker. Most observers also noted the Polynesians' violence: the human sacrifices and the cannibalism. The Maoris' flair in warfare was beyond dispute; so much so that when in the 1780s the British government had to decide whether to plant a settlement in

Australia or New Zealand—a decision of profound importance to that part of the world—it selected Australia. The Maoris seemed fearless, and were proven fighters. It was wise to leave them alone.

PART TWO

SIGNPOST

A HOST of Christians expected Christ to return or the world to come to a dramatic end in the year 1000. Instead, life went on, and the new millennium began and proceeded. This would be the most remarkable of all the 1,000-year periods that had run their course since the human race first left its African homeland. It would be remarkable not only for the quickening pace of change but for the recovery of the lost worlds.

All the human tribes had been loosely linked before the last powerful rising of the seas. A long chain of human contact linked the most southerly tribe in the world, amidst the tundra of Tasmania, with perhaps the most northerly, living near the chill land bridge joining northern Asia and Alaska. An unbroken chain of nomadic settlements crossed Asia to Europe and Africa; and it was conceivable that a new idea arising along the Yellow River might eventually reach, 1,000 years later, the Niger and the Nile.

Thereafter these human settlements were broken into large fragments. Virtually all contact ceased. Large populations of humans were quarantined by the rising seas. By the year AD 1000, the Americas had experienced more than a dozen millennia in which they were isolated from Asia and Europe. The continent of Australia had experienced long isolation from Asia. In the new millenium all these isolated places, and many more, were one by one to be reunited with the dynamic world-hub situated in Europe, Asia and North Africa. The effects of this process of rediscovery were to be earth-shaking, especially for the peoples who had lived in isolation.

The most unexpected part of this process of rediscovery was its source. It was initiated by a backward part of the world. Western Europe, which so far had made little impact on world history, was to become the dynamo. The Atlantic shores of Europe were to send out most of the ships which found the lost world. Even more unexpected, one part of the lost world—North America—was to rise to become the new global leader at the end of that millennium.

14

THE MONGOLS

IN HUMAN HISTORY the ocean was sometimes an insuperable obstacle to contact between remote peoples, while at other times the vast stretches of land were more of a barrier. What the sailing ships achieved in transport on the ocean, the horses achieved on at least one landmass. They slowly converted into a rough highway that wide transcontinental corridor of east–west grassland and mountain separating the contrasting civilizations of eastern Asia and the Mediterranean. It was to become an axiom of naval historians that whoever commanded the sea commanded the world. Likewise it could have been said that whoever commanded the steppes sometimes commanded the civilizations which stood at each end of them.

Occasionally the people of the steppes burst like a rocket upon the well-armed worlds at each end of the corridor. Several of their victories were remarkable. A westerly group, the Huns, stormed west and made the dying Roman Empire quake with fear. Nearly 1,000 years later an easterly group, the Mongols, combining bravery and cruelty and a touch of genius, conquered the largest territory ever held by one ruler up to that time.

The Mongols' early homeland lay well to the north of the silk route. At one time they probably lived near Lake Baikal, on the borders of eastern Siberia and what is now the Mongolian People's Republic. In about the 10th century they moved from northern Manchuria to eastern Mongolia. Later they gave their name to a dozen other nomadic peoples who joined them in the great conquest. The Mongols and their neighbors and rivals rarely if ever sowed a crop, they knew no irrigation, and they were not even settled peoples. In about AD 1000, the areas occupied by those peoples later called Mongols included the high plateau of the present nation of Mongolia. Indeed the average height of the lands forming that nation is about 1.5 kilometers above sea level. The snow-topped Altai Mountains stand to the southwest, but are not continuous enough to form a barrier debarring nomadic peoples from following west the long corridor of pastureland extending to Ukraine and the plains of Poland.

The families traditionally inhabiting these Mongolian steppes moved their livestock from pasture to pasture according to the changing seasons. They owned the sheep, goats, cattle and horses but the land itself was owned collectively by larger groups. Hardly a fence or enclosure was to be seen, but these skilled riders knew exactly the summer pastures on which they alone were entitled to graze their flocks and herds, and the wells from which they could pull up water. When the time came to move camp to summer or winter quarters, the oxen usually pulled the cart on which the heavy woollen tents were loaded. Possessing no large towns, their population in total was small.

The animals were their capital, their main source of wealth. Reluctant to eat into their capital, the Mongols preferred as much as possible to live off the dividends which came in the stream of milk. From the milk of their cows, sheep and goats they made butter, at least four varieties of cheese, the yoghurt now so popular in the west, a dried cream called urum, and a distilled liquor called *airak*. Even the hardy fast-galloping mares yielded their milk, which, fermented, was drunk with relish. In the grasslands and forests a few edible roots and grains were collected in season, and of course they hunted marmots, wolves, squirrels, steppe foxes and other wild animals, whose fur they prized.

In a normal winter the Mongols' herds and flocks survived even though no hay was stored for their benefit. They fed on the dry brown grass which lay beneath the ice and snow. Sometimes a herd of horses was driven deliberately through these white pastures so that their hooves broke the surface ice, allowing other livestock to find the dry grass below.

At first sight it was not an environment which would equip a people, few in number, for the task of toppling proud and populous civilizations.

But the men used horses with flair, fired iron-tipped arrows with accuracy as they rode, and could cover a vast terrain with speed. The women were competent as managers when the men were away on fighting or raiding expeditions; and indeed the women had a status which surprised many Chinese. In some ways the Mongols could be compared with the Vikings, who flourished a little earlier. What one people did at sea the other did on land. Both came from a harsh climate and thinly peopled territory, which is not necessarily an advantage but becomes one if, next door, lives a rich and populous empire which grows complacent and a little flabby.

THE MONGOLS ARE COMING!

Every shrewd emperor of China saw advantages in enticing the nomads to fight amongst themselves. In the 12th century they were as divided as they were to be united in the following century. In 1206, however, Genghis Khan, the chieftain of the Mongols, miraculously united these riders of the steppes. All clans or groups gave him loyalty: he had already killed or cowed those most likely to be disloyal. A magnetic leader, he was said by some to possess the mystical powers of the *shaman*, a kind of soothsayer revered by the pagan Mongols. With a mounted army of close to 130,000 men, his own genius in strategy and tactics, and a network of spies in enemy territory, he began to conquer. Thousands of his cavalry-men rode with a spare horse or two by their side so they could replace a tired horse if a long journey lay ahead.

Genghis Khan moved so quickly that surprise was often his weapon. He occasionally used the new invention of gunpowder if he had to be-siege a fortified town. Often he offered a city the chance to surrender. The price of surrender was one in every ten of the city's people and one-tenth of its wealth; and so his slaves and conscripted soldiers and wealth multiplied. Cities that did not surrender were besieged or stormed. Mas-sacre and butchery were the Mongols' trademark. They became so feared that they often found themselves pursuing the backs of the enemy.

Ruthless but intelligent vandalism was another of their weapons. They would destroy the irrigation systems that were the lifeline of many farmlands or lay waste to the land surrounding a besieged city so that its roadsides and fields were strewn with corpses. When advancing towards the walls of a well-defended city the Mongols would sometimes compel their prisoners of war to go ahead of them and form a human shield. And yet the Mongol leaders also enforced a strict discipline among their own people.

Enlisting more allies, recruiting or conscripting foreign soldiers, they more than replaced the men they lost through death, wounds or disease. The momentum of the simultaneous advance across Asia, both to east and to west, was terrifying to the people of cities who, thinking the Mongols were far away, suddenly saw them appear on the nearby hilltops.

China surely could halt them. At times its regular army consisted of more than 1,000,000 soldiers, and its output of suits of armor and weapons was prodigious. But inside China there was periodically a tussle between the generals, who sometimes amassed regional armies and took control, and the mandarins or bureaucrats who were close to the emperor. The mandarins were tight-knit: at about the time of the Mongols' invasion, four out of every 10 new members of the civil service were sons or grandsons of former civil servants or mandarins. As the mandarins handled the collecting of taxes and much of the administration, they treated the army less generously. So indirectly they weakened China's ability to defend itself.

The Great Wall of China could perhaps keep out the Mongols. It was a magnificent achievement in architecture and stonemasonry; but the extent of the wall's vulnerability can be measured by a fact not widely known in the west. During a span of 1,525 years, extending until almost the eve of the First World War, four of China's long-lasting dynasties were not created by the mainstream Han Chinese. Either they were of barbarian origin or were founded by ethnic minorities who lived on the inland fringes of northern and western China. The Great Wall was virtually of silk as well as stone, wonderful to see, impressive in its artistry, but easy to overcome. The vast region around Peking (Beijing) experienced, in the 800 years before the fall of the last Chinese emperor, a ratio of about one year of rule by a homegrown Han Chinese dynasty to two years of rule by groups reared on the outer side of the Great Wall: the Ming dynasty was the exception. Armed horsemen had simply leaped over the Great Wall. Nonetheless there remained a surprising continuity in Chinese history. What provided continuity was the well-schooled and distinctive mandarin bureaucracy.

The Great Wall of China was merely another hurdle for the Mongols to overcome. They captured Peking in 1215 and eventually made it the capital of China. To the south lay a huge area of country still in Chi-

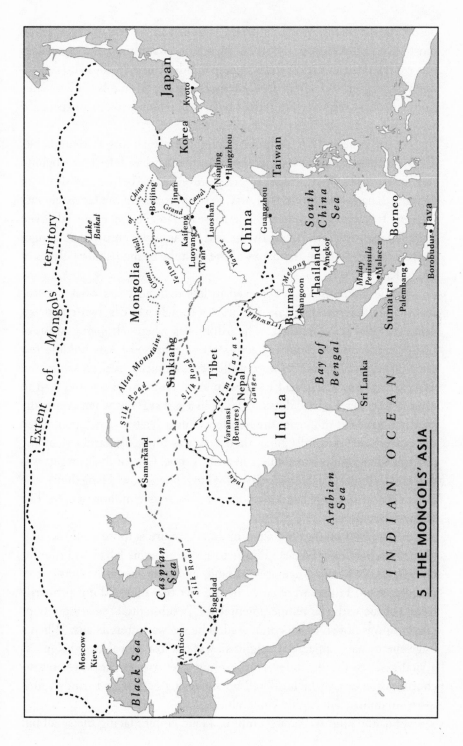

Extent of Mongols' territory

Lake Baikal

Japan

Kyoto

Korea

Mongolia

China

Beijing

Jinan

Grand Canal

Nanjing

Hangzhou

Kaifeng

Luoyang

Xi'an

Luoshan

Taiwan

Yangtze

Guangzhou

South China Sea

Great Wall of China

Yellow

Altai Mountains

Silk Road

Sinkiang

Silk Road

Tibet

Himalayas

Nepal

Ganges

Varanasi (Benares)

India

Burma

Rangoon

Irrawaddy

Mekong

Thailand

Angkor

Malay Peninsula

Malacca

Sumatra

Palembang

Borneo

Borobudur

Java

Bay of Bengal

Sri Lanka

Arabian Sea

INDIAN OCEAN

Samarkand

Indus

Caspian Sea

Silk Road

Baghdad

Antioch

Moscow

Kiev

Black Sea

5 THE MONGOLS' ASIA

nese hands, and the Mongols slowly subdued it. To occupy China, the most advanced nation in the world materially, was almost the equivalent of a central African nation today occupying the United States and replacing Washington as capital. In contemplating the Mongols, one conclusion is beyond dispute. There had been no conquest like it in recorded history.

At the other end of Asia the Mongols were almost as remarkable. They captured a succession of Islamic cities that had felt secure behind their high walls. In Ukraine in 1224—three years before the death of Genghis Khan—the Mongol cavalry were approaching the Christian city of Kiev. It did not fall quickly, but 16 years later it was captured. Even Baghdad fell to the Mongols. By the end of the 13th century the Mongol Empire stretched from the banks of the Danube to the fishing villages of Hong Kong.

While Genghis Khan achieved in less than 20 years what the Romans as conquerors had taken centuries to achieve, the two conquests cannot easily be compared. The Mongols, when advancing west of China, easily fought their way across a vast expanse of Asia holding few people. Their main targets were walled cities, crucial river crossings and mountain passes which had to be won at all costs. In effect they had to capture a scatter of small dots or islands in a vast sea. But when eventually they had to try to subjugate the Southern Sung dynasty which controlled the center and south of China, their task was probably harder than any accomplished by Roman soldiers in a short time. One of their targets was the rich and well-defended city of Hangchow (now Hangzhou), the largest city in the world and the home of close to one million people. The Mongols captured it.

It may well be that the winning of an empire is more easily accomplished on land than on sea. The victories of Genghis Khan and Alexander the Great over a huge area of land, and even the main victories of Napoleon and Hitler, were aided by the fact that they did not primarily have to cope with the temperamental sea. A substantial seafaring city or kingdom was not so easily conquered. The sea was often its ally. When a huge enemy navy appeared in sight, all was not lost. Local knowledge was a vital asset to the defender. An invading fleet, riding the waves or anchoring off a coast which offered no sheltering harbor and winds which were unfamiliar, was highly vulnerable.

Thus the mighty Persian empire, a land empire facing the small but rising republic of Athens, had suffered crucial defeats in the fifth century BC when its navy was twice hit by storms in the Mediterranean. Likewise in the 13th century the Mongols built an imposing fleet and actually landed troops on the Japanese coast, but were thwarted by the sea. In 1274 they lost 15,000 troops and sailors at sea. Seven years later a typhoon thwarted their attempted invasion. In the 16th century the Spanish, eager to invade Britain, were defeated more by storms at sea than by the enemy's navy. Later the English Channel proved one of the toughest enemies for Napoleon and then for Hitler. The sea tended to favor the defender. Thus if the cities of Samarkand and Peking, Herat and Kiev had been on the coast and not in the interior, and had to face the rampaging Mongols who arrived in fleets, they might have defended themselves with more success. To make such a comment is to place a land invasion in perspective and not to rob the Mongols of their glory.

The Mongols were fighters rather than administrators. They were more brilliant at winning an empire than at governing it and retaining it, though the Golden Horde did rule the south of Russia for two centuries. One of the Mongols' first achievements was to bring law and order to the long silk road: never before had it been under the control of one ruler. They even built new cuttings in high ground and a bridge here or there, with staging camps and simple hostelries along the way where merchants, their servants and pack animals could camp for the night. All kinds of cargoes came through, and it is recorded that between 1366 and 1397 the slave market in the Italian city of Florence sold 257 slaves, mostly young women, who had been brought along that road.

The safety of the road became a legend. It was said that travellers could even journey by night, presumably when the full moon was shining. A maiden travelling alone and "bearing a nugget of gold," it was said, could traverse the road with safety; and if she did not turn up at a staging post when expected, a search would be made for her. Ironically the road, busier than ever, was not quite so important to Europe, for its own silkworm farmers were now flourishing in the shade of the mulberry groves. Moreover the sea route to Chinese ports from the Middle East and India was now competing strongly with the overland caravans.

THE WANING OF CHINA'S
SCIENTIFIC STAR

A beehive of inventiveness, China still had much to teach the west. It had probably the most skilled farmers in the world even though some regions were backward. New breeds of rice were found by experiment, including one that resisted drought and an early-maturing rice that enabled an additional crop to be planted each year. The war against agricultural pests was ingenious. Likewise certain plants were burned to create thick smoke and so fumigate an area where insects were a pest. The wild chrysanthemum was burned and the ashes sprinkled on ponds to silence frogs that were croaking too noisily. Locusts, capable of causing famine when they attacked ripe crops, also attracted the problem-solvers; and live ducks were put in baskets and carried by laborers to the breeding spots of the locusts.

In the art of communicating, the most momentous event since the invention of writing was slowly beginning in China. Paper was being manufactured and the art of printing, using signs cut into wooden blocks, was being improved. Their oldest book dates from 868. The printing of a book instead of writing it out by hand was a wonderful opportunity to spread the message of Buddhism and also the precepts of Confucius, which every candidate for the civil service had to know. Long before a printed book was ever read in Rome, the Chinese were producing print runs which even today would be viewed as respectable. In 1273 a handbook for farmers and growers of raw silk was printed, and soon 3,000 copies were in circulation at a time when in Italy the same task would have called for a monastery full of monks to give up a whole year in order to write out the copies by hand.

In designing waterways the Chinese were masters. Whereas the Romans had been the masters of the aqueduct or elevated stone canal that conveyed freshwater to the cities, the Chinese were masters of the boat canal that crossed uneven terrain. China's Grand Canal, like its Great Wall, was built over many centuries. A Japanese monk visiting China in AD 838 was astonished to see a convoy of barges slowly sailing along the canal, with some of the barges lashed together so that they sailed three abreast, and the whole convoy being dragged by two water buffalo plodding along the bank. The canal carried grain from the farmlands, especially around the Yangtze River, to feed large cities.

As China possessed in abundance the three ingredients of gunpowder—sulphur, saltpeter and charcoal—it is not surprising that it discovered this explosive. A Chinese work of 1044 contains three different recipes for making military gunpowder, and almost certainly it was used from time to time in the following century. The Mongols themselves experienced gunpowder after they attacked the big city of Kaifeng in central China in 1232. A container of gunpowder was attached to a missile or lance, which was in turn hurled at the enemy. Called "the flying fire lance," it was more promising than devastating. When a firearm with a metal barrel was invented for the firing of the fire-missile, warfare would not be the same again.

On the cramped beach in the Italian holiday resort of Amalfi, once one of the foremost ports of the Mediterranean (its coat of arms is still on the Italian maritime flag), is a statue of an Italian said to have invented the compass. China, however, was almost certainly the inventor of that great instrument of exploration. It also invented the rod-and-bead abacus, which was a fine instrument for calculating before the invention of the present pocket calculator.

Several techniques for the building and sailing of ships almost certainly came from China, though some were used more effectively, and improved upon, in western Europe. From China came the spinning wheel driven by the action of the foot and a hemp-spinning machine driven by running water. Suspension bridges made of iron chains were built in China long before England made its famous iron bridge early in the industrial revolution. Five years before the arrival in England of William the Conqueror, a pagoda was made of cast iron in Hubei province: it still stands. In 1400 an observer with the gift of acute foresight might have thought that China was rushing, ahead of England, towards the world's first industrial revolution; but soon the rush was to slow down to a crawl.

In medicine and health the Chinese were vigorous in trying new remedies but also tenacious in clinging to old remedies, especially in herbal medicine, which was probably the main avenue of healing. Many of the Chinese used toothpaste and a cleaning brush—items unknown in Europe. Chinese physicians glimpsed the hazardous diseases which surrounded certain occupations—how the sharp dust raised by the drilling of holes in the underground mines weakened the lungs of the miners, how silversmiths inhaled the mercury they used in their craft, and how the cooks who constantly inspected the fire burning in their pastry ovens slowly impaired their own eyesight. In anatomy, too, Chinese scholars made advances. Whereas the Arabs, to the fore in many branches of science, were prevented by their Islamic religion from dissecting a corpse and so examining the human body, some Chinese experimenters felt no such inhibition. In the year 1045 they decided to use 56 political prisoners as guinea pigs. A slit was made in their heaving stomachs and their bodies, still breathing, were examined.

Liberty in China, as almost everywhere, was rationed. Even in AD 1200 several million Chinese were slaves. Some had been captured in war and enslaved; many were hereditary slaves presented as gifts to the Buddhist monasteries where they worked for the remainder of their life. Others were children or even adults who had been sold into slavery by a starving family. The largest owner of slaves was the imperial family, and 10,000 slaves could easily belong to one royal owner.

Chinese courts used enslavement as a penalty for certain offenses. The normal punishment of a murderer was prompt. He was executed, his family was enslaved, and his property was confiscated, six-tenths of it going to the family of the victim. When the Jurchens took over northern China in the 1120s they introduced a loophole. If a murderer could afford to compensate the family of the victim with livestock and other wealth, he avoided the death penalty and instead submitted to the cutting off of his ears or nose. This was in effect his convict insignia, engraved permanently on his face, though he was now a free man.

CHINA'S BLIND SPOT

The Chinese were on the verge of various impressive breakthroughs, but often they remained on the verge and stepped no closer. While many of their clever experiments were successful, few penetrated the entire country and eased the daily labors of the diligent workforce that worked its heart out seven days a week, year after year. And yet China was well ahead of Europe in its applied ingenuity in the thousand years before 1400.

The misfortune for the Chinese was that, having led for long in many branches of technology, they were hot and cold, inventive and lethargic, in that one technique which proved to be the gateway to the future. They failed at sea. True, they invented the compass, but they had no intense desire to sail into the unknown. They were skilled makers of maps but their best maps were of their own small-scale farming districts. A map of the globe was of little interest to them, for they believed that the fertile plains of China were the center of the earth, an oriental Garden of Eden, and that everything far from those plains was of lesser importance.

Chinese scientists still believed that the earth was flat with a definite rim long after that comforting idea had disappeared in Europe. They could see no point in the tantalizing theory—increasingly held in Europe—that by travelling west rather than east, a European ship would eventually reach China. For Chinese navigators in 1492, the corollary of that idea was that, by sailing east, they would eventually reach western Europe. If the Chinese had held that idea, their big ships might have set forth and discovered the west coast of the Americas long before the east coast was found by Columbus. But they did not believe the earth was round.

The Chinese showed high skills in the art of shipbuilding. In the years between 1405 and 1430, their admiral Zheng He supervised major voyages in large ships to distant lands. His Chinese fleet, when exploring far from home, mostly visited ports in Asia and the Indian Ocean which were well known to those sea captains who visited Chinese ports for commerce. Whether it could be called exploration in the Columbus spirit is dubious, and in any case the voyages ceased. Even Chinese merchants did not travel abroad. Already coastal shipping was curtailed in China; and the widened Grand Canal, reopened in 1411, was used rather than the sea coast for north–south transport. Remarkably, the Chinese shunned the sea, on which they were experts, at the very time when western Europe was embarking on distant oceans with startling results.

15

THE PERILS OF CLIMATE
AND DISEASE

A WARM PERIOD intervened during the Middle Ages, and the two centuries between the years 1000 and 1200 were perhaps as warm as the 1990s were to be in northern Europe. Harvests were scythed on lands which once had been seen as not worth ploughing, so frail were the summers. Vineyards flourished beyond the present limit of grape-growing. Even the far north of England made drinkable wine. In Scandinavia, large tracts which previously were covered with ice were now grassed enough in the late spring and in the summer for the feeding of livestock.

The island of Iceland was settled during the first hint of a warmer period. Lying on the edge of the Arctic Circle but gaining from the warmth of the Gulf Stream, it was settled by a few holy men from Ireland and then in 874 by Vikings from Norway. The Vikings were shaking northern Europe at the very time that the Islamic Arabs were stirring the Mediterranean and the Maoris were settling New Zealand. While the Vikings' warlike raids are renowned, their peaceful settlements were also effective; and eventually Viking towns and districts extended from the trading towns of Kiev and Novgorod in Russia all the way to coastal France, Scotland and Ireland, the Shetland and Orkney islands, the Isle of Man and Iceland.

Even icy Greenland, the largest island in the world, seemed to be a prize where, in these warmer years, Vikings might graze their sheep and smoke the fish they caught at sea. In the year 985, tiny ships set sail from Iceland to Greenland with some 400 settlers as well as sheep and goats, cows and horses, and probably bundles of hay. Most were Norwegians, but there was a contingent of Irish too. Landing on the more southerly coast of Greenland, the settlers thrived in the increasingly warm weather. In summer they cut the long grass, let it dry in rows of stooks and stacked it in haysheds, enabling livestock to eat well during the dark winter.

Houses and barns were built to withstand Greenland's long winters. Excavations carried out in recent years reveal the buried remains of very large farmhouses, with a barn and cowshed and sheepshed crammed alongside the bathroom and the few bedrooms. The houses and sheds were covered by a common roof, usually made of sods of turf cut from nearby ground, and the walls consisted of compact sods which were more than a meter in thickness. Here, in this cosy refuge from the winter, wool was spun and clothes were made. Probably those same clothes were washed with that fluid, rich in ammonia, which the Scandinavians carefully collected: cow's urine. Something is known of these settlers, especially the women. Bones excavated make it fairly clear that the women spent much of the day, while working, in a crouching position. The teeth of both men and women tended to be ground down somewhat and a likely explanation is that they ate sun-dried meat and fish which carried grit.

The population grew to 4,000 or 5,000 in less than a century and a half. The small Viking republic eventually possessed a nunnery and a monastery along with 16 churches and a cathedral presided over by the bishop of Greenland. The republic largely grew its own food but at one time exported livestock to Iceland and Denmark in return for grain and other commodities which its short summer could not adequately produce. It was the kind of busy settlement of which its founding families were proud: it seemed likely to last for 10,000 years.

Greenland and Iceland were stepping stones across the cold North Atlantic. America was the next stepping stone. The first European landings on the American continent were made by Viking expeditions just when Greenland was settled. Women went with the settlers to Newfoundland, and one expedition and its two ships were said to have been led by the woman Freydis, who used the axe as a personal weapon against her enemies with the same skill as the Swiss hero William Tell allegedly used the bow and arrow. Nothing came from these settlements. The American Indians had no reason to welcome the Vikings. The terrain, except for furs, had no commodity that would excite traders. If Christopher Columbus, five centuries later, had discovered that same coast instead of stepping ashore in the balmy West Indies, his name today would be no more remembered than Thorhall, Thorfinn and the Vikings who built huts and grazed livestock on the shores of Newfoundland.

COLD, WET AND HUNGRY

The warm seasons, after only a couple of centuries, began to alter. Even the Mediterranean island of Crete entered a colder phase in about the year 1150. In Germany and England the cold arrived maybe one century later, and most years between 1312 and 1320 were not only cold but also unusually wet. Rain, falling at an unwanted time, could be as devastating as drought. In several years the crops were so lean that only two grains— not the usual four—were the meagre harvest for every single grain that had been sown. As half of the grain had to be set aside as seed for the next year's sowing, a poor harvest imposed starvation on many people. In the space of six months in 1316 maybe one in 10 of the people of Ypres died of starvation or malnutrition. Here and there, human flesh was eaten. In 1330 began four successive years of famine in parts of France.

Religious processions held in western France reflected the poor seasons. Some included numerous emaciated, barefooted people, a few of whom were almost naked. Lean harvests affected the supply of cheap clothes as well as cheap food, for poor people made their linen from the flax plant, which was also affected by poor seasons. Indeed, land which was normally used to grow flax might be desperately needed for the growing of grain.

About the time that Greenland was settled, native Americans had moved into a fertile region of the Dakotas which, previously very cold, was now enhanced by the warmer seasons. After about the year 1250, the Dakotas became colder. Rings in the trunks of trees reveal that their annual growth, and probably that of maize, was somewhat stunted. As maize provided as much as nine-tenths of the food, a poor maize crop was a calamity. Moreover the herds of bison—the main source of meat—were culled by the lean years. Many settlers suffered from malnutrition, a deficiency of vitamin C and anaemia caused by a deficiency of iron. Human bones examined by archaeologists revealed signs of stunted growth.

At Crow Creek one group of these Dakota people occupied steep land above the flood plain of the Missouri River. While they could not protect their crops, they could defend themselves. Fearing an attack by rivals in about 1325, they worked hard to surround their cluster of houses with a wooden palisade or stockade and deep ditches. One ditch was about 2 meters deep and more than 6 meters wide: sufficient to slow down attackers and expose them to arrows.

The fortified village's ditch and palisade were not a strong defense. The village was stormed—a day of blood. In 1978 erosion of topsoil revealed a few relics, and excavation slowly unfolded the sequence of events. The houses were burned by the invaders, and at least 536 people, including one baby, were killed by heavy blows to head and body. Many of the victims were mutilated, the feet and hands severed and even the tongue torn out. Estimates of the age and sex of the human remains revealed an absence of young women. They were presumably captured and taken away, alive. The question of whether the warfare was normal, or was occasioned by the increasingly cold climate and a scarcity of food, cannot be answered with confidence.

As the decades passed, the climate of Greenland and the North Atlantic grew chillier. The barns which once were filled with hay now had gaps. Only three bundles of hay were gathered where once were four or five. Ships approaching from Europe or Iceland found packs of ice drifting in places where the sea was usually open. The colonists of Greenland waited in vain for the old-time summers which their grandparents had talked of. Farms and churches were abandoned. The young were few and a wedding became a rarity. In 1410 the surviving settlers went aboard waiting ships and sailed for Iceland and Norway. The European foothold on this cold land had lasted for more than 400 years. It was the equivalent of the Australian port of Sydney being settled in 1576 by Elizabethan England and then abandoned in the year 2000 because of deteriorating climate.

Greenland had no further contact with Scandinavia. Three centuries later it was rumored that a few families of European descent might still be alive in Greenland. In 1721 a ship sailed from the Norwegian port of Bergen with a Lutheran priest who hoped to find and baptize missing Viking settlers who, possessing no priest, had slipped back into heathenism. He found none to baptize. The Inuits had reoccupied the land.

The same change of climate must have affected the fisherfolk who plied their trade in the North Sea. In the 13th and 14th centuries the shoals of herrings multiplied, as if by a miracle. At the narrow outlet of the Baltic, the catches of herrings were huge. One chronicler vowed that the fish were so close together that they virtually formed an underwater wall through which the fishing vessels had to cut in order to reach port. Dutch and English vessels arrived to share in the catch. As fish, mostly preserved by salting, was prescribed in place of meat by Catholic edict for a total of more than 150 days a year, the market for salted herrings was large. Millions of European families must have rejoiced in the glut of herrings, which were shipped as far away as England and Holland.

The castle of Elsinore in Denmark, the setting of Shakespeare's play *Hamlet*, guarded one side of the narrow strait or Sound. Across the waters, on the Swedish shore, stood the port of Scania (Skanör); and it became the site of one of the busy trade fairs of Europe at the height of each fishing season. Each year the fair ran from about 15 August to 1 November, and its mainstay was the barrel of freshly salted herring. Around the 1420s, however, the traders who arrived heard increasingly gloomy news. The shoals of herrings were thinner, and salted herring was served less often on the dinner tables of northern Europe.

What caused the decline of the herring? Was it overfishing? Did disease or predators kill too many herrings? Or did the cooling climate impair their once-prolific rate of breeding? One climatologist has argued that the cooling lowered the salinity of the seawater, slightly altering the delicate balance of marine life, and reducing in number the millions of tiny marine organizms which the fish ate. Alternatively, the change of climate perhaps altered the volume of river water flowing into the Baltic and thereby lessened the salt content of a sea which was already low in salt by the standards of the world's seas. The decline of fishing at the mouth of the Baltic was to spark an interest in the rich cod-fishing grounds off the coast of Canada.

The phase of warmer climate had increased the rate of growth of population in Europe. Between 1000 and 1250 it grew rapidly. Then came cool years, leaner harvests and a slower growth of population.

There were more years of famine and more chances of epidemics. Europe was probably ripe for the Black Death.

THE BLACK DEATH

A frightening disease in Europe was not a new event. Leprosy, which is popularly regarded as a tropical disease, seems to have come with the returning crusaders who had caught it in the Middle East. They spread the infection. At first it was scarcely noticed, for its time of incubation can be as long as five years. Eventually hundreds of thousands of people were infected, initially in the ear lobes and the arms and legs, where nerve endings were destroyed. Numbness in the feet crippled many lepers. Medical opinion was astute enough to recommend that lepers should be isolated and given special care. By the year 1200, thousands of leper hospitals or hospices had been set up in Europe.

Most lepers were kept apart from healthy people. When begging for food in village streets, lepers would ring a bell to warn of their approach, and food was not handed to them but placed nearby for them to collect. In some old parish churches can still be seen a portal or window through which lepers, standing outside, could hear divine service.

Leprosy continues to flourish in tropical lands but in Europe it declined almost as mysteriously as it had begun. There was one notable exception. Leprosy clung to Norway, where, as late as 1873, one in every 40 residents of the port of Bergen suffered from the disease. Indeed it is now called Hansen's disease, in honor of the Bergen physician who diagnosed it.

Leprosy was already waning in Europe when a deadlier disease crept in. The Black Death of 1348 was not unique. It must have struck centuries earlier in Asia or Africa, but it left behind no detailed record of its casualties. A similar epidemic hit the Roman Empire between AD 165 and 180, and indirectly it promoted Christianity, for many Romans were impressed by the sight of Christians giving bread and water to victims who were too ill to move. About three centuries later another epidemic—a bubonic plague—came from India. It struck Constantinople in 542 and scythed its way across Europe. Most of those who died from this earlier wave of the "black death" were doomed within six days of showing their first symptoms—a headache, high temperatures, and the emergence on the skin of a lump or bubo about the size of an egg or small orange. Curiously, those victims whose flesh supported a very large lump were more likely to survive. China and Japan also suffered huge casualties from epidemics which perhaps resembled the Black Death. The Chinese city of Kaifeng is said to have lost several hundred thousand inhabitants during an epidemic in 1232. If the city was so stricken, the surrounding countryside must have been similarly devastated by the disease.

A plague is like a compulsive tourist. It takes heart when a new way of travel is opened up. The Mongol invasion, and its unifying presence over a vast area of Asia, revived trade along the old caravan routes and also provided a highway for the bubonic plague to move northwest towards Europe. In European ports, the rats and fleas they harbored were the carriers of the plague. After reaching Europe in 1348 it spread swiftly. Some cities—Paris, Hamburg, Florence, Venice—lost half or more of their population. Villages were more likely than cities to escape the infection. It spread slowly in winter, and rapidly in summer. All in all, perhaps 20 million Europeans died, or one in every three people. A monster of plagues, the Black Death was followed at intervals by lesser plagues.

In the midst of the misery and panic, scapegoats were found. Jews were persecuted even after the pope called on Catholics to treat them with some respect. At Basle in January 1349 a wooden house was built on an island in the Rhine, 200 Jews were forcibly placed inside, and the crowded house was set on fire. Two months later the Jewish people of the German town of Worms preferred to burn themselves alive in their houses.

The scarcity of food of earlier decades was replaced by a scarcity of labor. Farmland was no longer in short supply. In some regions of Germany, more villages were deserted than inhabited, and fields which had once been noisy with harvesters were weed-grown and silent.

THE ANCHOR OF HOPE

The Catholic church, centered on Rome, remained the most powerful institution of Europe. Plagues strengthened it more than weakened it, for it provided hope. All-embracing, it catered for merriment as well as sadness. Inside the village church the birthday of the parish's patron saint might be honored with a festival in which villagers would sing, dance, eat much and drink more. In larger cities some of the popular fairs—a blend of flea market, supermarket and buskers' parade—were staged just before a holy day. In Padua the 15-day fair was held just before the feast of St Anthony. In adjacent Venice the fair was held close to the feast of the Ascension. The holy day ended the fair.

Far from Rome, the Christianity practiced might be only a coat of varnish, or a rough undercoat of paint. Peasants worshipped not only Christ but also divinities whose names were not to be found in the Bible. In Russian forests, as late as 1550, many people worshipped the old god of thunder. In the cold mountains of Scandinavia, many people still revered Thursday as a holy day because it commemorated the god Thor, to whom they prayed.

In contrast, many medieval Christians were so dedicated that they turned away from the world and resolved to live out the remainder of their life in utter solitude, in a cell, nook or cave. Sometimes a bishop formally blessed the chosen cell, sprinkled it with holy water and doused the air with incense. Often the cell was adjacent to the parish church, or attached to a monastery or convent. Such men who cut themselves off from the world were called anchorites and the women were anchoresses, the names being derived from a Greek word meaning "to withdraw." Living alone in silence, they spent their days in prayer and penitence. As a useful pursuit some of the women embroidered clothes.

Julian of Norwich, before she became a solitary Christian, probably lived with her mother in the large English town of Norwich. At about the age of 30, she was paralyzed from the waist down and seemed to be on the verge of death. When the parish priest arrived on 8 May 1373 to administer the last rites, she could not even speak. He placed a cross before her eyes and said: "I have brought you the image of your Maker and Savior. Look at it, and be strengthened." She felt stronger. Hours later she experienced a religious awakening and saw a vision of Christ. Another 15 visions came to her in quick succession.

Regaining her health, she decided to live the solitary life. Years later she recorded her experiences, persuasively and tenderly, in a manuscript called *The Sixteen Revelations of Divine Love*. She recalled how the Lord appeared before her eyes and said confidingly: "I know quite well you want to see my blessed Mother, for, after myself, she is the greatest joy I can show you."

Julian continued her simple life for 40 years or more. Millions of women, had they heard of her, would have envied her devoutness. They felt certain that the Second Coming was not far away. Most Christians probably expected the great event to take place before AD 1500.

The numbers of the saints were increased every century, but the older saints were prized the most. One of the triumphs of the city of Constantinople, intent on justifying its claim to be the Rome of the east, was to snatch from the rival city of Antioch in the year 956 the arm bones of St John the Baptist. Eventually the city displayed several thousand relics that reportedly had been the limbs or personal possessions of major and minor saints. To touch or stand near the bones or frayed clothing of a long-dead saint gave hope to millions of Christians. Miracles might happen when they stood near these relics. Polycarp, the bishop of Smyrna, who was burned to death in about 155, was perhaps the first martyr to provide relics which were prized. His bones were "more valuable than precious stones and finer than refined gold." As the centuries rolled by, more relics—probably more relics than there were saints—entered into circulation. To place on a map all the Christian relics known to exist or claimed to exist in the year 1500 would have required a huge piece of parchment.

Italy was perhaps the largest repository of holy relics. In Venice the basilica of St Mark was said to possess a thorn taken from the crown of Christ as well as a nail from his cross. Turin's cathedral held the Holy Shroud that was said to have been wrapped around Christ after his body was taken down from the cross. The crown worn on ceremonial occasions by the kings of Lombardy held part of a nail said to come from Christ's cross; and in Milan in 1805 Emperor Napoleon felt proud to wear such a sacred crown. In Genoa the treasure of the cathedral of San Lorenzo was a precious cup, reportedly presented by the Queen of Sheba to Solomon—the same cup from which Christ was said to have drunk at the last supper. Naples cathedral prized its two glass flasks holding the blood of St Januarius. Twice a year the dried blood was said to change, miraculously, from powder into liquid. Some of the most prized relics had been stolen by the Venetians from Constantinople, which they sacked in 1204.

It is easy to deride the deep faith which was felt by millions of peasants, but holy relics had the power to comfort and soothe and inspire—a power not necessarily equalled by today's platoons of grief counsellors and medicine cupboards full of nerve-soothers. The relics were a blessing to millions who lived in those hazardous centuries when famine and disease were frequent companions.

The Middle Ages in Europe are often said to have run from AD 500 to 1500. Differing from the previous thousand years, and from the following 500, the Middle Ages were more inward-looking, and less enamored with individual achievement. That these ages had achieved less, materially, than the Roman Empire was not a source of disappointment. Most Christians probably believed that the Roman citizens in the years of their triumphs were essentially pagans, and that therefore many of their accomplishments were of little worth. The monastery, the convent, the anchorite cell and the act of praying were typical of this era just as the marching legion and the expanding province of law and order had been typical of Rome's empire.

Many of Europe's political and intellectual leaders in the Middle Ages did not feel inferior to the Roman Empire. Rather they disowned it. They believed that they were building their own empire, united by a common religion. They called it the Holy Roman Empire. It was a foretaste of the federal Europe of the latter decades of the 20th century.

16

NEW MESSENGERS

THE LONG Middle Ages or Dark Ages were not entirely suffocated by inertia. For the Vikings in the north of Europe and for Islam in the south of Europe they were not the dark ages but the light ages. Towards their end, in Europe as a whole, the sense of adventure and inventiveness was reviving. In the 12th century emerged the university—an institution which, eight centuries later, would circle the world. In the same century appeared the first windmills and also the first lock, an ingenious device which enabled sailing ships to follow the canal leading to the thriving Belgian port of Bruges. The skills of mining were about to improve, and in northern Europe a mineral that would be crucial for the future, black coal, was mined. At the same time, the deep-sea ship driven solely by the wind, with a magnetic compass to guide her and a sternpost rudder to steer her, was silently pointing to the possibility of exploring the wide Atlantic.

China remained a source of new ideas, including such remarkable innovations as gunpowder, paper and the technique of using ink. Not less remarkable was the way in which Europeans were welcoming these novelties and improving upon them. Nowhere was Europe so important as in the specialized crafts of clockmaking and printing. The clock was a medium which, like a soft metallic drum, subtly preached the message that time was precious.

The mass media were at work even in the Middle Ages. The bell, flag and smoke-and-fire signal were mass media and could send a message simultaneously to thousands of people. The sound of the loud bell, mounted on a high steeple in a medieval city, could be heard several miles away, though those within earshot had to assess whether the message called them to divine service or intimated that somebody of importance had died. In the evening the bell might be a call to worship or—if rung quickly—a loud warning that the enemy's ships were in sight on the rim of the ocean.

The colored flag, usually made of wool, sent a clear visual message to generations of people who could not read or count. As late as the 19th century a yellow flag signified infectious disease, and a white flag was a request for peace on the battlefield. At sea, for centuries, a flag flown upside down was a signal of distress, while a black flag flown outside a prison was a signal that a prisoner had been hanged. Fire and smoke were another medium, when war was in the offing. A succession of bonfires was arranged, each within sight of the other, and each fire could be lit in turn so that a silent signal announcing war could be relayed many kilometers to a capital city or a crucial port. Silent collective prayer was seen as another powerful medium.

Of the traditional media, the human voice was employed the most widely. Most news was passed on by word of mouth, whether on a Chinese roadside or in a Javanese temple. The human voice possessed a limited range, but most architects had an understanding of the theory of acoustics that enabled their buildings to project the sound of speakers and singers and musicians. Words spoken slowly and deliberately reached every corner of a large amphitheatre. In oratory manuals printed a century ago appeared the advice of the poet Alexander Pope to young and inexperienced speakers:

> Learn to speak slow—all other graces
> Will follow in their proper places.

The ancient Greeks, being masters of oratory, knew the art of throwing their voice to the far ends of a building. Christ and John the Baptist must have possessed voices that carried far. Those now living in the era of the loudspeaker and microphone do not realize how far an unaided voice can travel. In 1739 the young English evangelist George Whitefield was speaking in the open air in the American city of Philadelphia. Such a crowd gathered around in the hope of hearing him that Benjamin Franklin, standing on the fringe, wondered how many spectators could hear his words. Edging his way through the throng he mentally marked those outer spots where the speaker's voice was on the verge of becoming inaudible. After calculating how many people stood on average in each square yard, Franklin computed that more than 30,000 people were hearing Whitefield that day.

IN SIGHT OF THE CLOCK

In the late Middle Ages, the spoken word was first challenged as a medium by the printing press, but it was the clock which preceded the press as a medium of influence. It could not be foreseen that in Europe a day would arrive when nearly every adult would own a clock. Early mechanical clocks carried a huge face, were extremely expensive, and were made primarily to announce the time in public places. To manufacture a clock and another innovation of the era, the military cannon, required the services of highly skilled metalworkers, and indeed clockmakers were often gunmakers.

Residents of big Italian towns were the first to hear the chiming of a clock and to watch its hands move stiffly around the dial. The clock had to sit high in a tower so that people in the square and nearby streets could see its hand: usually there was an hour hand but no hand to show the minutes. Citizens might not yet be able to tell the time but at least they could nod approvingly when friends—eager to parade their knowledge— told them what the time was. Probably the first clock in Europe was installed in a large church in Milan in 1335; and the hourly sound of its bells could be heard throughout the night. In the following 20 years the northern Italian cities of Padua, Genoa and Bologna each displayed a tall public clock which chimed the hour, with one single chime announcing one o'clock and 12 chimes for midday. Paris went a step further, installing three public clocks and instructing church bellringers to watch the clocks closely and ring their bells every hour so that the entire city knew the time of day. In such cities the public clock must have been a persistent teacher of the art of counting—at least counting to the number 12—in the centuries before education became compulsory.

These early mechanical clocks were a link between the traditional world ruled by sun, moon and stars and a world which is now ruled by machines. Some big clocks provided knowledge which the booming profession of astrology required for its forecasting. The clock on the cathedral at Strasbourg displayed from about the 1350s a dial on which the positions of sun, moon and the main planets were indicated. The exact relationship between these heavenly bodies was a vital recipe for predicting when tasks and enterprises should be begun, indeed a guide to predicting the destiny of each individual. That a cathedral should combine a faith in Christ and a faith in the stars was not seen as heretical.

Strasbourg's clock was perhaps the most complicated machine of any kind seen in the world so far, but it was not yet accurate. The margin of error in a public clock could be as large as 15 minutes in a day, and therefore the clock required a skilled attendant to correct the time with regularity. Little by little the mechanism and accuracy of the clock was refined. By the early 1600s, rich merchants were buying expensive clocks for the walls of their own houses, and the city of Augsburg in southern Germany employed 43 master clockmakers as well as their assistants. Half a century later the master mechanic Christiaan Huygens introduced the pendulum to the clock, and that cut the margin of error to about 10 seconds in every 24 hours.

A tall public clock on a tower not only told the time: it also proclaimed that time was not to be frittered away, for the day of judgment would suddenly arrive and it would be demanded of everyone to affirm that they had used diligently the time granted to them by the Lord. In villages in 1600 the bell remained more important than the clock. At a thousand villages on Sunday morning the priest or pastor guessed when it was time to ring the bell for divine service, and his bell summoned the people. Sunset and sunrise, or a glance at the position of the sun in the sky, still ruled the beginning and ending of the rural day. The Roman sundial often served as a rough clock but in cloudy weather or at night it was unable to reveal the time.

PAPER AND THE BOOK

The western mechanical clock was exported to China, where it was marvelled at. From China, almost as if it were an exchange, came the genesis of an even more influential invention which was set to work in European towns. The invention was the art of printing on sheets of paper.

Paper and ink had reached Europe long before the technique of printing. Paper was first manufactured in China, Japan and Korea; and as early as the year 751, several Chinese artisans possessing the knowledge of how to make paper were captured and conveyed to Samarkand in central Asia where they revealed their techniques, thus manufacturing the first paper in very thick sheets in what the Chinese might well have called the Near West. This process eventually reached the Arab world and then Europe, where it slowly challenged the use of parchment. As parchment was made only from animal skins, and as a handwritten book of 200 large pages might consume the skins of about 80 lambs, a book consisting of parchment pages was far more expensive than one printed on the new paper.

The early paper was made from remnants such as old rags and ropes, and a waterwheel helped to convert these fibers into paper. In Italy an early papermaking town, Fabriano, still makes paper at the foot of a mountain range though the fast streams no longer turn the waterwheels. Once paper was being manufactured in Europe, the time was ripe for the coming of printing.

The Chinese made their letters and images not from metal but from wood and baked clay. The Koreans made movable type out of bronze as early as 1403 but their innovation did not influence Europe. The distinct printing advances about to be made in Europe involved the casting of individual durable letters of the alphabet out of lead, and the use of a heavy press to apply pressure so that the metal type imprinted the images in ink, firmly and sharply, on the paper.

Johannes Gutenberg, a resident of the German riverside city of Mainz, was perhaps the first European to print a book, using not only a press but also metallic type. His technique, when perfected, was like that used later by the typewriter. But whereas the modern typewriter requires merely four neat rows containing each individual capital and lower-case letter of the alphabet, Gutenberg's form of printing called for the making of hundreds of metal replicas of each letter of the alphabet. Inside the printing shop a small furnace heated an alloy of lead with a little tin and antimony. The individual letters, including the capitals and the lower-case letters, were then cast into molds. Each molded *a* and *b* was used many times before it became ragged or blurred. Printing therefore called for skilled metalworkers; and indeed Gutenberg himself had been a silversmith.

Gutenberg and his fellow printers set out, on a bench or shelf in front of them, dozens of the letter *a* and dozens of the letter *b*, and so on through the alphabet. From this assemblage they arranged or composed, with quick movements of the hand, the sequence of individual metal letters that formed a sentence and then a paragraph. A version of the wine press or the bookbinding press was used to press this page-shaped mass of metallic letters onto a fresh sheet of paper. The technique of printing from movable metal type was infinitely more suitable for European languages based on the simple Roman alphabet than for the 50,000 symbols of the Chinese language.

The printed pages were stitched together by hand and bound firmly inside a strong cover of leather or cloth, the art of binding having been mastered in the days of the handwritten book. From Gutenberg's printery the new techniques were copied and adapted. By 1480, printers worked in towns as far apart as Cracow, London and Venice. Most of the books they printed were serious and even learned—only the learned could read—and were in Latin. Books soon appeared in local languages with phrases culled from daily speech. The printing of sheet music, of which Venice became the master, was almost a revolution for musicians, who had needed a regiment of costly scribes.

Hitherto, the cost of producing a book by hand, on either paper or parchment, had been so expensive that most of the smaller churches in Europe could not afford a Bible. They made do with handwritten gospel books, which contained only those passages of the Bible required for saying the mass. These were the medieval foretaste of a *Reader's Digest* version of the scriptures.

The Bible benefited the most from the new technique of printing. The results are publicly displayed in the Washington Library of Congress. On one side is the Great Bible of Mainz, once owned by the dukes of Gotha, and written in Latin during the space of 15 months with a quill pen and perhaps a paintbrush, for each sentence begins with an ornate capital letter in red and black. This book spreads over a grand total of 459 pages of white vellum, made from the treated skin of calves, goats or newborn lambs. On some days in winter the scribe must have strained his eyes in the combination of faint daylight and candlelight. He must have been content when his patient handiwork was completed, on 9 July 1453.

Next to the Great Bible is the first edition of the Bible to emerge from Gutenberg's printing shop only two years later. Printed in the new Gothic typeface, it is modelled on the older Bible and similarly ornamented. Each freshly printed page was handed to a scribe, who hand-painted the first letter of the opening word of each chapter in royal blue and red. This early copy of the Bible is also printed on expensive vellum, though undoubtedly most copies were on paper. Initially printers tried to imitate the writer of illuminated manuscripts, but soon printers and writers would go their different ways. Thanks to the printing press, a cheap Bible was now possible.

An early printed book might carry a few illustrations. To produce an illustration a woodcarver took up a block of smooth wood and in the Chinese manner carved the illustration on the surface, from which an imprint was made with the aid of colored dyes. Before long, drawings were done not on wood but on shining copper plates from which they were imprinted on paper. Copperplate engravings, though expensive, outlasted wood and were capable of printing many copies before the impressions began to lose sharpness. The art of etching on stone was not devised until the late 1790s, when slabs were cut from an absorbent limestone mined in Bavaria.

Playing cards preceded books as printed objects. These cards, copied from the Saracens, enjoyed a minor vogue in Italy, Spain, France and Germany during the decade 1377–87, when initially they were painted by hand on paper. Wealthy English people adopted the pastime of cards in about the 1450s, which was the first decade of the printing press. The cards increasingly were printed from wood engravings. In most packs of cards used today, the king, queen and knave are still depicted in the costumes worn at the time of the invention of printing.

The technique of printing on paper was a social revolution. Europe was ready for it and eager to use and improve it, because the late 1400s were the time of its mental awakening. The printing press quickened that awakening.

Significantly, the urgent desire to spread a religious message, at first for Buddhism in China and then for Christianity in Europe, had been a spur to the inventing and utilizing of printing. Islam, however, had no time for the new device and actually shunned the printing press until the 19th century.

THE OTTOMAN CONQUESTS

In this time of quickening change, Europe was becoming more confident intellectually but was far from secure militarily. From the interior of Asia the Mongols had come galloping, and in their shadow came the Turks.

At one time the Turks were living mainly in Turkestan in central Asia. Effective warriors, they came west in stages and, taking advantage of the Mongols' advance, occupied many areas overtaken by confusion. The general of the Ottoman Turks was Osman I, founder of the dynasty. When he died in 1326 he was succeeded by strong leaders whose soldiers sometimes moved west as rapidly as a bushfire aided by a strong wind. The Ottoman cavalry rode ahead of the foot soldiers and the artillerymen, who used the new cannon with skill. No opponent could hold them for long.

By 1400 the Ottoman Turks held nearly all of the territory of the present Turkey and extended their rule far into Christian Europe. They held both shores of the Dardanelles, including the coastal strip which became the battlefield of Gallipoli in the First World War. They occupied long reaches of the Danube River and large parts of what are now Albania, Serbia, Kosovo, Bosnia, Bulgaria and Romania. In the Balkan lands the invading Turks found supporters as well as opponents. Many Christian peasants, irked by the rich landowners for whom they labored, silently welcomed the Turks, even accepted their religion, and joined their army as mercenaries.

The Turks surrounded the celebrated city of Constantinople almost completely by land and sea so that it became a tiny besieged island of territory. On 28 May 1453, the day when the last Christian service was performed in the cathedral of St Sophia, the Turks were at the high walls and about to enter Constantinople. After 11 centuries this famous city of Christianity was conquered. The Turks then moved into Greece, and three years later they captured Athens. In the south of Italy the port of Otranto fell to the Turks in 1480, which was only 12 years before the Italian-born navigator Christopher Columbus sailed forth on the voyage which discovered Central America. In the five years between 1516 and 1521, the Turks captured such diverse cities as Damascus and Cairo and Belgrade. At the very time when the Europeans were forcibly establishing their empires in America and Asia, the Ottoman Turks from Asia were forcing their way into Europe. They were now a European power.

The pope feared that the "infidels" might fight their way into the heart of Christendom. He called for a new crusade in which Christian rulers would drive back the Turks. Christian unity, he said, was a first commandment. But in any large region where many tribes, states and monarchs have long battled for supremacy or independence, unity is an unpredictable bird. The Sultan of Turkey sometimes eroded the unity by offering enticing deals to the commercial interests of Christian states. The city-state of Florence, now possessing its own ports at Pisa and Livorno, smiled on the sultan because he allowed the representatives of 60 of its trading firms to live in Constantinople. Four Italian cities, including Florence and Milan, paid the Turks to join them in assaulting their common enemy, the powerful republic of Venice.

That the Turks could be so tolerated showed a slight lapse of religious intensity in Italy around 1500. This same ebbing of Catholic fervor paved the way, inside Europe, for the rise of protesters or protestants who breathed religious fervor. Their main enemy was not to be the sultan: their enemy was the pope.

17

BIRDCAGE

WHAT HAPPENED in the western half of Europe just before 1500 was one of the most remarkable convergences of influential events in the known history of the world to that time. It was like a crossroad where, almost by chance, extraordinary meetings took place between navigators and painters, priests and teachers and scientists.

There emerged a new way of painting and sculpting and a fresh perspective in architecture which, seen as a whole, was called the Renaissance or rebirth. A religious awakening, the Reformation, swept across northern Europe. The technique of printing, a wonderful way of disseminating new and old knowledge, leaped from town to town. An entirely new world emerged with the discovery in quick succession of the American continent and an all-sea route from Europe to eastern Asia. Curiously this momentous cluster of events, each one coming so close to another, has no all-embracing name; and it is almost certainly too late to provide a name that will be accepted.

These events reflected new ways of seeing the world. Many artists and architects saw with new eyes the reality around them, whether the human body or perspective. Many theologians and preachers believed they had rediscovered human nature. Astronomers and navigators saw the map of the world with astonishment. All reflected a wish to bathe tired eyes with salt and see afresh. It would be surprising if these new ways of seeing the world, and the excitement that arose from them, had not been infectious. Printing helped to spread the infection. Along pathways which we cannot necessarily detect—for religion and art and navigation were almost different realms and were presided over by different people—these separate fields influenced each other. Thus Protestantism, one product of this excited time, was aided enormously by the invention of printing.

While these clusters of discoveries were in their way revolutionary, each arose in part from a veneration for the past. Many of the artists were enamored by the lost world of Greece and Rome and tried to recapture it. Some of the radical theologians were trying to recapture the virtues of religion as practiced along the Sea of Galilee by Jesus and his disciples, and also trying to distill the essence of the faded writings of St Augustine and early fathers of the church. Printers and their new craft gave their attention to printing the ancient Bible, to discussions of its meaning, and to resurrecting classical works. Even navigators at first were not searching for the new. They simply wished to find a route by sea instead of land to old China. At the same time, while initially enamored of the past, the theologians, printers, painters and navigators were all explorers. The times, the air, encouraged a sense of intellectual adventure, and all kinds of intellectual and cultural and scientific activities were therefore likely to gain.

This is not to suggest that the blindfold fastened by the past was removed suddenly. The process of unveiling the eyes took place bit by bit and was probably the most gradual in art and architecture, and it gathered momentum over three centuries. The magnificent Gothic cathedrals of France, England and northern Europe were mainly built in the 13th century. The revolution in painting also began early. In the Italian city of Padua in the year 1306, Giotto was conveying a wonderful impression of depth when he painted religious scenes on walls. In the view of many Italians he was an artist with unique eyes. In the 1380s in Prague cathedral, Peter Parler the Younger was producing busts, one of which was praised by critics as "the first real self-portrait of an artist known to us."

The urge to study mathematics in order to make perspective more powerful in architecture, like the determination to study anatomy in order to make painting more realiztic, gave many artists a new pair of glasses through which to see. Thus in the 1420s the mathematical Brunelleschi was designing the remarkable dome for the cathedral of Florence. Almost at the same time, in what is now Belgium, Jan Van Eyck found another formula which was not based on mathematics. He used oil instead of liquid eggs to bind together the home-prepared pigments with which he painted. The Renaissance continued to come in skips and leaps, and with it came a new way of seeing the world and its mysteries.

Around 1500 the new ways of seeing all seemed to flower. Just before Leonardo da Vinci completed his portrait of a young woman, "Mona Lisa," the Spanish found America and the Portuguese sailed into the Indian Ocean. Soon after, Michelangelo completed his painting of Old Testament themes on the ceiling of the Sistine Chapel in Rome. Martin Luther on the other side of the Alps was protesting against the heretical system of taxation by which Rome financed such displays of scarletry as the Sistine Chapel.

These far-reaching changes in the arts and religion, scholarship, printing and navigation are not often seen as tightly linked because each flowered in a different corner of Europe. Art and architecture flourished mostly in central and northern Italy and in the Netherlands; and religious reformers first blossomed in northern Germany and the Swiss lake-ports. Printing with movable type was invented in Rhineland Germany; and bold navigators set sail from the Atlantic ports of Portugal and Spain. The geographical spread of these dynamic regions is perhaps a sign of how far-reaching was Europe's invigorating mental climate. Significantly, this was the first time in European history when the major events were more to the north than south of the Alps and more on the Atlantic coast than the Mediterranean.

One part of Christian Europe did not contribute to the excitement. It had fallen into the hands of expanding Islam. In 1529 the Turks even besieged the city of Vienna. The Protestant Reformation was taking place within 300 kilometers of the advancing Turks.

In the western half of Europe these separate hubs of special activity sometimes overlapped. Columbus sailed west in command of Spanish ships but he himself came from the port of Genoa. Amerigo Vespucci, the adventurous navigator and explorer after whom America was named, grew up near Florence, where the Renaissance caught fire, but lived for a time in France and sailed in Iberian ships. The most learned man of the era, Erasmus of the Netherlands, spent much time in Switzerland, especially so that he could be near the printer of his books. Jan Van Eyck's most famous portrait was of a merchant and his bride, the merchant having come from Italy to trade in the Netherlands. Lucas Cranach, the fine north German painter, lived in the same town as Martin Luther, became an enthusiastic Protestant and actually painted portraits of Luther. Even straitlaced Geneva, which backed John Calvin, the Protestant preacher, had a special part in the renaissance of art. In 1444, almost a century before Calvin's years of triumph, the German-born artist Konrad Witz painted, for the altar in a Geneva church, the fishing scene from the Gospel of St John. His painting—still in Geneva—depicted the placid lake and its neat fish traps and fishing nets, with the grassed slopes of the Geneva countryside and the pyramid hill of Mont Salève in the background. In the words of one distinguished critic of art it is perhaps the first exact landscape "ever attempted."

This awakening taking place on so many fronts had a new patron. In mighty Rome the church was the patron of the arts, but the rich and rising commercial towns nurtured and financed many of these discoverers, whether in art or theology or navigation. The merchant houses of Florence and Genoa, Ghent and Nuremberg, Geneva and Zurich, Lisbon and Seville provided patrons and finance, and often an attitude sympathetic to new ways of seeing. These merchant towns held only a small fraction of the population of Europe, but they were vigorous.

The discoverers were like birds long kept in a large and wintry medieval cage called Europe. The cage door slipped ajar. The birds escaped, in ones and then in fours. In their new freedom they displayed their summer plumage and sang as never before.

OPENING THE BIRDCAGE

The birdcage was never opened with more optimism than in August 1492 when Christopher Columbus and his three small ships set sail from Spain on a hazardous voyage. His sailing might well be classed as the most significant event in the entire millennium.

An Italian called Cristoforo Colombo, he had gone in his twenties to live in Portugal, where one of his activities was trading in sugar. Much of Portugal's sugar came from the island of Madeira in the east Atlantic Ocean, and his wife came from the same island. When he set out in the direction of America he was to take advantage of the fact that much of the ocean ahead of him had already been explored.

More than 70 years before Columbus set sail across the Atlantic others had been mapping the route ahead. The island of Madeira was settled by the Portuguese in 1420. Eleven years later the Azores were discovered. Only a blob in the ocean, they were a long way towards the American continent, being about 800 sea miles from Lisbon and 1,000 from New-foundland. Portuguese ships also sailed south, hugging the African coast. West Africa was the main source of Europe's gold and a source of slaves and other goods, and therefore an attractive goal for traders. In the eyes of most Portuguese and most native African traders, a slave was simply a commodity, like gold or sugar or timber, with a market price to fit. Soon slaves were being shipped to Portugal.

In 1481 a Portuguese ship actually sailed some distance up the mighty Congo River: a sign of how strong was the urge to explore. Six years later the brave Dias left Lisbon to follow the Atlantic Ocean further to the south. For weeks, out of sight of land, he sailed right around the most southerly coast of Africa and then turned back. On his return voyage, closer to land, he saw the southern headlands and named one the Cape of Storms. Even then the art of public relations was in the air, and eventually the cape was renamed the Cape of Good Hope.

In essence, Columbus was planning to venture into an ocean of which much was becoming known and much was still a mystery. He had hoped for financial aid from Portugal, but that country was already succeeding with its own straightforward theories of geography. He turned to Spain for help. In the end he received finance from his old countrymen—certain Genoa merchants who were living in Spain—and from the King and Queen of Spain.

The long war between Islam and Christianity is said to have inspired mariners to seek a new route to Asia. It is often written that Columbus sought a back door to Asia and its riches because Islam now locked and guarded the front door. It is true that some 40 years before he sailed, the Turks had captured Constantinople and thus blocked the old supply route along which prized oriental goods normally reached the Mediterranean. In fact oriental wares continued to reach the Mediterranean, often by way of the Red Sea and Alexandria. Spain and Portugal wished to tap the oriental trade largely because, being highly valuable, it was worth tapping. They were also capable of tapping it because they now possessed new ways of building strong wooden ships, fitting them with more sails and larger guns, and new ways of navigating them in strange seas. For the first time in its history, Europe was capable of exploring far from home.

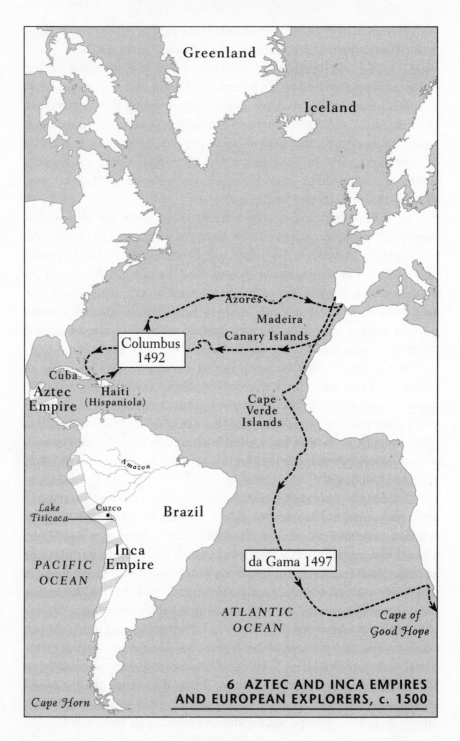

6 AZTEC AND INCA EMPIRES
AND EUROPEAN EXPLORERS, c. 1500

In Spain in August 1492, in the full knowledge that the world was round, Columbus set out to sail west in search of the east. He began to cross the Atlantic, believing that he was on his way to China. Such hopes now seem a little far-fetched, but he had reason to believe that he was actually crossing a narrow sea. At that time it was mistakenly believed that the oceans occupied only one-seventh of the surface of the globe and that therefore a very wide ocean simply did not exist. This was the belief of the ancient geographer Ptolemy, whose name was still revered more than a millennium after his death. He had written eight brilliant but speculative volumes while he was studying at the great library at Alexandria in Egypt; and had decreed that the Atlantic Ocean was much narrower than in fact it proved to be.

By chance Ptolemy's volumes, long lost to western Europe, had been published in a new printery in the Italian city of Bologna only 15 years before Columbus set sail on his first voyage. Ptolemy gave Columbus the reassuring belief that he did not have to sail far west before he would enter Chinese waters. Simple outlines of the Chinese coastline and ports were actually available; and it is possible that Columbus's destination was the southerly Chinese port of Swatow (Shantou) or Canton (Guangzhou).

With the coast of Spain far behind him, Columbus sailed confidently in a westerly or southwesterly direction even on dark nights. By night and day he was alert for the passing flights of birds, for he understood that earlier Portuguese explorers had discovered the Azores and other uninhabited islands in the North Atlantic by following what seemed to be the flight path of migratory birds. He was actually sailing in the direction of Florida when on 7 October 1492 he saw a wide-spreading flock of birds flying to the southwest. He changed the ship's course in order to follow them, noting hopefully that the sea breezes were balmy and scented "like April in Seville."

On the following night, in the moonlight, he heard more birds flying overhead. He felt confident that he was close to land and assumed that the land must be eastern Asia. There was surely no other land in what was—according to the most learned of geographers—that relatively narrow ocean separating Japan and China to the west from Europe and Africa to the east. Eventually a coastline came into sight. He must have felt a sense of triumph as he was rowed ashore. It was an island in the West Indies, but he thought it was India. Henceforth the people of the

Americas were to be called Indians, and Columbus himself, on his return to Spain, was to be honored as the Viceroy of the Indies.

After seeing the islands of Cuba and Haiti, Columbus returned to Spain in March 1493. The news of his discoveries created a level of astonishment perhaps exceeding that created by the first landing on the moon. On his second expedition, with 17 ships under his command, he established on the island of Hispaniola (Haiti) the first European town in the new hemisphere. In August 1498, on his third expedition, he actually reached the American continent and stepped ashore in the present Venezuela. When Columbus died in 1506 the extraordinary empires of the Aztecs and the Incas, far from the coasts which he himself had sailed, had not yet been seen by a European. He had unlocked the great door, but when he died the door was merely ajar.

While Columbus was exploring in the name of Spain, the Portuguese were continuing to explore with the help of their traditional ideas of the world's geography. This kingdom of one million people had poured brainpower and money into exploration, had half-paved the way for Columbus, and showed no intention of giving up. The finding of a new route to India was also Portugal's goal. Its navigators guessed that the easiest sea path to India was to circumnavigate most of Africa and cross the Indian Ocean.

Dias had already found a way around the Cape of Good Hope, though his ship did not reach Asia. Four years after Columbus returned from his first successful voyage to what he thought was Asia, the Portuguese planned their own large expedition to Asia by a different route. Vasco da Gama set sail from Lisbon in 1497 with three ships and a crew of 170. In sailing across the equator and around the south of Africa he spent more days out of sight of land than did Columbus on his first voyage. Perhaps no ship had ever been out of sight of land for so long. On the coast of East Africa he entered Islam's sphere of commercial influence and at the port of Mozambique he met Arab ships. Thereafter all was plain sailing. Indian pilots, Muslim by religion, actually guided him across the Indian Ocean to the west coast of India. Like Columbus he had found, with Muslim help, a new sea route to remote lands.

After an absence of 26 months, Vasco da Gama returned to Portugal with a sense of accomplishment, for he had reached Asia and so achieved what Columbus had failed to. Once ashore, he had to pass on information which suddenly saddened the news of the homecoming for wives, girlfriends, mothers, fathers and children of his sailors. Half of his crew had died during the long absence from home.

These voyages of Christopher Columbus and Vasco da Gama were amongst the most important events in the history of the world since the slow invention of farming, thousands of years earlier. The Portuguese voyage joined together two dynamic and rich parts of the world which previously were inaccessible by ship. The Spanish voyage brought together two inhabited worlds that had been far apart and unknown to each other. A comparable event will never happen again, unless advanced life is discovered on another planet.

THE HALLS OF MONTEZUMA

The Vikings, centuries earlier, had landed on a bleak and sparsely peopled part of the same continent as Columbus; and their landing led them nowhere, and was soon forgotten. But Columbus and his Spaniards landed closer to the hub of the Americas, where, unknown to them, were vast gardens, mines of silver and gold, grand cities and even empires.

The Maya was the first of the impressive civilizations to expose itself to the startled gaze of the Spaniards. In tropical America were small Maya cities with stone houses and temples and streets finely paved. In solidity and style they were a match for most places of similar size in western Europe and often were cleaner, though water was scarce. The Maya people turned out fine ornaments in pottery and specialized in an exquisite art form unknown in Europe, the shaping of the colored feathers of ornamental birds. They were skilled in crafting copper into war axes or peaceful implements but, like all other Americans, did not know of iron. Maya rituals and daily life were guided by calendars which were based on advanced skills in mathematics and astronomy. The scholars and priests practiced a distinctive way of writing based on some 800 signs or hieroglyphs, and they wrote on paper manufactured from the bark of the wild fig tree—a paper superior to the papyrus used in ancient Egypt.

The great era of the Maya, however, had ended by AD 800. The people were now divided into many factions, some of which were periodically at war. At one time their fine city of Teotihuacán with its wide central avenues had presided over the largest empire in the Americas, but its glory was fading. Further away were other signs of decay. The ruins of once-magnificent temples were now partly hidden by tropical forest, and even the tall Cholula pyramid—the largest structure in the Americas—was crumbling a little.

In the year 1517 the Spanish navigator Grijalva sailed from Cuba to the Maya port-towns on the mainland to the west, and in the course of nine months of leisurely sailing and numerous stays ashore he saw much that impressed him. In all he gave away to the Maya some 2,000 glass beads and several thousand iron pins and needles, the gifts of iron being especially welcomed. From time to time, however, he was forced to display his military might. While the Maya were shocked by the power of his cannons and gunpowder, they were sometimes able to retaliate effectively with their own simple weapons.

The Spaniard brought back to Cuba the news and rumors of the rich empire of Montezuma II, lying on the highlands further inland. The Aztec emperor was feared and resented by the Maya people on the coast; and any Spaniard venturing into his territory had to be audacious and well prepared. Hernán Cortés, chosen to penetrate the realm of Montezuma, was audacious but in some respects he was ill prepared. Aged 34, he was untested as a leader and fighter, though he had lived in the Spanish West Indies for 12 years. Shortish in build, he stooped slightly when he walked and was also bow-legged. The man who was to achieve one of the most amazing military victories on record did not yet cut a commanding figure.

With a small fleet of small ships, Cortés sailed from Cuba in November 1518. Amongst the 530 Europeans who accompanied him were 30 specialists in firing the crossbow: in fact more of his soldiers were specialists in bow and arrow than in firearms. In his ships were several hundred female and male Cuban Indians, many of whom were personal servants, as well as a few African slaves. On the decks were penned about 16 sturdy horses. They were a weapon of surprise, for no American had ever seen a horse. When they were landed on the shore the onlookers were as frightened by the sight of their big mouths as by their large hooves.

At Easter 1519, Cortés and his party halted their journey into the interior and spent three weeks at the Central American town of Potonchan, where on Palm Sunday they erected a Christian cross in the town square and organized a holy procession in which a likeness of the Virgin Mary was held up so that the puzzled inhabitants could gaze at her. Before leaving the town, Cortés was presented with a vivacious woman who could speak the local languages he needed, for one language was familiar to the

Maya along the coast and another was spoken by Emperor Montezuma in the interior. Cortés soon rejoiced in his gifted interpreter. Having spent his childhood in Medellín, a Spanish town with a mosque and synagogue as well as Catholic churches—a town more cosmopolitan than almost any in western Europe—he would have known the dangers that could arise in a strange land simply through a misunderstanding of manners, customs and language.

Baptized into the Christian faith and christened Marina, the interpreter soon learned to speak Spanish. Her value to Cortés was, in the words of one historian, "certainly equivalent to ten bronze cannon." Guide and interpreter and adviser, Marina was his mistress too. Through her words the strange land that he was about to enter became intelligible.

He already knew that Montezuma's city, called Tenochtitlán, lay on a plateau about halfway between the Atlantic and Pacific oceans. Breathing a rarified air nearly 2,500 meters above sea level, it stood on an island set in a long lake with mountains nearby. Mexico City occupies the site today, but the lake has vanished.

To visit the city from afar was one of the most remarkable experiences the entire world could offer. Travellers passed high mountains, one permanently capped with snow and many of them wooded, before at last reaching a plateau from which they looked down and saw the lake and glimpsed in the distance the stone pyramids which were a landmark of this civilization. Three main causeways led across the lake to the island city and its 200,000 people. It was one of the world's largest cities, and a few of those Spaniards who had travelled widely in Europe before setting out for the New World knew that only the city-ports of Constantinople and Naples were as large, while it was understood that even in China not many cities were larger.

The area of the Aztec empire itself was almost as large as modern Italy and its people numbered six or eight million. They excelled in the crafts of building and architecture, and were goldsmiths and jewellers of the first order, highly competent in mathematics and adept at agriculture, cultivating a variety of plants as well as keeping turkey and muscovy duck. Admittedly they lacked some of the major inventions adopted or contrived by the Europeans, for they were unfamiliar with bronze and iron and screws and nails, they lacked the wheel, and they possessed no mechanical pulley, no gunpowder and no deep-sea ships. As their civilization was much younger than those of Europe and Asia, and as the population they could call upon for inventions was smaller, the Americans' achievements were not to be despised.

The way of life of the island city had the orderliness and discipline often found in a military people. It was an ascetic and even puritanical regime. Alcohol was made from the sap of the cactus plant and consumed; but drunkenness was normally permitted only in people of high estate. Adultery, if detected, could lead to the sentence of death.

A calendar of 360 days, based on the solar year, had to be followed with strict attention. A specific day and even hour of the day ordained almost every activity, including when the maize must be planted. There was even a correct day on which to be born. Some infants, however, were unlucky enough to be born on one of the five annual days which were classified as odd ones, being those needed to fill up the calendar's quota of 365 and a quarter days. In addition certain years were designated in advance as momentous—every 52nd year, to be exact—and were nervously awaited. If the world was to end, it would probably end at the beginning of that 52nd year.

The sacrificing of human lives almost dominated the calendar of the city. The act of sacrifice was more like systematic butchery than a religious festival. In the previous century, when ritual sacrificing had become more frequent, thousands of chosen victims, most of whom were male, could be killed in the same month. As the afterlife was seen as more important and infinitely longer than this life, a girl and boy who were led to a temple to be ceremonially killed at least had the consolation that their reward would be lasting.

The execution was carried out with high drama, presided over by priests, justified by ideology, and even welcomed by some parents, especially the poor, who came forward with their own children. Prisoners of war torn from their homeland and a very different religion could not be expected to view the sacrificial altar and the stone knife in the same consoling light. To be held down on the altar already stained with blood, and see a priestly hand clutching a blade of sharp flint, was the last conscious sight for tens of thousands of victims. The heart was skillfully cut from the body and then burned ceremonially. Often the limbs of the victims were eaten by chosen warriors and rulers. The deluge of sacrificial blood was the Spaniards' main justification for conquering the Aztecs, instructing them in the merits of one god rather than 200 gods, and compelling them to be baptized as Christians.

The feeding of such a large city was a feat of skilled organizing and hard manual labor. The city was stocked with food, grain, firewood and building materials by people who served as pack animals. The American continent possessed no wheeled vehicle; and even if there had been a cart, no horses or bullocks were available to draw it. Firewood and foods could be carried in boats a short distance along the lake; but the long-distance items were brought from as far away as the Gulf of Mexico by a procession of human carriers shouldering special packs capable of holding close to 25 kilograms in weight. As parts of the road went up steep slopes, the human carriers had to be strong. Understandably they carried such items—cocoa beans, cotton armor, gaudy feathers and honeycomb—as were valued highly in the Aztec city. Amongst the cargoes carried on their sore backs were also those special commodities which distant peoples were forced to send as taxation or tribute to the mighty Montezuma.

Much of the soil around the lake was fertile. For some 4,000 years it had been cultivated with relatively simple implements of wood and in recent centuries it had been sustained in its fertility by manure carried from the city and irrigated by channels of water diverted from the lake or springs. Crops of prolific maize, along with beans, greens, chili peppers, squashes and other vegetables and fruits, came from the terrain near the lake. Maize more than any other plant was the secret of this successful economy. One square kilometer planted with maize could feed three times the number of people living on the wheat or rye grown on a European area of similar size. Occasionally a drought brought a lean harvest or a flood damaged crops. How such a huge city managed in a year of a poor harvest is not clear.

The Aztecs preferred military solutions to civic dilemmas. When short of food, they would send out armies to forage in distant regions, and employ the new prisoners of war to act as carriers of the confiscated food. The penalty was that neighboring peoples hated the Aztecs.

The conquest of Montezuma's city was boldly planned by Cortés. He knew that from the start of the fighting he would be hopelessly outnumbered. Though he possessed guns and gunpowder—and just over a dozen horses—his men mostly fought with crossbows and swords which were, if anything, only slightly superior to the enemy's bows and arrows, clubs, wooden spears, slings and stones, and their swords which lacked even an iron blade. Moreover he was fighting far from home, in terrain that the enemy knew intimately. On paper his disadvantages were far larger than his advantages, but he was bold as a fighter and ingenious as a leader. He gained vital support from nearby peoples who, hating the Aztecs, were only too eager to serve the Spaniards as advance scouts, carriers, suppliers of food and fighters, if called upon. He even gained subtle support from the leading Aztecs who thought, when he arrived in November 1519, that he might be the reincarnation of a god whom they had long expected. Cortés's was one of the most astonishing victories of which world history contains a record.

Montezuma II, with his dark features and aquiline nose and courtesy and eloquence, humbly surrendered. Cortés took over the empire and even the emperor's children. He had a child by one of the beautiful daughters and escorted home three of her brothers as if they were his personal trophies.

Cortés, possessing far more wealth than he cared to reveal, returned to Spain in 1540 and lived out his final years near Seville. Later his remains were taken to Mexico, the land of his fame, and reburied. The procession of reburial was exactly the opposite for Vasco da Gama, the hero of the new Portuguese empire. He died in India and was buried at the Indian port of Cochin, where the site of his grave can still be seen in the church of St Francis. Later his bones were conveyed across the oceans and buried again in Portugal. Likewise, Columbus's body was also moved, as if it were a piece of valuable furniture. Buried in Spain, he was reburied with honor in Spanish America on two occasions, and then returned to Seville, where he lies in the mausoleum built for him.

At the time of their death and long after, these navigators and explorers were heroes, and their places of burial and tombstones were venerated in the Old World and the New. But several centuries later, after the peoples they had colonized set about the rewriting of the story of their own traumatic past, they virtually spat on the bones of Columbus, Vasco da Gama and Cortés.

The appropriate balance between praise and blame is not easy to calculate. One fact is beyond dispute. When Europe and the Americas were suddenly face to face for the first time, the confrontation was on a scale of bewilderment that was without precedent in the history of the world. The confrontation should have entailed far less cruelty; but bewilderment, confusion and aggression were inevitable.

18

THE INCA AND THE ANDES

THE EMPIRE of the Aztecs had crumpled. Far to the south, in the distant Andes Mountains, was a relatively new empire that seemed more formidable. Ruled by an emperor known as the Inca, it was much further away from the new Spanish ports in the Caribbean. Moreover its cities and villages had a protective rampart of mountains and gorges.

The middle and lower slopes of the Andes, and the adjacent Pacific coast, had long been occupied by gatherers and hunters. A backwater of the human world, the area began to stir itself about 3000 BC, when it domesticated three useful breeds of livestock—the llama, alpaca and guinea pig. A thousand years later its people were cultivating maize and the potato, two valuable plants which were unknown in Asia, Africa and Europe. In irrigating their crops they managed to cope with geographical obstacles more difficult than those faced by the valley cities of the Middle East. By the time of Christ the Nazca people were driving tunnels into hillsides in the south of Peru in order to divert the underground streams for the purposes of irrigation. Their building of agricultural terraces and aqueducts became impressive. Their skill in domesticating an increasing variety of useful plants was equally to be admired.

To metallurgy they were latecomers. Metals were not utilized here until several thousand years after they were being smelted and hammered along the eastern Mediterranean. Not until about AD 900 did the people of the Pacific coast and the Andes first see bronze ornaments and instruments. Fortunately their region was rich in tin and copper, the ingredients of bronze, and so they became producers of metals and manufacturers of various bronze tools including axes, chisels and knives. Iron, however, remained unknown to them.

While the Middle Ages for Europe were, by certain materialist definitions, the "dark ages," the same years in the Andes were the "light ages." The towns and villages along the Andes were being altered by new technology, new crops and new instruments. In some ways the small states of the Andes in AD 1400 resembled the rival Italian city-states of the same time, except that the Andes had a multitude of separate states, many of which occupied a single valley and its surrounding slopes. The corrugated landscape made for isolation. At least 20 distinct languages were spoken, and maybe 100 or more ethnic groups each occupied its territory on the middle and lower slopes of the mountains and on the narrow strip of Pacific coast. Then, in a short space of time, one superpower began to fight its way to the fore. It was in command when the Spaniards arrived.

Warfare between these dozens of groups or mini-nations had recently become almost a habit. In the course of the more serious of the wars the enemy's irrigation schemes and gardens—the results of generations of labor and ingenuity—were damaged, women and children were taken prisoner, and livestock and crops were destroyed or plundered. Even "the stones they had used for grinding" their grain were snatched away from some of the vanquished. In this long bout of fighting the Incas proved themselves superior, and from about the year 1438 their territory began to expand.

Originally from the highlands around Cuzco in the present Peru, the Incas numbered maybe 40,000 people. After a succession of wars and threats of war they won dominance over all other groups and ruled a total of 10 or 12 million people. Their domain, in the month when Columbus first landed in the Americas, made the empires of Spain and Portugal seem small. The Incas ruled all the way from the present Colombia and Ecuador in the north to central Chile in the south. Today five separate republics occupy the territory once ruled by them. Stretching over 36 degrees of latitude, the Inca lands were the equivalent of a European empire extending from the coldest parts of Norway to the mountains of northwest Africa.

Such was the extent of the Inca empire that soldiers despatched from

the center to a distant outpost might spend 60 or 80 days on the road before they finally reached their destination. It was easy to walk such long
distances because the empire was drawn together by a wonderful network
of roads. The ancient Roman and Chinese roads and bridges had been
the more remarkable, but no other early empire could match the Incas'
roads, which their corps of forced laborers constructed. Eventually the
Inca roads stretched over 23,000 kilometers—long enough to cross Asia
at its largest width. The two main roads ran parallel, one following the
Pacific coast and even crossing the desert of northern Chile, and the
other following the mountains. The mountain road, the busier of the two
arteries, went up and down a thousand hills. In places it was more than 25
meters wide but in steep pinches it was more like a zigzag path. As the
Incas owned no wheeled vehicles they did not have to worry if the road
was excessively steep or unusually narrow. When a marsh had to be
crossed, a narrow embankment was made of earth or stone. When a river
had to be crossed, a pontoon bridge—a floating walkway—was built.
When a gorge blocked the progress of the road, a suspension bridge of
thick rope was constructed to span the gap. Some of these bridges were
still in use three centuries later.

Across the bridges, perched high above the rushing streams, ran the
official messengers. They were neither barefooted—they wore sandals
made of untanned leather and tied by a woollen cord to the feet—nor
bareheaded. On the long stretches of level road the messengers moved at
an impressive pace. The speed at which their news travelled was expedited by the relay system: every few kilometers along the highway was a
hut where another messenger was waiting. In the space of one day a message might travel up to 240 kilometers.

Urgent goods as well as messages were carried by the relays of messengers. Thus a parcel of fresh fish would be carried a long distance for
the enjoyment of senior officials in the capital city of Cuzco. Along this
road a high official himself could be carried if he so wished, the normal
conveyance being two parallel poles carried by four men, with a seat in
the middle for the exalted one.

The roads could be useful for an invader, but for a time the Incas
were supreme. Fine generals, skilled in tactics, led their armies. While
the Incas supplied the senior officers, the subdued peoples supplied the
humble foot soldiers, both women and men. If a particular captive group
was trusted, it was permitted to put forward its own officers. If those offi-

cers proved disloyal, however, they were arrested, paraded in shame in the Inca capital and eventually killed, their cleaned-out skulls sometimes serving as drinking vessels. Spies and police were necessary to hold together an armed force in which the Incas were far outnumbered by their former enemies. And yet it was not entirely an empire of unwilling subjects. The Incas had brought peace to a war-torn region. They had also brought a willingness to cooperate, so long as the minority group surrendered without fighting. In that sense they were like the Mongols, who, just two centuries earlier, had usually been lenient towards those central Asian enemies who quickly surrendered.

Some of these alien regiments must have been unfailingly loyal to the Incas in the face of heavy loss of life on remote battlefields. The Lupaqa provided 6,000 soldiers to fight for the Incas, yet after 20 years only 1,000 were alive. Amongst the subdued peoples, those fit individuals who did not join the army were likely to spend much time as conscripted laborers. Each year one conquered group might be compelled to send to Cuzco 200 men and 200 women to build stone walls or carry grain. Another band of 100 people might be summoned to serve on the trunk road to Cuzco, where they sang on ceremonial days. The Incas were clever organizers and efficient gatherers of taxes, whether in labor or in provisions. Their record-keeping was thorough, and they conducted a census of each locality every year, thus accumulating possibly the finest population statistics the world had known up to that time.

Along the trunk roads might be seen, in certain years, a procession of people walking long distances to a new homeland. The Incas, like the rulers of the future Soviet Union and other empires, knew that the dispersal of alien peoples, and the mixing together of different ethnic groups, lessened the chance of an organized rebellion. On the same trunk roads walked soldiers on their way to distant regions where patrol duty was needed or fighting was likely. Warehouses, spaced along the road and serviced by vanquished peoples, supplied them with food.

People shared the road with that other beast of burden, the llama. When washed down by the rains, many of these woolly pack animals displayed handsome white coats with black or brown spots. A member of the camel family, though lacking the conspicuous hump, a llama could carry a load weighing 40 or 50 kilograms, thereby compensating for the absence of the wheel in Andes civilization. When making long journeys on the mountainous roads these sure-footed carriers were often accompanied by a reserve team which could take up the load when the main carriers became exhausted. One of the virtues of llamas was that they could travel for a couple of days without one drink of water. Moreover, when they finally halted in the evening, they did not have to be fed with costly hay and grain carried from afar; instead they grazed along the side of the road or near the night's stopping place. A cupped pair of hands full of maize was sometimes placed under their mouth as a bonus. The animal, however, was not imbued with a permanent wish to please. When tired or annoyed it might direct a flow of foul-smelling spittle at its shepherd or driver.

SUN, MOON AND THUNDER

The Incas were intensely religious. Important decisions were preceded by pleas to the gods—would they bless this military campaign or this coming harvest? The sun and moon were gods whose help was humbly requested. The sun, as the giver of heat, was seen as friendly and so the afterlife was lived in warmth. In contrast the hell of the Incas was a cold place.

The sun was the male god, and from him the emperor claimed descent; and so he ruled by divine right. The sun regulated the calendar, and in each year that December day when the sun came furthest south of the equator marked the beginning of the Incas' calendar. Thus their year began, in hot weather, almost at the same time as the year began in Europe, in cold weather. Their solar calendar, being an expression of the will of god, determined the exact day on which they planted their crops. Indeed, five successive months of the 12-month calendar were named specifically after the season then prevailing. Thus the month of the Small Ripening was followed by the month of the Great Ripening, and then came the Garment of Flowers, the Dance of the Young Maize, and the Song of the Harvest. A night calendar was also revered, for it determined when ceremonies in honor of the moon and stars should be held.

The sun god had his favorite plant and its leaves produced coca, which was spiritual in its qualities. Originally the tropical bush producing coca grew along the eastern foothills of the Andes, but it was domesticated and then transplanted to gardens on the lower slopes of the ocean side of the Andes. It was planted on flat terraces, painfully constructed from steep slopes, and water was conveyed to the terraces in long canals crossing the parched ground. As the coca crop was highly valuable, stone fences or walls were built to protect it from thieves and possibly also to prevent grey foxes from entering the garden and urinating on such a sacred crop.

Coca leaves were carried in baskets and fiber sacks along the highways to the capital city, where they were available only to the high officials of the kingdom and to the custodians of the temples. Mixed with lime, coca was often chewed in such a way as to bring a bulge to the cheek. It also transmitted an excitement to the mind, thus aiding the making of prophecies in those temples devoted to the worship of the sun. From the same plant came in modern days the minor additive which, until 1905, was part of the recipe for the drink Coca-Cola, and also the drug cocaine.

Of all the world's known societies prior to the last 100 years, the Incas should probably be ranked, in their attitude to women, within the highest cluster. Women not only had the right to own property but also possessed their own powerful god. Of the two main deities of the Incas, the moon was the goddess of females, and they served as her priests. The moon presided over the fertility of women: she protected them during the birth of a child. Women's economic role was as honored as that of men, and burial ceremonies paid tribute to her work and her needs. Whereas in the grave of a man was placed the hoe with which he had gardened, a woman was buried along with the wooden rod or spindle on which she had wound or twisted threads of new cotton. Even skeins of cotton were buried with her so that she could make cloth for the afterlife.

In the Andes region the god who was the most feared, before the Incas gained sway, was the bringer of thunder and lightning. He remained influential even when the new Inca gods assumed the center of the divine stage. On the edge of the villages many families built shrines to this powerful god who sent the lightning and thunderstorms which, in the mountains, often brought the heavy rain that was needed when the gardens were parched. He drew his rainwater, it was believed, from that luminous stream so visible at night, the Milky Way.

The sacrificing of animals, especially guinea pigs and the worthy llama, was a vital part of religious rituals. After a chosen llama was ceremonially slaughtered, its warm innards were inspected for portents of the future. For such grand events as a coronation, or in making the danger-spiced decision to go to war, the sacrifice of a human being was demanded. Children aged from 10 to 15, being considered purer than adults, were usually selected. It was deemed an honor for one's child to be chosen. It was not, however, such an honor that an Inca child received preference over a child of a subjected group.

In the regions far from the walls and temples of the capital city, a human life might be deliberately sacrificed at an appropriate time of year in the hope that the gods of fertility would bless the growing crops. In the very high mountains, where the growing season was short and a brief and dry summer could be disastrous, the sacrificing of a young girl was an insurance policy.

In the spring of 1995 one such Inca sacrifice was uncovered by the thawing of the snow 6,000 meters above sea level. The girl had been sacrificed during the very last decades of Inca rule, and possibly in a year of drought when a human sacrifice seemed the only hope of beckoning down the rain. Frozen and therefore well preserved, she was found to be about 13 years old and apparently in sound health on the eve of her death. Wearing a dress made from fine llama wool, she must have walked or been carried up the steep slopes from a village lying far below. She carried a doll—it was found in her blanket. Perhaps alcohol or drugs were given to her so that she would feel less pain when, at the moment of sacrifice, a fatal blow was delivered to the side of her head. Her dead body was placed beneath a stone platform, and statues of gold and silver—the metals of the upper orders of society—were deposited nearby. Bags of maize lay almost within reach, perhaps so that she would not starve in her afterlife.

Given the frequency of ritual sacrifice, human blood was so plentiful that it could be used in medical experiments. There is evidence that, long before a blood transfusion was successfully practiced elsewhere in the world, the Incas succeeded in transfusing human blood to the body of a sick person. As nearly all native South Americans were of the same blood group, the transfusion of blood from one person to another was safer than in Italy where blood transfusions, involving more than one blood group, were boldly attempted, perhaps for the first time, just one century after the collapse of the Incas' kingdom. Another skill of the Incas was in surgery. They could cut a segment of bone from the skull of a wounded or sick patient, or scrape clean the bone in its set position, without necessarily damaging the brain. A delicate operation, its success rate was probably as high as 60 per cent. This achievement suggests that these pioneering Inca surgeons used antiseptics to ward off infection.

THE LADDER OF THE ANDES

It is possible to understand the economic life of the Incas and of the many mini-nations which preceded them only by grasping the unique geography of the Andes. The terrain and climate were so diverse that as people walked to higher ground they virtually entered one new country and then another and another. Close together in the Andes, as if standing on a sloping ladder, were four distinct climatic and geographical regions, of a kind which normally are separated by thousands of kilometers of ocean or land. The four regions were separated by gaps in altitude rather than gaps in latitude. It was somewhat like Norway sitting on top of Holland which in turn sat on top of Sicily. These distinct regions were linked by zigzag mountain paths and occasionally by roads, rather than by a long ocean voyage.

On the slopes and bottom of the valleys lay a warm and dry region which, with the aid of irrigation, could produce fruit, cactus and even maize. In the middle ground, which was at least 500 meters above sea level, stood the zone best suited to agriculture. Here at one time the forests grew, but they were chopped down and replaced, in the more favorable places, by a chessboard of gardens. Here grew maize and beans, squash and the grain *quinoia*, which was rich in protein.

Much higher was a third rural zone, cooler and moister. Here grew an astonishing diversity of potatoes and tubers—perhaps 250 varieties in all. The potato, along with a supplement of grain, was the raw material for a biscuit mixture which was prepared and then exposed to the cold winds and, in effect, dehydrated. The potatoes so preserved were placed in adobe storehouses where they lasted during the long winter months— a sure supply of food at a time when not a blade of grass grew on these snowy slopes. As the dried potatoes were light, large quantities could be carried cheaply to other villages. They were also stacked in the roadside warehouses from which the armies were fed as they travelled.

Even higher than the potato country were the alpine pastures resorted to in summer. The climatic contrast between these highest and lowest zones was like the difference between the French Alps and the desert of Algeria. On the high pastures few trees offered shelter, the rains were plentiful and the winds bleak. On much of this high ground grazed the flocks of llamas. When an animal was slaughtered its meat was cut into long strips and dried in the sun.

In the lower and warmer country maize or Indian corn was not only the main source of grain but also the main ingredient of the beer called *chicha*. Women were the preparers of beer, and in the first stage they chewed the grains and selected fruits and then spat them into a pot of water. The saliva in their mouths broke down the sugar in the fruit and grain, and so helped the fermenting process. The resultant beer was high in alcohol.

The early South Americans had remarkable success in discovering or domesticating plants that are now known in many corners of the world. They tamed the potato, the sweet potato, the tomato, various beans, the cashew and peanut, coca, hot peppers, squash, manioc or cassava—known in Europe as tapioca—and the pineapple. Maize as a garden plant originated independently both in South America and in Mexico.

Here too grew rubber trees and a distinctive species of cotton used for making fishing nets and lines. When the nets were laid out in the shallow coastal waters they were kept afloat by another agricultural product, the gourd. Like a huge pumpkin or marrow, the gourd was often hollowed out to form a capacious container which was capable of holding up to 30 liters of liquid. To fill a gourd to the brim became the common way of measuring grain in the Andes, just as to fill a bushel or box was once the common method of measuring grain in Europe.

The mountain peoples, so conservative in religion, were unusually inventive. The Incas, devising a method of building in stone without using mortar, erected public buildings on a large scale. The Andes peoples extended the use of bronze from ornaments to workday implements; and soon bronze axes, knives, chisels, crowbars and heads of clubs became common items in their domain. They invented the crowbar, using it in mining, and also devised a highly effective spade for gardening. They learned how to use rivets and solder metals.

This was a civilization largely of its own creation. What it borrowed from Central America and the Aztecs was probably much less than it devised on its own. The civilization was all the more impressive because it arose in a part of the world which did not serve as a vibrant intersection of cultures but was simply a dead end.

THE FALL OF THE INCAS

The Incas had held their empire of mountain and plateau and desert, of sweaty jungle and everlasting snow, for less than a century when the Spaniards arrived at its fringes. Spain's influence came in the form of diseases, which spread swiftly amongst the native peoples. The emperor of the Incas, having been engaged in frontier wars, was returning south towards Inca territory in about 1525 when he was struck down by a mysterious disease. The onset of his death was swift. The question of who should succeed him was, for the Incas as for many European monarchies, a crucial and divisive question. Suddenly the dominance of the Incas was endangered by civil war even before the real enemy arrived.

On many occasions leaders within the world's most influential centers of power have fought amongst themselves, seeing themselves as immune to outside attack at the very time when they are no longer supreme. The ancient Greeks did this once too often. Even Europe was to slip into that trap of overconfidence in 1914 and again in 1939. Likewise the Incas fought amongst themselves not knowing that a powerful and unknown enemy, the Spaniard, was almost at their door.

The Incas were even more exposed to that other enemy—the new diseases which arrived with the invader. In the history of the inhabited globe up to that time—so far as can be ascertained—the people of only one other large area had lived in utter isolation for countless generations and then suddenly had been reunited with the wider world. The Japanese, few in number, had been isolated from the Asian mainland by wide and impassable seas. For scores of generations after the rising of the seas they probably had no contact with the outside world. There is no clear record of what happened when, some centuries before the birth of Christ, the Japanese were fully exposed again to the outside world. It is not known whether their health was impaired and their population initially reduced by the arrival of new Asian diseases to which they had no immunity. But it is known what happened to the tens of millions of Americans who, their long period of isolation coming to an end, were suddenly exposed to strange diseases.

When Christopher Columbus discovered the Americas, smallpox was rife in the Europe he had left behind. A few Spaniards unknowingly carried it in ships crossing the Atlantic. By 1519 the disease had reached the island of Espanola, where it killed perhaps one-third of the population. It was a secret and unintended weapon of the Spanish soldiers who vanquished Mexico. It was also potential gunpowder for the soldiers who, in 1532 under Francisco Pizarro, set sail from Panama in an attempt to conquer the Incas. That tiny force of Spaniards and horses needed a special weapon, for they were fighting far from home and were hopelessly outnumbered. But they pressed forward with ease. In November 1532 the Spaniards easily captured the Sun God, the Inca emperor Atahualpa. In the following year they captured Cuzco. Smallpox, that invisible ally, was already leaping ahead of the Spanish soldiers and killing large numbers of Incas.

The speed with which smallpox killed was itself a cause of despair for those who watched, helpless. Incubated in only 12 days, the disease showed its presence in a quickened pulse, a feeling of dryness in the mouth, a pain in the pit of the stomach, acute aching in the back and often vomiting. On the third day red spots appeared on the face and then on the neck and the wrists, finally speckling the whole body. Those who survived the disease developed pimples and scabs which began to fall off around the 16th day of the fever, sometimes leaving pitmarks which permanently disfigured the face. The pockmarked face, already a common sight in the streets of Vienna and Madrid, became familiar in the Americas. It was the hallmark of the lucky survivors.

By the 1530s smallpox was raging—or had done its worst—all the way from Bolivia in the south to the Great Lakes in the north. There was something mysterious about the way it arrived, retreated and then struck again. The long immunity experienced by some peoples was also puzzling. Iceland, in frequent contact with Scandinavia year after year, did not become the victim of an epidemic until two centuries after smallpox had devastated the Mexicans. When smallpox invaded Iceland in 1707, it quickly killed one in every four people. In Europe the peak of the disease was also in the early 1700s, when it caused at least one in 10 of all deaths in some lands.

Meanwhile in villages and wigwams, on the high slopes of the Andes and on the hills across the Missouri, the nightmare of another disease descended. Measles arrived soon after smallpox; and often it was difficult to determine which of those two infections caused the sprinkling of red spots on the skin. Typhus also arrived: it was relatively new to Spain itself, having been observed first in Spanish soldiers who had just returned from the island of Cyprus. In crept influenza, first noticed in the Americas in

1545, and whooping cough, diphtheria, scarlet fever, chicken pox and even malaria, all of which appear to have been new to the inhabitants and therefore were the more deadly.

How many people died of disease in Mexico alone during the first half-century of the Spanish coming has been the topic of endless calculating and learned guessing. Perhaps eight million Mexicans were alive when Cortés arrived; and half a century later the population was reduced to less than one-third. In the empire of the Incas, far south, the death toll also numbered millions, while in some of the less populous regions maybe eight of every 10 people died.

Even those native Americans who were taken back across the sea to western Europe as objects of display or affection were prone to catch the new diseases. Ten West Indians were escorted across the Atlantic by Christopher Columbus to Spain where in the royal court they were paraded as trophies along with vivid American parrots; but only two of the 10 people saw their home again, the remaining eight having died in the space of a year. The Frenchman Jacques Cartier returned from Canada in 1534 with 10 American Indians, and nine were to die from European diseases, the sole survivor being a girl.

At first the impact of the Spanish people—as well as their diseases—on the native Americans was disastrous. Civilizations were shattered. Cultural and economic life largely disintegrated in the main towns though it survived for many decades, less altered, in sparsely settled areas. Millions of people died, while others merely exchanged the Inca form of slavery or subjection for the Spanish. For the defeated perhaps the main solace in the long term was Catholicism, which came to dominate Latin America.

The magnitude of these shattering changes can perhaps be grasped by imagining that the invasion had been in the reverse direction and that the Aztecs or Incas had arrived suddenly in Europe, imposed their culture and calendar, outlawed Christianity, set up sacrificial altars for thousands of victims in Madrid and Amsterdam, unwittingly spread disease on a scale that virtually matched the Black Death, melted down the golden images of Christ and the saints, threw stones at the stained-glass windows and converted the cathedral aisles into arms or food warehouses, toppled unfamiliar Greek statues and Roman columns, and carried home to the Mexican and Peruvian highlands their loot in precious metals along with slaves, indentured servants and other human trophies.

19

REFORMATION

IN EUROPE, the all-powerful Catholic church was in peril. It tolerated too many back doors and trapdoors which permitted the rich and the unworthy, on paying a prescribed fee, to hope that they could slip safely into heaven. The saints, it was believed, guarded a storehouse of mercy and indulgence from which they could distribute a portion to those wealthy sinners who at the last moment wished for salvation and could afford to pay for it. Some indulgences and concessions, given in return for money or for services rendered, rested on a sound spiritual basis. Thus in 1095, during the crusades to rescue Jerusalem from the infidels, Pope Urban II promised to forgive the sins of those crusaders who crossed the seas "out of pure devotion and not for the sake of gaining honor or money."

Money donated for the building of cathedrals was also acknowledged by a holy receipt or passport which could be shown to the eternal gatekeeper. When the grand church at Speyer in Germany was being rebuilt in 1451, at least 50 priests sat "in their stoles" and, after hearing confessions, granted forgiveness to those pilgrims who donated money. A quarter of a century later the pope allowed indulgences to be sold for the sake of people now dead and residing in purgatory. In short, the rich could pay hush money for sins committed by dead relatives who, at the time of their death, might have felt no need for forgiveness. The poor, because they were poor, were largely denied this concession.

SELLING THE BLOOD OF CHRIST

The church engaged professional collectors, like charity's fundraisers of today, and they sold indulgences. As the medieval church, far more than most Christian groups today, believed in eternal punishment, the selling of exemptions and reprieves was sabotaging a key tenet of its theology. It was almost selling out the church for a few gold coins. John Calvin, the Geneva reformer, was to accuse some of the collectors of spending their commissions on "strumpets, pimps, and gluttony." He pointed out that Christ shed his blood for all; and yet here were agents virtually selling his blood, at so much a spoonful. The Catholic church still had a host of worthy priests, monks and nuns, utterly dedicated, but the exceptions were many.

Martin Luther, a north German priest, began to question the straying church. The son of a successful miner, he was professor of biblical theology in the small town of Wittenberg. At first there was little sign that he would rebel, for the church had promoted him as a favorite son. Doors were opened for him and he strode through. By the standards of the time he travelled much, and even crossed the Alps and worshipped in Rome. He knew Greek, was scholarly as well as devout, was widely read in the scriptures, and had the oversight of a dozen nearby monasteries. He was aged 33 when he rebelled.

Martin Luther detested the practice of selling indulgences or priced packets of forgiveness. Indeed when a Dominican priest sold indulgences to simple people and convinced them that thereby they were "saved" from eternal damnation, Luther was angry. On 31 October 1517, on the eve of All Saints' Day, a notable day in the calendar, he posted his protests in Latin on the door of the castle church in his town. His manifesto contained 95 points or theses, the first of which began: "Our Lord wished the entire life of believers to be one of penitence." His point was unmistakable to those who crowded around the door. Why should worshippers be penitent when some hucksters were actually excusing people from the need to repent—in return for a few coins.

Luther can still be seen as in the flesh. The fine German painter Lucas Cranach knew him and captured him on canvas. Here is a strong and slightly coarse peasant face, with small shrewd eyes, hair covering his ears and a little stubble on his face, as if he only shaved himself every few days. The nose is lumpy with strong nostrils, almost as if he is sniffing for the smell of his dinner. The face suggests that he is a hearty eater but it also conveys an ascetic quality. If one saw this strong-looking man walking along the street, or standing in the pulpit on Sunday, the combination of peasant strength and alertness would command attention.

That he was two distinct persons in the one body struck observers. At the Black Bear Inn in the German town of Jena three travellers, all businessmen, began to talk in the presence of a man carrying a sword—the carrying of swords being a sign of the troubled times. The travellers discussed religion, a hot topic. Not knowing that the armed man was Luther, one of the travellers said what many other Germans were probably saying: "Either this Luther is an angel from heaven, or he is a devil from hell." Luther, not offended at the remark, was generous enough to pay for their dinner. Often, however, he did take offense. And he did not quickly forgive.

Like most religious reformers, he did not wish to leave the Catholic church, but he was driven further and further towards a point from which he could not turn back. The church understandably dictated the terms on which he could stay. He could not accept them.

THE INK OF THE REFORMATION

In German-speaking cities alone, more than 200 printing presses seemed to be almost waiting for that event which they were so effortlessly to aid: the Protestant Reformation. The Catholic church's monopoly of the Bible was about to be ended by an invention partly borrowed from a land where the name of Christ was almost unknown. The Bible was a precious handwritten book, so scarce that in many churches the only copy was chained to the reading desk. For the first time in Christendom the gospels were to become available at a price which a village church or a moderately wealthy merchant could afford. A pamphlet containing a simple sermon could now reach, through the might of the printing press, more people than one sermon had ever before reached. No previous evangelist had ever had such a powerful assistant.

Martin Luther saw the printery as God's gift to his work. He wrote religious pamphlets and handed them to the printer along with his latest sermons. He began to translate the Bible into German, completing it in powerful and simple prose in 1534.

Wittenberg, a town with a mere 2,000 people, boomed briefly as the heart of the German printing industry. The scent of fresh paper and strong ink must have pervaded some of the town's lanes on the hot days of summer, when the windows and doors of the printeries were wide open. Whereas only 150 different books were printed in all Germany in the year of Luther's protest, 990 books were printed in 1524—just six years later. More than half of those books were printed in Wittenberg. Most were in favor of Luther. To him the printing press was a team of horses "whereby the Gospel is driven forward."

Luther was a protester, or a protestant in the vocabulary of the times. While his protests were somewhat political and social, they were primarily religious. Partly through his influence, hundreds of towns in Europe were shaken by a remarkable religious awakening. Millions of people felt that God was by their side. They could not express adequately the joy and sense of release and relief they felt.

As well as a sense of peace, urgency was in the air. What if one died tomorrow and, unprepared for sudden death, was judged to be unworthy of a life in heaven and was hustled down into hell, there to live in pain and torture for eternity? Luther had that fear when he decided to become a monk. He confessed that "he felt walled around with the terror and agony of sudden death." That terror traditionally led a host of Catholics to help the sick and the poor, and so win favor in the eyes of Christ; but Luther came to believe that good works were not enough. A person could do endless good works but thereby feel a worldly pride. He came to think that salvation lay not in doing good but in a simple, self-forgetting faith in God. Tens of thousands who heard him preach were profoundly moved by his arguments and his passion.

A PROTESTANT IS A PROTESTER

The lightning with which Luther lit the skies might have slowly faded but for the efforts of the French-speaking preacher John Calvin. Born in the north of France and educated in Paris, he lacked the magnetism and some of the glamour of Luther. When he preached, he showed little sense of theatre. It was his original mind, arresting message and nervous sincerity that impressed those who, eager to hear him, stood shoulder to shoulder in the big church by the lake at Geneva.

Political and religious enemies he made with ease. In 1539 he was expelled from Geneva. When he returned, after three years, his tenure was not secure. The arrival, from 1546, of hundreds of religious refugees from France began to tilt opinion in his favor within this small mercantile city and its surrounding farmlands and villages. Geneva was now ruled by Calvin, those clergymen known as the Company of Pastors, and the city-state authorities. It became the religious and moral showplace of Europe.

Every reformation and revolution carries a tension between those who insist that everything must be reformed and those who say, after the first bout of reforming, "We have gone far enough!" Calvin aroused animosity even amongst his own supporters by denouncing as papist many of the old Christian names so popular in the city. In 1546 the Company of Pastors, without formally announcing its policy, resolved that babies brought before them for the ceremony of infant baptism should be given sound biblical names and not the names of local Catholic saints. A barber of the town brought his baby son to the crowded church to be christened Claude—one of the three most popular names in Geneva—but the pastor solemnly christened him as Abraham. The barber snatched the child away and carried him home. There was uproar in the congregation and in all those places where gossip was exchanged.

Conscious that Geneva would be judged everywhere by its high standards, Calvin tried to enforce those standards. As he argued in his *Sermons on Micah*: "I say that once we have made a profession of faith like ours, we are more severely to be condemned if we do not deal fairly and equitably with our neighbors, or if we indulge in any violence, force, crookery or deception."

A centerpiece of his doctrine was a belief which now is highly controversial but seemed reasonable and even congenial to people living in a more religious era. He believed in predestination. He believed that God in his all-seeing wisdom knew in advance how each human life would unravel. In essence, some people from the day of their birth were predestined to win a place in heaven. Others were destined to fall by the spiritual wayside, and nothing they could do would alter their ultimate fate. Mainstream Catholic doctrine said a person might be saved by good deeds, and Luther said that people could be saved only by their deep faith in God's mercy, but Calvin dismissed these views. God was all-powerful and only his decision could save a person's soul. To us the doctrine seems preposterously unfair. Calvin would have argued that our concept of fairness was irrelevant. In his own opinion, and in God's view, all people were in one sense worthless. The fact that so many were ultimately saved was a sign of God's overflowing generosity to those who had no innate right to generosity.

The theological justification for Calvin's view could be found in many passages of scripture. Letters written by St Paul insisted that God made his decisions "not according to our works, but according to His own purpose and grace." In lucidly outlining his argument, Calvin stood intellectually on the shoulders of earlier Catholic theologians, the foremost of whom, St Augustine, had preached in North Africa more than 1,000 years previously. Calvin was not unlike Mohammed, who believed that God ordained far in advance what each single human being would do, whether good or evil.

Pastor Calvin's stand on predestination was both reassuring and electrifying to his flock. In a typical Calvinist congregation some listeners were probably terrified by this creed which Calvin expounded in long sermons constructed on the stepping stones of biblical texts. Most of his listeners, however, joyfully assumed that they were already amongst the chosen ones and had been chosen at birth.

Geneva was relatively tolerant towards heretics, whereas almost every other European city of comparable size was quick to execute the heretics who refused to be silent. Calvin had been accustomed to dispute publicly with his strongest critics, but occasionally he and his Company of Pastors would instruct the civic leaders to expel a critic from the city. Thus Jerome Bolsec, who had ceased to be a Carmelite monk and had become a doctor and disputer, was expelled from Geneva in 1551.

Two years later Michael Servetus, a clever Spanish-born medical practitioner and radical theologian, arrived in Geneva. He should not have arrived expecting mercy. Previously an inhabitant of France, he had been tried by Catholic authorities in the city of Lyons and sentenced to be burned to death because of his radical views on Christ. Miraculously he escaped from Lyons and made the short journey to Geneva. Attending a service in the cathedral, he was recognized and promptly arrested at Calvin's request. In court he was tried over a period of two months. That a trial, in a century of swift trials, should last for so long was a tribute to the thoroughness of Geneva. On 26 October 1553 he was convicted of heresy and sentenced to be burned to death. On the following morning, on a hill outside the city, he was tied firmly to a heavy wooden stake and his body was surrounded with dry firewood and the yellowing oak leaves of autumn. Attached to his waistband were his own writings directed against both Calvinism and Catholicism. The fire was lit. The agonized cries of Servetus would be heard for centuries to come.

In these emotion-charged years, a host of ordinary people showed courage in clinging to their old faith or in embracing the new. Of course most, when threatened with death or prison or the loss of property, fell in with the view of those who governed their land. But hundreds of thousands took risks in flirting with the new faith or clinging to the old. Summer was especially the season for spiritual rebellion, and on Sundays in warm weather the reforming preachers would hold religious services in barns in the countryside, or by streams where their converts could be baptized, or in the open air by roadside hedges—out of reach of the authorities who would have halted a strange religious service held in a street or square of their city. Sometimes several thousand people would walk from the nearest town to share in these occasions. Sometimes they walked by indirect routes to the place where the "hedge service" was to be held, so that its location would not become known to the town's law enforcers.

The letters of the day enable us to eavesdrop on one of these secret Calvinist services. It is a Sunday afternoon during the summer of 1566. At the foot of a small hill not far from the Belgian town of Ghent worshippers and curious spectators are quietly assembling. The service is to commence at 3 p.m., or so the word of mouth has announced, but there is a fear that the preacher—a stranger to the town—might be arrested. So the service begins one hour earlier. Already assembled are onlookers as well as distinct groups of devout people, each group having 30 or more members with its own teacher or leader: "closely packed small companies made up of men, women and young girls."

At the foot of this hill many of the devout carry a book of psalms printed cheaply and in metrical form. The singing of the psalms, with an accompanying instrument, can be heard by those latecomers approaching the secret place of assembly. The preacher himself sits on the hill. Short in build, aged about 30, he holds a felt hat in his hand. He speaks, we are told, "bare-headed and with quiet authority." How closely the people must have listened to the exciting but dangerous message that was banned in the villages and towns from which they had walked.

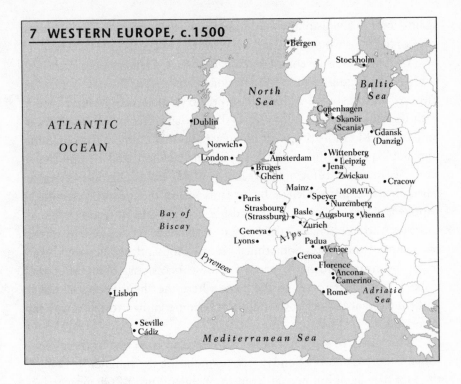

7 WESTERN EUROPE, c.1500

Bergen

Stockholm

North Sea

Baltic Sea

Copenhagen
Skanör (Scania)

Gdansk (Danzig)

ATLANTIC OCEAN

Dublin

Norwich

London

Amsterdam
Bruges
Ghent

Wittenberg
Leipzig
Jena
Zwickau

Cracow

MORAVIA

Mainz
Paris
Speyer
Nuremberg
Strasbourg (Strassburg)
Basle
Augsburg
Vienna

Bay of Biscay

Geneva
Lyons

Alps
Zurich
Padua
Venice
Genoa
Florence
Ancona
Camerino

Lisbon

Rome
Adriatic Sea

Seville
Cádiz

Mediterranean Sea

WOE, WOE, WOE!

A far-reaching revolt against the Catholic church came from the sects called Anabaptists. Named after the Greek word for "rebaptized," they were the militants of the Reformation. They first appeared in Zwickau, to the east of Wittenberg, and then surfaced in Zurich and hundreds of other towns in northern Europe. When driven from towns they were willing to worship in the fields in the warmer months and baptize adult converts by immersing them in running streams. They came in many varieties and nursed many beliefs. Most opposed the idea of infant baptism, believing that it was too precious a gift to be bestowed on day-old infants who were unable to make a conscious decision to live and die for Christ. More than any other protesting group, the Anabaptists were powerful amongst the poor. Most had a strong sense of community, viewing each other as brothers or sisters or even as comrades. Some of the sects were primitive socialists. The sects' leaders, at risk to their life, were disposed to poke out their tongues at those who ruled.

The Anabaptists were denounced as mad or evil by Luther, Calvin,

Zwingli and the preacher-heroes of the early Reformation. They were seen by many rulers as the scum of the Reformation. "Anabaptist" became a term of abuse. Notorious were the five female and seven male "strippers" who in Amsterdam in 1535, to emphasize that they preached only the naked truth, took off their clothes and ran along a street calling out "Woe! Woe! Woe!—the wrath of God." The 12 Anabaptists were executed. Feared as opponents of the religious and social order, Anabaptists almost everywhere were persecuted. A legion of them bravely clung to their faith and many paid the price. In Holland and Friesland alone, some 30,000 were killed in the 10 years after 1535; and yet it was in this region that they survived.

A PROTESTER FROM ITALY

Calvinism, which began to flower in the decade of Luther's death, gave the Reformation new energy. For 40 years the reform message took wing, landing in districts far from its birthplace. For a time it seemed that most of western and central and southern Europe might be converted to one of the competing new creeds. Most of northern Germany fell to the Lutherans. From Finland to Denmark and Iceland they took over the cathedrals. In Poland and Hungary the Calvinist creed swept through towns, making its mark especially with wealthier families. Holland and the island of Britain—except for the Scottish Highlands—were won by the reformers. Into France walked or rode a long procession of young pastors from Geneva and they won wide support in the seaports, especially along the Atlantic coast. Even Italy was penetrated. The Anabaptists worshipped in Vicenza and other sects took root in nearby Venice. Reformers were worshipping around the famous old university of Bologna, and fervent congregations sprang up in cities along the northern Italian plain ranging from Milan to Modena. John Calvin himself had travelled in his younger days from his citadel of Geneva to the Italian city of Ferrara, where the duchess gave him her secular blessing.

The career of an Italian evangelist, Bernardino Ochino, is a mirror of the fervor and tumult of the Reformation and of the way in which the Church of Rome also raised reformers on its home soil. While Luther was still a novelty, the Italian religious order which had been founded by St Francis of Assisi gave rise to an even more puritanical wing, the Capuchins. Beginning in the Marches, amidst the sugarloaf hills near the

Adriatic port of Ancona, the early Capuchins came to prominence in 1523 after a plague struck the town of Camerino. There they cared for the abandoned sick and the poor. Their strong preaching and good works—and the simplicity of their daily life, the coarse clothes they wore and the mud huts in which they lived—helped to inspire disciples. Here was a home-grown reformation within sight of Rome at the very time when the first Reformation was bubbling and steaming on the far side of the Alps.

Ochino, originally a follower of St Francis, became the Superior of the Capuchins in 1538. A magnetic preacher, he began to preach facets of Lutheranism in Catholic pulpits. Fearing persecution, he wisely fled towards safety. Crossing the Alps to Geneva, he satisfied the strict questioning of John Calvin and became more or less his follower. After serving as pastor of the Italian Protestant congregation at the rich German city of Augsburg from 1545 to 1547, he was forced to flee from pulpit after pulpit. He preached in England for some six years and then moved to Zurich, Nuremberg and finally to the distant Polish city of Cracow, usually finding a congregation of devout Italian exiles to whom he preached but usually provoking a ruler who forced him to move on. He was aged 77 when he finally settled in Moravia, near the present borders of Poland and the Czech Republic. His last place of exile, it was the home of the most unyielding of the pope's enemies, the Anabaptists.

The Protestants turned against many of the hallmarks of Catholicism. The Catholics believed in grand religious ceremonies and rich processions and jewels in the miter of the archbishop. In contrast, many of the reformers insisted on simplicity, and even when rich they preferred a church without stained glass in the windows. Catholics believed in a holy circle of saints whose help could be invoked; but many of the reformers dismissed the saints as needless intermediaries standing between the humble Christian and Christ himself. Catholics believed that all infants should be baptized as servants of Christ almost as soon as they were born, but many reformers believed that a true Christian should only be baptized when old enough to make a firm decision. Catholics often decorated the walls of their church with statues of Christ; but the reformers cast out the statues, along with the Virgin Mary.

Catholics believed in the authority of the pope and his preachings, for he was the embodiment of a series of laying on of hands beginning with the apostle Peter. Reformers, however, believed in the direct authority of the Bible. It conveyed the word of God, they said, and therefore it surpassed the word of St Peter. Catholics believed in the guiding power of the priest, but many reformers believed in the priesthood of all believers. In their eyes the humblest Christians who faithfully read the Bible and waited humbly for God's inspiration conveyed as much spiritual authority as the Catholic parish priest. Catholics prayed and preached in Latin but many reformers preached in German or Dutch or French; and Calvin himself insisted that French, not Latin, was the language of Geneva. Catholics had long abandoned the idea that priests could marry but now Protestants revised the idea. Luther himself married a nun, as did Ulrich Zwingli, who was the prophet of Zurich.

The new Protestantism fostered dark and light shades of revolt against the Catholic church. Most Calvinists, believing that there should be no majestic music and no lofty choirs, emphasized the singing of the whole congregation, with their voices unaccompanied by instruments. The word was all-important: music was simply a servant which carried the word. In treating music both as an aid to worship and also a seductive snare, the early Calvinists were almost like Muslims. They echoed that plea for simplicity which had been made in the Middle Ages by Cistercian monks.

On the other hand, the Lutherans maintained the rich musical tradition of northern Germany, which, with their aid, flowered astonishingly just two centuries after Luther first made his protests. In northern Germany two young musicians, Handel and Bach, had each made a pilgrimage on foot to the port of Lübeck to hear the special religious services for which the Lutheran organist Buxtehude provided the music. George Frederick Handel was himself the grandson of a Lutheran clergyman. Johann Sebastian Bach wrote nearly all of his magical output of music while working as a Lutheran organist, cantor or director of church music. Most of his oratorios and cantatas were written for the Lutheran congregations at two large Gothic churches in Leipzig, which, in the three-hour service that began every Sunday at 7 a.m., allocated half an hour for a cantata that Bach usually composed and conducted for 30 or 40 singers and instrumentalists. A church service of long duration was a characteristic of the first three centuries of Protestant ardor.

SHARP SWORD AND CUTTING WORD

The Catholic church examined itself critically after Luther and Calvin had held up their Bibles in protest. It prohibited the main abuses, some of which were far from as frequent as Luther had argued. The selling of indulgences by a professional collector of revenue was curbed by the Council of Trent in 1562. A bishop could no longer be absent from his own diocese for long periods. The music and the liturgy—almost as diverse as that of Protestantism—were taken in hand. The new baroque architecture, which especially flourished in Spain and the Spanish Indies, became a new affirmation of faith within a rejuvenated and chastened Catholicism. Seminaries were opened in order to train young clergy. New religious orders brought purpose to the church; and the Jesuits and Capuchins joined the old Catholic orders in sending missionaries to new lands.

After 40 years the tide turned against the protesting Protestants. In central Europe most of the rulers, determined that all people should belong to one religion, their chosen religion, began to harry the protesters. To practice a dissenting faith was to practice treason. The strongholds of the Protestants were now confined to northwestern Europe: to Scandinavia where their victory was complete, to England and Scotland, to most of the principalities of northern Germany, to Holland and to certain cities and cantons of Switzerland. In all these lands the Catholic faith was banned.

Likewise in Catholic lands—and they held most of the population of Europe—the worship of any other faith was banned. Wars often determined which religion was the victor. Battles in the European countryside had been frequent long before the Reformation, but religious passion ignited the gunpowder.

The early decades of the Reformation resembled the early years of Islam. The reformers depended on the sword as well as the word. Luther's message could not have won a huge territory on both shores of the Baltic without the support of princes and regiments. Zwingli, a former priest, was acclaimed as a reforming preacher by the rulers of Zurich. When war broke out with Catholic armies he was not merely the chaplain in his Protestant army, for he wore a steel helmet and carried an axe and long sword. Raised by the sword, he was killed by the sword. Calvin succeeded only because he was backed by the rulers of the Swiss republic of Geneva. In France his doctrine, failing to win over the monarch, began to lose its strong footholds in the south and west of the land. In Paris on St Bartholomew's Day in 1572, some 20,000 Protestants were slaughtered.

How should the new churches of the rebellion, having rejected the authority of Rome, be governed? The reigning kings or princes of such newly Protestant lands as England and Denmark took over the broad governance of the church, with the added bonus of being able to confiscate the lands and other treasures of the monasteries, convents and bishops' palaces. Gustavus Vasa, King of Sweden, even confiscated the bells of the Catholic churches. The Protestant church became in one sense the spiritual arm of the state. The bishop appointed by the king generally controlled ecclesiastical affairs, with the king at first looking over his shoulder. The Reformation served to promote nationalism and the power of the secular ruler. But even in Catholic nation-states such as Portugal and France, the ruler tended to supervise or control the church.

While the Protestants tended to centralize power in most of the lands where they were victorious—or where they were allowed by the ruler to be victorious—they also initiated a democratic stream. Calvinism set up a system of governing the church in which the senior members of the congregation were influential: there were no bishops and no ultimate authority. Like Lutheranism it preached that the Bible and not the church was the ultimate court of appeal, and to the Bible every devout and intelligent Christian could appeal. In Calvinism ordinary people had more influence than in any Catholic congregation.

In the end the Protestants made no headway south of the Alps or south of the Pyrenees. Their unexpected triumph was on the far shores of the Atlantic. Whereas Spain refused to allow Jews, Muslims and Protestants to emigrate to its new colonies, Britain and Holland allowed Protestant dissenters to sail away to the new American colonies. In Boston and other New England towns the Calvinist Reformation burned with a fierce flame.

The rise of the United States, its distinctive culture, its early fostering of intense debate and its ultimate democracy probably owed as much to the Protestant reformers as to any other single fact. From America, in the 19th century, the evangelical Protestant missionaries were to penetrate much of the world. Today, the church is far more dynamic in Congregationalist Samoa and Methodist Fiji than in Luther's town of Wittenberg or Calvin's city of Geneva.

Many of the spiritual offspring of the Anabaptists, wishing to escape persecution in Holland and England, made the voyage to North America. It was in Baptist churches, above all others, that African-Americans found their spiritual home. The Reverend Martin Luther King Jr, the fighter for civil liberties in the 1960s, was a southern Baptist. The "strippers" of Amsterdam, if they were resurrected, would be intrigued to learn that in 1999 the president of the most powerful nation on earth was a Baptist.

WOMEN AND THE BOOK

At first the Reformation seemed to be a blow to women. Probably the only institutions in the western world in which women held power in their own right were the convent and the monarchy. Women governed the female convents; and when a convent held valuable properties in a city, the woman in charge held additional power. Thus in Zurich the abbess of the Benedictine convent helped to administer the town. The closing of the powerful convents in most of the states that were now Protestant indirectly reduced the power of women. There was one compensation. Most Protestant churches believed that as many people as possible, whether women or men, should read the Bible; and that led to the opening of more schools which taught reading and writing.

Initially, few women were literate. In the English diocese of Norwich in the 17th century, only about 11 per cent of women were literate. Even male laborers as a group were slightly more literate than women. On the other hand, 65 per cent of yeomen or male small farmers were literate. Steadily the rate of female literacy began to grow. Prussia, a Lutheran stronghold, made education compulsory for boys and girls in 1717. Scotland and the Netherlands, both of which were Calvinist strongholds, encouraged literacy. In the Dutch city of Amsterdam in 1780, a remarkable 64 per cent of brides signed the register when they married, while the others clumsily drew a cross in the place where their signature of consent was called for. In England, about 1 per cent of women could read in the year 1500, but this had risen to 40 per cent by 1750. Belatedly, Catholic countries followed this revolutionary trend.

The improved ability to read and write was a prelude to the extension of the right to vote. If, as late as the year 1900, most western Europeans had been illiterate, the trend towards democracy would not have travelled far.

The Russian church, in contrast, turned its back on literacy. No Christian church in any other nation had as many adherents as the Orthodox church had in Russia; but its priests were poorly educated, and many were far more skilled in chanting from memory—or from forgetfulness—than in reading the scriptures. No Russian university taught theology; and the typical priest assumed a spiritual and intellectual authority higher than his powers of advocacy merited. The authority of the priest was cemented because few of his congregation could read the Bible.

The Bible in the modern Russian language could be found in no bookshop or church until Tsar Alexander I welcomed in 1812 a local branch of the British and Foreign Bible Society, a society skilled in distributing bibles in English-speaking lands. Even this first Russian attempt at unlocking the closed Bible was thwarted by the clergy. The full Bible, with testaments old and new, was not freely available in modern Russian until 1876, by which time even Karl Marx's secular and "seditious" bible was available to those brave enough to ask booksellers who were brave enough to keep a copy. It is just possible that a more educated clergy and a Bible-reading public would have allowed the Russian church to hold the middle ground and retain some sympathy amongst intellectuals. This vacant ground, however, was to be pegged out by atheists and rising communists.

WATCH OUT FOR THE WITCH

The surging interest in religion took unusual forms. More evil was detected as well as more saintliness. In many parts of Europe witches were multiplying, or so it was said.

In an era of religious fervor, belief in mercy and goodness went hand in hand with belief in the power of evil to ruin people's lives. Evil was personified in the witch. When tragedy appeared it was increasingly attributed to the plotting of a witch. When an economic blow struck a village or family, a search was made for the offending witch. Most accusations of witchcraft arose out of the quarrels, tensions and hardships of daily life. Personal quarrels were magnified by the increasing faith that God was everywhere and that his adversary the devil was also prowling every-where, after dark and in broad daylight. The encountering of witches was like the sighting of flying saucers in the second half of the 20th century. Once the idea caught hold of a region, it spread with speed.

In Europe during the three centuries between 1450 and 1750, most of the 100,000 or more "proven" witches were concentrated in a small number of regions. In the southeast of Scotland and in eastern France, witches were said to be especially active. In the Swiss district behind Lausanne on Lake Geneva, and in the German archbishoprics of Cologne, Würzburg and Bamberg there were widespread outbreaks of witchcraft that excited the people. In Europe over a long period, close to one in three of detected witches lived in Germany.

There were patterns in the spread of witchcraft. Thus in England and Hungary nine of every 10 convicted witches were women, though in Iceland and Estonia most of those accused and convicted were men. Of the tens of thousands of people sentenced to death for witchcraft in Europe, three of every four were women. Many were old and disfigured but some were young and pretty, and a few were children. In Britain a typical female witch was either a spinster or a widow, was old and poor, and tended to quarrel with her neighbors. Being poor she was sometimes a burden on the local government or on her neighbors. That did not make her popular.

Contrary to an impression widely held today, most of those who accused a woman of being a witch were women. Accusations usually arose from the activities where women came together—the raising of children, the household's daily tasks, the tending of cows and poultry, the bringing in of the harvest and sometimes the gathering of sticks and light firewood. Accusations stemmed often from events surrounding the birth of a child. A miscarriage might be attributed to the witchcraft of a female neighbor. The death of a mother while giving birth to her child might be attributed to the interference of the devil, who shrewdly chose a woman of the village to do his evil work. An accident to a young child, the death of a calf or lamb or the failure of the harvest was often attributed to a witch. In villages where starvation was not far away, the witch was seen as a deadly enemy who had to be confronted and conquered.

Witches were forced to make a confession before the courts passed sentence. While some confessed voluntarily, most had to be tortured before they were willing to claim that they were servants of the devil. A thumb might be placed in the screw, an excruciating torture. The woman might be placed on the rack and her limbs stretched until, the pain being unbearable, a confession was extracted. A common method of extracting a witch's admission of guilt was the strappado. The person's hands were first tied behind the back, and the body was hoisted from the floor by a pulley to a considerable height. The body was dropped, the fall was halted suddenly, and the resulting pain was intense. There were brave women who under terrible pain clung to their innocence.

The methods employed against witches reflected the practices of the times. Hundreds of different crimes were punished by death, and so the putting to death of witches—they were condemned criminals—was not in itself unusual. Likewise, torture was widely used as a way of preparing other suspects on other charges for a quick trial.

The intensified pursuit of witches in western and central Europe between 1580 and 1640 was probably aggravated by economic hardship. Religious tensions also sharpened the search for witches, and they were often found in towns or regions where rival sects were face to face. A land with religious unity was much less likely to produce accusations of witchcraft. Russia was almost devoid of witches. In Ireland, Poland, southern Italy and several other Catholic lands and regions the arresting of witches was rare.

In an ultra-religious era, nearly everyone believed in the power of organized evil. It was assumed that the devil was at large in the world, with a million pairs of evil eyes and a million pairs of hands, and that he was choosing witches as his personal servants. It was believed, and even more so in Africa than Europe, that witches did immense harm to human lives. This emphasis on the might of evil—and it is no longer prominent as a belief in western civilization—was the essence of the crusade against witchcraft and the justification for the cruelty inflicted on witches.

The tragedy was that western civilization, when at last it ceased to believe in witches, was also ceasing to believe in humankind's immense capacity for evil as well as good. In the first half of the 20th century, millions of educated and cultivated people were not prepared for the ruthless way in which Evil, by whatever respectable name it adopted, would so devastate Europe that the era of the witches seemed a mere mishap.

20

VOYAGE TO INDIA

PORTUGAL to India became a regular sea route. It was the most arduous that the world had so far known; and the voyage to the Americas had no counterpart. Four or five ships set out each year from Portugal to India, and their captains planned the voyage carefully so that they could make best use of the winds and curb the prospect of encountering dangerous storms or hazardous coasts. The favored time to sail from Lisbon was in the first half of March, for this would allow them some six months to sail beyond the Cape of Good Hope and some way into the Indian Ocean where the winds were likely to turn in their favor. There, if they were too late, they might encounter difficult winds that would persuade them to turn back to a place of shelter. A voyage to India could last a year or more if it was commenced at the adverse time of year.

Some Portuguese ships called at Brazil on the voyage out, but most ships called at no port. Indeed in the early years the captains knew no African port where, on calling, they could feel welcome or even safe from surprise attack. Once a well-loaded Portuguese ship had passed the most southerly coast of Africa and turned north, she usually sailed through the wide Mozambique Channel which separated Africa from Madagascar. The captains' hope was to reach this strait just when the north-east monsoon—their sworn enemy—was fading away, to be replaced by a tailwind which would blow them quickly to India. Most Portuguese ships preferred to hug the coast, and to give them a haven a fort was built in 1595 at Mombasa in the present Kenya. Sailing further north and following the coast almost to the Red Sea, the ships then turned east, following the Arabian or Sabaean coast and so making their way towards their Indian destinations.

Leaders in Europe took an interest in this most exotic sea route across the northern Indian Ocean, an ocean they could not hope to visit. When John Milton in England wrote his poem *Paradise Lost*, he added the lines:

> As when to them who sail
> Beyond the Cape of Hope, and now are past
> Mozambique, off at Sea North-East winds blow
> Sabaean Odours from the spicie shoare
> Of Arabie the Blest.

The voyage to India was not only at the mercy of the winds. Even a fast voyage could be an ordeal. The soldiers and merchants who came aboard at Lisbon were not mentally prepared for such a long and tempestuous ordeal. In 1573 an Italian priest watched many passengers walking aboard as if they were embarking on a day excursion rather than a long voyage that might be their death. Some carried only a shirt, two loaves of bread and some cheese and a jar of marmalade. The ship also supplied rations—mainly hard biscuits, dried fish, salted meat and wine. The food could be heated only when the sea was relatively smooth. A wooden ship was always in danger of catching fire, and cooking fires were allowed only on deck in a few boxes filled with sand.

After a few weeks the freshwater, which was usually stored in wooden casks, began to taste foul. It also became scarce as the voyage went on, and so the washing of the face let alone the rest of the body was not a frequent event. With so many people crammed together, and with the ship spending much time in the tropics, and with no fresh fruit or vegetables, disease spread with ease. In the years from 1629 to 1634 more than 5,000 Portuguese soldiers set sail from Lisbon but fewer than half reached India alive. Most ships carried a surgeon whose favored remedy was simply to bleed three or four liters of blood from a sick patient. The cure rarely worked miracles.

The main Portuguese harbors in India were Goa and Cochin, both standing on the west coast. The sight of the sails of a Portuguese ship approaching these harbors, the long voyage almost over, was as exciting to Portuguese living in the ports as to those standing on the decks of the incoming ship. Hawkers would load their little vessels with fresh fruit, vegetables and nuts and hurry out to sea in order to meet the tall sailing ship. Musical instruments would be merrily played as the Portuguese, leaving their ship to ride at anchor, were rowed ashore where news of two remote lands would be exchanged.

India had long traded indirectly with Europe. Some of its wares were well known in Venice and Lisbon long before the time of Vasco da Gama. The overland caravan routes between the Persian Gulf, the Red Sea and the Arabian Sea on one side and the Mediterranean on the other were old. One sign of the antiquity of these links awaited the first Portuguese to walk the streets of Cochin. There they found a small and isolated colony of Jews. One can still enter the small synagogue in the city of Cochin, but its worshippers are few.

Goa, standing further to the north, replaced Cochin as the chief harbor for the Portuguese; and indeed it remained a province of Portugal until the 20th century. From Goa would set out, once a year, a large ship loaded with trading cargoes for Malacca (Melaka) on the Malay Peninsula and for Macao in China and so to Japan. Again the captain would try to adjust his time of sailing to gain the benefit of the monsoons of the western Pacific. The start of the new monsoon was like a traffic light, proclaiming the green or "go" signal to ships coming from one direction and the red or "stop" signal to ships coming from another.

The cargoes exchanged between Asia and Europe were mostly high-priced luxury goods that could afford the high costs of transport. They were goods destined for only the top layer of society both in Asia and Europe. In China and Japan would arrive scarlet cloth, woollen apparel, crystal and glass, Indian chintzes and Flemish clocks. In the hold of the ship returning to India and eventually to Europe were Chinese silk and silken goods in large quantities as well as exotic medicinal ingredients. Another item of "cargo" might consist of Chinese slaves or servants.

In Goa at certain times of the year the Portuguese ships prepared for their homeward voyage. In addition to Chinese goods they took on loads of pepper—western India was the home of pepper—and cinnamon and other spices. There also was carried aboard containers of nitrate of potash, which was the crucial ingredient of gunpowder; indigo dye; cotton piece goods; and eventually Indian diamonds that came from the mines of Golconda. Such cargoes made India seem magically rich. About the year 1600, in the eyes of most Europeans, the name India was a synonym for dazzling wealth. Several of William Shakespeare's plays display that dazzle. Thus, Troilus says of Cressida: "her bed is India; there she lies, a pearl." In the play *Twelfth Night* Maria is addressed as the golden girl, "my metal of India." To resemble shining metal from India was to be doubly precious.

In addition to the cargoes which were carried aboard on the backs of Indians and literally crammed into the Portuguese homeward-bound ships there were personal cargoes which were placed or roped together on the open deck, where they would be exposed to spray and salt wind. Every member of the crew had a right to load cargo and sell it in Lisbon. Even the ship's boy had the right to fill one-third of a wooden chest with cinnamon—if he could afford to buy the spice in the Indian street market. The officers and crew indeed held the sole right to use the open decks as a storage place for their personal cargoes. The decks were packed high with bundles, packages, wooden chests and crates to the point of making the ship unstable in certain winds. A walk along the deck was like an obstacle race.

The voyage home was riskier than the voyage out. Even the departure from the Indian port could be risky. The monsoon almost blockaded the port of Goa for three months of summer, making it easy to enter but very hard to leave. To set sail at Christmas or soon after was easiest, for the monsoon had changed direction. The stretch of Indian Ocean and the rocky coast near the approaches to southeastern Africa were the most hazardous, especially if the ship was delayed and did not reach that stormy zone until May or June when the winter winds were strong. The list of wrecks on the route between Lisbon and Goa was terrifyingly long. In the years 1590–92, 17 ships left Lisbon for India but only two returned safely. In the 100 years after 1550, about 130 of the stately and rather cumbersome sailing ships were lost. Most of these were wrecked, and nearly everyone aboard perished in the sea. For a few days the lighter crates might be seen bobbing on the waves. At home in Portugal, in cottages and merchant houses, the relatives waited and waited for sons and fathers and cousins and uncles to return. After two or three years, they gave up hope.

Some of the returning ships were captured by pirates and enemy vessels not far from Europe. The cargo was confiscated along with the ship.

Curiously the Portuguese in India made more profits by trading within Asia than by the long-distance trade to their homeland. Even when driven from some of their richest trading posts in South-East Asia, they remained busy on the Asian trade routes. One of their successes was the carrying of Indian cotton and calico textiles to the Indonesian islands and returning with spices and sandalwood and other aromatic woods for India. In Hindu funerals mourners liked to be purified with the scent of the yellow aromatic sandalwood cut on the island of Timor, not far from northwestern Australia.

This roundabout sea route past the Cape replaced in economic importance the long caravan trails and silk roads that for centuries had traversed the center of Asia from the Black Sea to the walled cities of China. One century or so after the sea route was established, the Dutch language could be heard in the riverside alleyways of Canton and Portuguese was becoming the pidgin language of the Asian trade and the precursor to pidgin English, while a few pots of Japanese or Chinese tea—bought at astronomical prices—were being brewed in western Europe.

Priests had rounded the Cape in early Portuguese ships. One of the first was Francis Xavier, an early Jesuit who vowed to lead a life of poverty and dedication. Arriving in India in 1542 he made the Portuguese port of Goa the base for missionary voyages. He was not the first Christian in India—several congregations of Syrian-speaking Christians existed on the Malabar Coast by AD 600—but he was dynamic. He travelled as far away as Japan, where he won converts. His fellow Jesuits later had temporary success in China where the Italian Matteo Ricci devised a ritual that allowed Chinese converts to venerate their ancestors as well as Christ.

The Catholics far more than the Protestants were the early missionaries in the New World, and their courage in venturing there was to have far-reaching effects. They were to the fore partly because in both the Americas and Asia the two pioneering European colonizers were Catholic nations. Indeed Protestantism was not born until a quarter of a century after Columbus sailed. But even if Protestantism had arisen a little earlier, it is not certain that it would have been so enthusiastic in sending out missionaries.

Perhaps nothing did more to restrain Lutherans, Calvinists and Anglicans from organizing missions to the heathens than the fact that most of their clergy, as part of the revolt against the papacy, were married. To encourage a wife and young family to accompany a clergyman to an unhealthy tropical port in America, Africa or Asia in 1600 was an invitation to an early death. Furthermore the Catholic church had relative unity—a powerful aid to the spreading of its message.

Long after Protestant nations had become the dominant traders and governors in India and most of coastal Asia, they were slow to foster the work of missionaries. It was not until 1704, more than a century and a half after the death of Francis Xavier, that a Protestant king, Frederik IV of Denmark, founded a missionary outpost in India. In the British parts of India the capitalist East India Company was in charge, and for decades it had no time for missionaries preaching in its midst. Britain's state church, the Church of England, did not even send a bishop to India until Reginald Heber, already popular as a writer of hymns, set out for the rising city of Calcutta in 1823. His task was enormous. That his diocese or domain at first embraced not only India but also Australia was an indication that missionary fervor did not run to boiling point in the state church of what was now the world's largest empire.

The arrival of the Portuguese had less effect on India in the medium term than the arrival, less than a quarter-century later, of an Asian power. The Mughals, variously known as Moguls and Mongols, fought their way through narrow mountain passes into northern India and set up a dynasty that lasted for about a quarter of a millennium. The first ruler, in 1526, was a descendant of Genghis Khan and Tamerlane. He despised India's way of life and compared it unfavorably with life in the lush valleys of central Asia. Where, he asked, were the fine horses—vital to a Mughal— and the tasty meat, the grapes and melons, the candles and chandeliers, the fresh water and the baths and the ice?

The Mughals were yet another wave of the emigrations from central Asia to more favored parts of eastern Europe, China and India. Slaughter was part of the initial conquest, but the Mughals' rule, by the standards of the time, was orderly. In painting, carpetweaving, glassmaking, architecture and other arts they made more of a mark on India than did the early Europeans. When the emperor's wife, named "The Chosen One of the Palace" or Taj Mahal, died in childbirth in 1631, the emperor in his grief assembled a team of 20,000 workers to build at Agra a mausoleum of white marble and red sandstone that became known as one of the wonders of the world.

At that time the Portuguese and other Europeans held only a straggling chain of forts and harbors along the coast of India. They had created nothing that could even sit in the shadow of the Taj Mahal. In a sense the Europeans were traders rather than colonizers; and the safest bays and river-mouths along the coast were more important to them than the soils of the inland. The Dutch and the British had now largely displaced the Portuguese from India's attractive trading posts. In the Indonesian archipelago the three powers jostled for control, with the Dutch the winners and the Portuguese clinging to the crumbs.

The Indonesian archipelago was a special prize for European traders. It was becoming the biggest producer of pepper in the world and was for a time the only producer of cloves. Situated not too far from India and very close to the Asian mainland, the Indonesian islands had long been reached by each gust of religion blown from Asia. Merchants had brought their creeds along with their trading goods; missionaries had arrived to spread the word. Palembang in Sumatra was the focal point for the region's trade with China, and in the 600s it listened closely to the Buddhist missionaries, some of whom came from China and others probably from India. Buddhism was strong in Java by the year 800, and the monumental temples at Borobudur are witnesses to its wealth. Islam was a late arrival, probably being transmitted from India and even Arabia by traders and sailors. One of the earliest-surviving signs of Islam's increasing strength in the archipelago is a tombstone found in eastern Java and carved in about the year 1082.

The long string of Indonesian islands had no political and economic unity, and those at the eastern end had little contact with those at the western end. Rulers fought one another. Their merchants competed for trade in pepper, nutmeg, cloves and those other spices which made some of the islands so prized. By 1650 four major states still held power in the archipelago, with Bantam and Mataram centered on Java, Achin centered on Sumatra, and Macassar to the east. If the sultans of the Indonesian archipelago and Malay Peninsula had united, they could have kept at bay the European ships. They were happier to fight and argue rather than unite. Within 30 years they were to be at the mercy of the Dutch.

SPIKED BY DISTANCE

In Asia these Portuguese, Dutch, British and French empires—and the extension of the Spanish empire in the Philippines—at first occupied only a necklace of steamy Asian ports and a few inland trading depots. They could be called empires only with hesitation. Their power, away from the coast, was usually weak. Compared to the Roman Empire their personal and conscious imprint on the lands in which they intruded was at first soft and seemed to be temporary. In many, their main impact was through the diseases they unconsciously carried. The cultural impact was weak because so few Europeans settled in the ports and trading posts, being deterred by the hot climate, the fear of tropical diseases and the distance from home. Europe's impact on nearer America, especially its temperate zones, was much larger than its impact on Asia.

Even as late as 1650, Europe was far from becoming the master of most of the narrow straits and mountain passes which controlled the trade of the world. Europe was too divided to be able to dominate vast tracts of overseas land. Wars between European rulers were frequent. Moreover Europe could apply in Asia only a fraction of its military might: Asia was simply too far away. Distance in effect still spiked Europe's guns and retarded its fighting ships.

In eastern Asia the advance of the Europeans, so confident in the first century, was halted. Japan, which at first was friendly to alien merchants and missionaries, had sent a deputation of four youths all the way to Europe, where in the 1580s they were handsomely treated by the mighty of Madrid, Lisbon and Rome. Early in the following century the Japanese had second thoughts. They expelled nearly all Europeans and killed many Jesuit and other priests who did not wish to be expelled. Only Dutch traders were permitted to make occasional visits. When actually doing business in a Japanese harbor they were almost prisoners of war, and were not allowed to bury their compatriots in Japanese soil and could not conduct religious services amongst themselves.

China, dominant in its own part of the world, extended its long land borders in the 18th century. It occupied Tibet and eastern Turkestan, areas which it had long regarded as within its sphere of influence. Rarely before had China commanded so much of the silk road. At the same time, some of the Indian rulers took a lesson from the Chinese and defied the Europeans. In June 1757, one of the blackest months in Britain's colonial history, more than 100 of its soldiers died while imprisoned in the Black Hole of Calcutta.

On the nearer shores of the Indian Ocean, the Europeans were far from triumphant. In East Africa for nearly two centuries the Portuguese had held the key port of Mombasa, which lay on their route to India.

Now their grip was threatened by the Sultan of Oman, whose headquarters were near the mouth of the Persian Gulf. In 1696 the sultan's navy sailed south from Oman, laid siege to Mombasa, and after three years captured it. In that corner of the Indian Ocean the sultans of Oman were supreme. Indeed in 1840 the sultan moved his residence from Oman to the busy harbor on the African island of Zanzibar some 3,000 kilometers away. Not often in the history of the world had a ruler moved his capital city from the Northern to the Southern Hemisphere.

While western Europe was revelling in a phase of global conquest, central Europeans still lived in fear of the Ottoman Empire. Turkish armies camped outside the gates of Vienna in the summer of 1683, and once again they laid siege to one of the mightiest cities of Christendom. Now it was the Turks' turn to retreat. In the late 1680s they were driven from Buda, being one half of the present city of Budapest, which they had ruled for more than a century. They lost the city of Belgrade and even, for a few years, Athens. For lovers of art the defeat of the Turks in Athens was to prove a calamity, because, in the course of the fighting, part of the Parthenon was toppled. Soon the Turks regained Athens and they ruled it until 1829.

The Turks also clung to the Holy Land and much of the Middle East. There was no starker sign of the limits of influence of Christian Europe than that the city of Jerusalem, century after century, remained in Islam's grip.

In 1600 and 1700 the rise of Europe to dominate much of the world was not preordained. Its strength was more visible on the maps of the world than it was in reality. So far its victories were more in coastal America than in Asia and Africa. It had made little impact on Japan, China and the Ottoman Turks. And yet its confidence and commercial drive, its wide-ranging technology, and its prowess in war—even when hopelessly outnumbered—were portents of the coming era when it would shape a diversity of cultures far more extensive than Rome had ruled.

21

THE NEW WORLD BEARS GIFTS

THE SPANIARDS colonized vast areas of the Americas and many islands in the West Indies with a tiny force of soldiers, sailors and civilians. By 1600 they were dominant in Central America and shared South America with Portugal. Spain and Portugal had won the first phase of colonization and conquest partly because they were strong in seafaring and partly because they were also the two European countries which were closest to Central and southern America. After 1600, however, they began to lose impetus.

The new phase in colonizing the Americas belonged to France, Holland and Britain, seafaring nations which also had a geographical advantage over the Mediterranean states. By 1650 their little ports, wooden fortresses and fur-trading posts in North America dotted the Atlantic coast and the near interior. France was busy in Canada and on two of the West Indian islands, Martinique and Guadeloupe. Britain held colonies extending along the Atlantic coast from the island of Newfoundland— which it shared with the French—to New England, Virginia and the West Indies. Even the Danes were soon to set up plantations in the Virgin Islands. Of the states in western Europe only the Germans were missing.

On the Atlantic coast of North America the Dutch and the Swedes each held colonies that broke the continuity of the chain of British coastal colonies. New York was founded by the Dutch, and the island of Curaçao in the Caribbean was Dutch too, while Delaware was Swedish. Thus a traveller who decided to journey on foot along the shore from English Boston, which was then a village, all the way to Washington, which was not even a village, had to pass for part of the way through Dutch and Swedish territories. In total, six western European nations held colonies in the Americas, but the Spanish and Portuguese territories were still paramount and together they probably produced the most wealth.

The Europeans were beginning to dominate the Americas, but the stream of influence ran in both directions. Up such rivers as the Thames, Tagus and Loire came a range of new food-plants and medicines from America. Never before in the history of the world had so many valuable plants been transferred from one continent to another.

A SUPERMARKET CROSSES THE ATLANTIC

Maize was the most remarkable of the new plants, and Christopher Columbus himself carried seeds back in his ship. Maize, or Indian corn, had the amazing ability at harvest time to produce, for each grain planted, far more grains than wheat or rye could. Maize did not spread with miraculous speed, but it eventually reached farms in the warmer parts of Europe. By 1700 the tall green stalks of maize could be seen waving in the breeze in much of rural Spain, Portugal and Italy, where they were transforming farming and leading to an increase in population.

The American potato was to northern Europe what maize was to the south. The Irish welcomed the potato, for on their tiny plots of land it grew more calories than any other known crop. It was growing in County Down by 1605, and by the end of that century the hot potato was the chief food of Ireland's poor. From Ireland, curiously, seed potatoes were taken to North America, where this South American food was still unknown. Germans also rejoiced in it, knowing that a crop of potatoes—unlike a crop of ripe corn—was not easily damaged or destroyed by a rampaging army.

In European gardens could also be found other American novelties: the sweet potato, the red capsicum or pepper, the tomato—which was astonishingly slow to please European palates (it was still a novelty in Britain four centuries after Columbus returned)—and the artichoke, which gained in France an early popularity far exceeding that of the tomato. The place of origin of some of these novelties was not recognized by the average gardener, for their names were a camouflage. As French explorers were first to introduce the long thin beans from Canada, they were known in some European lands as French beans. Mystifyingly a new kind of artichoke, also introduced by the French from Canada, was called the Jerusalem artichoke.

Turkey, the only meat to be introduced from the Americas, was equally disguised by its European name. In fact, the names "turkey cock" and "turkey hen" were first given to the exotic guinea fowl seen by European explorers off the west coast of Africa and then were transferred to the tall Mexican birds which eventually reached European farmyards. The turkeys, which strictly speaking should have been called *mexicos*, were popular on Spanish and English dinner tables as early as the Christmas of 1573.

That lands as far apart as Turkey and America should be viewed as the same by cooks in the kitchen was a sign of how much mystery centered on the whereabouts of East and West. Even American maize was called turkey corn or turkey wheat by European peasants who rightly marvelled at these prolific plants unknown to their grandparents. In Holland and England another wonder bulb of this era, the focus of a speculative boom in the 1630s, was initially called the Turk's cap. More formally known as the tulip, it originated—unlike the turkey—in Turkey itself. On the other hand, the tall tulip tree, with its tulip-like flowers, was first found in the moist cold forests of North America.

From the Americas came such delicacies as the pineapple—to be eaten only at the tables of the very rich—and the capsicum pepper, as well as such luxuries as cocoa and tobacco. Like nearly all the transatlantic novelties, tobacco spread slowly across Europe; and two centuries after Columbus's first voyage a typical rural worker in Poland and Sicily probably had not yet sniffed for the first time the sweet aroma of burning tobacco.

The monarchies of Europe were not sure how to handle this new fashion for smoking tobacco in a pipe or sniffing it in the form of snuff. Some kings tried to ban it. In Russia a smoker could be punished by the amputating of his nose. Other countries which held tropical colonies tried to ban the growing of tobacco on their home soil so that it could be grown in their colonies and then imported through a port where a tax could be collected on each lot of tobacco carried ashore. England set up colonies in Virginia and Maryland mainly for the growing of tobacco. France encouraged the growing of tobacco in its own West Indies islands but also permitted it, under strict supervision, in Alsace and a few other home provinces. Distant Turkey was to become one of the most enthusiastic growers of American tobacco which—to increase the confusion— became known as Turkish tobacco!

The traffic in minerals, in the short term, was the most dramatic of all the Atlantic trades. The first prize for the Spaniards in Central and South America was gold and silver. Once they gained full control of their American territories and sent forced labor to work the mines, they would ship home, in heavily armed convoys, so much silver and gold each year that monetary inflation began to convulse Spain and then Europe. There will always be debate about the role of precious metals in igniting Europe's inflation of the 16th century, but one fact seems clear. The dramatic bouts of inflation across the western world have coincided with the fighting of large wars or, even more significantly, a major change in the supply of just two crucial commodities: precious metals in earlier centuries and oil in the inflationary 1970s.

In the early ships which carried precious metals and precious plants and seeds across the Atlantic came another tourist. The disease syphilis almost certainly came from the Americas. There it originated as yaws, which mutated into syphilis. An examination of skeletons in the Americas provides evidence in favor of an American origin. The new disease, once it spread in Europe, was not given an American name. In some parts of southern Europe it was called the Venetian disease—for that luxurious city was viewed suspiciously as the home of licentiousness—and in other lands it was called the Neapolitan disease or the French pox. Syphilis became common in the 1500s; and a gnawed or nibbled appearance of the nose was often a symptom.

A PEACOCKS' PARADE

The European voyages also tapped Asia. For centuries a stream of Asian wares and plants had crossed the width of Asia by land but now it flowed along the sea lanes. Chinese tea found its way to Europe, as did the secret of porcelain and many other manufactures.

Kaolin, the raw material for porcelain, was a word which originally seemed strange to most European ears. The word was actually the name of the hill in China where the soft white clay was mined. Known as k'ao-ling, it produced, in the hands of skilled potters and in their kilns, the first porcelain.

An enterprising French priest sent samples of kaolin to Europe around 1700 and pointed out that it was vital for the manufacture of porcelain. Soon prospectors found similar deposits of kaolin in Germany, France and England. Mixed with water, the clay was molded under pressure into the shapes of cups and plates, and in the high temperature of the kiln they retained their shape. When held aloft the china was translucent. In Europe the first true porcelain was made at the Meissen factory in Saxony in 1707. Later the same kaolin clay was to be used in the making of paper, rubber, paint, ink and other products.

From China came garden flowers new to Europe. The chrysanthemum was a favorite. Solely a yellow flower until the eighth century, it was honored in China as the floral aristocrat, and praised by poets in verse. It adorned the street markets in parts of China after the summer flowers had passed their prime. The petals of another species were not only admired but turned into a wine which was ceremonially drunk on the ninth day of the ninth lunar month. By the year 1600 the Chinese had bred some 500 varieties, of which a few reached Europe in the new wave of floral imports.

The fact that so many popular western flowers originated in China was sometimes obscured by the new names assigned to them in the course of their westward journey. Thus the Chinese origins of the common camellia, first seen in England in the year 1702, were concealed by its botanical name, *Camellia japonica*, which suggested Japan. Curiously the word "camellia" was even more of a smokescreen, for it derived from the surname of Father G. J. Kamel, a Czech priest who served in the Philippines and lent his name to the novel flower.

The New World also gave to eager Europeans a delight which was not common. It gave them bright colors. As late as the year 1500, most cities and villages had been drab in their colors. A cottage might be whitewashed but rarely was it painted. Timber houses looked drab, though in Holland the bricks then in favor emitted a cosy red glow. Admittedly stone houses could be enhanced by the color of the stone, but the building stone was usually chosen not for color but convenience. In many cities the stone was naturally dark, and over the years even pale stone was slowly discolored by wood smoke—a foretaste of what coal smoke would do more thoroughly. Admittedly in some medieval cathedrals the stained glass was beautiful when the sun was shining, but the color was heightened because so much in the city streets was dull.

Europeans' clothes were usually drab, except those worn by the rich. Goods were not packed in bright colors because any form of wrapping was expensive, and wrapping paper was a sheer extravagance and never colored. Banners and flags were attractive because they were far richer in color than the clothes worn by most citizens. In Europe some of the wonder of spring came from the fact that winter was dark and gloomy and suddenly here was a blue sky, dazzlingly white clouds, green grass and trees in blossom.

It was the ancient Phoenicians who found, in a species of shellfish in the eastern Mediterranean, a purple color which was so rare and brilliant as to be chosen as a royal color. The Roman Empire supported many dyeing workshops, one of which has been excavated at Pompeii. Most of the dyes commonly used in Europe came from local plants such as woad and madder, but the range of colors was limited, the process of dyeing was expensive and beyond the income of the poor, and sometimes the dye on the linen and wool did not last long.

One of the miracles from the newfound Americas was new colors. Mexicans, long before the coming of the Spaniards, had observed how a wingless insect, feeding on the cactus plant, contained when pregnant a vivid scarlet color. The dried bodies of 70,000 insects were required to produce just half a kilogram of cochineal powder; and this powder, when treated with ingenuity, produced a variety of colors ranging from crimson to carmine. In the early 1600s, Cornelis Drebbel, a Dutchman working in London, found that the dissolving of pewter in nitric acid produced a mordant which enabled cochineal to create the most vivid of dyes. Scarlet had long been the name of a color used for banners and clothes, but the scarlet freshly made in England from cochineal dazzled the eye. The new scarlet became a buzzword, and was even conferred on scarlet fever, which in the 1670s was first diagnosed as a disease in its own right rather than a form of measles or smallpox. Likewise the cochineal color entered the palate of artists, enabling them to paint landscapes with such watercolors as purple lake, crimson lake, Florentine lake and carmine.

The sea route around Africa opened up a cheap source of the color blue. Indigo, the plant from which the best blue was extracted, was farmed in Bengal. Cut in the fields and carted in bundles to the drying yards and water tanks, the indigo plant released its indoxyl by a process of fermentation. For many centuries small and expensive consignments of Indian indigo dye had occasionally reached the Mediterranean by the overland route, but now it began to arrive in thousands of wooden chests stowed in Dutch and Portuguese ships. Additional supplies soon came from plantations in Spanish America where the indigo plant had been transplanted. In Europe indigo, now much cheaper, was seized on with delight by hundreds of workshops which laboriously dyed textiles and clothes. Indigo produced such a brilliant blue that the blue color traditionally extracted from the European woad plant seemed dull. Soon, in the more fashionable precincts of Amsterdam and Venice, men and women wearing coats and hats, capes and tunics of bright indigo blue paraded themselves like peacocks.

The woad industry, employing thousands of European farmers and carters, resented this Indian intruder which threatened their livelihood. At Frankfurt in 1577 the German Diet banned the importing of this "devil's dye," and France copied the edict. Ultimately the intruder was victorious over the simple woad plant and showed the extent of its victory by disporting itself not only in blue but in other combinations devised by ingenious dyers, including an indigo red and an indigo brown. Even the French army abandoned its russet uniforms and dressed in blue.

From tropical America came logwood, soon to be a vital source of black dyestuffs. When a tree was chopped down there was exposed an inner wood, darkish red in color and smelling faintly like a violet that had been freshly picked. In European dyehouses the logwood produced a dye which was increasingly used to blacken woollen and cotton cloth. No dye could surpass it in cheapness until the synthetic dyes made from coal tar stormed the market in the 19th century.

Colors may seem to be a mirror of the vanities, but they were central to the rise of Brazil, now one of the most populous nations. The Portuguese were the first to assess the coast of Brazil. Thirteen of their ships, sailing towards the southern tip of Africa and so on to India, were deflected by the tropical winds to the coast of Brazil, where they spent a week in April 1500. Thereafter Portuguese ships occasionally used Brazilian harbors as a halfway house on the long Indian route. They carried away Brazilian people, monkeys and parrots in small numbers—as captives and curiosities—but their main prize was the logwood tree. It was so valued in Europe that it led directly to the opening of the port of

Pernambuco where, protected by a coral reef, Portuguese ships could safely anchor. A lesser variety of the tree grew in the East Indies, and was already known as brazilwood. So the land of Brazil received its new name.

The brazilwood tree, not at all glamorous with its crooked trunk and prickly leaves, grew in dry and often rocky soil near the Atlantic coast. Stripped of its thick bark and soaked in a tub of water, the inner wood produced a red color known sometimes as the juice of Brazil. The juice, prized by dyers in Europe, was applied to wool, cotton and silk. Like experienced chefs, the dyers devised their own recipes. With the aid of numerous boilings and dryings of the wood, various incantations and the adding of a dose of stale urine or ox gall, they brought forth a variety of reds, scarlets and purples.

The French wished to share in the precious woods and were the first to settle beside the wonderful harbor of Rio de Janeiro, there depositing an uneasy mixture of Catholics and Protestants from Geneva. Their settlement of Henryville finally fell to the Portuguese in 1560 and henceforth the French tongue was rarely heard along the Brazilian coast. Steadily sugar plantations, worked by African slaves, replaced the brazilwood trees in economic importance, and Brazil by 1640 was the world's main producer of sugar.

MUSK, OPIUM, CLOVES:
DOSES OF EXCITEMENT

Many tiny packages, boxes and casks came in the new cargoes to European warehouses and were deemed as precious as gold. From China came caddies containing small quantities of that precious ingredient of medicine, perfume and the art of embalming—musk. Dry and light, dark in color, it sometimes resembled dried blood in appearance. Cut from a sac in the abdomen of a small male deer that flourished in the mountains of central Asia, it was sewn up in a small skin by Canton operators, but some traders were known to adulterate it and then sew up the sac again. In the era of few painkillers, musk induced drowsiness. The first edition of a celebrated encyclopaedia vowed that it was better than opium, for it did not leave an aftermath of "stupor or languidness." By the 17th century the Chinese were importing from the west opium itself, which they smoked in pipes or consumed as a pain-stifling medicine. Imports were so strong that in 1729 the Emperor of China tried to ban the smoking of opium, a ban which failed to halt the inflow of opium extracted from poppies specially grown in British India for the illicit Canton market.

Everywhere the market for new medicines was large. Europe then suffered much from malaria, and in the marshes of Italy it was virulent. A cure was offered by the bark of a Peruvian bush, the *cinchona*. The Spaniards were slow to realize the bark's merits, and did not send samples of it to Europe until 1633. Mainly imported by Catholic priests, it was at first known as Jesuit's bark. That the crucial ingredient in the bark was quinine was discovered by the French during the time of the Napoleonic Wars.

In Europe cloves from the Indonesian archipelago were prized as a medicine, especially for toothache, as well as a spicer of food and drink. The fruit of a majestic evergreen tree, cloves first saw the light as flower buds before changing their color to green and then to a vivid red. Reaching the market in the shape of small dark-brown tacks or nails, with a hot taste and a fragrant smell, cloves were snapped up by traders. The Dutch, eager to corner the world's valuable market for cloves, permitted it to grow in only five islands near Amboina (Ambon). In the year 1667 alone they planted 120,000 clove trees on Amboina and busily uprooted thousands of clove trees on other islands. Likewise they tried to confine the nutmeg tree to the Banda Islands, in the hope that a monopoly could be created.

In the eyes of most merchants, pepper was the prize in South-East Asia. A creeper that clung to the branches of trees, its berries were picked when bright red and then spread on mats under the hot sun, where they were allowed to shrivel and become black. From the west coast of India and from Sumatra, pepper was shipped increasingly to the markets of Amsterdam and Antwerp. It was so costly that in many European kitchens it was kept in a tightly guarded wooden pepperbox shaped like a cylinder. Only a small box was needed, and the powdered pepper was sprinkled on special meats as meticulously as if it were gold dust. William Shakespeare's nimble mind once selected the typical pepperbox as the image with which to portray a hiding place that was so tiny as to be laughable: "Hee cannot creep into a halfe-penny purse, nor into a Pepper-boxe." Once the spice of the well-to-do, pepper became less expensive and its consumption soared. Eventually, like many items of food that were once expensive, pepper lost some of its glamour as it became cheaper.

From the east the Europeans were more likely to carry home exotic foods than recipes. And yet some recipes travelled, and chefs as well. In the port of Macao, close to Canton, Chinese cooks were purchased and then shipped to kitchens in Portuguese Goa and even to Lisbon, where by 1600 a Chinese cook was no longer such a curiosity. His face might be stared at, but his meals were marvelled at.

Not only the meal table of the wealthier Europeans but also the face of agriculture itself was being altered. The voyages of Columbus, Vasco da Gama and other European sailors across the Atlantic, Indian and Pacific oceans promoted a revolution in the world's agriculture. Alongside the cargoes stowed on deck or locked below were small consignments of seeds and seedlings which eventually were carried, by a series of deliberate and chance happenings, to every continent. Coffee, cotton, sugar and indigo plants went to the Americas to be grown on a large scale, with their harvests being exported to Europe. From America the returning slave ships carried across the Atlantic seeds, tubers and cuttings which were the nucleus of what became extensive crops of maize and sweet potatoes and cassava in African valleys and plains.

The horses and mules shipped on deck in small numbers from ports such as Lisbon and Bristol transformed the carriage of goods in the Americas and even the daily life of the native Americans on the plains. To Argentina went cattle and to Australia went sheep, and ultimately the one land held more cattle and the other held more sheep than had been pastured on any land in Europe. Cocoa had been first grown in Mexico, but soon the Spanish were growing it in plantations in Venezuela and the French and the British were growing it in the West Indies, for the habit of drinking sugared chocolate was spreading from Spain across Europe. Cloves were grown not just in Dutch Indonesia but eventually in Zanzibar and on the island of Réunion. Many valuable plants, native only to one region of the globe, were treated as if they were a precious patent, but soon the monopoly was broken. Agricultural espionage is an older profession than industrial espionage. In the space of three centuries, dozens of useful plants went to far-off lands.

A similar transfer of plants and animals had happened again and again in the distant past, whether 10,000 years ago in Asia Minor, 5,000 years ago in northern Europe or in the early Christian era in central Asia.

But this latest exchange spanned much of the surface of the earth and was conducted with unprecedented speed.

Here was an early version of the information revolution, rather slow, with the erratic sailing ships serving as a lifeline along which was carried an incredibly small number of seeds, seedlings and breeding animals. Its effects were only slowly appreciated. Nobody in 1492 could have predicted what had been unleashed, nor could they—200 years later—predict what was still to be unleashed. The same unpredictability was to be true of the steam revolution, and is probably true of the information revolution in which satellites and computers, fiber optics, microchips and the fax and Internet were driving forces in 2000. A remarkable journey had been commenced but nobody knew where it would end.

New lands became dominant in producing once-unfamiliar crops, ranging from coffee and sugar and potatoes to indigo, cotton and tobacco. A global market in foods and fibers was developing. A semi-global network of finance was emerging, in which prices and interest rates dominated the scoreboard, and merchants in Amsterdam and London collectively exercised an economic influence exceeding that of individual monarchs. The economy of the 20th century could sometimes be glimpsed in the future.

CARNAGE AND EXTINCTION

During the expansion of Europe and the swift international interchange of plants and raw materials, casualties arose. Many birds, animals and plants were endangered by the arrival of new people, new animals and new guns and snares. The uninhabited tropical islands of the Indian Ocean and the sparsely inhabited plains of the Americas were especially vulnerable.

On the volcanic islands of Mauritius and Réunion had lived for countless years a flightless bird, the dodo. A member of the pigeon family, big and docile, with thick horny legs and white feathers and an unusual head, the bird lived safely, assailed by no predators. Its body was so large that, when plucked, it would not have fitted into a domestic cooking oven. Fortunately there were no ovens and no people on these islands, which lay far out in the Indian Ocean. Then the European explorers arrived, bringing pigs and rats. The eggs laid by the dodo in nests on the ground were vulnerable. The population of the birds quickly fell, and their final decline was hastened by the capturing of specimens which were taken home for naturalists and sensation-seekers to marvel at.

The last-known dodo, caught on the island of Réunion, is said to have died in a French ship sometime before 1746. The phrase "dead as a dodo" became a synonym for extinction. In every region of the New World a variety of species, whether the passenger pigeon of North America or the marsupial striped "tiger" of Tasmania, went the way of the dodo.

22

THE GLASS EYE OF SCIENCE

SCIENCE was stirring itself in Europe. Ceasing to crawl, it began to walk and even to run. It was running for some time before it passed China in most fields, but by the 1520s there were strong signs of its gathering speed. The same printing presses which were expounding Luther were explaining the latest discoveries of science. The printed page travelled with ease, whereas the typical European scholar did not. Most of Europe's famous scientists of 1550 had never met most of their foreign contemporaries face to face, even when they lived only a few hundred kilometers apart.

Each decade was now studded with innovations in science and technology. The 1540s was like a launching pad. In 1542 Andreas Vesalius published his eye-opening book on anatomy. In 1543 Copernicus explained his sensational ideas on astronomy, while Georgius Agricola published a pioneering work on geology in 1544. One year later Ambroise Paré increased the skills of surgeons by expounding his novel ideas on the treatment for gunshot wounds. In the following year Gerhardus Mercator announced that the earth has a magnetic pole. It was in this decade that the Italian city of learning, Padua, made two innovations in the study of medicine by opening the first theatre for anatomy and the first botanical or herbal garden; herbs were still an integral part of medicine.

New advances came from studying the sun and earth and stars. In this field the mighty discoverer was Nicolaus Copernicus, a Polish scholar, who used all his powers of measuring and observing as well as that uncommon activity known as "thinking" to prove that the sun was at the center of the universe. He dethroned the planet earth, a victory so momentous that it seemed at first to challenge the Bible and the very essence of Christianity, which saw the earth as the center of the universe.

Copernicus began to dethrone the earth in about 1510, soon after Columbus and his voyages of discovery had enlarged it. The victory of Copernicus, however, was not assured even after he died in 1543. In a sense his insight is only half-grasped even today. Common speech and poetic imagery still imply that the earth is the center of the universe. Each morning, in the mind's eye, it is the sun that rises and not the earth that sets.

An emphasis on measurement and observation, indeed a whole new scientific method, drove these advances. Anatomy gained from the new eagerness of Italian medical schools to dissect the human body rather than rely on what old Greek scholars had written. The Christian embargo on dissecting a body was eased. An autopsy had even been sanctioned on the body of Pope Alexander V after his mysterious death in 1410. The brilliant young Flemish doctor Vesalius frequently dissected bodies, and at the University of Padua he taught his bold findings in the 1540s. He rewrote the old anatomy books. In the same university the Italian anatomist Gabriele Falloppio discovered the tubes linking each ovary with the uterus. His brief career illustrates how certain intellectual disciplines and trades, now apart, were once linked. In Padua he was not only professor of anatomy and director of the botanical gardens but the practical maker of a new contraceptive: a condom made from pigs' intestines.

The wave of discoveries, made on many scientific fronts, were the work of hundreds of hobby scientists, stargazers, medical men, and clergymen with an hour to spare. Most of these scientists would now be called amateurs, but the best had the brilliance of a modern star. Many were all-rounders who were intent on solving a cluster of intellectual riddles. Thus Isaac Newton, who was acclaimed in his lifetime as the greatest of all physicists, investigated theology, chemistry, astrology, astronomy and the making of telescopes as well as the laws of motion and gravity. Rarely in the 16th and 17th centuries were famous scientists full-time investigators, and rarely did they live long lives. Isaac Newton was unusual in that he lived into his eighties, at which time he possessed all but one of his teeth and an eyesight so keen that he needed no spectacles. Such was his versatility that he could have made his own spectacles.

A breakthrough in science is said by some observers to be no more than the application of common sense, but several of these theories seemed to defy the common sense of their time, both the spiritual and the secular versions of common sense, and so were not readily accepted. Many discoverers wisely hesitated to publicize what they had found, whereas today's discoverers are tempted to leap into print without a day's delay. Copernicus spent one-third of a century nursing his central idea before he was persuaded to entrust it to a book. Newton is said to have glimpsed his major discovery in physics while watching an apple fall from a tree in an English garden in 1666, but 21 years passed before he expounded his theory in print. William Harvey, the English physician who discovered that the blood perpetually circulated, lectured about his discovery for a dozen or more years before he put it on paper in 1628, publishing it not in London but in a German city.

While the printer disseminated many of the discoveries, the priest and parson were tempted to impede them. Religious leaders opposed or were highly suspicious of several revolutionary ideas in science. The very idea that natural laws, hitherto unknown, operated in the universe, and that similar laws might be found to be operating in the human as well as the physical realm, was a potential danger to a religion which preached that God, all-wise and all-knowing, presided over every corner of the world and could suspend natural laws and work miracles. Even China, which was sympathetic in most eras to most sciences, set up religious obstacles to the investigating of the stars, for the stars gave rise to predictions, which were a prerogative of the emperor.

In Europe the Protestants on the whole were slightly less hostile to new science; and they helped England, once a weakling in the realm of learning, to become a leader. Century after century Britain's minor Protestant sects provided a haven for some great scientists who were unorthodox in religion. Thus Isaac Newton and Joseph Priestley, the discoverer of oxygen, were Unitarians; and in the 19th century Michael Faraday, a theoretical pioneer of electricity, was a devout worshipper in the tiny Glassite sect. In contrast, Spain, whose mental climate was hardly a hothouse for science, produced more saints than scientists. And yet scientists were needed to explore and explain the wonders of the new lands unlocked by Spain. Its king was so keen to recruit the famous Swedish botanist Linnaeus that in 1755 he even promised him the freedom to practice his Lutheran religion in Madrid.

GLASS AND THE TRANSPLANTED EYE

The scientific revolution was a marvellous advance in the way the world was *seen*. Whereas, before 1550, the skilled worker in metals was responsible for such advances as the mechanical clock and the printing press, it was the skilled worker in glass who facilitated such later discoveries as the microscope and telescope. Glass became the scientist's transplanted eye for seeing the invisible.

The ancient Egyptians had produced the first vessels of hollow glass. The Syrians invented the blowpipe for blowing glass into round thin-walled vessels in about 200 BC, and the Romans manufactured a rough glass which was usually a little muddy but at its best was clear. The Romans could manufacture a mirror—it stems from a Latin word meaning "to admire"—but as a means of acquainting a child with its face, the Roman mirrors were not much clearer than a still pool of dark water.

It was Venice, the silicon valley of its era, which improved on the old Roman methods of making glass. The glassmakers of Venice had become so numerous, and the fires burning in their workshops posed such a danger of setting fire to the whole city, that in 1291 the government moved them to the adjacent island of Murano. The first mirrors or looking glasses of any clarity were made in Venice about 1500, and the Venetians kept secret their novel process of manufacture for more than 150 years. Whereas the Romans backed their mirror glass with lead, the Venetians used an amalgam of mercury and tin. The mercury was not favorable to the health of the glassworkers but the mirrors themselves were eye-openers. Mirrors did more than anything to enhance Venice's reputation as the home of luxurious, vain and maybe immoral feminine wares: a reputation already created by Venetian gloves, fans and those embroidered Venetian breeches which tightly fitted the legs.

A revolution in science was also in the hands of the glassmakers. The power of curved glass to magnify an object under examination had been known even before the rise of Greek civilization; but specific glass lenses for use in spectacles and reading glasses were not invented until about 1300. Spectacles preserved in the Deutsches Museum in Munich date from 50 years later; and it was possible for a physician doing his painful duty during the Black Death to put on his spectacles in order to examine more closely the skin and tongue of victims. Just over a century later the German city of Nuremberg was a gathering place for the makers of spectacles. The reading glass was bringing contentment to more and more people whose eyesight was dim; and when printed books came into vogue the demand for spectacles increased, especially amongst men and women who wished to read in the poor light of a northern European winter.

The illuminating power of glass was dramatically revealed in the seafaring town of Middelburg in the Netherlands. In 1608 Hans Lippershey, a maker of spectacles, began to construct useful telescopes. To the astonishment of those who employed his telescope, they could clearly see a person standing 3 kilometers away. The instrument was a boon for military men, sea captains, merchants and scientists. The idea but not the telescope reached Galileo Galilei, who was teaching mathematics at Padua in northern Italy. Making his own version of what he called a "spy glass," he was delighted to find that it could magnify by a ratio of three. Grinding his own glass lenses he increased the ratio of magnification to eight and then 32.

In the nearby city of Venice, merchants and shipowners carried the exciting telescope to the top of towers and, looking out to sea, saw ships which were invisible to the naked eye. As one ship arriving with a large cargo could dramatically affect the prices of the pepper and other wares it carried, the possessor of a telescope could make money by speculating on the strength of commercial knowledge which only he possessed. The telescope was a clever instrument for what now might be almost called "insider trading."

Galileo's improved telescope was achieving in the skies what Columbus and Magellan had done by sailing the seas: it was mapping new worlds. Through his telescopes, mostly made from Venetian glass, Galileo inspected the moon, which he described as a "most beautiful and delightful sight." He also detected what nobody else had seen—the moon's craters and unpolished surface. He discovered four new planets, was the first to see the spots on the sun, and found that the Milky Way consisted of stars.

He also came to the same conclusion as Copernicus: that the earth was not the center of the universe to which every other heavenly body paid court. This insight carried profound implications for certain sentences in the Old Testament which Galileo denounced as written by the ignorant for the ignorant. The church raised a heavy hand against him in 1616 and an even heavier hand after he persisted with his theories. He spent the last eight years of his life under house arrest on his little farm near Florence.

To the telescope, the Dutch and Italian glassworkers added the microscope. Anton van Leeuwenhoek, who sold dress materials and clothes in the Dutch town of Delft, became a master maker of microscopes. With a magnification of at least 270, his microscopes saw far more than had ever been seen by human eyes. In 1677 he described for the first time the spermatozoon. He described with accuracy the red blood cell. His microscope enabled him to puncture various widely held myths: that the flea was born out of sand and that the eel was hatched out of dew. One of his most useful finds was that a flying insect laid the eggs that produced the weevils which ruined wheat and flour held in storage. Meanwhile in England, Robert Hooke, while looking at plant tissues under the microscope, coined the crucial word "cell." It was not yet realized that all plants and animals consisted of cells.

The microscope was an eye-opener for botany and zoology. At the very time when the exploring of new lands multiplied known plants and animals, the Swedish botanist and physician Carolus Linnaeus turned all his attention to plants. Even when he was only eight he was known as "the little botanist." In 1732, at the age of 25, he set out to explore parts of Lapland, where he marvelled at its plants. In the following 20 years he devised and perfected his method—soon to be the whole world's method—of classifying all living things by giving them two Latin names, the one specifying the broad genus and the other the particular species.

What Linnaeus did for the classifying of plants, other scientists, south of the Alps, achieved in the classifying of time. The reform of the calendar was a snail-like process. In the heyday of Rome, Julius Caesar and his advisers had reformed the calendar by abandoning the cycle of the moon and turning to the solar year. The solar year extends over 365 days, five hours, and 48 and three-quarter minutes; but those overhanging hours created a difficulty for the new calendar. Julius Caesar adopted a sensible compromise. His calendar, later named Julian in his honor, assumed for the sake of simplicity that the sun ran its annual course in 365 and a quarter days. Accordingly it counted 365 days for every first and second and third year, and 366 days for every fourth or leap year.

Caesar died long before the inherent difficulty of his calendar became prominent. The awkward fact was that his calendar in each succeeding century fell a little further behind. Indeed in each year the calendar lost just over 11 minutes and in its initial 1,000 years it lost about seven days. It also interfered with the fixing of Easter Sunday, an event unknown in Julius Caesar's time, but later of profound importance.

At last, in 1582, Pope Gregory XIII acted decisively. Using the computations of the Naples astronomer and medical man Luigi Ghiraldi, the pope announced his solution. In that very year he would eliminate the 10 days running from 5 to 14 October. In short, the calendar would be brought up to date with one stroke of a quill pen. The future would also be handled with the same decisiveness. As a long-term corrective the new Gregorian calendar would embrace a leap year in 1600 and 2000, though not in the intervening years of 1700, 1800 and 1900.

Those living in Spain, Portugal and Italy would long discuss the memorable October of 1582. Ten days, to their puzzlement, simply vanished from their life. A few months later France and the various Catholic states of Germany lost their 10 days. Protestant countries, however, were not sure whether they should follow a reform initiated by a pope. England continued to follow a different calendar to that which prevailed in Catholic France and Spain. When it was Christmas Day in England it was already January on the other side of the English Channel. In Germany two towns only a few kilometers apart followed a different calendar, depending on whether they lived within a Lutheran or a Catholic state. In 1700, after more than a century of confusion, the German states agreed to share the Gregorian calendar.

When Britain at last adopted this new calendar, 11 unlived days had to be deleted. Thus in 1752 its calendar jumped overnight from 2 September to 14 September, a change that made for dislocation in many quarters and consternation in others. In London a mob in an understandable state of confusion was heard to chant: "Give us back our eleven days." Russia and several other nations within the Eastern or Orthodox church continued to follow the old calendar. Russia was to wait until the year of its communist revolution, 1917, to adopt what the pope and Italy had initiated more than three centuries earlier.

The search for new ways of counting and measuring was hastened by the variations and confusion in the existing ways of measurement. In weighing goods the regions of Europe used varying measures, as did

China and India. The measuring of a mile was a subject of argument and doubt whenever a border of European lands was crossed by a traveller. An English mile was 1,760 yards, an Italian mile was 2,029 yards, an Irish mile was 3,038, a German mile was 8,116, and the Swedish mile exceeded 10,000 yards.

At least hot and cold were now measured with more precision, though not with total agreement. In 1714 Gabriel Fahrenheit, a Baltic inhabitant who became a maker of instruments in Holland, invented the mercury thermometer. On his scale the boiling point was pegged at 212 degrees, but a few decades later a new scale was invented by the Swedish astronomer Anders Celsius, who set his boiling point at 100 degrees. These disagreements were aggravated in 1799 when revolutionary France introduced the metric system of weights and measures, with its simple logic and its verbose names.

Builders and engineers, like the makers of instruments, experimented. Iron was taken up by builders. On the south coast of England the Eddystone Rocks, lying near the sea lanes and the major port of Plymouth, were a hazard for sailing ships; and a lighthouse was declared to be vital. As a lighthouse was not easily built on such a stormy ledge, perhaps iron might do what stone and wood alone could not. In 1699 Henry Winstanley fixed iron stanchions to the partly submerged rock itself, and on the stanchions he built a wooden tower with stairways, balcony, weathervane and turret. An ornate building, it resembled a private grandstand surrounded by wild sea. In 1703 Winstanley was marooned in his tower during a storm, and he and the tower vanished into the sea. But it was a foretaste of the many new areas in which iron could excel, and by the end of the century England was building iron bridges and iron engines.

The scientific method was welcomed by a few German theologians and employed to impugn such miracles as Noah's Ark, which had supposedly been built when a great flood was about to endanger all living things. Similarly, many traditional churchmen began to use a similar technique to try to defend the authenticity of the Ark. The first edition of the *Encyclopaedia Britannica*, published in Edinburgh in 1771, included a long article defending the Ark. It was depicted as a three-decker ship built of cypress and capable of serving as a floating wildlife sanctuary. The lowest deck was for the beasts, the middle deck was for the foodstuffs they would eat in the course of one year, and the top deck was shared by cages or spaces for the birds and a kind of penthouse built for the eight members of the Noah family. One nagging doubt was whether the Ark would have had enough room to hold specimens of all the world's living creatures. The encyclopaedia reached a reassuring conclusion which would surprise those who marvel at the diversity of nature in the whole world: "the number of species of animals will be found much less than is generally imagined, not amounting to an hundred species of quadrupeds, nor to two hundred of birds."

IN SEARCH OF VENUS

James Cook's first voyage of exploration in the Indian and Pacific oceans was driven by the demands of science. It was confidently predicted that on 3 June 1769 the planet Venus would briefly cross the face of the sun. Here was a rare chance to learn the exact distance of the sun from the earth—a calculation which, if accurate, would provide vital information for astronomers as well as for ships trying to learn their exact position at sea. On this day of the transit, however, it was possible that the sky might be clouded in Europe, and so the chance to observe would be lost. The decision to seize this opportunity to observe Venus was intensified by the knowledge that the transit would not happen again until 1874.

Britain decided that the most promising place to observe the transit of Venus was on the newfound island of Tahiti, where it was assumed with cheerful optimism that the sky was always clear. The voyage to Tahiti in the far Pacific was meticulously planned. Perhaps the boldest scientific expedition the world had known, a minor foretaste of the moon probes of the 1960s, it was staffed by a tiny team of scientists more talented probably than any previous team which had been assembled for a long expedition. In his ship *Endeavour* James Cook prepared room for an artist—accurate artists were in effect the "photographers" of the era—and the finest collection of astronomical and navigation instruments ever to leave Europe. With him sailed the dashing young English botanist Joseph Banks and his coterie of servants, and the Swedish botanist Daniel Solander. With him went the finest glass telescopes and the finest mechanical clock. Science was the first-class passenger in Cook's wooden ship.

In due course the ship reached Tahiti. A portable observatory was erected, the instruments of science were cleaned and assembled, and the observations were made on the day of days. A haze around the sun, however, made them of little use.

Cook then proceeded to carry out his instructions to search for the great south land which, it was believed, must surely lie somewhere in the vastness of the Pacific Ocean. It had long been an article of faith that to maintain the sheer balance of the ever-spinning globe there must be an equal amount of land in the Southern as in the Northern Hemisphere. Somewhere a continent must lie, hidden. The theory was incorrect, but the conclusion culled from it turned out, by accident, to be correct. Australia was the missing continent, and Cook first saw it at daylight on 20 April 1770.

In fact, various Portuguese, Dutch and British sailors had already seen—or been wrecked upon—parts of the south, west and north shores of Australia. It was Cook who found the more attractive eastern coast where most Australians live today. In company with Joseph Banks he so praised its grasslands, soil, fish, natural vegetation and harbors that it was later seen by Britain as a promising site for a colony.

After returning to England, Cook sailed again to southern seas. At high risk to his two wooden ships he sailed south to the wild seas and winds beyond the Antarctic Circle. In three successive summers, he sailed closer than any previous navigator to that frozen continent. Again and again he found bays of ice, actually sailing into them in the hope that he might find land at the far end. At Christmas 1772, almost the warmest time of the Antarctic year, his sailors' hands were numb when they tried to tie and untie the ropes. A gale brought sleet and snow which froze the sails. Below deck the ship's tailors were busy making caps of red baize for the sailors and lengthening the sleeves of their jackets so that their lower arms could be protected from the bleak weather. Cook persisted in his belief that beyond the ice lay land—if only he could find a channel by which to reach it.

Without knowing it, Cook sailed right around Antarctica. Indeed, the sea of floating ice was so hazardous that he thought no other ships would ever venture further south. Eventually he returned to England, where his reports of the swarms of fur seals living on islands nearby helped to spur expeditions of sealers and whalers who further explored these seas in later decades. The actual land of the Antarctic, beyond the ramparts of ice, was not sighted until 1820, and decades passed before the jigsaw of the long coastline of icy cliffs was pieced together. Here was an area of land larger than the United States, covered with thick ice and topped by mountains rising even higher than the European Alps. Slowly it would be realized that this vast refrigerator of a continent had profound effects on the level of the world's seas and on the winds and climates of a vast area of the Southern Hemisphere.

Cook was a true child of the new age of measurement. On this second voyage he carried the novel chronometer, an accurate and delicate watch invented by James Harrison. Cook was the first navigator and explorer to be able to calculate accurately, in all weathers, the position of his ship on an east–west line: in short, he could determine his longitude. When mapping new lands and reefs, he made charts of unprecedented accuracy.

In making several of the longest voyages in human history, Cook harnessed the latest medical knowledge. He suspected that a shipboard diet consisting of nothing but flour, salted meat and a daily ration of spirits was itself the cause of the scurvy that caused pain, debilitation or even death on long ocean voyages. In sympathy with this age of science, he resolved that whenever his ship entered a harbor he would search for fresh greens and other vegetables which might remedy what is now known to be a deficiency of vitamin C. In New Zealand he collected leaves and cabbage-palm hearts, and with the twigs and leaves of a native spruce he brewed a beer for his sailors. They were unusually healthy because he took care.

In 1776, James Cook prepared for his third voyage into the cold extremes of the Pacific Ocean. The north end of the Pacific was almost as mysterious as its southerly or Antarctic end. Like other sailors and merchants Cook held the hope that to the north of the present Canada he might discover the "north-west passage," a route which, if it were free of ice during the summer, would be a short cut linking western Europe and China. Such a route would supplant the incredibly long, slow and stormy sea voyage around Cape Horn. Cook failed to discover the north-west passage, but it did exist in ice-blocked form and was first traversed by an oil tanker about 200 years later.

Captain Cook realized that the Pacific Ocean, which for so long had been unknown in Europe, was almost becoming the Europeans' own toy harbor. The Spanish held most of the Pacific coast of America, the Dutch held the Indonesian archipelago, and the Spanish held the Philippines. Even the Russians, in their slow expansion eastward across Asia, were assembling a loosely held colonial empire which extended all the way from Moscow to the shores of the northern Pacific, where the chill Siberian port of Okhotsk was the empire's most easterly town. Now, through Cook's explorations, there was the prospect that the British might found their own Pacific colony in eastern Australia.

Cook's voyages into the Pacific and Indian oceans were in effect like switching on a time machine. Many Pacific islands, settled by the sea-skilled Polynesians in the course of several thousand years, had remained in isolation until Cook arrived. At such strange meetings between such different peoples and cultures there was bound to be some puzzlement and suspicion, even with goodwill on both sides. Captain Cook, normally tactful in his contacts with native peoples, was the victim of a misunderstanding. In 1779 in Hawaii he was clubbed to death.

23

DETHRONING THE HARVEST

In Europe and Asia, the typical family lived close to the breadline. Whether in 1500 or 1800, in France or in China, most families either owned no land or such a small holding that it could barely feed them even in a prolific year. Countless males and unmarried females left their tiny farm or their rural village to work on other farms or at other trades. Often they received free meals while on the job, and those meals represented a considerable part of their earnings.

Much of the rural work fell to women or young children: the weeding of gardens and crops, the shepherding of geese, the carrying of water from the well to the house, the spinning of fibers and making of cloth, the brewing of homemade beer, the foraging for the herbs that served as medicines, and the gathering of firewood for the stove and manure for the garden.

Scavenging and foraging were almost a way of life. A peasant owning one cow and a tiny pocket of land might send his children out each day in summer to cut grass on the roadside, some of which was preserved as hay to feed the cow in the winter. In forests mushrooms and wild berries were sought, and birds' eggs were collected. In many parts of China the population of birds declined, so intensive was the use of land and so eager were the hunters of birds and the collectors of eggs. Daily life, in every part of the world, centered on the production of food.

In 1800, in the whole world, a few millions were still nomadic hunters and gatherers but most were farmers. Their daily life was ruled by the sun and the rain. From the shores of the South China Sea to the shores of the lakes of inland America the triumphant event of the economic calendar was the bringing home of the harvest, a task performed by women and children and men because, once the grain was ripe, all hands were needed to reap it and bind it and carry it to a place of storage. In most parts of the world, though not in the fertile tropical valleys of Asia, the harvest was a once-a-year event.

Grain dominated the meal table to a degree which is now unimaginable in a prosperous country. Much of the grain was eaten as bread or damper but some found its way into mouths in the form of porridge and soup. Gruel, served piping hot, was eagerly devoured in winter. In hungry times, water was plentifully added to a small amount of flour in order to give temporary relief from hunger. One homespun recipe for gruel was "nine grits and a gallon of water." In Russia and Poland the *kasha*, a gruel made from rye, was thin and watery after the leaner harvests.

In many European lands the grain, especially barley, was also used for brewing beer. In England home-brewed beer, drunk at nearly every meal, was almost as essential as bread in the daily diet. Children drank it each day. At a well-known boarding school in London in 1704 breakfast for the boys consisted of bread and beer, while the poor people living at the workhouse received beer at nearly every meal. Tea, widely drunk in China, was a drink only for the well-off in Europe. Coffee was also a luxury, except in such coffee-growing lands as Arabia and Brazil.

In Europe and Asia the various grains must have provided more than 80 per cent of the diet of a typical household. In Europe the bakehouse in the village street was in effect a simple supermarket with two kinds of bread for sale. Dearest was a loaf of wheaten bread, baked from almost-pure flour, while the cheaper loaves consisted of bran and second-rate grain. Bread was the "staff of life"; and some bakers were tempted to adulterate it or to sell loaves that were less than the official weight. Their bread being central to daily existence, bakers were often controlled by special laws, and could be hanged for selling underweight bread. The price of bread was often the barometer of social stability. A rise in the price of bread often denoted the likelihood of unrest.

The failure or half-failure of a harvest was frequent all the way from Sudan to China. In Finland in the early 1690s a long famine killed one-third of the people. France, which in a lush year could almost overflow with cream and honey, suffered a nationwide famine in 16 of the 100 years after 1700. That century which ended in revolution was probably the worst for harvests since the 11th century.

The coming harvest was often mentioned in the prayers of young unmarried women. If the harvest was plentiful, their long-planned marriage was likely to take place. If the harvest was lean, the marriage was postponed. Women in western Europe did not usually marry until they were aged 24 or 26. Late marriage was the main reason why a typical woman gave birth to only four or five children. The big family of eight or 10 children was to be more common in the late 19th century.

A fine harvest was not enough. Sometimes it was at risk when the granaries were invaded by mice. During a plague of mice, cats soared in value. Dick Whittington, the country boy who rose from nothing to become the Lord Mayor of London in 1397, is said to have made his first step to riches by entrusting his cat to a sailor who, voyaging to the Mediterranean, sold it to a Moorish king whose granary was besieged by mice. The exact truth of this story is in dispute. What is not in dispute is that similar stories, told to children in Denmark and Germany, Russia and Italy, affirm that cats could make the difference between plenty and famine.

Cats were kept in houses, granaries and barns less because they were pets than because they were mouse-hunters. When in 1755 Dr Samuel Johnson produced his dictionary of the English language, he bluntly defined a cat as a "domestick animal that catches mice." But surely a cat was entitled to be stroked and petted for its own sake? Johnson disagreed, labelling the cat as "the lowest order of the leonine species." Less than 20 years later, the first edition of an encyclopaedia showed that Johnson's prejudice was widely held. The volume denounced the cat as "full of cunning and dissimulation," a tormenter, a born thief, "totally destitute of friendship" and very lazy. The cat was kept "not for any amiable qualities, but purely with a view to banish rats, mice, and other noxious animals." Not until about 1800 did the romantic movement, and its adoration of the countryside and simple rural ways, begin to raise the cat in the esteem of the western world.

Traditionally each grain of wheat that was planted in the ground yielded only a few grains at harvest time. In the Netherlands and France between, say, 1500 and 1700 the average yield was perhaps seven to one.

In northern Russia the yield was often only three to one. After such a harvest, about one in every three grains had to be stored as seed for next year's harvest. This posed a dilemma if famine set in. With the children crying for food, the temptation was to eat some of the grain that had been set aside as seed for the next harvest.

In Europe the main cereals harvested by the regiments of scythe-carrying reapers were wheat and rye. Crops of millet also occupied a vast expanse in northern China and Africa as well as in Europe. Though the grains of millet were coarse, they lasted up to 20 years; and in the 16th century millet was kept in the granaries of the fortified ports of the Venetian empire as an insurance policy against famine or siege. Oats, another widely used grain, were fed to working horses that pulled large wagons in peacetime and heavy guns in wartime. In the age of the horse, oats served as the equivalent of cheap diesel fuel; but in poor northern countries such as Scotland the same oats were also the food of the poor. In his dictionary Dr Samuel Johnson wrote pointedly of oats: "A grain, which in England is generally given to horses, but in Scotland supports the people." Rice was the main crop in the warmer parts of China and could also be seen in Italy. Maize, the wonder crop from the Americas, was increasingly grown on river flats in southern Europe but the price of its wonderful yields was often an exhausted soil.

Of the food consumed in a typical European or Chinese rural household, all but a fraction was produced locally. Salt was the one common food to be carried long distances. In 1500, the salt traffic earned fortunes for carters and shippers. The city of Venice had a virtual monopoly of the salt collected along the Adriatic, and the shipping of salt helped to maintain its economic ascendancy. The warmer part of the Atlantic coastline of France produced salt—by evaporation of seawater in summer—and this salt supplied England and the rich Baltic ports. Between 1427 and 1433 a count was made of the ships which entered the Baltic port of Tallinn. Of the 314 ships, an astonishing 105 came with cargo from the saltworks in the Bay of Bourgneuf in France. The Baltic was the home of the herring trade, and the salting of fresh herrings called for a little mountain of salt each year. The German or Hanseatic port of Lübeck was the king of the herring, and it was fortunate enough to cart salt on the short overland route from the German town of Lüneburg, where salt was mined. To own a salt mine in Europe was to own a goldmine. In China the government decided that it could gain easy revenue by tightly controlling the sale of salt.

Upper Austria held rich deposits of salt that were excavated by underground miners. Mozart was born in a salt town—"Salzburg" virtually means "salt town"—and from the nearby mountains each week set forth a procession of small carts carrying nothing but rock salt. Through the cobblestone streets of medieval Munich as many as 10,000 salt carts a year passed by. Usually the raw salt mined underground required treatment. To purify it called for iron boilers or vats filled with brine, with a fire roaring underneath day and night.

Small villages might run out of salt while waiting for the winter snow to melt. Housewives rejoiced when the wagon—or in China the salt barge—at last arrived with bags of salt. Most villagers bought little salt and used it frugally—a mere "pinch of salt" was sufficient. The frugality with salt points clearly to the people's precarious standard of living in the era before steam transport dramatically transformed the distribution of salt and grain.

Sea salt or kelp produced soda, which in turn was an ingredient of soap. In much of Europe the other ingredient of soap was tallow—the fat of animals—or a mix of olive oil and rapeseed oil. To make soap was therefore to use raw materials which would otherwise be eaten. In times of starvation the making of soap, and even the act of washing with soap, was like taking food from the mouths of the hungry.

Indians and Turks were more interested in soap and personal hygiene than Europeans. Indeed western Europe was more regular in washing its face and hands back in 1300 than in 1800. The Black Death probably made people suspicious of baths as places where infections might be caught. Baths were seen too as hothouses of moral laxity. In Germany, Frankfurt held 39 public baths in 1387, but a century and a half later—with a new self-consciousness towards nakedness—it held only nine.

Health suffered as the inland cities became larger. No large city had a system for disposing of sewage. The river was the favorite outlet, and someone's sewage, after floating 200 meters downstream, became someone else's washing water or drinking water. In eastern Asia, on the other hand, the sewage from villages and towns was often carted to the surrounding fields and put on the soil as fertilizer. The defect of this method was that many people, in consuming food grown on manured soil, infected their digestive tracts. In Thailand as late as 1970, perhaps two of every three rural people suffered from these infections.

While the population of Europe was usually rising, it was cut back by occasional disasters. Thus, during the Thirty Years' War which tore across Germany like a cyclone in the years 1618 to 1648, deaths through fighting, dislocation and malnutrition were possibly on a scale unseen in any later war. Germany lost perhaps one-third of its population. While the war was raging, Italy was hit by plague. In 1630 about one million people died on the plains of Lombardy, with Bologna and Parma and Verona losing half of their population in a year. During the two major wars of the 20th century, only Leningrad (St Petersburg) and a few other Russian cities suffered losses of similar magnitude.

For the typical laboring family in some regions of Europe and China, lean years were punctuated by an occasional year of abundance. From about 1570 luxuriant harvests became less frequent in the north of Europe. The climate was colder, and Baltic ports such as Riga were closed by ice more often. Near the Mediterranean the olive groves and their young fruit were hit more often by frost. Called in retrospect the Little Ice Age, this new era of climate continued for about 300 years.

Thousands of French, Swiss, Italian and Austrian farms on the foothills of the Alps were devastated by the colder seasons. Glaciers, most formidable around 1600, reached the houses of villages on the lower slopes and crushed them. The villagers had time to flee but many lost house, vegetable garden, barn, woodheap and grassy strip of pasture: they lost everything. In 1616 in a French-speaking village in the Chamonix valley only six of its 21 houses remained. The glacier, crawling along, was an object of terror.

Small processions of villagers, led by a priest or even a bishop, went to the edge of a glacier and prayed that it might halt. Sometimes the processions went far into the mountains, with the people, bareheaded out of respect, singing hymns as they climbed. At the glacier they stopped while mass was performed and the ice sprinkled with holy water.

The prolonging of winter and the spread of the glaciers tended to cut off Europe's south from its north. Between Italy and Germany the mountain passes, accessible in the time of Luther, could be dangerous even in the early summer. Not every part of Europe, however, suffered from the changing pattern of weather. Dozens of farming regions still received more than enough sunlight to ripen crops in a typical year. Germany had highly favorable years for wine between 1603 and 1622. Moreover, during these three centuries of a colder climate, wiser farming methods could compensate.

As for China, it suffered from its own run of natural disasters in every century: its epidemics, droughts, floods and fires as well as that pervasive self-inflicted disaster, a long war. In northern China in 1557 one earthquake killed 830,000 people. A long drought would have killed many more by way of starvation and the diseases that were aided by malnutrition. China was more vulnerable than Europe to natural disaster.

Increasing population in Europe and China called for more crops. Between 1500 and 1800 the number of small landowners grew by millions. They cultivated areas previously covered by forest and marshes. Chinese peasants went to the far south and west and took up poor lands. Many Europeans moved as tenant farmers into the hills of central France and Tuscany, where they eventually built simple two-storey stone houses which today, after renovation, are the charming holiday homes of Dutch bankers and English politicians. Where peasants stirred the poor soil with a hoe and planted beans and maize and vines, holiday-makers now bask in the sun, drinking chilled wine on terraces which, decade after decade, were built up with soil carried in a never-ending procession of baskets from a valley far below.

A vast area of land had to be set aside to grow natural fibers for blankets and clothing. Whereas today much clothing is made from synthetics, as late as the year 1800 all the raw materials of clothing came from farms. Land which might have been set aside to grow food had to grow the flax or hemp from which linen sheets and shirts were made or, to a lesser degree, the mulberry leaves with which silkworms were fed. Likewise, land was needed to feed the sheep which supplied wool and the various animals which, in death, supplied hides for the making of leather. In Japan it was common to wear a leather garment when outside the house, and in Europe most boots and shoes were made of leather or wood. Likewise, additional land was needed to grow crops such as woad and indigo, from which were extracted the colors for clothing.

Linen was one of the major products of northern Europe. An ancient textile woven from flax, it provided mummy-cloth for the Egyptians and clothes for millions of ancient Greeks and Romans. In early modern times, linen was widely used for sails for ships, white cloths for tables and sheets for beds (for those who could afford such a fine wrapping) as well as for making trousers, overalls, heavy pinafores and even underwear.

The Dutch painter Rembrandt, around 1651, sketched with pen, ink and brush a "view of Haarlem." The Dutch town and its towerlike churches stand in the distance, while on the outskirts rise the big arms of the windmills. But in the foreground are neat rows of what at first sight seem to be small hothouses covering an extensive area of pasture. In fact they are a patchwork of linen cloth, spread out to dry in the fresh air and sun. Wherever linen was woven, these spacious "bleaching fields" were needed in order that the fresh but dirty linen could be whitened. It was washed and rinsed, washed and rinsed for maybe 48 hours before it was "spread on the field to dry." And when it was completely dry it was treated again in a large copper vat and then, early in the morning as a rule, it was "spread on the grass, pinned, corded down, exposed to the sun and air, and watered for the first six hours," and not allowed to dry. After lying there all day and night, it was treated again in the copper vat, and so this sequence of long wetting and then slow drying on the grass was repeated, with the final adding of a little milk to aid the whitening process. So the drying fields were used again and again.

Vast areas were set aside for the growing of wool and flax. Nearly every village from Bavaria to East Prussia worked its linen looms. Wool was spun in hundreds of thousands of cottages by women and children, who were the chief spinners. Poor children tried to scavenge for their own use the bits of wool tugged from sheep by thorns and brambles.

Cotton, a foreign crop, was a special help to Europe. Grown in India or on slave plantations on the far side of the Atlantic, calico and other Indian goods helped Europe's population to expand by allowing more of its own land to be cultivated for food. Manufactured cotton, especially Indian calico, was shipped in large quantities to Britain before that nation became a great manufacturer of clothes from imported cotton. After 1820, wool also arrived in increasing amounts from Australia and New Zealand. Without the wool and cotton increasingly imported from the New World, Europe would have had to divert huge areas of its own soil to the growing of linen, flax and other raw materials.

In China, cotton was far more important than wool as a material for clothing. Increasingly replacing hemp as a fiber, cotton was using up vast expanses of farmland by 1400, and at picking time bales of cotton filled the thousands of little boats that sailed along Chinese rivers and canals to the towns. Many farmers alternated crops of cotton with rice. Some regions were such specialists in cotton that they had to import much of their food from adjacent regions.

In the year 1800 most people in Europe did not buy even one item of new clothing from shops or fairs. They made clothes at home, inherited them from the dead, or bought them second-hand from the female dealers who dominated this branch of clothing. Within each family there was a busy unpaid trade in clothes. Garments normally passed from sister to younger sister, brother to younger brother, and were patched and restitched and mended and darned as they changed hands. One of the perks of being a servant was to receive second-hand clothes handed down by the master or mistress. The clothes might be a little frayed, but were received with outstretched arms.

It was an enormous effort for Europe and Asia and Africa to produce enough food and clothing to keep their people alive and well. Sometimes the effort failed, and millions of people had empty bellies and threadbare clothes. If one village was hungry it could not expect outside help, partly because the next village was also likely to be hungry. Each village was usually a world to itself.

When in 1773 London's formidable man of letters Dr Johnson visited the island of Coll, which lay about 20 kilometers west of the Scottish mainland, he depicted a place which, being self-sufficient in almost everything, was typical of nearly the entire world at that time. Its people grew wool and flax, from which they made linen and woollen clothes and then dyed them in the simplest way, using a moss for the color red and heath for the yellow. They made their own candles. They made leather from animal hides and turned it into boots, though most of their children presumably walked in bare feet, for leather was expensive. The islanders grew their own grain, and what little meat they ate was from their own goats and sheep. They built their own smoky huts, the smoke curling up from the peat which they themselves dug up and burned, for this bare windswept island grew no trees from which firewood could be cut. There was only one shop and no church, though a dignified old Presbyterian pastor, dressed in black, preached regularly in a hut.

The landlady of the house where Dr Johnson stayed, for there was no hotel, informed him that she had never visited the Scottish mainland. When he expressed surprise, his companion Boswell tactlessly pointed out that Johnson himself was only now venturing on his very first trip outside England. Johnson replied that he had no need for travel as he was a citizen of the prince of cities: "Sir, by seeing London, I have seen as much of life as the world can shew."

Houses in Asia and Europe and Africa were of the simplest: most would now be called slums. In Europe and China the shared bed was normal, and three or four children crowded into it. Sometimes the whole family slept together on a homemade mattress filled with straw collected on the farmlands and renewed each harvest time. Rushes cut on the edge of a nearby swamp might form the covering of the wooden or earthen floor. In winter the house was usually cold—the bed was warmer. The Chinese sensibly tended to warm the family's shared bed rather than the whole room, and millions of Chinese families slept on a brick rectangular box heated by a brazier.

In large towns, many people living together in one room generated heat. Even if a fire was burning in that room in the depths of winter it radiated scant heat, partly because firewood had to be used frugally. The fuel had to be gathered in the forest and carried in the arms or on the shoulders to the home; and that required hours from the small stock of leisure time. Sometimes there was no forest nearby, and so fuel was very scarce for poor people. Cheap firewood in the year 1500 was more vital to the average home than cheap oil was to be in the year 2000.

A house chimney was a small hole in the roof. The smoke hovered inside the house and provided heat as well as smarting the eyes. Even in daytime a house was usually lacking in light, and window-openings consisted not of glass but of wooden shutters which, on being flung open, let in cold as well as light. In Europe in the 1400s the house window, though small in area, became more common. In very grand houses, small windows of glass were increasingly fitted into those wall openings which previously were covered by oiled cloth, wooden shutters or bits of animal horn pieced together. The glazed window was almost normal in Vienna in 1484. Two hundred years later the Royal Hall of Mirrors at Versailles was perhaps the most astonishing interior of a building to be seen in the world up to that time and a dazzling display of what glass could achieve. Many peasants who heard about it could only marvel, for in their village not a glass window was to be seen.

The forest was one of Europe's strengths, providing timber for building ships, carts and houses. The building of a noble palace could eat a small forest. The builders of Windsor Castle near medieval London used a total of 3,994 oak trees as well as a quarry or two of stone. Later the expense of transporting timber from the receding forest to town was one reason why so many European towns were built of local stone, mined in nearby quarries.

In China and India and Europe, wherever the population was large, the pressure on forests was intense. As town and farmland expanded, the forest retreated. The salt-mining and metalworking industries were devourers of whole forests; and one large ironworks might use 2,000 hectares of forest in a year. Many blast furnaces operated only one year in three, and then had to wait for the forest to regrow so that more trees could be chopped down for the making of the charcoal consumed in the furnaces. In 1556 the mining expert Georgius Agricola, in his massive handbook on mining and metals, warned intending mine-developers in Saxony that a mine was worthless unless a forest stood nearby or "unless there is a river near, by which he can carry down the timber." In other words, no forest—no mine. Owners of many large estates systematically planted trees and monarchs passed laws to preserve the new and old forests; but poor people in their constant search for firewood ripped up new hedges and trees.

The scarcity of wood explains some events which are easily misinterpreted. Thus when the acclaimed film *Amadeus* depicted the burial of the composer Mozart in Vienna in 1791 without even a coffin to contain his remains, the audience was quick to surmise that Mozart must have been a pauper. In fact, three years previously Emperor Joseph II had banned burial in coffins, partly to encourage simplicity in the place of extravagance and to encourage the body to return to the soil. But an important motive was to economize on the use of wood.

When firewood became scarce, ingenious substitutes were tried. The straw of the sugarcane was burned in Egypt, dry cow dung was burned in India, and the skins of crushed olives were burned in some Greek islands. Coal as an alternative to wood was slow to compete. In the north of China, where the forests almost vanished in some regions, coal was even used for house-cooking. Its offensive odor led to the development of coke as a fuel. In the north of England and France in the 1200s coal was being mined, and English coal was carried in sailing ships across the channel to the Low Countries city of Bruges. In the London riverside suburb of Wapping the coal-burning kilns sent such fumes adrift over London that in 1307 they were forbidden to burn coal as fuel. In the following five centuries more and more coal was shipped to London, making it perhaps the first big town in the world to use coal on a large scale, whether in the kitchen stove or the factory. As the forests became thinner and more people scavenged wood, use of the alternative fuel was encouraged.

There were limits almost everywhere on cities growing beyond a certain size. A city could not grow too large simply because it could not secure in its neighborhood the food and firewood it needed. A town of, say, 30,000 people needed firewood on such a scale that 600 or 1,000 horsedrawn carts would arrive each week with loads of firewood. The town needed another 200 cartloads of grain in an average week. As horses or oxen pulled the carts, a large area of land had to be set aside to provide grass or hay for them. Normally the countryside could not sustain a large city. A freakishly large city like ancient Rome or modern London could be sustained only by bringing food and fuel long distances by sea and river.

China's cities, for unusual reasons, could grow to a size unknown in Europe. For a long period China's farmlands had been more productive than Europe's, simply because they grew high-calorie rice rather than low-calorie wheat. Amongst the advantages of rice was that less of the harvest had to be set aside as seed for the next crop. A rice crop in China could yield twice as much food as a wheat crop of the same area in Europe. This meant that in China in the era of poor transport a compact rural district could grow the food that would support a relatively large city. Firewood and building timber remained a problem, and sometimes wood was floated, in the form of a raft of logs, down the fast rivers to the cities.

A city enjoying a warmer climate could manage with less fuel. This is one reason why Italy could support quite large cities even in 1850. The Italians experienced a shorter winter than did the people of northern Europe, and seem to have shivered bravely. Leigh Hunt, an English poet who lived in Italy after the Napoleonic Wars, was one of many foreigners who complained of the cold Italian houses. He could afford to buy fuel, but little was for sale.

It was almost an unbreakable rule of economic life that the labor of most people was needed simply to grow food and fibers and cut firewood. About 15 per cent of the population of a region could live in a city, and the remainder had to work the land with their hands and feet and all their strength. The lowlands near the mouth of the Rhine were the startling exception. In the Dutch republic in 1675, an astonishing total of 45 per cent of the people could live in cities because of unique natural advantages. Their fuel was peat cut in the surrounding bogs—a peat bog was virtually a rich forest that could be exploited year after year—and sent to the city along the canals and rivers. It is estimated that, if no peat had existed, Holland would have had to set aside one-quarter of its area for firewood-producing forests. Without its cheap river transport it would have had to employ 110,000 horses to cart the fuel to the cities. In turn that marching army of horses would have consumed hay and oats on such a scale as to commandeer one-third of the nation's arable lands.

The need to spend much time and devote much land to growing fuel for heating and lighting, and the raw materials for warm clothing, was a perpetual curb on the standard of living of much of Europe. In contrast, tropical peoples, in their standard of living, easily kept pace with Europe until the 18th century partly because they needed little clothing and warming fuel. They needed fewer calories, for they did not have to ward off the winter cold. In fact, several fortunate parts of the tropics even possessed a supply of cheap lamp oil. Burma produced oil for some generations before the liquid was dramatically discovered by drilling a hole in Pennsylvania in 1859. In one small district in Burma's interior, amongst the sandhills, wood-lined shafts went down about 60 or 70 meters, and the oil was hauled to the surface in an earthenware pot tied to a rope. A visitor to Burma in 1826 counted, at two small river ports, 206 local boats waiting to take on a cargo of oil. Perhaps half of the households of Burma used this cheap, green, strong-smelling oil in their night lamps, for it was far cheaper than the sesame and other vegetable oils used for lighting.

THE BREAKING OF AN OLD DEADLOCK

For maybe 4,000 years the standard of living of the average person in Europe, Africa and Asia had risen little, if at all. There had been abundant years and terrible years, minor rises and falls in people's material well-being and an increase in the luxuries available to the rich; but for the two-thirds of the population living on the lower rungs of the economic ladder, daily life was a struggle. Between 1750 and 1850, however, came hints of a dramatic change. Britain especially showed signs of a leap forward. Its population grew rapidly but the standard of living of most families was also rising above its humble base. Prosperity was increasing not because of a fortunate sequence of fine summers and lush crops, but because of the application of ingenuity to daily work in all its forms, on sea and land, on farms and in factories.

At the time it was impossible to understand the cause of the increasing prosperity, and even now it is not easy, but a long-lasting deadlock was being broken. The deadlock rested on a shortage of land and food. In the closely settled regions of Europe, all the land was already being used for crops and animals and the growing of timber. But if coal and, later, oil could be used as fuel instead of timber, and if the steam engine could replace horses and oxen for transport, ploughing and other heavy work, a vast area of land would be released for the growing of food for human consumption. In effect the farmlands for the first time could feed and support very large cities.

When farmers became more skilled in breeding livestock and plants, and in maintaining the fertility of the soil, then one small farm could produce more food than ever before. And if transport was improved by canals and stronger roads and later by railways and steamships, then each district or each country could specialize in the kind of economic activity for which it was best suited, and exchange its products in return for others. In essence, if ingenuity was applied to all kinds of daily work, and not least to transport, the output of food and other products would multiply faster than the population increased. And more food, fuel and shelter and clothes and leisure would potentially be available for each family, at least in the more efficient nations.

This interplay of events and trends was to shape the following two centuries. It was to disrupt all traditional ways of life, but its rewards would be large. In the favored countries the standard of living of the people standing on the lower rungs of the income ladder would become almost as high as the standard had traditionally been for those standing on the upper rungs.

PART THREE

24

THE FALL OF A PACK OF CARDS

UNPREDICTABLE EVENTS, or the coincidence of vital events happening side by side, play their part in history. In the emerging of the United States of America, the South American nations, South Africa, Canada and Australia the unforeseen mixture of events was especially powerful in the final decades of the 18th century. Many of those events pirouetted around the fortunes of France, whose influence was as decisive when it was losing as when it was winning wars. The French language, of all the European languages, held the strongest claim to be the international language when these events began to unfold, but when they had finally unfolded the foundations were laid for English to become the global language of the 20th century.

In 1750 the continent of America had been split into two or three overlapping worlds. Dozens of native tribes and mini-nations were still self-governing, especially in the cold extremes of the north and south and in the prairies of North America, but their influence on the wider world was faint. In contrast, many parts of the continent under European influence—and they were mostly near the coast—were brimming with vitality and a sense that the future would be overflowingly in their favor. The population of these colonies was growing, their wealth was soaring and their influence on western Europe and western Africa was pervasive. And yet they were governed from Paris and London, Lisbon and Madrid—an arrangement that had persisted for generations but might not last forever. By 1750 the combined economic strength of the European colonies in the Americas was probably greater than that of most individual nations in Europe.

For a long time the intriguing question was not whether America would become independent but on which European nation it would remain dependent. In 1763, at the conclusion of the Seven Years' War between France and Britain, control of Canada and Nova Scotia passed from France to the victors. In the eastern or more European half of North America, Britain now held a dominance that seemed likely to grow. Nearly all the way from Hudson Bay in Canada to the Gulf of Mexico, Britain was in control. Moreover most of the colonists of North America favored continuing British control. Strongly supportive were the colonists of Boston, New York and Philadelphia, many of whom had fought in the recent war. They had no wish to be governed by Catholic France or its commercial regime.

Once the war ended, relations between Britain and her colonists in North America lost a layer of the old warmth. The cost of fighting the Seven Years' War had doubled the national debt of Britain, but the American colonists contributed little towards meeting that debt. A vital source of government revenue was the duties collected on imports, but many American importers tended to evade duty, preferring to smuggle into their home ports such items as West Indian molasses, which they then distilled into rum. Massachusetts alone had more than 60 rum distilleries relying on smuggled raw materials. Rum was only one of the American channels of tax evasion. As a result, the average North American colonist in the early 1760s paid one shilling in taxes whereas the average Briton paid 26 shillings. The attempts to correct this distortion were to cause resentment and anger.

THE UNPREDICTED UNITED STATES

Many of the American colonies already had parliaments through which they could vent their grievances. The parliaments by their very nature provided an emphatic hint that these colonies, if necessary, could govern themselves, completely free from British control. The 13 British colonies at one end of the terrain now called the United States each operated their own parliament. Rhode Island and Connecticut even had the right to elect their governor, in sharp contrast to most of the colonies, which accepted a governor sent from Britain. Already the Americans had a framework for independence. They did not agree, however, whether they should seek independence, for the loyalists were dominant in Canada. Even in the 13 colonies to the south those loyal to Britain were initially more numerous than those who believed ultimately in rebellion. The colonists were predominantly of British descent or birth, the main exceptions being the Germans in Pennsylvania and that one-sixth of the population consisting of black slaves, who had no political voice.

Britain and the 13 colonies drifted apart. In 1775 armed colonists began to fight the British garrisons. The rebel leader was George Washington, an American-born plantation owner who had fought against the French as a militiaman. In the first 12 months his forces gained spotted success. Capturing Montreal they were weakened by an outbreak of smallpox and failed dismally to drive British troops from Canada. But Washington drove the British from the port of Boston and thereby showed such a prospect of military success that he began to win substantial and secret support from France and Spain, who were Britain's old enemies and eager to retaliate by stealth. In May 1776 France and Spain gave Washington secret aid in money, gunpowder and weapons. American private ships also received the right to use French ports as bases from which to attack British ships. Without that aid the American rebellion would ultimately have been defeated.

Emboldened by the support now promised, and spurred by the bold action of the colony of Rhode Island in breaking away from Britain, 56 rebel leaders signed their own American declaration of independence on 4 July 1776. In defense of their stand they could not appeal to the familiar symbols of power and loyalty, the king and the parliament. They simply appealed to their own people. It was a document with revolutionary implications for the western world and, in the course of time, for the entire world.

If the war was to be won, sea power was all-important. The European navy that controlled the Atlantic could send its own reinforcements to North America or prevent its opponent from sending for help. Britain was the main naval power but after 1778 its superiority was diminished by the interference of the French navy and by the open enmity of Holland and Spain. The war dragged on, becoming another seven-year war. In 1782 it was still deadlocked, with the British navy subdued but far from defeated in the west Atlantic and a British army still entrenched near the city of New York. In November 1782, Britain accepted peace rather than continue such an expensive war.

The United States was at last free and independent. Under the peace treaty it possessed nearly all the territory—Florida was the exception—stretching inland as far as the banks of the Mississippi River. It was still impossible, however, to conceive that this baby nation of colonists, holding fewer than three million people, would eventually become important. One obstacle to success was high, and seemed permanent. The United States even in its own territory was hemmed in by other European powers.

Britain itself could patrol the coast of the new United States. It owned Canada and, following the peace treaty of 1763, it owned Florida. Therefore, along the Atlantic coast the United States was open to potential attack by British naval vessels operating from Florida in the south and Canada in the north. But in the peace negotiations which in 1782 ended the American War of Independence, Britain decided, during its discussions with Spain, that it would prefer to surrender Florida. This news was heard with dismay in Florida, for it had become a haven for British loyalists moving south from New York and other places rather than live under the new republic. The news was even more shattering when the reason for Britain's abandonment was made known. It had preferred, when offered the choice, to retain the limestone rock and small harbor of Gibraltar, at the mouth of the Mediterranean, and surrender the vast land of Florida. So Spain took over Florida and thousands of British loyalists sailed away.

Independence was a boon, but the United States was still sandwiched by Britain, which held Canada, and by Spain, which held Florida, Louisiana and vast lands to the west of the Mississippi. As a result of diplomatic negotiations in Europe, Spain also held both New Orleans and St Louis, though they had been founded by the French. For the next third of a century, Florida remained a Spanish territory.

Meanwhile the land borders of the United States had a definite end. Most of the territory in the present United States was in the hands of colonial powers. If those boundaries had endured, the United States, with its vast resource bowl and its ability to attract immigrants, might some day have become an important power in the world but it would have had no hope of becoming one of the supreme powers. Confined to the eastern

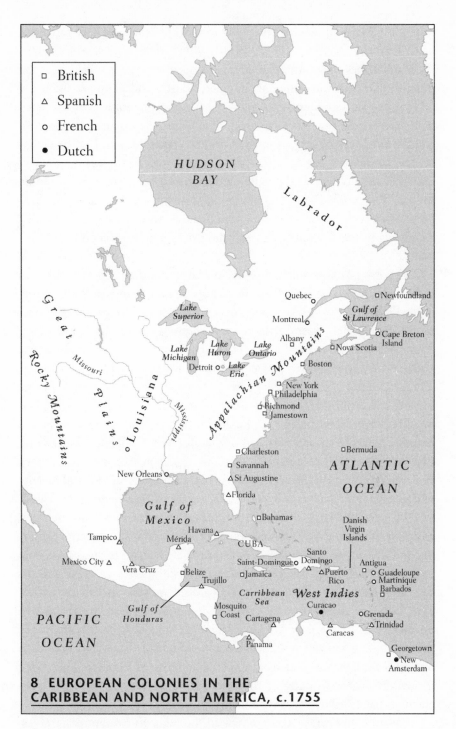

□ British

△ Spanish

○ French

● Dutch

HUDSON BAY

Labrador

Great Plains

Rocky Mountains

Missouri

Louisiana

Mississippi

Appalachian Mountains

Lake Superior

Lake Michigan

Lake Huron

Lake Ontario

Lake Erie

Detroit ○

Quebec ○

Montreal ○

Gulf of St Lawrence

□ Newfoundland

○ Cape Breton Island

□ Nova Scotia

Albany □

Boston □

□ New York

□ Philadelphia

□ Richmond

□ Jamestown

□ Charleston

□ Savannah

△ St Augustine

△ Florida

New Orleans ○

Gulf of Mexico

□ Bermuda

ATLANTIC

OCEAN

□ Bahamas

Danish Virgin Islands

Tampico △

Havana △

Mérida △

CUBA

Santo Domingo ○

Antigua □

○ Guadeloupe

Mexico City △

Vera Cruz △

Saint-Domingue ○

Puerto Rico △

○ Martinique

□ Belize

□ Jamaica

Barbados □

Trujillo △

Carribbean Sea

West Indies

Curacao ●

Gulf of Honduras

Mosquito Coast □

Cartagena □

Grenada ○

△ Trinidad

PACIFIC

OCEAN

△ Panama

Caracas △

Georgetown □

● New Amsterdam

8 EUROPEAN COLONIES IN THE CARIBBEAN AND NORTH AMERICA, c.1755

side of the Mississippi River, its population would for long have remained inadequate.

Sometimes events in retrospect seem neat and predictable but at the time, looking forward, they are tangled, untidy and peppered with the unpredictable. The victory of the rebel American colonies, with French help, had strong repercussions in France. Much debt had been incurred and the king had to increase taxes in order to fight the war. But the events on the far side of the Atlantic had shown that even the most powerful monarch was vulnerable if people, in demanding more freedom, stood up to him. The outbreak in 1789 of a popular revolution in France, the outcome of a whirlpool of major and minor causes, was strongly propelled by the revolt in the United States and the principles enunciated in that revolt.

Erupting in Versailles and Paris in May 1789, the French Revolution at first seemed to be a declaration of hope rather than a prelude to turmoil. By July, however, a mob was running loose in Paris. In the next month the French assembly issued a declaration of "the rights of man." Such declarations, to be almost a monthly event in some years of the late 20th century, were a rarity as well as an act of treason in the 18th century. Three months after the declaration, the extensive properties of the Catholic church in France were nationalized, and many priests as well as royalists were wisely fleeing the kingdom. And yet the collapse of the old regime in France initially pleased or delighted many liberals. In London in February 1790, where the democratic tradition had long been more vigorous than in France, the House of Commons could still debate whether the tumultuous events in France were to be welcomed or feared.

By 1791 the King of France was a captive in his own land. In 1792, amongst the new laws, marriage was permitted without the clergy presiding and divorce was liberalized. In September of that year was passed an unusual law whereby any clergyman denounced by six or more citizens for "uncitizenly behavior" was liable to be deported, and at the end of that year three ships, carrying 550 convicted priests, set sail for the area in northwestern Africa later known as Spanish Sahara. A month after they sailed the king himself was executed for the crime of treason. Less than nine months later was issued an official manifesto, of a kind unimaginable in western Europe in any of the previous 1,000 years. It virtually proclaimed that Christianity was abolished in France.

Meanwhile France was at war with the main European monarchies.

Fervently it proclaimed that it had a duty to impose its own popular secular revolution on all the lands it conquered. Originally for the French people, the revolution was now marked "for export." But the command of the revolution, and therefore its message, was slowly passing from the hands of radical politicians into the hands of a young soldier. Napoleon had enjoyed his first celebrated victory at Toulon in 1793, when he was in his mid-twenties. He proved to be a brilliant general who thought that almost nothing was impossible, and for nearly two decades his faith was fulfilled. In 1799 he became the head of government or first consul of France. In 1802 he became ruler for life, with the power to decide who should be his successor. Two years later he became emperor, and in Paris he was formally crowned by Pope Pius VII.

The new United States stayed out of the French revolutionary wars, thus refusing to continue an alliance with the nation which had probably saved it from military defeat in the late 1770s. Thereby it launched that long tradition of self-imposed isolation from events in Europe. As before, the quarrels in Europe provided an opportunity for the United States to expand. Napoleon had taken back Louisiana and the western side of the Mississippi from Spain, which was too weak to say no. In 1803 he was desperate for revenue and decided to sell to the United States all the land on the western side of the Mississippi River. Known simply as the Louisiana Purchase, this secured for the United States, at three cents an acre, ownership of North America's longest river system and a vast expanse of land running all the way from Canada down to the Gulf of Mexico. This transaction embraced the territory now occupied by one-quarter of all the states in the USA.

If this tract, far larger than any European nation except Russia, had remained in French hands, or if it had passed into the hands of a group of French-led colonists, there might in the end have been two rival but independent Americas, with one displaying the stars and stripes on the eastern seaboard and the other displaying a version of the French tricolor in the far interior. Would the United States later have been able to annex Texas and California if a French land barrier had continued to intervene? It is likely that the USA would have remained a middle-sized nation with its only ports facing the Atlantic Ocean.

What Napoleon sold in 1803 was land belonging to many native American tribes or nations. Originally it was the intention of the British and perhaps the French rulers that these tribes or nations should be able to retain most of their western lands. In 1763 the British, still in control of much of North America, tried to draw on the map a Proclamation Line across which white settlers must not trespass. The line ran along the mountainous watershed dividing the short rivers that flowed towards the Atlantic from those that flowed inland to the great Mississippi. The native Americans were permitted to retain the western lands or in effect the vast interior, but not for long.

Soon the line reappeared further to the west, like a vanishing trick. After the United States became an infant nation, the official dividing line between native Americans and Europeans suddenly found itself further west at the Ohio River. Before long the line was on the banks of the Missouri, and so it chased the sunset. The rights of the native peoples were pushed westward or ignored. If they had been a united people they might have succeeded in halting the expansion. But they had never been united; and indeed the European colonizers had long discouraged unity. Much of the history of the world has been shaped by disunity.

THE FALL OF THE HOUSE OF SPAIN

The United States, in winning independence, set a precedent that was more infectious than could have been predicted. One of the sugar colonies in the West Indies was the first to follow the path of the new United States. Santo Domingo, a long and mountainous island, was held by the Spanish in the east and the French in the west, where the colony was called Saint-Domingue. The French Revolution temporarily weakened France's control of its colony. Likewise the message of the revolutionists that all people were equal was seized upon in 1791 by those inhabitants of the French colony who decidedly were not equal: the African slaves on the sugar plantations owned by the French and the mulattos who were neither slaves nor citizens. In a sudden uprising they took control. In 1794 the French planters, many of whom had crossed to the continent and settled in Louisiana, persuaded the British to reconquer the colony: Britain needed little persuading, knowing that the uprising of slaves here might be followed by uprisings in British slave colonies. But the British failed in their attempt at conquest, losing some 20,000 men to yellow fever or the weapons of the African-American defenders.

In 1801 France sent across the Atlantic a powerful fleet to regain control. Two years later, with the war resuming in Europe, France withdrew from the island. In the following year a black man proclaimed himself the emperor of the new nation of Haiti. After nearly three centuries the Americas again possessed not only an emperor but a tiny nation which, in the words of the English *Annual Register*, "presented an image of liberty and equality highly captivating to men groaning under degradation and bondage." Now the Americas had two independent nations: the USA and Haiti.

The turbulent events in Europe paved the way for more independent nations. When in 1808 Napoleon invaded Spain, the Spanish colonies on the far side of the Atlantic were given their chance to take the side of Spain or seize their liberty. By 1810, all the way from Spanish Mexico to the Spanish colonial ports near the Andes, there were civil wars or wars of liberation, battles on sea and land, executions of mutineers and innumerable reprisals. Along the River Plate was seen the strange sight of the town of Buenos Aires proclaiming its independence while its rival port of Montevideo, remaining loyal to the motherland, showed its loyalty by bombarding Buenos Aires. The virtual end of the Napoleonic Wars allowed Spain, liberated at last, to resist the attempts of its colonies to liberate themselves; but it was too late.

By 1821 the present map of Central and South America had largely taken shape, with a free Mexico, a new cluster of Central American republics, a free Peru, a free Chile and a free Paraguay, along with a free Republic of the River Plate which later was divided into Argentina and Uruguay. One year later, Brazil completely broke away from Portugal and became a monarchy. Three years later Bolivia was formed, taking its name from Simón Bolívar, its liberator. In North America too the Spaniards had finally withdrawn, having ceded Florida to the United States.

Slavery still persisted in many parts of the Americas. There were more slaves, in fact, than ever before. While the United States imported no more slaves, it still employed the slaves in its possession, and their numbers were multiplying. Brazil and Cuba were strongholds of slavery. In 1850, perhaps one-quarter of Brazil's population was living in slavery, and the nation still depended on the sweat of slaves to grow sugar and coffee and other tropical products, to run the mule trains in the interior, and to serve as maids, prostitutes and porters.

Whereas in 1775 the seafaring nations of western Europe had laid claim to the Americas all the way from the icy tundra of the north to the rocky tip of South America, they had largely retreated in the next half-century. Their quarrels and rifts undermined their empires. Most of their colonies became independent.

By 1830 the Americas largely consisted of independent countries. In the north the main exception was Canada, where rebellions were to break out against British rule in both Upper and Lower Canada in 1837. Britain replied by granting to Canada a level of independence which, had it also been granted to the North American colonies before they rebelled in the 1770s, would have kept them on side, perhaps for several generations. The other European colony in North America was Alaska, where the Russians traded in furs, Russian Orthodox missionaries conducted their missions and the occasional Russian ship arrived bearing stale news from St Petersburg. Alaska was to be purchased by the United States in 1867.

South of the Gulf of Mexico, in 1830, the movement towards independence was almost complete. Hardly a European flag was to be seen, except on the masts of visiting ships. The only Europeans holding high ceremonial positions in most of Central and South America were ambassadors and consuls. Only a few insignificant European colonies existed on the South American mainland, the main cluster being in Guiana where the British and French and Dutch each possessed a strip of territory. Only in the Caribbean did the European powers remain supreme, and even there Haiti was independent. Britain still held Jamaica and much of the West Indies, France held Martinique and other islands, the Danes held part of the Virgin Islands, and Spain clung to Cuba, the richest of all the islands. Never perhaps in the history of states had such a huge area been rearranged so quickly; and yet the languages and religion and many of the social and political institutions of the conquerors largely remained in place. Even slavery remained in place.

In this sequence of events—falling into place like a pack of cards, in retrospect, but really so unforeseeable—the Americas was not the only continent affected. Just as the fluctuating power of England, France and Spain had repercussions on the long-term question of who would own the Americas, likewise the connecting sequence of events in the Americas had repercussions on Australia, South Africa and other lands.

BEYOND THE CAPE OF GOOD HOPE

The loss of many of its American colonies served to turn British attention away from the Atlantic Ocean to the Indian and Pacific oceans. The war against France, beginning in 1792 and continuing on and off for nearly a quarter of a century, provided Britain with opportunities to seize French colonies and some Dutch possessions, for Holland had become a satellite of France. In that huge arc of sea stretching from the Cape of Good Hope to Cape Horn, Britain had not been the dominant power, the Portuguese and the Dutch in turn being the leaders. Whereas Britain's main possession in those seas in 1780 was a foothold in various parts of India, it became far and away the dominant colonial power in that extensive part of the globe in the following half-century. It controlled the key port of Cape Town and the coast of South Africa, the strategic islands of Mauritius and Ceylon (Sri Lanka), most of India, parts of the Malay Peninsula and all of Australia, along with potential or real control of New Zealand, many other islands in the Pacific and much of the Pacific coast of what is now Canada. Indeed at one time Britain seemed likely to win control of the Dutch East Indies.

Britain was now stronger in the Indian and Pacific oceans than it had ever been in America. In Asia and the Pacific it now governed a population dwarfing that which it had governed in America. Largely defeated in one continent, it had turned to new oceans and quickly built up the largest empire the world had seen.

One change set in motion by these events was the rise of English to become, in the second half of the 20th century, the first language that could be called global. In 1763, outside the British Isles, only about three million people spoke English as a first or second language, and nearly all of them lived in North America. Nothing did more to give English an opportunity in the long term to become a global language than the consolidation of a huge territory into the hands of the United States, and Britain's acquiring of so many scattered colonies in the Indian and Pacific oceans. If the United States had remained small in area, clinging only to the Atlantic seaboard, and if most of India had never come under British control, the prospect of English becoming a global language would have remained small.

The collapse of one card sometimes brought down another card. Britain did not plan to place a settlement on the eastern part of the Australian continent which Captain Cook had discovered. The plan was forced upon it by the rebellion in the American colonies. Britain had been sending many of its convicts to its southern ports, where in effect their services had been auctioned to slaveowners and they had been used as overseers. The final breaking-away of the Americans forced Britain to look elsewhere for a place to which convicts could be usefully sent. "Usefully" was the key word, for Britain ran a mercantile empire and tried to use labor in the interests of its own shipowners and merchants. Britain's first thought was that convicts sentenced to transportation across the seas should help build a new British naval base on the long trade route to India.

The deserted and desolate Das Voltas Bay in southwestern Africa was selected as a potential port of call where British ships, with the aid of convict labor, could be repaired, take on firewood and freshwater and fresh vegetables, or shelter in storms or in time of war. But the captain of the naval vessel *Nautilus*, which inspected the bay, was not impressed. Britain searched elsewhere and eventually chose eastern Australia as a place where convicts could advance Britain's political and economic interests.

On the strength of reports brought home by Cook's *Endeavour*, the British government selected Botany Bay, the sandy shores of which now hold the runways of Sydney's airport. Cook and Banks enthusiastically reported that the bay had fertile meadows, a tropical climate which could grow rice as well as wheat, and at least one stream that ran throughout the year with sufficient flow to turn the waterwheel of a mill. All these boasts were errors, understandable in visitors who had spent only a week in a region previously visited by no European. Naturally the local Aborigines knew the bay and its vegetation and climate with as much intimacy as Banks knew the climate and botany of Lincolnshire, but there was no attempt at conversation by either side and no common language even if they had shared enough trust to sit down and try to chat.

The British government decided to harness convicts, male and female, and their guards—the marines—as their first settlers. It was hoped that in the tropical paradise of Botany Bay the convicts would soon grow all the food they needed. Nearby lay a bonus. On the uninhabited Norfolk Island, northeast of Sydney, grew a unique and tall pine which seemed likely to provide first-class masts for British fleets, and a superior species of the flax plant which, it was hoped, would produce fine sailcloth and rope for the British navy.

A British fleet carrying convicts and marines sailed into Botany Bay in January 1788. They soon discovered in that hot month that the landscape was not the green utopia which had been seen in cool April some 18 years previously by Cook and Banks. Abandoning Botany Bay and resuming their voyage for a few hours along the coast, the 11 ships straggled through the gap in the perpendicular cliffs and entered sunlit Sydney Harbour in which, the commander observed, space existed for 1,000 ships to gather in safety. It was one of the finest harbors in the world, but its encircling shores would prove to be as dismal for a would-be farmer as those of Botany Bay.

Twenty-four soldiers and convicts were promptly sent to colonize the forest-clad Norfolk Island. Running into "a perfect hurricane, with a most tremendous sea," the ship finally reached the lonely uninhabited island. Its crew were optimistic until they slowly learned, by trial and error, that many of the mastlike native pines were either weak or rotten behind the bark. Moreover the unique flax plant, even when Maori flaxworkers were imported to treat it, did not produce the sailcloth desired. In the long history of the creating of European colonies far from home, whether in Asia or the Americas or tropical Africa, severe setbacks were probably as common as early success.

At Sydney Harbour the new colony struggled to grow enough food. Only when the colonists crossed the narrow coastal spine called the Blue Mountains and began to disperse huge flocks of sheep on the vast warm inland plains did Australia emerge as a place of importance in the eyes of the world. A generation later, tens of millions of people facing the cold winters of the far Northern Hemisphere were clad in clothes or sleeping beneath blankets made from Australian wool.

The Aborigines who quietly peeped at the British ships roped to shoreline trees, and watched the building of huts and stores, the boiling of water in pots, the noisy firing of guns, the quick lighting of fires and the felling of trees with axes made of iron—all metals being unknown to them—could only wonder at these activities. It was possibly the strangest set of encounters in the recorded history of the world, for the ways of life of these new and old peoples were much further apart than when the Spaniards confronted the Aztecs, the Portuguese first met Arabs in East

Africa, the Dutch first settled themselves at the harbors at Cape Town and Jakarta, and even when French and British navigators came face to face with the Polynesians who had long lived on the islands of Tahiti and New Zealand.

In contrast, the peoples of Australia were still quarantined from nearly every radical change that had happened in most other parts of the world during the last 10,000 years. The gap between the newcomers and the natives was almost a chasm. The Aborigines' talents, so different to those of Europeans, could rarely be comprehended or appreciated by the newcomers. There was no way in which they could initially understand that most Aborigines had a knowledge of several languages and several dialects, an extensive knowledge of the botany and zoology of each region, subtle as well as simple skills in hunting and fishing, and a diet offering more variety than that available to most people of Europe. They could not possibly understand that the Aborigines, in their marriages, diet, rituals and concepts of ownership and land, obeyed a set of long-held rules that, though difficult to fathom, in some senses were as sophisticated as the rituals guiding the aristocracies of Stockholm and Warsaw.

Nor could the Aborigines understand the British way of life, laws and institutions, religion, manners and dress, modes of farming and manufacturing, the acts of reading and writing, the hoarding of food in barrels and bags and storehouses. They could not glimpse the depth of scientific knowledge in the civilization which the newcomers—so many of them uncivilized—had left behind. The technology of the strangers, whether large ships or firearms or ticking clocks, was baffling. The Aborigines had no hope of comprehending where these people had come from and how long they intended to stay.

On many parts of the long inland plains Aboriginal women and men, seeing the extraordinary newcomers for the first time, had to find ways of explaining them. Were these the ghosts of dead Aborigines returning to familiar haunts? When a rider on horseback came into view the puzzle was just as intense, because at first sight the rider and horse were indissolubly part of the same strange creature. Domesticated animals were entirely new to the Aborigines, who sometimes assumed that the sheep and cattle must be the wives travelling with the white men.

The Aborigines of Australia did not defend their territory effectively. Compared to the New Zealanders they lived in less populous groups, were not so well organized, did not build forts, and did not easily unite with neighboring groups in order to resist an attacker. Decade after decade, this unaccountable procession of white faces and new animals was moving further into the sparsely peopled continent. Region after region was taken over from indigenous peoples who had possessed them for countless years. In a thousand isolated places there were occasional shootings and spearings. Even worse, smallpox, measles, influenza and other new diseases swept from one Aboriginal camp to another, just as they had raced through the Americas when the first Spaniards arrived there nearly three centuries previously. The main conqueror of Aborigines was to be disease and its ally, demoralization. They formed a corrosive, tragic mixture. To this tragedy scientists, in this first age of science, had no answer.

After half a century or more, most European observers predicted that the day would come when the Aborigines would be reduced to a few hundred and then would vanish. Similar forecasts were made of the native Americans and of the Maoris of New Zealand, whose land the British later occupied. Decades would pass before the swift decline in the population of these peoples was to be reversed.

25

BEYOND THE SAHARA

FOR CENTURIES, most of Africa was virtually beyond the reach of the peoples and empires of Europe. Maybe it was more accessible in Roman times than later. Indeed the Romans colonized Africa with more success than possibly any other European power before 1900, though they colonized only the northerly fringes. The Romans ignored the distant lands on the far side of the Sahara, though a few of their towns lay in oases in the North African drylands.

How far was the Sahara a barrier that blocked the movements of peoples and how far was it a mirage? It is one of the tantalizing questions of world history and not likely to be answered with certainty. A lot of evidence suggests that the desert was such a formidable barrier that, until modern times, it prevented European and Asian empires from entering most of Africa. Indeed the heart of Africa proved to be less accessible to scores of generations of Europeans than did the heart of Asia, which was much further away from Europe.

It was easier to travel from Rome and Paris and reach distant Asia than it was to travel into nearer Africa. In contrast ancient Rome was not threatened, nor were ancient Cairo and Carthage and Constantinople, by invaders from the distant parts of Africa. Without doubt, the Sahara desert was a geographical barrier more formidable than any in Asia.

Moreover it was too large for any of the surrounding countries to control completely.

THE PUZZLE OF THE DESERT

This largest desert in the world covered one-quarter of all the land of Africa. Consisting of expanses of rock as well as sand, it was vast enough to cover continental USA. Perhaps it should be likened more to sea than to land—a dry sea into which people ventured, sometimes losing their life while journeying between the distant desert-ports. Like a sea it concealed pirates who swooped on traders. Like the sea it was swept by storms, and sensibly the Tuareg people wore cloth veils across the mouth as a guard against the biting, flying sand.

Here and there, rising from the desert, were rocky mountains which caught the rain. Much of it pattered down in a few cloudbursts and was quickly evaporated by the sun and burning earth. The desert shifted, and over the millennia it shrank or expanded as climate changed a little or as goats and cattle fostered erosion in the outlying zone of thorny bushes and prickly grass.

The Sahara Desert was not necessarily a more forbidding obstacle than the European Alps. The Alps were a barrier between Germany and central Europe on the one side and Italy and the Mediterranean Sea on the other, though the barrier was less forbidding in summer when the snows melted and the mountain paths and roads were open again. But there was one difference. The incentives to cross the Alps were stronger: Italy, with its art and history and religion, was a magnet, especially to people of the same culture. Moreover Italy held out the charms of its climate, seeming ever so sunny and seductive to pilgrims and travellers from the cold north. As the German painter Albrecht Dürer exclaimed in October 1506 when he was about to return home from Venice: "O, how cold I will be away from the sun; here I am a gentleman, at home a parasite." The Sahara, unlike the Alps, did not separate two regions with different climates and products.

The desert was far from a complete barrier. Caravans of camels crisscrossed it. Century after century Islamic traders crossed it and won a host of converts. Potentates from western Africa crossed it, and in 1324 the Emperor of Mali arrived in Cairo where he was long remembered for the gold he sprinkled—almost as if it were confetti—on those he favored. European merchants crossed the desert more than is realized. In 1470, at the time of the Renaissance, merchants of Florence were observed trading in Timbuktu, on the far side of the desert. They even pointed out that the local African textiles resembled those of Lombardy. But a white skin was rarely seen in the wealthy, walled, irrigated towns on the edge of the Sahara. In the 1820s, the sight of a visiting European man drew women in their thousands just to stare at his salt-colored skin.

With its waving date palms visible to the approaching traveller, the tropical African town of Timbuktu for long conveyed an aura of mystery to the ears of Europeans who heard its name. In 1826 Major Alexander Laing, the British explorer, called it the "far-famed capital of Central Africa." By European standards it was almost a city. For at least 600 years this bustling oasis had been famous for its trade in slaves, dates, grain, salt gathered in the desert and kola nuts collected from forests, and, above all, for the traffic in gold. Timbuktu was a collecting place for west African gold which, before the discovery of America, was perhaps Europe's chief source of the precious metal.

Timbuktu stood almost in the western Sahara but its people had to ride or walk only 20 kilometers to drink the water of the River Niger. The town was an inland depot for the northern third of Africa—a depot for caravans crossing the Sahara and for loads carried on the heads of porters or on the backs of asses and oxen from Sudan, and a terminus for the occasional cargo from southern Europe. It was approached less frequently from the closer coast of western Africa than from the Mediterranean coast and the inland Moroccan town of Marrakesh. In the late 1500s, Marrakesh welcomed mules and camels laden with Timbuktu gold along with the occasional cargo of slaves. One consignment of 15 virgins was especially noted. Significantly the commodities which crossed the desert and its expensive trade route were those which, like gold and ivory and pretty women, commanded a high value per kilogram. For much of the world's history items traded over long distances had tended, especially when transport was dear, to be of high value. They alone could justify the costs of cartage.

Just as Africa's desert was one bulwark against outsiders, so too were its rivers. Africa was deficient in long navigable rivers, with the exception of the stately Nile. It held few of those high mountains whose melting snows helped rivers to flow strongly in summer, when the flow was most needed.

Africa had its share of long rivers, but most were interrupted by waterfalls, rapids and cataracts. No ship could pass up or down the turbulent, frothy stretches to be found in nearly every major river. The Zaire and the Congo had their rapids. The flow of the majestic Zambezi was interrupted by the Victoria Falls. The history of Europe would have been different if the Danube, Rhine, Rhône and Elbe had also been interrupted by waterfalls.

Navigable rivers promote trade and the exchange of ideas; but Africa had only one long and navigable river, the Nile. It may be that Egypt's success as a creator of civilization owed much to the role of the river valley as a highway and source of food and to the fact that the river entered the sea not far from the center of other early civilizations. If the Nile had flowed into the ocean in western Africa, its influence would have been less.

South of the Sahara, in the vastness of tropical Africa, there was no river to match the Nile. Moreover Africa as a whole was weak in those gulfs and deep bays, those tongues of sea which enabled a sailing ship or galley to penetrate a considerable way towards the interior. Whereas more than 33 per cent of the landmass of Europe was peninsula and island, only 2 per cent of Africa was so shaped. These were considerable disadvantages for Africa, to which must be added the vast area of jungle.

To travel in the heart of Africa was slow and difficult. Few rivers penetrated far inland. The host of isolated communities was reflected in the diversity of languages, and even today Africa has one-third of the world's living languages. If dictionaries by chance had existed in the year 1800 for all the central African languages, and if foreign travellers had decided to equip themselves thoroughly for a journey halfway across the continent, their pack animals would have been weighed down with books. But could they have used pack animals? The answer points to another of the accumulating obstacles facing Africa.

In the moist woodlands of tropical Africa the bloodsucking tsetse fly, no larger than a housefly, was a danger to all beasts of burden, infecting their blood and weakening them with sleeping sickness. In about one-quarter of the area of Africa the infection killed all domesticated animals except poultry. Humans were not immune. Of an emperor of Mali it was written in the 1300s: "His end was to be overtaken by the sleeping sickness which is a disease that frequently befalls inhabitants of those countries and especially their chieftains. Sleep overtakes one of them in such a manner that it is hardly possible to wake him." It is probable that the incoming Europeans with their unprecedented mobility helped to spread the disease.

Malaria, sleeping sickness and other tropical diseases helped to build a wall around tropical Africa, dispelling or killing outsiders as well as Africans. The sleeping sickness especially obstructed economic development. The lack of farm animals in such a big area not only deprived Africans of protein in their diet but also robbed them of beasts of burden, and so they themselves had to become the beasts of burden, the carriers and packhorses. The absence of domesticated animals meant that manure was scarce, and so crops lacked the fertilizer available in other parts of Africa where, the tsetse fly being unknown, herds of cattle flourished.

Other obstacles limited useful outside contact with the African heartland during the last five millennia. Perhaps Africa possessed less than its share of the natural resources Europe and Asia craved. Maybe it also lacked the botanical diversity of Asia. If central and southern Africa had produced the world's first tea and coffee, pepper and nutmeg, silks and dyestuffs and a variety of other products that tingled the palates and aroused the acquisitiveness of the peoples along the shores of the Mediterranean, the geographical barriers inside Africa would have been less significant. Barriers are not a deterrent if something valuable lies on the other side.

So the Sahara Desert, the dangerous African rivers, the relative dearth of attractive natural resources and the diseases did form obstacles, but they do not completely explain why so much of Africa, for so long, was less attractive to European eyes. Certainly the desert could be crossed by those determined to cross it. Islam crossed the desert and occupied much of western Africa. The traffic in west African gold crossed the desert with ease. At about the same time metallurgical skills probably crossed the desert to western Africa; and a bronze and a brass age flourished belatedly—with fine artists shaping and decorating metals for the royal courts—in the present Nigeria, the Ivory Coast and Ghana.

For many centuries it was Asia, as much as Europe, which influenced Africa. The Indian Ocean was the main gateway to eastern Africa, and the ships or dhows sailing from Persia, India, Arabia and even the Indonesian archipelago often entered the fine harbors of East Africa. They were busy at a time when no Europeans were to be seen there. On the island of Zanzibar the Persians were settled for maybe 500 or more years before the first Portuguese sailed past.

The places standing near the crossways of the world have advantages. They are stimulated by new ideas—as well as crushed by new armies. Africa, apart from its Mediterranean coast and strips of its east and west coasts, was too remote to be stimulated.

THE TRAFFIC IN SLAVES

Africa for long exported a controversial commodity which was in high demand almost everywhere. That commodity was the slave.

It must be said at once that slavery was nearly as important in the history of a variety of other countries and tribes. Ancient China possessed slaves by the millions, and the practice of selling people into slavery in China was not banned until 1908. Indians owned slaves before and after the time of Christ. Many tribes and some states in America, long before the coming of Columbus, owned slaves and half-slaves. Europe's serfdom, which survived in Russia until the very decade when slavery ended in the United States, was a version of slavery.

A slave was a familiar sight in the Greek city-states. In Sparta the slaves or helots far outnumbered the free people. In lands ruled by Rome slaves were to be seen on thousands of rural estates. In the silver mines in Spain in about the second century BC, maybe 40,000 slaves were at work. They were the backbone of many agricultural countries where hard labor was required. Each slave was in effect an extra pick or axe or shovel, an extra hand at harvest time, an additional pair of hands in the building and road-mending gangs or the household kitchen. So long as these slaves produced more than they ate, they were an asset.

In many parts of the world it was almost a rule of warfare that prisoners were either killed or enslaved. As wars were frequent, the count of new slaves in each century was high. To be a slave was preferable to the alternative—to be a corpse. Slaves were black and brown and white, for color did not exempt one from slavery nor recommend one for it. Early Christian leaders regarded slaves as spiritual equals, as St Paul made clear, but they did not call for them to be liberated and so become their equal on weekdays just as they were equals on the Sabbath.

Early Christianity, like early Judaism and Islam, understood that slavery was an ancient and useful institution, and not to be meddled with. Learned and compassionate opinion in the 21st century cannot understand how slavery for so long could have been accepted without question, but then this new century is the heir to ideas of human equality and dignity which were uncommon in earlier centuries. Moreover today the prosperous countries have no economic need for slavery. Thanks to technology, they have a glut, not a scarcity, of unskilled muscle power. Moreover they have a new and tireless slave known as fossil fuel, which was not known to early civilizations.

Long before European ships began to carry slaves from Africa, the Africans themselves were busy traders in slaves. Even in the heyday of the Atlantic slave trade, more of the new slaves were set to work inside Africa each year than were sold abroad. Since 1500, more African slaves have probably been sold to Islamic lands than to Christian lands, and Muslims have been the main slave-traders in Africa. Presumably there was an active slave trade in Africa long before Islam arrived.

Inside Africa many people were enslaved by their own kinsfolk. Fathers sometimes sold their own children into slavery, and brothers sold brothers. Maybe half of the slaves who ended their days in foreign lands or regions had been enslaved by the African group or society of which they were a member. Slaves were usually debtors, criminals, misfits or rebels and they were especially prisoners taken in war. The various buyers at the slave markets had distinct preferences. In the Niger region the favorite slaves were Sudanese women, often dark copper in color, expressive of face, handsome of figure and easily trained for household tasks. In the Muslim world most slaves worked in the house and, it is said, were not treated unkindly by the standards of the time.

In the 16th century most slaves exported from western Africa were women and were sold to Islamic lands. A century later most slaves were men and were shipped in European-owned ships to Christian colonies in America. The Portuguese pioneered the slave trade to the Americas—they already used African slaves in their own sugar plantations in the Cape Verde Islands and in Madeira—and the British and other seafaring nations soon joined in the highly profitable but callous trade. A long strip of coastal western Africa, stretching from the Senegal River to Cameroon, supplied most of the slaves; and in the busiest years of the 1700s they were shipped across the Atlantic at the rate of 100,000 a year.

Working in sugar, tobacco and cotton plantations scattered all the way from the mouth of the Amazon to Jamaica and Virginia, they did not see their homeland again. Most of the sugar eaten in Europe was grown by African slaves working in exile.

The voyage in little sailing ships across equatorial waters from western Africa must have been an ordeal. Most slaves were crowded below in the hot darkness, often in chains. Their supply of drinking water was meagre, and they had not previously been at sea. For the European crew the voyage was often as hazardous, and many died of tropical diseases. In Britain one of the arguments later invoked in order to abolish the slave trade was that a crowded slave ship was as deadly for the British crew as for the black slave.

Generations of African-Americans were born into slavery but few escape routes were open to them. A baby born to a black mother and a white father—the father was usually the owner or overseer—was virtually free. Another path of escape was simply to run away. Many slaves ran in fear of a coming whipping, or as a result of a whipping. Sometimes dogs pursued them. Many of those who did escape to a nearby forest or swamp voluntarily returned to slavery with its secure supply of food and shelter and the consoling religious faith of their fellow slaves.

Slavery was a lottery in its tempo of work, its punishments and its rewards. Much depended on the personality of the owner and his wife and his overseer—who was often black—and on the attitudes of the government under whose laws the slave worked. Almost certainly the United States was superior to Brazil and other lands in its treatment of slaves, and some observers of American slavery agreed that on a typical cotton or rice plantation, the cabins of the slaves were at least as comfortable as those of poorer people in Scotland and Sicily. But outside the cabins there was no freedom.

In the popular movies of today it is the voyage of free European emigrants that typifies the new settling of America. For the best part of three centuries, however, most immigrants to the Americas were African slaves. By 1820 the West Indies had received eight times as many black migrants as white migrants, and nearly all the black migrants were slaves. Brazil by 1820 had received six times as many Africans as Europeans, and they still maintained their African cultures and languages at a time when in the United States the original African languages had virtually vanished. Indeed the map of Brazil was divided into horizontal bands, with Africans from Angola dominant in the north, west Africans in the middle band, and slaves from Mozambique in the band centered on Rio de Janeiro.

The ports of the United States received in total, by the year 1820, slightly more African slaves than free European immigrants; but the Europeans—with the benefit of a lower death rate and higher birth rate—formed the great majority of the American population. After the 1820s African immigration was to decline, for the very concept and legitimacy of slavery was under assault.

It almost seemed that Africa now was jinxed. The home of the human race, a continent so centrally placed, it had become strangely isolated. It seemed cut off from the throbbing parts of the world. Its geographical selling point by the 16th century was that it could supply millions of slaves, acclimatized to working in tropical heat and living only a short sailing distance from the rising plantations in the Americas.

26

NOBLE STEAM

IN 1801, the *Annual Register*, a popular book which chronicled the year's events, declared that the outgoing century had been remarkable. Science and technology, more than in any previous century, had leaped ahead. While Europe was often at war with itself, it was busy spreading science, religion and civilization into the remotest forests and gorges. The editors of the book regretted, however, that some of the barbarous tribes who had for the first time set eyes on European explorers and traders were "not only ungrateful, but jealous and hostile to their disinterested bene-factors." The idea that other peoples might actually prefer their way of life did not fit easily into European preconceptions.

Never had there been such exploring "of the most remote and un-known regions of the globe." The thirst for knowledge, claimed the *Annual Register*, had supplanted the thirst for gold and conquest. Never had long-distance trade so increased. On the familiar sea lanes the sailing ships were much faster than before; and even the long voyage from Europe to India was no longer feared as an ordeal.

WHEN TOURISTS WERE RARE

The world had shrunk but even rich people did not travel far in search of knowledge or pleasure. A queen rarely travelled outside her realm. Only a

323

few European missionaries crossed the seas to work in strange lands. In eastern Asia a few pilgrims sometimes travelled far to visit the great Buddhist shrines, but few Islamic pilgrims travelled far to worship in Mecca. Scholars—and in every nation they were few—stayed at home and learned of the world through books. When the young London poet John Keats wrote the words "Much have I travell'd in the realms of gold, and many goodly states and kingdoms seen," he signified that he travelled by reading. At that time he had never moved far from his birthplace. He was to die young, in Rome, but he went there only because he suffered from tuberculosis and hoped to find a sunnier, healthier climate.

William Blake, a gifted poet who was one generation older than Keats, penned the promise that the people "shall build Jerusalem in England's green and pleasant land"; but England was the only land he knew. A Londoner, he knew the River Thames and its rowing boats and the floating shops of the hawkers, but he did not see the sea itself until 1800 when he was aged 42. Renting a cottage only a short stroll from the beach he was surprised by "the shifting lights of the sea."

In the world as a whole tourists were few. To cross the Alps was still an adventure and people talked of it for the remainder of their days. It was the French conqueror Napoleon who, with the help of 30,000 men, was soon to build the first road across the Alps, using the Simplon Pass to link France and Italy. No country of Europe had a guidebook for the use of travellers—Switzerland was to be the first.

The most travelled people in the world were not scholars and priests but ordinary European and Arab sailors, who, in their mobility, were the air crew of their day. Between 1700 and 1800 the largest category of long-distance travellers in the world consisted of those who had no wish to travel: the millions of African slaves led as captives across their own continent or shipped across the tropical sea to the Americas.

The world was composed of tens of thousands of small, self-contained localities. Even to sleep one night away from home was an uncommon experience. This was true of China, Java, India, France or Mexico though not of Australia and its Aborigines. People spent their whole life in one place, and from it came nearly all the food they ate, and the materials they used for clothing and footwear. Here originated the news and gossip that excited or frightened them. Here they found their wife or husband.

A holiday by the beach or in the mountains belonged to the future. Spa towns, where people drank the mineralized waters for the sake of their health, were the only specialized tourist towns in Europe. In these "watering places," tourists drank the waters according to a strict formula that prescribed so many jugs or glasses a day. In the early 1800s perhaps the most international of the spa resorts was Carlsbad, a pretty town hemmed in by steep granite hills and pine forests a few days' ride from Prague and Leipzig. In 1828 an average of no more than 10 visitors arrived each day in order to take the extended course known hopefully in Carlsbad as "the cure."

Over time, a procession of minor royalty and major musicians including Bach, Beethoven, Chopin and Dvořák came to Carlsbad for the waters, classical music and companionship; and here too arrived—in three successive years—the little-known polemicist Karl Marx. Eventually this Bohemian valley-town acquired English and Russian churches where visitors worshipped in their own language before returning to the pavilion to partake of more medicinal water. Its main spring still rises in a hot perpetual stream, and the water still has an excruciating taste which improves with amnesia.

The industrial town, not the spa and holiday resort, symbolized the new era. In the north of England, especially from the 1780s, arose factory towns full of ingenious but uncomplicated machines which spun and wove wool or cotton. The machines needed an army of helpers for which children in large numbers were recruited.

England applied to the making of iron and copper, spoons and rails, pots and pans the same ingenuity which it had recently applied to the manufacture of textiles. Visitors from abroad marvelled at the vigor of Manchester, Leeds, Sheffield, Birmingham and the new industrial cities, but they threw up their hands when they toured the factories and mines and counted how many little children were employed. An American describing a Yorkshire woollen mill in 1815 noted that about 50 girls and boys were at work, arriving at six in the morning and leaving at seven in the evening. In winter they arrived in the dark and left in the dark. The eldest child was not over 10 years of age. All were smeared with the dirt and grease of the raw wool they handled. Everywhere in the settled world the standard of living partly depended on the hard labor of children, but the new factory—unlike such rural jobs as the minding of geese and the milking of cows—was a tireless tyrant which demanded the day-long attention of the children, even when they were on the verge of falling asleep through exhaustion.

Visitors deplored the cloud of coal smoke hovering above these cities on windless days. London was regularly polluted by coal smoke, even when William Wordsworth visited the city and penned his touching verses entitled "Composed upon Westminster Bridge." He proclaimed London as one of the most beautiful sights on earth, and he marvelled that it was so "bright and glittering in the smokeless air," but its residents were all too familiar with the smell, taste and sight of coal smoke. Perhaps Wordsworth saw little smoke because he entered London early in the morning. At that hour a few hundred thousand home fires were not yet lit for cooking and, being warm weather, a fire was not required for heating. If he had returned to London in winter he would have noticed the pall of black smoke; and if he had returned in 1850, the last year of his life, he might have been forced occasionally to grope his way through dense fogs, of which coal smoke was a prominent cause.

THE STEAM HORSE

The mechanical and human energy expended inside the new factory was an eye-opener. Often a waterwheel on a fast stream supplied the motive power for the factory's machines. Increasingly the latest factories used coal and steam power, but for a time the noisy steam engine gave little sign that it would transform the world.

Steam as a driving power was first used effectively in the tin and copper mines of England. Many of these mines were deep, and as their workings became larger and deeper they attracted so much underground water from near and far that they became an unwanted reservoir. To pump out the water, and to pump every day and night of the year, was an essential task if the mine were to remain accessible to miners. Manual pumps had long been used to lift buckets of water, level by level, from the depths of the mine to the surface where the water could be allowed to run into the nearest stream. The major problem was the amount of sheer energy needed to work the pumps. Men and horses could be used, but even horses were needed in large herds. In some mines of no great depth a team of 120 horses, working in relays, had to work the pumps.

What if steam power replaced horsepower? In 1698 Thomas Savery applied steam, produced by coal, to work the pumps in a Cornish mine. Eleven years later a Devon blacksmith, Thomas Newcomen, built a reciprocating steam engine which was even more efficient. Handsome steam-driven pumps were installed in the tin and copper mines of Cornwall and the new Newcomen–Savery steam engine could do what otherwise a huge army of men or horses had done. To this kind of engine James Watt, a Scot, brought vital improvements. His wonderful device of 1769, the distinct condenser, eventually produced about three times as much steam or energy from the same ton of coal. In the 1780s he again showed his ingenuity by turning away from the backward and forward movement of the piston and producing instead a rotary motion, which enabled steam to turn wheels. Nearly every big step in the evolution of the steam engine was made by resourceful Britons trying to solve practical problems arising from the daily work in new and expanding industries.

The Cornishman William Pryce, in his *Treatise on Minerals* published in 1778, calculated that a powerful steam engine operating pumps in a deep mine could now do the pumping for which a total of 1,230 horses, working in relays, might otherwise be needed. Rightly he called it that "noble machine, the fire engine"; but for long its power and potential uses were not comprehended by intelligent observers.

The use of steam in textile mills and in mines created a sense of awe. But the steam engine had little effect on the whole world of commerce until its power was applied to transport. The shriek of a steam locomotive was first heard in the north of England, the heart of the infant industrial revolution. The puffs and whistle cries of the locomotive at first startled many people and frightened the horses working on the roads and grazing in the pastures nearby. The speed and power of the locomotive astonished the first passengers. They were almost blinded by the steam and coal smoke.

In land transport this was probably the most important invention since the Roman road, and infinitely more productive. Even when a railway train was pulled by horses on a track of iron rails—and the first railway wagons in Hungary and the USA were harnessed to strong horses—the cost of carrying goods was dramatically reduced.

The first steam train ran between Stockton and Darlington in England in 1825; and its main cargoes were coal and other minerals. France opened its first steam railway in 1828, Austria in 1832, Germany and Belgium in 1835, by which time the first train was about to reach the city of London. Into the countryside in Europe and the United States went an army of railway builders, defacing strips of peaceful landscape with their railway cuttings and their impressive clay and earth embankments. By the early 1850s remote provinces of the New World were building their first railways—Egypt, Mexico, Peru, Brazil and eastern Australia.

The United States saw the immense value of railways in crossing the continent, especially in a westwards direction; and by 1846 its railways covered the same mileage as its fine network of canals on which horse-drawn barges travelled. Even backward Russia decided that a railway should link its capital St Petersburg with the inland city of Moscow. The tsar himself took up a straight ruler and pencilled on the map the route which this railway should follow. It is said that he marked a straight line between the two cities, except for the place where his thumb accidentally obtruded over the edge of the ruler. The railway builders dutifully followed his accidental detour.

Before the age of steam it was difficult to imagine a sailing ship or a wheeled vehicle arriving on time. Admittedly a horsedrawn coach might arrive punctually in a distant city, but on many wintry days it was delayed by floods and snow and fogs, and even on fine days it could be retarded by heavy traffic on the busier stretches of the road, or an accident to a horse. In contrast the train had the track to itself. It usually arrived at each station at the exact minute specified.

The brand-new word "timetable," a symbol of the modern breathless world, was coined in England in 1838. In the following year the booklet called *Bradshaw's Railway Timetable* could be bought in bookshops by those who travelled frequently by train and wished to plan their journey in advance. The idea of a timetable and an exact time of sailing was also adopted in the busier ports. Whereas in 1800 a sailing ship would advertise that it hoped to set sail on a long voyage on a certain day provided that all cargo by then was safely loaded, a mail steamer in 1850 announced that it would definitely depart on a certain day, and might even name the hour of the day.

Not everyone welcomed the new railway. Many rural folk, assuming that they would never possess enough money to buy a ticket for a train, could see no purpose in it. The shattering noise of the passing trains, they thought, would frighten the cows into giving premature birth to their calves. George Eliot in her novel *Middlemarch* recorded other fears:

"Women both old and young regarded travelling by train as presumptuous and dangerous." No bribe, no command, would persuade them to "get into a railway carriage."

Those who lived through the first 30 years of the railway age realized that the world had changed forever. The novelist William Thackeray, writing in the early 1860s when England became the first country to be crisscrossed by railway lines, spelled out the magnitude of the change. He recalled how some 40 years earlier the Prince of Wales had set out in his own horsedrawn coach from Brighton to London, having arranged for relays of fine horses to be ready along the road, and every few miles his tired horses were speedily unharnessed and fresh ones took their places in front of the carriage. But his journey, the fastest that money could then buy, was incredibly slow and expensive compared to the modern train on which thousands of people travelled each day. Thackeray thought that the train had so changed daily life that the railway embankment was like a wall that divided past and present. Climb the embankment, he wrote, and stand on the railway line "and look to the other side—it is gone!" An old way of life, in which few people travelled far from their native village, had vanished.

The black steam locomotive butted its way into nearly every facet of life. The brewery in a market town found itself for the first time competing with beer brought cheaply from afar by train. Fresh eggs and meat reached the city from far away. City fashions quickly reached the draper in the remote valley. People could attend a friend's funeral held in a distant town: a visit almost impossible in the earlier era of slow communications. In most countries a national daily newspaper was feasible for the first time because a fast mail train could convey bundles of newspapers to most towns on the very day of publication. The newspaper was also cheaper, for it was printed by a steam printing press devised in Germany.

Almost everything, from postage and holidays to war, was transformed by the iron rails. The quick war between France and Prussia in 1870–71 was heavily influenced by the organizing skill of Prussian generals in using trains to bring their huge army together and disembark it at crucial parts of the French border. The Prussians poured into France while many French soldiers, still in their home towns, were buttoning on their tunic or saying goodbye to their girlfriend.

Steam was slower to transform transport on sea than on land. The early steamships were wooden paddle-steamers, useful around harbors and on short voyages, but unable to make long voyages unless they used their sails as well as their coal-burning engines. By 1840 fast steamships were regularly crossing the North Atlantic, at the very time when European immigrants were crowding into America. Charles Dickens, the famous novelist, decided to visit the United States with his wife Kate and they boarded the steamship in Liverpool in January 1842. Encountering wild seas—both were seasick for at least five days—they observed with some dismay that at night the flames danced above the top of the tall red funnel and that the funnel itself was in danger of being toppled by the gale. On steamships the fear of accidental fire was high.

As the screw propeller replaced paddles, and iron replaced wood in the ship's construction, and as engines became more efficient, the steamship could travel far before it needed to take on another cargo of coal for its voracious engines. Meanwhile fast sailing ships became faster; and when rich gold was found in California in 1848 and in Australia three years later, magnificent clippers were built to carry gold-seekers there. For passengers as distinct from cargo, the future lay with the steamships, which became bigger and stronger. A crucial advantage of a steamship was that it could sail in windless weather, even reverse in narrow spaces and voyage along a narrow canal—tasks impossible for a large sailing ship.

The steamship made it feasible to build the narrow Suez Canal. It joined the Mediterranean and the Indian Ocean in 1869, and obviated the long slow voyage around Africa. India was suddenly tugged closer to Europe. For a voyage between Bombay and southern France the Suez Canal shortened the sea distance by 56 per cent, between Bombay and London by 42 per cent. Between Melbourne and London, the Suez Canal cut the length of the voyage by nearly one-quarter. It was a further tribute to steam that the canal was dug out of the desert, partly with the aid of steam shovels. As a result of this initiative by French financiers, the Middle East—once the hub of the known world but now a backwater—became important again. The discovery of oil in Iran four decades later was to increase its importance.

In 1873, tens of thousands of readers were excited by Jules Verne's new book, *Around the World in Eighty Days*. The hero of the book was an Englishman with a French servant. He "made a bet of 20,000 English pounds that he would successfully go round the world by ship, train and simpler conveyances, returning to London in eighty days." When he set out on his first day, boarding the train that ran from London to Dover, he knew that he would gain from the new time-saving routes, including the Suez Canal, new railways crossing India, and the transcontinental railway crossing the United States. Verne's book was just in time. A world tour, planned in advance with the help of the timetables of railways and fast mail steamers, was soon a common occurrence.

Steam engines were not the end of the fast changes in transport. Operators of the first railway trains decided that they needed a courier to run ahead of the trains. They adopted what was christened the telegraph—a word which stemmed from the coupling of two ancient Greek words meaning "from afar" and "to write." A telegraph was a single line of iron or copper wire, resting on a succession of tall posts and running alongside the railway line. With the aid of an electric battery, the wire carried signals from one station to the next. One signal might warn an approaching locomotive that the railway line was already occupied. Another signal might announce that a train had broken down and an emergency locomotive was needed. The railway companies agreed, for a fee, to allow other organizations and individuals to send commercial messages along their telegraph lines. Probably the first public telegraph line in the world ran, in 1843, alongside the English railway linking Paddington station in London with the town of Slough.

THE MESSAGE THAT OUTRAN THE SUN

Inventors were quick to improve the telegraph system first used on English railways. Dr Samuel Morse, an American, devised an early version of his morse code for the Washington to Baltimore railway in 1844. To build an overland telegraph line usually cost less than 1 per cent of the sum needed to build a railway for the same distance. Many telegraph lines were built between towns which possessed no railway. By 1849 a web of telegraph lines spanned 15,000 kilometers in the United States.

To send the telegraph wire under oceans and straits was the next ambition. The favored solution was to enclose the wires or cable in a padding of gutta-percha, a kind of india rubber collected from the sap of a tree in the Indonesian archipelago. In 1850 a telegraph line crossed the seabed of the channel between England and France. To cross the North

Atlantic was a more testing task. A cable laid painstakingly on the seabed by a deep-sea ship was completed in 1858, amidst jubilation. Alas, it conveyed messages only for a fortnight.

Much of the dramatic news from the American Civil War in the early 1860s had to be conveyed from the United States to Europe by ship. For a time it was possible to send a telegram along the new line from New York to California but not to London. A permanent cable across the Atlantic was finally laid in 1866. Within a decade a combination of overland and undersea telegraph lines reached nearly all the main cities of Asia, Africa and South America.

The telegraph wires and cables had almost reached the most remote of the Australian colonies by the mid-1870s. They strode on long legs across Asia and then, on land and on the bed of the sea, across the Indonesian archipelago. Reaching the north coast of Australia at Darwin Harbour, the wire ran south on a procession of poles across the arid wastes to Adelaide, on the southern coast. One line already went east to Melbourne and Sydney, on the Pacific Ocean, and another was built across the desert to remote Perth, on the Indian Ocean. Yet another telegraphic cable crossed beneath the Tasman Sea to New Zealand. It was now possible to send a telegram to London from nearly every remote port of Australia and New Zealand.

These delicate lines were vulnerable. When a storm blew trees onto a telegraph line, when a ship's anchor cut an underwater cable, or when Aborigines in the heart of Australia cut off the wire in order to manufacture a new spear-point, cities and nations would be completely cut off from the outside world. After some days or weeks the broken line was repaired, and countries were again united by this expensive but delicate wire running across the world.

As the electric currents faded after they had travelled a few hundred kilometers, repeater stations were built in the wildernesses. There, in permanent isolation, at all hours of the day and night, telegraph operators waited for the occasional signals to arrive. Faithfully they tapped out a repeat of them so that they sped to the next repeating station. News of a possible war in France reached a remote French colony, news of the death of a mother in Ireland arrived quickly in a daughter's house in Boston, and news of a typhoon wrecking ships on the China coast quickly reached a merchant in India. Only the wealthy, however, used the early telegraph because each word was costly.

With good fortune a message could cross the world in 24 hours. A magical, record-breaking night was 16 February 1871. From Karachi, then in British India but now in Pakistan, a telegram was cabled to London. Passing through the repeating stations it reached London in 50 minutes. In contrast the sun next day would take four and a half hours to traverse that distance of almost 9,000 kilometers, thus prompting an English journalist to report this swiftest of telegrams with the headline "The Sun Outdone." The same message would have taken weeks to reach London by mail steamer.

It has become almost normal to view far-reaching inventions as the work of one or two lonely individuals, standing far above the ruck. But invention is the outcome of a team game as well as a contest between individuals. The struggle to devise and improve steam engines, railways, steamships and telegraphs, ironworks and textile machines took place in many nations and hundreds of go-ahead workshops. Some of the major changes stemmed from a multitude of contributions by now-forgotten people. Only a few of the inventor-heroes are remembered.

Nothing so far in the history of the world had done as much to unite all lands as this slender thread of wire crossing steppes and plains, jungles and icy valleys, factory suburbs and mountain villages, and the very bed of the sea. Part of the magic of the telegraph was the sheer wonder that a message could travel unseen along wires. A new intellectual vogue for extrasensory perception, for spiritualism, and for a belief that the dead could tap messages to the living, owed much to the telegraph. More widely held was a faith that the telegraph would inaugurate an era of world peace: a faith resting on the assumption that if only national leaders could talk to one another they would live in peace. But the telegraph was to send not only affirmations of friendship but declarations of war.

In 1876, just when the international telegraph was reaching the remote parts of the world, the telephone was born in North America. Business houses living nearby could talk to each other once the telephone wires entered their building. They could not dial directly to a nearby phone but depended on a long line of women, working in a central exchange and commanding a row of plugs and switches which, manipulated by hand, linked one phone to another. When the women went home for the night, the telephone lines became silent. The first automatic telephone exchange was built in the Indiana town of La Porte in 1892. Germany, now to the fore in adopting new technology, built an automatic exchange at Hildesheim in 1908. So far these automatic exchanges served only local calls.

A conversation on the long-distance telephone remained difficult, the voices being distorted and not easily heard. When Boston and Chicago were linked by phone in 1893, that seemed about as far as the voice could travel over land; but within a quarter of a century the east and west coasts of the United States were linked by phone.

The ocean was even more of a hindrance to the telephone cable. England and France were linked by underwater phone in 1891 but the wider oceans remained impassable for wires. For decades the long-distance call on the telephone was only for those with a large business or a high income. A telephone cable was not laid across the seabed of the North Atlantic until 1956, and human voices were audible then at the Scottish and Canadian ends only because of the advent of the vacuum-tube amplifier.

The excitement of these new inventions can hardly be conveyed to present generations whose sense of wonder has been almost saturated by wave after wave of innovations. But even in those decades lived people who scoffed at the telegraph and other new devices. Henry David Thoreau, a thinker and eccentric who lived in a hut in the woods near Boston, put forward this argument in 1854 in his book *Walden*: "Our inventions are wont to be pretty toys, which distract our attention from serious things . . . We are in great haste to construct a magnetic telegraph from Maine to Texas; but Maine and Texas, it may be, have nothing important to communicate." He added the sobering thought that "the man whose horse trots a mile in a minute does not carry the most important messages."

THE RUSH TO THE SMOKY CITIES

The family farm was still the focus of millions of dreams and hopes, especially in the New World where land was cheap and abundant. During the numerous centuries before governments provided social security, a farm—if it was large enough—was itself the main form of social security. Providing food and shelter and the raw materials of clothing, it also kept the family together, for most sons and daughters could live and work there before their marriage, and the parents could live there in old age—if they lived to old age. In the New World those who could not be usefully employed on the family farm could carry their experience, muscle power and determination and take up cheap virgin land somewhere else and build their own log cabin or hut. In a range of countries from Chile to the Transvaal, struggling new farmers were defeated by drought and pests, debts and poor prices, but the dream of being a farmer remained alive.

A vivid snapshot of the farmlands of Massachusetts survives from about the year 1820. Winter has set in, and in the weak light of the afternoon the small farm of the Whittiers is full of bustle. Women are at work in the kitchen. In the barn the old horse is "whinnying for his corn." In the stalls the cattle are being fed with the hay that was made in the summer. The rooster is crowing, an east wind is blowing and heavy snow is expected. The logs and sticks of sawn firewood are being carried indoors and piled in readiness for the lighting of the fire in the room where the family gather after the day's work is almost over. That night the snow falls. Next morning, the boys of the farm put mittens on their hands and set out to shovel away the deep snow and clear a thin corridor from the house to the barn where behind the closed doors the draft animals are waiting to be fed. These simple scenes are described in John Greenleaf Whittier's poem "Snowbound," first printed nearly half a century later.

There were similar scenes in farms stretching from Ohio to Sweden and Siberia, but it is Whittier's poem that caught the feeling of snug security which so many farming families felt when their own ceaseless work had provided them with all they needed for the long winter. So they sat, the uncle smoking his pipe and dispensing folklore about moon and clouds, the mother spinning wool on her hand-turned wheel, and a story being read aloud, until they saw the time of the "bull's-eye" watch on the wall was close to 9 p.m., their time to go to bed.

Even as the Whittiers sat at their fireside, there were signs in one or two European lands of one of the extraordinary changes in human history, a change which is still embracing country after country. In a few nations, most people were no longer tilling the soil. England and Belgium were perhaps the first nations in Europe, probably in the world, where the majority of the workforce was no longer needed for the producing of food. Only 30 per cent of the English workforce was needed for rural pursuits. In Australia, Chile and Argentina a similarly small part of the workforce was needed in rural industries. Those lands were now producing far more food—and also wool and cattle hides—than they themselves could use. A way of life which had slowly emerged some 10,000 years ago and spread across virtually the whole globe was about to be supplanted as the main provider of daily work. Most farms were producing more than in the past, and needing the labor of fewer people.

England and Belgium were showing the way. In contrast, in France and Italy about 60 per cent of the working population worked the land. In Asia probably no region employed less than 70 per cent of the people in agriculture. English farmlands needed fewer people than in the past because they were more productive. They had new breeds of livestock, new ways of rotating crops and fallowing the land, heavy draft horses equipped with ingenious collars and drawing stronger ploughs. They gained from the draining of marshes, the manuring of the soil and the mechanization of farming. The steam engine was even dragged onto the larger farms. The steam-driven threshing machine, separating grain from chaff, could be seen on many English farms by the 1830s. It helped to dispense with that army of labor which for thousands of years had been needed at harvest time.

A simple measure of the increased supply of food is that serious famines, so common in France in the 18th century, become rare after 1800. The scarcity of food in Ireland and the lower Rhine in the 1840s was the last death-dealing famine in western Europe.

Another trend was visible in Europe: the population was increasing more rapidly than at any time since the years of warm climate between 1000 and 1250. Why the population was increasing was eagerly debated, but too many factors were at work to sustain a simple answer. Certainly people were living longer, and Sweden was remarkable because in 1850 the average life expectancy of its newborn females had risen to 45 years—a rise of maybe eight years in just over half a century. Plagues were fewer, and the knowledge of how to combat disease was increasing. Furthermore, in much of Europe each hectare of farmland produced more food for the multiplying population. Between 1750 and 1850, Europe's population jumped by more than 80 per cent, a rate of increase which was viewed as astonishing—until the population of nations of the Third World began to grow at a more astonishing pace after the Second World War.

What was happening in Britain and a few other industrialized nations was a foretaste of the whole western world in the 20th century. Across Europe most of the cities and towns grew, and several became as large as China's largest. By 1800 the population of London had passed one million. By 1860 it was three million—by far the largest city the world had known. Early in the new century, by some reckonings, London was to hold close to 10 million people, and they consumed wheat and butter and jam, bacon and mutton and apples which came not only from English farms but in ships from distant lands. Most of the increase in population in western Europe took place in cities. In 1600 Europe had held a mere 13 cities possessing more than 100,000 people. In 1900 there were to be 143 such cities.

The rising cities themselves were dirty, and most houses were small and lacked facilities for washing more than hands and face. At the end of the century, in the German city of Breslau, six or more persons were commonly living in one room. In Vienna, which by 1900 was one of the five biggest cities of the world, nearly half of the people lived in dwellings which consisted only of one room with perhaps a small kitchen attached. Some of these houses, bereft of even an outside window, were incubators of infection.

Even in 1850 most houses in some of the finest cities did not have access to clean running water. Large cities usually lay beside a river, and water for cooking and washing was fetched from the polluted river or from nearby wells. Most people carried the water along the street to their house in a wooden pail or bucket. As water was scarce the washing of clothes was infrequent. In any case the washing of the naked body was believed to drain away essential oils and so allow disease to gain a bridgehead in the body. People who wished to wash could visit public bathhouses, but these baths were less plentiful and less popular than in ancient Roman cities of much smaller size.

Sewage found its way to the rivers and, flowing downstream, polluted the water used by the next city. Death-carrying infections were spread by poor sanitation. Asiatic cholera had first appeared in eastern Russia in 1823, and nine years later a fierce strain of it reached New York, filling the streets with apprehension. It came again and again to Europe, filling the corners of many cemeteries about once in each decade. Russia, one of the less sanitary countries, lost a quarter of a million people through cholera in 1892, at a time when fatal epidemics were becoming less frequent elsewhere.

Increasingly engineers built reservoirs for supplying freshwater to cities and laid underground pipes and dug tunnels to carry away the city's daily sewage. The death rate of the cities also fell because of advances in medicine. It was in the mid-1870s that the German bacteriologist Robert Koch made the momentous discovery that bacteria—so tiny that millions could inhabit a drop of spit—caused disease. In 1876 he found that certain bacteria caused anthrax in sheep and cattle and occasionally in human beings. In 1882 in Berlin he announced that he had located the bacterial cause of tuberculosis—a disease first identified by the ancient Greek Hippocrates and long known as "the captain of the men of death."

The ease of travel in the age of steam expedited this lightning run of medical discoveries. Koch hurried to Egypt, hoping to study the latest epidemic of cholera, but he arrived just in time to learn that it was over. Later he sailed in a mail steamer through the new Suez Canal on his way to the home of cholera, India, and there in 1883, with the aid of his powerful microscope, he made his discovery of the bacillus that carried the disease.

Likewise the ease of travel between Europe and India helped to locate the cause of malaria. Ronald Ross, a medical officer working in India, occasionally travelled to England to keep up with the latest research in bacteriology, and home in India he used his knowledge to investigate the causes of malaria. In 1898 he discovered that malaria did not emanate, as had traditionally been believed, from marsh air or from stagnant water. Instead it was distributed by the bite of what he called "the dapple-winged mosquito." Thus he located the cause of this most catastrophic of all tropical illnesses. One long-term outcome was to be a massive increase in the population of many tropical lands.

DEATH OF A COMPOSER

In Europe, perhaps for the first time, it was healthier to live in a large city than in the countryside. Indeed the death of Russia's most famous composer, at the height of his fame, aroused puzzlement and indignation largely because he died just when the city at last seemed the safest and healthiest of places.

The musician Tchaikovsky was aged 53, and his fame was rising: *The Nutcracker* was his recent triumph. On Saturday 16 October 1893, in St Petersburg, his sixth symphony was heard for the first time. The audience was eager and expectant but slightly disappointed. After all, he was a genius, and therefore a failure was inadmissible. On the following Thursday he felt ill, and calmly enquired whether he had caught the unimaginable—cholera. A frequent drinker of water at his meals, he possibly had drunk tainted water. He was beyond help, and died at 3 a.m. on the following Monday. Dressed for his funeral in a black suit, he was laid on white satin in readiness for the politicians and the musicians, the high and the humble, who poured in to gaze on him before his coffin was carried to the Kazan cathedral. Some 60,000 people sought tickets for his funeral service but only one in 10 could be crammed inside.

Why should this gifted musician die from a disease of the poor and the hungry, and why should he die in the medical safety of a big city? Some suggested that it was suicide; others vowed that it was cholera. A scapegoat was needed and was sought. The public turned against the physician of the dead composer.

It was a mirror of this inventive, confident earth-shaping century that, in many European circles, death was no longer seen as an act of God which could occur at any time. In many circles the human race was overoptimistically seen as the architect and inventor of its own future. God was being challenged in his own heaven by engineers, shipbuilders, bacteriologists, surgeons and all the other heroes of the new technology, and by political leaders who let it be known that they were now tackling many of the world's long-standing ills, including poverty and slavery.

27

WILL ALL BE EQUAL?

THE CRUSADE to abolish slavery was in part an equalitarian crusade, led by people of compassion. Victory against the slaveowners, however, depended on more than compassion. The crusade on both sides of the Atlantic was led by increasingly wealthy nations which no longer depended on slavery for a significant part of their wealth. Thus in the 1790s, Denmark abolished the slave trade in its West Indian islands and revolutionary France abolished slavery in its colonies. It was easier for these European nations to liberate slaves still at work in their tropical colonies: their whole economic life was far less dependent than the USA on the work of slaves.

The United States was late in throwing its weight against slavery. Admittedly the nation was born out of a rebellion which emphasized freedom, but its people had been rebelling against the rule of another group of whites, not against the rule of white over black. At that time, an attempt to abolish slavery would have incurred a heavy economic loss to every section of the United States, including those states that did not own slaves. It would also have divided and destroyed the nation.

In the United States the hostility to slavery came later, when the nation ceased to depend so heavily on agriculture. The spearhead against slavery was in the wealthy states of the north, which depended not on slaves but on ironworks, factories, free farms and shipyards. In their hands the United States was becoming a great industrial power; and by 1860 its output of iron and steel—now the barometer of industrial success—was ranked third in the world, with only Britain and France ahead of it. The Americans could now afford to wind down or even abolish slavery, but the political and economic cost was still high. The crusaders, most of whom were devout members of churches, were willing to pay the price, though the real cost was likely to be carried by the slave-owners themselves and the states whose economy depended on slavery.

ABE LINCOLN'S THREE MINUTES

In the United States the importing of new slaves was already banned, thus forcing the plantations to rely on the sons and daughters of slaves. The labor of slaves was still considered vital to daily life in the subtropical southern states; and in 1861 eleven of these southern states rebelled. They seceded from the United States and created their own nation, the Confederate States. Amidst this tension Abraham Lincoln was inaugurated as president of the old United States. A month later, in April 1861, the Civil War began, with a Confederate victory at Fort Sumter in South Carolina.

Lincoln did not bring his nation into the war primarily to abolish slavery. He fought initially to preserve his country and its unity in the face of the secession of some of its oldest and most important states. Lincoln was trying to find a compromise. If necessary he would allow slavery to continue, so long as the nation remained one. He simply wished to save his nation from a harsh amputation.

It now seems slightly strange that this most famous of the world's democrats should be proclaiming the brand of political equality known as democracy while tolerating, reluctantly, the harsh inequality of slavery. But democracy in its modern version was still in its infancy, while slavery in stark contrast was an old, vigorous and long-continuing institution. Moreover the United States had been built on the federal principle—that a variety of states could gain strength from their unity but cling to their political and economic differences. The essence of federalism was that enemies and opponents could coexist, and Lincoln had to cement that coexistence. In 1861, in his eyes, the sin of the slave-owning south lay less in its support of slavery than in the unpalatable fact that it opposed federalism and the very existence of the United States.

The hero of the war against slavery came from humble stock. In 1816 his parents had moved from warm Kentucky to the more northerly state of Indiana where they were small farmers. Abraham Lincoln, who was then aged eight, learned how to handle an axe and became adept at the strenuous work of chopping down trees and splitting them into the rails from which, at that time, tens of thousands of simple farming fences were being constructed across the North American plains. When as a young lawyer he entered politics, his supporters called him "The Rail Splitter," but Lincoln by then was more proud of the education he had won for himself than of his earlier life as a son of toil.

His mother and father worshipped at the Separate Baptist Church, one of the many splinters of Protestantism that flourished in North America, and like most believers in that sect they opposed horseracing, dancing, the drinking of alcohol and the keeping of slaves. Their opposition to slavery was based not only on religion but also on their own financial interests. In such slave states as Kentucky, the Lincolns and other small white farmers had trouble in competing with the big farmers who employed the cheap and unfair labor of slaves.

Like most politicians in a democracy, Lincoln had to swim with the stream if he was to summon the popular support required for big tasks. He swam with the stream, even on the topic of slavery. As president his inaugural pledge was "not to interfere with slavery." At that time he was far from a moral crusader. While he held definite personal views about slavery, he was not an advocate for the equality of black and white people. He was simply governing a divided nation and trying hard in his first year in office to divide it no further.

In 1862 he supported the idea of creating a separate nation in Africa for blacks, "for the good of mankind." When black leaders said no he accepted their no. A year passed before he finally conferred freedom—still a theoretical freedom—on the slaves living in the northern states. He did not abolish slavery in the southern states: indeed the constitution of the country had to be amended before slavery could be abolished. He was slowly becoming an abolitionist through a series of sidesteps and shuffles and tiptoes, some of which were propelled by the course of the Civil War itself.

Soon after the victorious battle at Gettysburg the Union's dead were reburied in a neat war cemetery, to be dedicated on 19 November 1863. The main speech, anticipated to be two hours long, was entrusted to Edward Everett, who had been president of Harvard University and secretary of state. Everett was expected to suggest that concessions be offered to the southern slave-owning states. Lincoln for his part decided to offer no concessions to slavery. Chewing over what he might say as the second speaker on the platform, he instinctively decided to appeal to the uppermost principle, the rights of all peoples to determine how they should be governed. In his own hand he wrote out half of his short speech before he went in the train from Washington to Gettysburg, where he completed it.

For the ceremony in the cemetery Lincoln dressed himself in a new black suit and a stovepipe hat that made him seem even taller than he was. The hat was circled by a black band of mourning, so placed not to commemorate those killed in battle but his own young son, Willie, who had recently died after a short illness. Lincoln listened to Everett's long speech and then stood up and delivered his own speech in the space of about three minutes. Offering lofty thoughts, he was also self-effacing. He contrasted the day's speeches, so ephemeral, with the sacrifice of the soldiers who now lay in the neat rows of graves: "The world will little note, nor long remember, what we say here."

Lincoln himself would have been astonished to learn that the words of his speech would endure. After all, it consisted of only a few sentences. Yet it had an eternal sound. It concluded with a sentence that would remain alive: "we here highly resolve that these dead shall not have died in vain—that this nation, under God, shall have a new birth of freedom—and that government of the people, by the people, for the people, shall not perish from the earth."

At first sight it is puzzling that such a fervent democrat, leading a nation which was to become the symbol of democracy, should express the fear that some day democracy might perish from the earth. But in 1863 a democracy, of the kind practiced today, was still a rarity. Many Americans thought that theirs was perhaps the only true democracy in the world, and yet it gave no votes to women and no votes to slaves. Americans saw republicanism as the essence of democracy, and so they did not take seriously such rival New World democracies as Canada and Australia, which, enthroning the popular vote and standing independent in virtually everything except foreign policy, positively preferred to remain satellites of Britain. Democracy was still an experiment, and few countries had so far tried it. Lincoln could not be completely sure that the American experiment, in the face of the south's determined effort to secede, would last.

Lincoln's stand for the unity of his nation was to be, in the history of the enlargement of human freedom, even more influential than his campaign against slavery. If the United States, from the 1860s, had been divided into two nations, with little in common, then the influence of North America on world affairs would have been much weaker, and the outcome of the Second World War might well have been different.

Just before the victorious end of the four-year war in 1865, Lincoln was at ease, watching a play in a Washington theatre, when he was assassinated. Slavery was already doomed in the Americas. It was abolished in the United States in that year, and was increasingly challenged in Cuba and Brazil. No new slaves were arriving there from Africa, and the babies born into slave families were declared to be free. At last, in 1886, slavery was abolished in Cuba and two years later the last slave was liberated in Brazil. In many parts of Africa and a few scattered parts of Asia, slavery continued. It was not officially abolished on the sand-swept plains of the African state of Mauritania until 1980. Nations continue to condemn it, even in the 1990s, but here and there it persists.

REBELLION IN CHINA

The two most deadly wars in the long period of peace between 1815 and 1914 were fought inside nations rather than between nations. Moreover they were fought inside important nations and so the final outcomes had strong potential effects on the weights and balances of world power. While the American Civil War is still widely known—television and films have revived the memory of it—the other war, the Taiping Rebellion, is little known outside China. The dead in the American Civil War exceeded 600,000 but in the Chinese war the dead perhaps exceeded 20,000,000, making it more deadly than the First World War.

This uprising of simple peasants was a clamor for equality at a time when population was soaring and farmland was scarce. The nutrition and housing of most Chinese peasants were poorer than those of most slaves in the United States. But poverty and hardship do not automatically lead to an uprising: if poverty actually led to rebellion, the history of the world would be nothing but a chain of rebellions. A spark was needed and was provided by Hung Hsui-chüan.

Hung was born near the southern port of Canton (Guangzhou), in a Chinese region which was often sprinkled with foreign ideas. He had the ambitions of a bright Chinese youth, but between 1828 and 1843 he failed four times in his exam for the civil service. As this exam was the gateway to prestige, his repeated failures spread over 15 years were an acute personal humiliation. Hung was compelled to be a village teacher instead of an honored bureaucrat—until he fell under the spell of an American missionary, a Southern Baptist who, without realizing it, rekindled the ambition in the frustrated teacher. Receiving Christian visions, Hung wrapped them in Chinese patriotism and set about leading the people towards "the Heavenly Kingdom of Great Peace." In Chinese the phrase for "great peace" is *taiping*, and that name was given to the rebellion he led.

Hung gained early support from the Hakka, the dialect group to which he belonged. Originally emigrating from central to southern China, the Hakka saw themselves as a distinct people and, more significantly, were seen as distinct by other Chinese. Energetic workers, they thrived on small farms and were skilled in that vital calling of the hillsides—the burning of charcoal for the iron industry and for villagers' cooking stoves. Converted by Protestant missionaries, many became missionaries themselves.

This Chinese messiah was in his late thirties when he propagated his views. In part a puritan, he opposed such common pleasures as opium and gambling and such Chinese traditions as the binding of female feet and the worshipping of ancestors. His appeal to peasants lay partly in his promise to confiscate the farmlands of the rich landlords who owned more than half of the land in China. Many peasants were also delighted to hear that Hung's heavenly kingdom, while spanning the world, would be centered on China. He further appealed to nationalism by opposing the Manchu rulers, who were seen as outsiders in the south.

He affirmed his own distinctive version of equality, extending it to women, whom he proclaimed as equal to men, though the two sexes were to be kept apart on public occasions. Soon his rebel army held 100,000 female soldiers, under the command of his sister.

Marching through the welcoming countryside, Hung's troops were bound to win early victories while the government, in disarray, was assembling its forces. Surprise was on Hung's side. His troops captured the river-city of Nanking (Nanjing) in 1853, a victory which was almost the equivalent of the Confederate army capturing Washington, D.C., during the American Civil War. Town after town, city after city, perhaps 600 in all fell to his armed forces, which eventually numbered close to one million.

When a town was ransacked, the Buddhist pagodas were often a target. The most celebrated pagoda in China and perhaps in the world stood high above the tiled roofs of Nanking, which was now the seat of government of the Taiping Rebellion. Completed in 1430, known as the Porcelain Tower and rising to nine tall storeys, its walls were bright with glazed porcelain. Green, red, yellow and white, the pagoda was like a shining jewel case. Often painted by visiting European artists and printed as a wall picture, it became as well known "in the nurseries of England as one of the Seven Wonders of the World." Hung destroyed it.

This amateur theologian and general preached his own blend of Confucius and Christ. There was also an equalitarian strand, and if he had controlled the countryside rather than the cities he might have redistributed the land on a large scale and set up communes. But he found it easier to win battles than to make use of his victory to administer the new territories. In 1856, a turning point, the senior ranks of the rebels were split by personal disputes and thinned by a purge. Thereafter the troops had less success.

On 1 June 1864, after nearly 14 years in the field, Hung stared at the certainty of defeat. On that day he committed suicide. But the Taipings had shaken what seemed unshakable. Thereafter the prospect of rebellion was enhanced in the minds of a host of Chinese intellectuals and dissidents. The fighting example of Hung deeply influenced the nationalist Dr Sun Yat-sen, who, half a century later, was to overthrow the Emperor of China. Even the communists, who later overthrew the nationalist republic, were helped by the gale which Hung had unleashed.

AN AGE OF SOCIAL EXPERIMENT

The seeds of the plant Equality had lain in the earth for thousands of years. Those Greek philosophers known as the Stoics emphasized that all human beings, whether slaves or free, shared the power of reason and a capacity to show goodwill, and that these qualities distinguished them from other creatures. The Roman Empire and the concept of natural law emphasized common rights; and in the year 212, most freeborn men of the empire received citizenship and so became equal before the law. Christianity was not yet very influential in the Roman Empire. In any case most Christians accepted the continuation of inequality in the material world while agreeing with St Paul's edict that all who loved Christ were spiritually equal. Christ's preaching, however, did include a strand strongly disapproving of inequality. The rich, he warned, were shackled by their riches.

These ideas of equality, though of small influence in the Middle Ages, were revived by the Renaissance with its stress on individuality and by the Reformation with its insistence that all who humbly read the Bible were entitled to be their own interpreters of God's word, and even entitled to be their own priests and pastors. An emphasis on equality led to an emphasis on education for all. Those Protestant lands which built schools assumed that every child had potential, and that reading and writing were the keys to unlocking it. Democracy in the United States owed much to the hundreds of thousands of literate people who, governing their own congregations, believed that they should also be entitled to sit in local parliaments.

In Europe in the second half of the 19th century the demand for economic equality became loud in certain years. It was louder in the cities because it was easier to organize unofficial protest movements in cities than in a village. The call for equality was also spurred by the sharp extremes of wealth. Whereas the monarchy, the nobility and large landowners and merchants had often been conspicuously wealthy, the rise of factory owners who earned vast sums in their own lifetime heightened the sense that their wealth had been created largely by the sweat of their present employees. Demands for economic reforms were spurred by the increase in unemployment in bad years, and the fact that to be unemployed in a big city was to be more helpless than in the countryside where at least firewood could be gathered and where relatives might be called on for food and shelter.

Most of the strong protest movements were in the cities; and in 1848, the year of revolutions, they were on the brink of success. Whereas many of the early protests wanted nothing more than cheap bread in a year of dear bread, the new reform movements were often comprehensive and sophisticated. In 1848 Karl Marx and Friedrich Engels, the young German architects of what became communism, displayed an insight into some of the directions being taken by the fast-changing European economy. Marx predicted with acute foresight that in the industrial nations the new machines and skills would produce enormous wealth and a wide gulf between rich and poor. His goals included the abolition of private property and the defeat of its owners. By 1875 he was dramatically emphasizing equality: "From each according to his abilities, to each according to his needs." He borrowed that catchy slogan from the French anarchists, who were far more numerous then than the socialists.

Economic reformers did not have to point to the need for action. In Italy a host of little children walked barefoot in the middle of winter. In big German cities a host of families each lived in an apartment of just one room. In Russia countless families shivered in the cold in winter because they could not find enough fuel to keep the fire alight. In industrial cities, unemployment in some years of the 1880s exceeded 10 per cent; and most of the unemployed were people who were eager to work and had a lifetime's experience of hard work. The business cycle or trade cycle, the slow swing between economic boom and depression, was now a feature of economic life in industrialized Europe, and levels of unemployment rose and fell like a yo-yo.

It is often implied that the rise of socialism, anarchism and other economic reform movements was simply a result of the acute hardship visible in Europe. If such movements are primarily a sign of hardship they would have been more advanced in Calcutta and Cairo than in Berlin and London. Periodic hardship was a spur to these protesters but not the only spur. More important were their improved means of publicizing and organizing. Radical groups gained weight from the congregating of workers in suburbs where they could easily be organized into trade unions and political parties, and from the decline in the official censorship of radical newspapers and the increased numbers of workers who could read those newspapers. In 1867 the two most celebrated German socialists were elected to the Reichstag, though five years later they were sentenced to prison. As voting rights were extended, left-wing parties could be found in nearly every European parliament. In France in June 1899 a socialist, Alexandre Millerand, became a member of cabinet.

Initially the demand for equality was heard less in economic than in political life, where the slogan of equality did not represent such a strong threat to the wealthy. To ask for the right to vote was less demanding, less revolutionary, than to demand that all land be redistributed equally amongst poor and rich. The right to vote was a rarity even in Europe. In 1800 only a tiny proportion of the world's nations possessed a parliament exercising even a modicum of power, and only a limited number of citizens were allowed to vote in elections or sit in those few parliaments that did exist. The English-speaking world was to the fore in parliamentary government, but the so-called mother of parliaments on the banks of the Thames was far less democratic than the United States during the early decades of the 19th century.

In the late 1850s three of the five Australian colonies served as a political laboratory, and there nearly every man gained the right to vote, including the right to vote by secret ballot and the right to stand for the lower house of parliament. At that time the five major European nations—Britain, France, Germany, Austria and Russia—were far behind Australia, Canada and the United States in their pursuit and practice of democracy.

At the end of the century, New Zealand and Australia were still pioneers in extending democracy. Indeed the wide extension of voting rights and the practice of paying members of parliament led to the election of the world's first government to represent primarily lower-paid workers, small farmers and small shopkeepers. The first Labor government came to power in Queensland in December 1899 but held office for only six days. It was a foretaste of an era when most of Europe would be governed intermittently by social democratic governments.

THE CHOSEN WOMEN OF WYOMING

Women gained from the new interest in equality, though voting rights came to them in slow steps. The American territory of Wyoming was the first to give women the right to vote. It made this radical change in 1869, in the hope of attracting more women to settle in its gun-carrying, masculine territory and so give a softer tone to a frontier society. A year later the nearby state of Utah gave women the vote. As Utah was largely a Mormon society, and many of the householders lived with several wives, it could not be easily classified as a haven of feminism. The effect of the new law was simply to give long-resident Mormon families more votes, at the expense of newcomers to Utah.

To admit women to a medical school was also an audacious step. In the United States, Miss Elizabeth Blackwell, obsessed with the desire to study medicine, had to engage various private tutors before at last, in November 1847 at the age of 26, she was admitted to the medical school at tiny Geneva College in a small town in New York State. Her victory was premature; and at first she was not allowed to attend practical classes and view the human body in company with men. She graduated 14 months later, gained more experience at St Bartholomew's Hospital in her native England, and eventually opened an infirmary in New York for poor women. A forerunner of the animal liberationists, she expressed mistrust of the pioneering work of Pasteur and Koch because they experimented on animals. When in 1864 the University of Zurich decided to admit female medical students and treat them as if they were equal to men, Dr Blackwell wondered whether this might be a sign that the tide was turning. She was mistaken.

Even in Europe one generation later a woman working in the professions was a rarity, except in teaching. The first female scientist to win world esteem was probably Marie Curie, the Polish-born physicist who in France in 1898 coined the word "radioactive" to describe one of her findings. At that time a woman in a parliament was still unknown in the entire world, though Queen Victoria, the formal head of the largest empire, had already reigned for 63 years—a "term of office" longer than a female prime minister in any democratic country will ever experience. Not until 1924 did the world's first female cabinet minister, Nina Bang, take office in Denmark.

The stirrings of a welfare state in western Europe were another sign of the vogue for equality. If all peoples in a nation were worthy, should they not be cared for by the government when they were ill, old, permanently deprived of work or absolutely destitute? In Germany in the 1880s, Bismarck set up a scheme of national insurance, while in Denmark, New Zealand and parts of Australia the old-age pension was in place by 1900. Under pressure from trade unions, Australia introduced the bold idea of a basic wage for factory employees. In a variety of nations the tax system was altered to reduce the tax on small incomes and to increase it on large incomes. Somebody had to pay for the welfare. The rich were the popular choice.

Even in prosperous cities many families with a regular income lived precariously by today's standards. In the English city of York, a family of five who sat towards the bottom of the income ladder could not afford the luxury of beer or tobacco, a halfpenny newspaper, or the postage for a letter. They did not have enough weekly income to place a small coin in the collection plate of their church, and they could not afford a Christmas present for their children unless they themselves made the present.

Sometimes they would take their Sunday clothes to the pawnbroker on Monday morning in order to have enough money to buy food until payday arrived. For the family of a breadwinner who suffered an accident at work or a bout of sickness, the loss of income was shattering. If the husband died, the widow had to take in boarders—if there was room to spare—or washing. With luck she might remarry.

There was one consolation. These families usually enjoyed a higher standard of living than their grandparents had known in their rural village. Furthermore they lived longer, and in more comfort, and were the beneficiaries of more education.

The rising call for equality, vigorous in European-peopled nations in the period from, say, 1840 to 1914, expressed itself in the new call for democratic government. It expressed itself in the idea of primary education for all boys and girls and in the principle—almost universal in Europe by 1900—that every young man should be ready to serve in the armed forces: an equal right to die ran alongside an equal right to be educated for life. Likewise the rising popularity of team sports, largely English innovations, carried an innate belief in fairness and equality. The two teams of footballers, cricketers or other sports players had to be equal in numbers: a rule unknown in business, warfare, politics and most other competitive activities.

This wave of ideas, equalitarian and liberal, burst onto the religious arena. Hitherto most governments had given strong preference to adherents of the official religion. In Britain as late as the year 1820, the law emphasized the inequality of religions. Thus Catholics and Jews could not vote or sit in parliament, and Baptists and most Methodists could not teach in universities. Members of the nonconformist religions could not be married in their own church by a pastor of their own religion. Long before the end of the century, however, adherents of all religions became equal in most respects within the British Isles, though not in every European nation.

The European surge towards equality expressed itself in a growing suspicion of hereditary rights and a preference for some form of republicanism. Venice for centuries had been a powerful aristocratic republic, and Italy in the Renaissance was dotted with small republics; but the rise of a powerful United States and the new chain of South American republics was the herald of a more republican era in the entire world. France, after abolishing and then restoring the monarchy, became a committed republic in 1870. Brazil, which by now was the only surviving monarchy in the Americas, became a republic in 1889. China, perhaps the oldest continuous monarchy in the world, became a republic in 1912. In Britain, Austria-Hungary, Russia, Germany, Italy and most other European nations the monarchy, reduced much in power, seemed likely to survive; but the turmoil late in the First World War removed three of the powerful monarchies of Europe, and they were not restored. Most of the new nations founded in Europe after the war chose to be republics. Of the surviving monarchies, most were held in tight rein by their parliaments. But the waning of the monarchy was no guarantee that democracy would triumph.

THE BOTTLES OF EQUALITY

This thirst for equality was a hallmark of the era, but the equality was labelled and sold in bottles of different shapes and sizes. In some bottles so labelled lay a sparkling brew of inequality. Nationalism was in one of those bottles. While every citizen of a nation might feel a sense of togetherness and equality in the presence of kinsfolk, the equality did not so easily extend to people of other nations. While a keener appreciation of equality was in the air, it might not always extend to people belonging to other income groups and social classes. In addition the feeling of equality might not be shared by rural people and city people in the presence of one another, and it might not be extended to new immigrants.

The interest in equality sometimes clashed with the interest in race felt by many Europeans. A characteristic of the second half of the 19th century, the fascination with race stemmed from an unusual mix of factors. This was a century when the search for general laws about human nature—and the confidence that such generalizations could be found—was intense. Charles Darwin and Karl Marx were only two of the searchers; and Darwin, as the foremost and ultimately the most influential biologist of the era, did much to concentrate public attention on the long-lasting differences between species. Therefore it was easy to slip into the argument that just as Arab horses were different from Cossack ponies, so Africans were perpetually different from, say, Slavonic peoples. At the same time the dramatic increase in contact between people who had long been apart, geographically and culturally, drew attention to the sharp differences that did exist—differences which were wider than probably exist today. Much of this comment on race was neutral but some was aggressive.

Western European peoples were enamored by their own progress in this age of steam and compulsory schooling. From the lofty platform on which they stood, it was easy to think that they were inherently superior, mentally and physically, and would remain so. That their civilization was far ahead of central Africa's and even China's they had no doubt; and certainly it was far ahead in a material sense.

When, in March 1905, Kaiser Wilhelm of Germany pronounced that "Germans are the salt of the earth," he was only saying what many other leaders might say about their own people at a time of excessive patriotism—a patriotism which seemed almost necessary when international tensions were rising. But some scholars and politicians had no time for this concept of clear-cut races with innate virtues and defects. Many who did believe that there was something special about their own branch of European civilization were romantics and often generous in spirit. Many were eager to spread their culture amongst colored peoples in their own colonies. That this surging tide of racial and nationalist ideas could carry such grave dangers was appreciated almost nowhere in Europe.

The Jews were ultimately to be the tragic victims of this tide of ideas, but in 1900 the signs were few, outside the Russian Empire, that this tide was necessarily malevolent. The Jews, for the first time, were permitted to rise to the fore in public life in many European nations. With growing confidence they proclaimed their unity by displaying, more than ever before, the star of David as their symbol. Jews seemed to be one of the special beneficiaries of the equalitarian tides of the time. Indeed Germany was seen as relatively friendly, and thousands of Jews emigrated to Berlin, Leipzig and other German cities where they graced professional and intellectual life, were prominent in music, painting and writing, and built handsome synagogues.

The main home of the Jews was in central and eastern Europe. In a wide band of country running from the Baltic Sea to the Black Sea, a distance of more than 1,200 kilometers, the Jews averaged more than 10 per cent of the total population in every major district. This band of territory included much of western Russia and the eastern fringe of the Austro-Hungarian Empire. It embraced such large cities as Warsaw, Kiev, Cracow and Odessa, but the Jews formed a majority in no city where they were prominent.

Russia governed most of this area and, unlike most other European nations, tightly restricted the rights of Jews. They had to live in specific areas, the so-called "Pale of Settlement," and could not enter certain professions. In scattered towns there were riots against Jews: in the port of Odessa in 1905 some 300 Jews were killed. To emigrate to the United States was one way out of the peril. As a people Jews were easily identified, for they worshipped on Saturday. For religious purposes they spoke and wrote their own language, Hebrew, and in everyday discourse they mainly spoke Yiddish, a dialect of medieval German. In a few European circles they were the target of Christian bias, being seen as the descendants of those who allegedly had crucified Christ. The Orthodox church in Russia and the Assumptionist Fathers in France were sometimes vigorous in expressing this hostility towards Jews. Some European theologians and intellectuals even argued that Christ was not a Jew.

As bankers and moneylenders the Jews were often prominent. Some of the anti-Semitism, particularly in years of serious unemployment, had an economic edge. It was directed against those rich Jews who formed a tiny minority or against the Jewish moneylenders operating in small towns in eastern Europe. The criticism was sharpened by the contemporary emphasis on equality and on the need to cut down tall poppies. Many Jews were tall poppies. Anti-Semitism, especially when directed against the rich and successful, was labelled by the German leftist politician August Bebel as a kind of socialism—"the socialism of fools."

Many sections of European society showed no unease towards Jews. In some nations, nothing prevented talented Jews from rising to positions of prestige. Late in the 19th century, whether in the arts or sciences or medicine or the law, Jews were prominent out of all proportion to their numbers in western Europe. In England, where they were few, they were able to attain high office. The conservative prime minister presiding over England from 1874 to 1880, the eloquent Benjamin Disraeli, was descended from Italian and Portuguese Jews; and his own father when young had frequented the synagogue. Disraeli, however, would probably not have won high office if he had been a mainstream Jew.

It was Mrs Benjamin Disraeli who, during the fashionable horseracing season, introduced young Lord Rosebery to a shy, intelligent 17-year-old Jewish heiress, Hannah de Rothschild. A member of a famous Jewish family of financiers, Hannah became engaged to marry Lord Rosebery. The opposition to the marriage came not from the London press but from the *Jewish Chronicle*, which expressed "the most poignant grief" at the news that she was marrying outside her race. She married Rosebery but did not desert her faith. The marriage did not impede his elevation in 1894 to the prime ministership of what was then the most powerful nation the world had known.

From this slow enthroning of equality, several hundred million people living in Africa and Asia did not gain. The demand for equality and freedom in much of Europe coincided with some loss of freedom in parts of other continents. With so many Asian and African peoples now ruled by distant European monarchs or parliaments, it was not easy to talk convincingly of equality in Cairo, Tashkent, Shanghai or Calcutta. For perhaps the first time in human history, equality was widely lauded as a goal and virtue, but ironically hundreds of millions of people lived under colonial rule. Indeed, most lived under the colonial rule of those European nations which were foremost in preaching equality.

28

A GLOBE UNWRAPPED

IN BURMA in 1900 the typical shopkeepers near the Rangoon River knew far more than their mothers about happenings in Europe. Schoolteachers in African villages knew something about China, a land which their grandmothers might not even have heard of. A skeleton of knowledge about remote lands was now in the curriculum of a thousand schools. Colored maps of the world became commonplace. It is doubtful whether in the days of Napoleon more than a fraction of the people in Europe had ever set eyes on a map of the world; but a century later most of Europe's schoolchildren had seen such a map or a globe and could even recite the names of rivers and mountains in each continent. In the 19th century, in most countries, the knowledge of the average person had grown, but the knowledge of the specialists soared.

It was the last age of global exploration. In almost every decade of the 19th century, a major geographical discovery was made: the finding of the sources of the River Nile; the first ascent of the Matterhorn and other mountains which had previously been seen as unclimbable; the discovery of the sources of the Amazon, Mississippi and Congo rivers; expeditions into the sunburned interior of Australia; the finding in Greenland of the world's largest glacier, the Humboldt; and voyages up the forest-lined rivers of New Guinea. One of the few symbolic landmarks still unvisited was the South Pole, which was to be reached in 1911 by the Norwegian explorer Roald Amundsen—just five weeks ahead of the Briton, Robert Scott, who died in the snow. Many of these remote landmarks now being seen and mapped by people of European descent had long been seen by natives of the regions. The Europeans put them in perspective and printed them on the maps.

New insights into the long history of the world came from some who travelled far. Charles Darwin sailed slowly around the world in a British naval vessel in the 1830s, visiting places as inaccessible as the Galápagos Islands in the eastern Pacific and gaining the knowledge that led to his theory of biological evolution, first published in 1859.

In the straits and islands of South-East Asia, another British naturalist independently discovered Darwin's theory, as well deducing the existence of a remarkable dividing line separating the habitats of many species of plants and animals. Alfred Russel Wallace, teacher and surveyor, was in his mid-twenties when he fell in love with natural history. Deciding to collect exotic birds, partly for the pleasure of those European collectors who wished to stay at home, he sailed in 1848 to the Amazon River to collect and conserve. On his return voyage the ship caught fire, and many of his specimens and zoological notes were lost.

Wallace was not deterred. Setting out for the Indonesian archipelago he moved from island to island, collecting specimens of every living thing that was garish and extraordinary. In 1858 at the port of Ternate in the Moluccas he caught malaria and in his delirium must have wondered whether, like his brother, he would die in a faraway land. In 1862, his collecting and observing almost finished, he returned with the first living birds-of-paradise to reach Europe. Wallace's alert eyes and powerful memory assembled the facts that enabled him to prove that between South-East Asia and Australia, and especially visible between the islands of Bali and Lombok, was a deep and permanent sea barrier, now known as Wallace's line.

It was not yet realized that a new dimension of the oceans was waiting to be explored. Whereas the human eye can see, at least in clear weather, the highest mountains on earth, it cannot see the chains of mountains lying on the seabed, for the sea blocks out the sun's light. Few educated people knew that the seas occupied more than twice as much of the world's surface as did the land. The existence of ranges of mountains far beneath the sea was not known, though the American oceanographer Matthew Maury shrewdly argued in 1855 that far out in the Atlantic

Ocean was what he called the "shallow middle ground." Early attempts to lay a long telegraphic cable across the seabed between the United States and the British Isles proved that the bed of the ocean was far from flat.

A British wooden vessel, HMS *Challenger*, was equipped to sound out ocean beds in remote parts of the world. She set sail in 1872 and systematically dropped overboard a long wire-line to measure the depth of the ocean. Her first major discovery was a winding chain of mountains which lay far below the surface of the Atlantic and ran along the seabed in a north–south line. At no place did this Mid-Atlantic Ridge come close to the continents of America and Africa.

In 1874 *Challenger* ventured far to the south, becoming the first steamship ever to cross the Antarctic Circle. In dredging the bottom of the icy Antarctic ocean her scientists found fragments of continental rock which had been smoothed by glaciers. This discovery, conveying the firm suggestion that a big landmass lay to the south, was the most persuasive evidence so far found for the existence of an Antarctic continent as distinct from a small land or a cluster of islands. Near the west coast of South America, *Challenger*'s scientists and crew found and broadly defined another chain of underwater mountains, the East Pacific Rise. Several of these mountain chains extended for a longer distance than any range of mountains mapped on land.

In the 20th century the deepest parts of the ocean were discovered to lie as deep as the world's loftiest mountains were high. Mount Everest in central Asia is more than 9,000 meters high; but in the north Pacific Ocean a trench running between the islands of Guam and Yap has been measured as even further from the surface of the sea. It was not yet sensed that below the seabed lay a wealth of minerals. More than a century after *Challenger* completed her voyage, one-quarter of the world's oil was being tapped from fields offshore.

The sea still covered mysteries. Were the continents, now far apart, once joined tightly together? A young German meteorologist, Alfred Wegener, after travelling to Greenland, made a sweeping observation of profound importance. In 1912 he devised the theory of continental drift. He suggested that there had originally existed only one massive continent, that tropical Africa and South America had once been joined but that North and South America had not always been joined, that the Himalaya Mountains arose from the pressure of continents slowly colliding, and that present continents were not fixed in position but were either slowly moving apart or coming closer. His brilliant ideas were deemed preposterous and only won wide respect in the 1960s, long after his death.

THE LURE OF THE FARAWAY

With the widening knowledge of the globe and the influence of the romantic movement came a realization that the world was sprinkled with unfamiliar places that could elicit gasps of wonder from lovers of nature. The ancient Greeks had listed their wonders of the world, nearly all of which were buildings created by their own artists and architects within a small radius of the cities of Athens and Alexandria. In 1900, by contrast, many travellers preferred the grand spectacles of nature to the grand buildings of Greece and Rome, China and India. Some pointed to Niagara Falls, the Swiss Alps, the Himalayas, the harbors of Hong Kong and the table-shaped mount of Cape Town, the trees of Yosemite in California, New Zealand's Milford Sound and the muddy Irrawaddy in Burma, while others collected a different set of colored postcards. The assumption that these marvels could in no way be imperilled was more confident than it is today.

Many fortunate travellers marvelled at the volcanic terraces and rock stairways on the North Island of New Zealand. One wide terrace was a delicate pink with crystals like rosy icicles. The waters of the other terrace were wonderingly described by the English historian J.A. Froude in 1885: "The hue of the water was something which I had never seen, and shall never again see on this side of eternity." It was not the color of the violet or the harebell—the flowers he loved—nor sapphire or turquoise. A master of English prose, he confessed he could find no way of conveying "a sense of that supernatural loveliness." One year later the pink and white terraces were utterly destroyed when stones, ash and hot mud poured from the nearby volcano.

For perhaps the first time in human history, a few people of talent were resolving to live in, not merely travel to, faraway and mysterious parts of the world. There they were eager to bathe in local culture rather than simply propagate their own culture as missionaries, medical officers or merchants. In 1890 Robert Louis Stevenson, the Scottish-born author renowned for his books *Treasure Island* and *Dr Jekyll and Mr Hyde*, set up house with his extended family in the coastal hills of Western Samoa, within sound and sight of the sea and its reefs. In the following year the Frenchman Paul Gauguin, a stockbroker, left his wife and five children in Paris and set sail for Tahiti to begin a fresh life as a painter and "hippy" in the tropics. Both the Scottish writer and the French painter were to end their days in the South Seas. Long after he was buried on the hilltop above his house, Stevenson's elegant prose conveyed the romance of the South Seas to a vast reading audience. "Song is almost ceaseless," he wrote of his Samoans. "The boatman sings at his oar, the family at evening worship, the girls at night in the guest house, sometimes the workman at his toil."

In 1901, in the arid center of Australia and far from the nearest railway, a miraculous thread was tied between the 20th century and the era of the nomads. Professor Baldwin Spencer and F. J. Gillen captured the dances of Aborigines on one of the first movie cameras and recorded their haunting songs on the wax cylinder of a phonograph. As the learned visitors had no battery or electricity, they were forced to crank the handle of the camera continuously to supply the motive power. Moreover they had no alternative but to arrange the heavy camera for long periods in a set position, so that it pointed continuously in the one direction. Spencer decided to direct the camera towards a group of nearly naked men performing the dance of an ancient rainmaking ceremony, with the dust rising from their bare and pounding feet. The dancers, wisely not interested in posterity, suddenly began to make "a wide semicircular sweep" and slowly they passed out of the camera's vision. Thus much of the precious film was wasted.

It was a remarkable occasion and time signal. Here were the representatives of a dying way of life that had dominated the entire world in 10,000 BC, standing face to face with the latest step in technology. The dancing Aborigines retained the sense that they were in command, that they and not the strange intruders held the key to the universe. While they danced, their voices—for they were impressive mimics—imitated the cry of the plover bird. The Aborigines believed that their imitation of its cry would entice rain to fall on the dusty ground, which had long been parched.

In the shrinking of the world, the surviving remnants of the hunters and gatherers, once all-powerful on the face of the globe, were the most drastic losers. Later most of their descendants would probably gain from readmission to a wider world; but the generation which faced for the first time this new, powerful and incomprehensible European way of life—so many years removed from their own style of life—could only feel bewildered. They had occupied their lands for thousands of years, and their future had seemed eternal. In that sense they were exceptionally privileged. They had been able to retain, far longer than all other human societies, a traditional way of life based on the luxury of a tiny number of people possessing vast and often attractive spaces. But in the end the demise of the old nomadic way of life had been spurred by its inefficient and aristocratic monopoly of what was becoming the world's scarcest asset, land on which to grow food and find shelter.

The material advance of the human race and the multiplying of its numbers in the previous 10,000 years had come largely from the skilled and ingenious use of land, plants, animals and raw materials. Much of it had come from the more intense use of land for farms and flocks. Now, in Australia and the icy fringes of the Northern Hemisphere and the arid corners of the southern half of Africa, the last of the nomads were being called upon, with unanswerable urgency and sometimes with violence, to stand aside or join in. How could they join? They lacked the skills and attitudes, values and incentives which would enable them to take part with ease. The process of dispossessing—now suffered by the surviving nomads in Australia, Canada, arid southern Africa and the northern tundra—had already affected nomads who once inhabited nearly all of the world. Moreover in other lands the earlier generations of nomads had had some chance of joining in the new way of life because, in the inaugural era of farming and herd-keeping, the new way of life was not far removed from their own. In the late 19th century the steam-engine societies displacing them had little hope of understanding, and often no wish to understand, the complexity of the takeover which they were swiftly carrying to a conclusion.

THE SEA CARPET

New shipping routes were joining the continents, uniting them with a speed and safety not seen before. In 1900 lighthouses stood on most of the capes fronting the world's sea lanes. The southern tips of the continents of America and Africa and Australia held their lighthouses, and in the darkness the lights beaming from these lonely headlands were landmarks for deep-sea captains. Many narrow straits in the East Indies and

West Indies displayed a strong light at night. In Europe various islands virtually popping out of the lonely sea warned of their presence at night, and it was the German island of Heligoland in the North Sea which operated the most powerful night-light the world had seen.

The ships which sailed past the white lighthouses reflected the new web of commerce. Shipping was cheap; the cost of carrying goods was cut. Bulk commodities such as coal and wheat, cotton and pig iron and petroleum, were carried cheaply from one end of the world to the other: and yet a few lifetimes ago, only precious commodities such as pepper, ivory and gold could afford to be carried long distances in ships. The children of the lighthouse keepers at Cape Horn, if they were curious about the ships passing by, could discern in fair weather a straggling procession of stately tall-masted sailing ships carrying nitrate from the dry coast of Chile all the way to Germany where it was becoming prized fertilizer. They could perhaps see ships carrying bales of wool or a consignment of copper concentrate from Australia to England, or oregon timber to Europe from the northwest coast of America. The Panama Canal, that remarkable short cut across America, was not completed until 1914.

Money and technology had their own web of connections. A railway in the Argentine or Queensland might be financed by English money. A mine in Siberia or an oil well in Sumatra might be financed by German or Dutch money. Just as capital crossed the world in an unprecedented flow, so did people. Free or half-free migration had never been on such a large scale, whether Germans and Irish flocking to the United States, Italians and Iberians to South America, Japanese to Hawaii, Britons to Canada and New Zealand, Chinese to the Malay Peninsula and Java, Welsh to Patagonia, or Indians to Fiji and Natal.

Carriers of culture also crossed the world in unprecedented numbers. Christian and medical missionaries, women and men, poured into China, India, Korea, Polynesia, New Guinea, Sudan, German South-West Africa, French Indochina and wherever they were permitted to enter: in practice they were permitted to enter almost every land during the heyday of Europe. In Africa one of the famous explorers was David Livingstone, a Scottish mill hand who became a Christian missionary, while the Alsace-born medical missionary Albert Schweitzer spent most of his life helping victims of leprosy and sleeping sickness in Gabon. Missionaries such as the Belgian-born Father Damien, who died while helping lepers in Hawaii, were folk heroes in an era when it was not yet thought quite right to acclaim footballers as heroes. Musicians also criss-crossed the world, and at the turn of the century the young Italian tenor Enrico Caruso divided his year between opera houses in Buenos Aires, New York and Europe. Global empires made it easy to lay down professional pathways across the world, and many academics and bureaucrats spent their working life far from the land of their education.

This many-sided process was to be given, at the end of the 20th century, the name of globalization. It was certainly international and global but it was also rabidly national. While the world was becoming one, it was also remaining divided. The map was fragmented into empires controlled from Europe. Much of the world had been divided amongst European imperial powers by 1850, and the final phase of subdivision took place in the following 50 years when colonies as far apart as New Guinea and East Africa were acquired by Germany, tropical Congo was taken over by Belgium, parts of northeastern Africa fell to Italy, New Caledonia and much of Indochina were taken by France, a vast area of crag and plain in central Asia was absorbed into the Russian Empire, and a string of islands and large patches of mainland fell to Britain, which was far and away the largest owner of colonies. Many strips of the Chinese coast fell into European hands, while Taiwan was occupied by Japan. Even the United States reluctantly entered the race, buying Alaska and capturing Spanish colonies stretching from Cuba to the Philippines. By 1900 most parts of the world were governed by Britain, France, Holland, Spain, Portugal, Russia, Germany, Belgium, Italy and a few other colonial powers.

The colored maps of the world were dotted and dashed with the red which was widely used by map-makers to symbolize the British Empire. Queen Victoria, who was to die in 1901, ruled an empire that would have made even the Mongols blink. Hers was the first empire on which the sun never set.

THE PALE EMPIRE OF IDEAS

While the Roman Empire in its extent and longevity was a marvel, several empires which were flourishing by 1900 were larger. Russia, the United States and China each occupied an expanse larger than that of the old Roman Empire. Likewise the empires of Britain and France across the seas were vaster in area than the total of Rome's colonies, though Europe's control of daily life in its colonies probably was less pervasive than that of Rome within its empire.

There are two categories of empire. One is the physical, consisting, like the Roman and British empires, of colonies and dependencies. The other category is the pale empire of ideas. In the 19th century, Europe spread in influence even more through its empire of ideas than through the possession of new colonies. Just as Buddhism had spread from India into China without even the aid of a conquering army or the establishing of a physical empire, so the spread of Christianity, a knowledge of world geography and the physical sciences, and many other messages of western civilization did not necessarily depend on the presence of a European army and navy.

At the same time a pale empire of ideas—much paler—was extending in the opposite direction. Around 1900, a river of powerful ideas quietly flowed from Africa and Asia to European civilization. In art, French cubism was much influenced by west African art. Famous writers such as Jack London and Rudyard Kipling saw virtues in the Inuits and the Indians. In the social sciences two giants of the infant century, Freud and Durkheim, thought that the sick or ailing society in Europe could learn from Australian Aborigines. A new respect for nature in sections of western society meant that those so-called primitive people who lived close to nature on the other side of the globe were accorded virtues previously ignored. The founding of the international Boy Scout movement in 1907 reflected the belief that much could be learned from the wolf as well as from the books of Cambridge and Tübingen.

KNOWLEDGE: A NEW REAL ESTATE

Secular knowledge was in the ascendant, though it owed much to religious impulses. Ever since certain wings of Protestantism had encouraged the idea that everyone should be his own priest, and even her own priest, an ability to read had been vital. Protestant Prussia, Holland and Scotland—each of which was relatively small in population and area—led the way in literacy and so in the general pursuit of knowledge. Scotland's places of learning continued to produce so many talented young men that the country could not use them effectively; and so they trooped south to London where the book-publishing industry, probably the largest in the world, became almost a Scottish home away from home. Engineers, politicians, explorers, inventors, soldiers, merchants, teachers, philosophers and divines, speaking with a Scottish accent, were foremost in the British Empire and beyond.

The Jews also came to the fore in seeking education. They could not own land in most European countries; but medicine, science, business, a few of the universities and certain of the learned professions were opening their doors to Jews in the 19th century. Their role in the knowledge industry was far more influential than their small numbers would have suggested. Knowledge was their real estate, their title deed.

Traditionally in most parts of the world the ownership of land had conferred income, social status and political rights on those who owned it. Knowledge was now challenging the economic role of land, though it was not yet making deep inroads into the status of land. By 1900 nearly as many people probably made a remunerative and satisfying living in the USA, France, Britain and Germany from knowledge as were making it from ownership of land, minerals and other natural resources. Knowledge was the new frontier. There was virtually a rush for knowledge just as there had been a rush for gold in California and Australia half a century previously.

Knowledge was often a disciplined and confident force and it marched readily across national boundaries. It was a form of international currency, and the possessor often moved from nation to nation with some ease. Just as the gap in wealth and prestige between the owner of a small strip of land and a huge estate was wide, so the gap between the owner of a small parcel and a large parcel of knowledge was also becoming wide. That sort of knowledge which was utilitarian and tended to increase personal or national wealth was valued more highly than other sorts. The dispensing of newly acquired knowledge, especially in medicine and engineering and the basic and applied sciences, was increasingly the goal of those new universities and technical institutes which by 1900 were to be found in every major city on the globe. An ability to expand knowledge was almost the hallmark of the leading nations; and no other period had seen such an accumulation of useful knowledge. Albert Einstein, the physicist, was widely seen as the genius of the first half of the 20th century; but who could say so with certainty, for the learned theories formulated by this brilliant and unassuming German Jew were understood by few. In contrast Erasmus the Dutchman, who was seen as the genius of the 16th century, was an all-rounder. Each field of knowledge was now the domain of specialists, and few specialists jumped the high fences designed to separate them from outside fields.

Specialization was the secret of Europe's success but it carried great dangers for the specialists, even more than for the civilization that gained from their research. It was sometimes complained in a whisper—for the thought was heretical—that if knowledge and indeed wisdom were really so important, why were most of the specialists satisfied with the possession of such a small and concentrated morsel of knowledge?

From this invasion of knowledge no land could hide. Japan had had periods of hiding and yet had retained vitality and inventiveness in its isolation. In the late 1500s, at the close of its first period of contact with Europe, Japan manufactured more muskets than probably any other country in Europe. In the 1850s it put out its hands to the world again, opening its ports to foreign ships. In the 1860s it began to model its army on the French and its navy on the British. In 1876 its ban on the wearing of swords was another sign of the rejection of its feudal past. The building of railways—fiercely opposed by some Japanese—was one more. The reshaping of Japan was brisk and decisive. In 1895 it was victorious in its short war with China and 10 years later it won—to the surprise of the world—its short war with Russia.

China's long and proud phase of self-absorption, in contrast, ended in some humiliation. In many of its ports the Europeans made their own laws, and Shanghai was fast becoming a European city. Christian missionaries poured in to spread their message, many facing death when they preached in the remote countryside. In June 1900 there was a rebellion against foreigners, and the German ambassador in Peking was killed. Foreign armies quickly arrived to put down this uprising. The throne of China, once all-powerful, was soon to collapse. There was even a prospect that China would suffer the fate of Africa and be partitioned amongst the European powers.

It was an extraordinary somersault in the relations between China and Europe. If such a humiliation of a throne and a culture had been possible in, say, the year 1400, it would have been the Chinese who sent Buddhist missionaries to Dublin, who operated the customs houses in Hamburg and Constantinople, and who threatened to partition Europe if the people did not behave themselves.

Around the world most of the locked gates were flung open, but not those of Mecca. It remained a forbidden city to unbelievers. Every so often furtive sightseers made the journey to Arabia, only to betray their ignorance of the rituals at sacred sites where, it was rumored, some were judged to be Christians and promptly executed. Many Arabs setting out on the legitimate pilgrimage now liked to wear colored Manchester textiles, and their weapons used gunpowder. The overland pilgrimage was no longer such an ordeal. In 1909 the pilgrimage, for long dominated by strings of camels and a vast concourse of pilgrims on foot, was transformed when the first steam train arrived in Medina with pilgrims from Damascus.

THE RISE OF NORTHWESTERN EUROPE

For several thousand years there were only two long-standing centers of innovation and economic power. One was eastern Asia and the other was the Mediterranean, especially the lands near its eastern shores. Of the influential western empires before AD 1500, the Egyptian, Mesopotamian, Greek, Roman, Hellenistic and Byzantine empires lay in this relatively small zone. The eastern Mediterranean was not only the birthplace of the three most influential western religions—Judaism and its offspring, Christianity and Islam—but also the cradle of most of the vital western innovations, ranging from farming and metallurgy to writing, arithmetic and even the state.

Later, political and economic power and sheer inventiveness moved away from this hub in the eastern Mediterranean and its hinterlands. The seat of power moved to the North Atlantic coastline. South of the Alps was superseded by north of the Alps. The old ports of the Mediterranean were challenged by the river ports and harbors of western Europe. The demise in the relative power of such cities as Athens and Alexandria, Rome and Constantinople was matched by the rise of Lisbon, Seville, London, Amsterdam, Antwerp and Paris: all cities on the sea or close to the sea and looking out to the west. Later, Berlin and St Petersburg became part of this new focus, for their nearest commercial outlet was the North Sea. This shift towards northwestern Europe was more decisive and long-lasting than any comparable shift in eastern Asia. There, the northern half of China remained the hub of power, though in the 20th century there was a swing in relative power towards Japan, South Korea,

Taiwan and Hong Kong. In some ways this lesser swing in power from China towards the maritime lands nearby was paralleled by the shift from the landlocked Mediterranean to the Atlantic coast of Europe.

The ascent of northwestern Europe to a dominance on the world stage, such as was never achieved by the old eastern Mediterranean and Asia Minor empires, could not have been predicted in the year AD 1600. The ascent was not inevitable, but, in retrospect, a few powerful factors were promoting it. With the discovery of the Americas and the opening of the long sea route past the Cape of Good Hope to India, the East Indies and China, northwestern Europe held an advantage. Admittedly it shared this advantage because the west coast of Italy and the Mediterranean coast of Spain were in as favorable a position as Amsterdam and London to tap the wealth of the New World across the ocean.

Protestantism was part of the new dynamo of northwestern Europe. This religious movement mainly flourished on the north side of the Alps. Almost certainly it was easier for a reformation to succeed when it was far from Rome and from those other Italian cities and princedoms with an affinity to the papacy and an economic and emotional interest in supporting it. Moreover the Reformation in its early years was adopted and promoted by the exponents of that commerce and capitalism, much centered on textiles, which was already vigorous in parts of northwestern Europe. With some notable exceptions the Protestant creeds were more sympathetic to the spirit of inquiry which the growing science and technology needed. At the same time it is reasonable to suggest that Protestantism, and especially Calvinism, was as much the offspring as the parent of the different spirit increasingly visible in northwestern Europe.

Geography promoted the rise of northwestern Europe in another way. This cold region with its long winters was a heavy consumer of fuel. As England and Belgium and other parts of the region began to run out of a cheap supply of firewood they turned to shallow coastal beds of coal. It so happened that this region was wonderfully endowed with coal compared to Italy, Greece, Egypt, the Fertile Crescent and all the lands of the eastern Mediterranean and the Persian Gulf. In turn the mining of coal led, though not automatically, to the steam engine and the coke-burning blast furnace. The steam engine was the most powerful agent of globalization so far experienced, for it led directly and indirectly to the engine in cars and aircraft, and to the age of gas and oil.

Coal and steam helped to enthrone northwestern Europe as commercially and politically supreme. This was also the first region of the world to import, on a large scale, raw materials and food from afar. For the first time in the history of the western world a cramped region supported a huge population at a relatively high standard of living. Here the population was even more densely settled than in China. For long it was the main source of those Protestant emigrants to Boston, New York, Philadelphia and those seaboard provinces that became the economic powerhouse of the new United States. This emigration, rather than weakening northwestern Europe, bolstered its global trading links and its cultural and political influence.

So a mixture of major and minor factors helped northwestern Europe to supplant the warmer and drier Mediterranean and Middle East. Geography alone, though a major factor, was not enough. The history of the world is dotted with geographical advantages that were shunned or squandered. Western Europe exploited its geography with a spirit of intellectual and commercial adventure such as the world had possibly not seen before.

The United States displayed the same spirit of adventure, with even more effect. A vast bowl of resources and a dynamo of knowledge, it was potentially richer than northwestern Europe and by 1900 held more people than any two western European countries combined. It was also united whereas Europe was divided. Nothing was to do more to mold the 20th century than the increasing unity of North America and the increasing disunity of Europe.

29

THE WORLD WARS

A HISTORY of the world could be so written that it was almost dominated by the wars between clans, tribes, nations and empires. Countless wars, recorded and not recorded, have taken place even in the last 10,000 years. Certainly, peace is the more normal condition than war, but war and peace are linked in their causation. Thus a memorable period of peace can depend on the outcome of the previous war and the enforcement of that outcome. Peace between the nations of a region is often the result of an agreed pecking order which has been arrived at either by war or by the threat of war.

In Europe in 1900, alas, there was no agreed pecking order. And yet there were widespread hopes that the nations would fight less frequently. Nations consoled themselves that their economies were now so interdependent that they could not fight for very long because they would run out of munitions, food and raw materials, not forgetting money. Some commentators even thought war itself might slowly vanish. Those who argued that a lack of a common language led to misunderstandings, which in turn led to war, now offered their solution. A new and synthetic international language, Esperanto, was spreading like a bushfire in the early 1900s. Similarly, tourism across national borders was flourishing, and it was commonly predicted that people who met foreigners in their happy travels and holidays would surely be reluctant to put on military

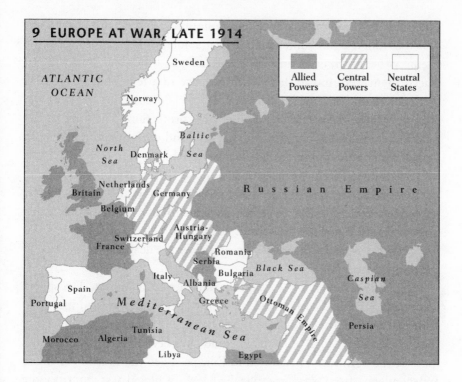

9 EUROPE AT WAR, LATE 1914

uniforms and fight them. But in the course of human history most of the intensely fought wars have been fought between neighboring countries.

Europe's last major war, fought between France and Prussia in 1870 and 1871, had been swift; and so the short war was thought to be the likely pattern of the future. The First World War was approached in the belief that war itself was still a quick and efficient solver of problems. Both sides expected to win. They also expected to win quickly, for military technology seemed to be more decisive than ever before.

A DEADLOCKED WAR

The war began in August 1914 and was expected to be won before Christmas or soon after. When the Germans and their ally, the Austro-Hungarians, clashed with the Russians in eastern Europe, and the Germans fought the French and British armies on the plains of northern France, and the Austrians fought the Serbs, the war seemed to be moving swiftly towards an early conclusion. Germany was the early winner but casualties were huge.

The firepower of the latest machine guns, and of the heavy guns drawn by horses, was so devastating that soldiers advancing towards the enemy were mown down in their thousands, and the thousands who replaced them were mown down. In the space of a few months, on most battlefields, soldiers had to dig hundreds of kilometers of trenches and arrange walls of barbed wire for their own protection. The long battle-field trench, deep enough for a soldier to stand upright and not be seen by the enemy nearby, was really a form of shield.

So the opposing armies ceased to move swiftly as in past wars, and the war became defensive. Any attempt by one army to leave the shelter of the trenches and storm forward usually led to the capture of only a tiny strip of ground—before the rain of shells and bullets from the opposite line of trenches forced a retreat. On such days the deaths were counted in the thousands.

It was also a far-flung war and that sharpened its impact. The spread of French, British, German and other European colonies had increased the risk that a European war would become a global war; and indeed in the 18th century a total of five wars could have been called global, though most of the fighting was centered in Europe. Even the War of American Independence from 1775 to 1783 had been a global war. In 1914 the presence of new German colonies in lands as far apart as northern China, Western Samoa, New Guinea and East Africa and the presence of rival British and French colonies nearby served as a fuse that carried the war almost instantly from Europe to remote tropical harbors. Indeed it was a world war in 1914, when the main colonial battles occurred, much more than it was in 1918. On the other hand, the Second World War was more global in its last year than in its first year.

Meanwhile in Europe, on most battlefronts in the last weeks of 1914 the war had reached a stalemate. What was intended to be the Great War of 1914 became the Great War of 1914–15; and still the months ticked away. In April 1915, in an attempt to end the stalemate, the British and French with Australians and New Zealanders launched a new front on Turkish beaches near Gallipoli, at the mouth of the Dardanelles. They hoped to defeat Turkey in a few weeks, use the liberated Dardanelles as a sea route to ports in southern Russia and so send arms and munitions which would equip the huge Russian armies. In turn it was hoped that the Russian armies would apply pressure on the Germans on the Eastern Front. The Turks, however, defended ably. They dug trenches as their shield, deadlocked this sector of the war and forced the invaders to with-draw at the year's end.

The military deadlock defied the predictions of all but a few gifted generals and armchair strategists. Nothing like it had been seen in the history of the world. It is common to blame the generals. But in most of the countries at war, even the mothers and wives and girlfriends were initially supportive and for long they were even resigned to the slaughter, believing with the aid of wartime propaganda that the perpetual bloodshed would miraculously terminate in the defeat of the ex-hausted enemy.

The war, with all its surprises and uncertainties, was spiced with "ifs." If Russia could have been propped up in 1915, the tsar and his ministers might have maintained control of their restless country. But failure in three successive years of fighting amputated the leg of the already hob-bling tsar. In 1917 two revolutions in quick succession broke out, and Lenin and his communists took control. Russia withdrew from the war.

Until the 19th century every vehicle travelled on the surface of land, sea or ice; but that iron rule was quickly broken by new aircraft and sub-marines. Aircraft were used in warfare by the Italians who invaded Turk-ish Libya in 1911. In the final phase of the First World War, flocks of tiny aircraft flew high over the Western Front to observe the enemy's activi-ties and positions, and big airships flying at less than 100 kilometers an hour dropped bombs on a few British, French and German cities, inflict-ing damage that gave no real indication of what aerial bombing would do in future wars.

In this war, the submarine and its torpedo were far more important than air power. It was the Austrian navy which, in the Adriatic in the 1860s, developed a self-propelled torpedo capable of travelling under the water and exploding when it hit a ship. A surface boat fired the torpedo, but its approach was easily seen by an alert enemy. A vessel hiding be-neath the sea was the solution. In the 1880s the French devised the un-derwater ship or submarine, driven at first by an electric motor and later by the new petrol or diesel engine.

At the outbreak of war in 1914 the Germans owned the best sub-marines. Their first remarkable victory was early one morning in the sev-enth week of the war. A submarine patiently waiting in the North Sea sighted three English cruisers. In a short time the cruisers were sunk, and 1,400 sailors were drowned. The German shipyards built more and more of their long cigar-shaped submarines and sent them quietly out to sea where they preyed on the cargo ships carrying food and metals and munitions from the Americas, Africa, Asia and Australia to British and French ports. Occasionally they sank a passenger ship. The loss of lives when an iceberg sank the *Titanic* two years before the war was tiny compared to the loss of seamen and civilians by submarine warfare in the same cold Atlantic. In April 1917 alone submarines sank 354 oceangoing ships. This astonishing success had its price. The United States was still neutral but some of its ships were sunk. Nothing did more to anger Washington in 1917 and to force it into the war. At the start of 1918, Germany still possessed a fighting chance of winning the war or negotiating a favorable peace. Russia had already been knocked out of the war. The United States, entering late, was not seen as likely to exert a powerful influence. Furthermore, Germany's main ally, the Austro-Hungarian Empire, was still holding firm the mountainous front line against Italy. In great heart the Germans commenced an offensive which, in March 1918, won much ground and pushed close to Paris.

Slowly the fortunes of the war swung against Germany. It suffered because the access to food and raw materials, and the power to produce munitions and men, favored its enemies. Its front lines were dinted by hammer-blows. By September 1918 Germany's allies were about to wilt. The Bulgarians surrendered. The Turks, fighting to hold their old empire in the Middle East, were close to surrender. The Austro-Hungarian Empire was about to break into splinters, and in October both Yugoslavia and Czechoslovakia proclaimed themselves republics. In Germany, as winter approached, the morale of civilians and even soldiers was failing. Food and clothing were scarce, the enemy blockade having done its damage. On 3 November 1918, German sailors mutinied at Kiel. On 9 November a socialist revolution captured Munich, while the Emperor of Germany, Kaiser Wilhelm, abdicated in Berlin. Two days later, on 11 November, Germany and its allies signed the armistice.

For soldiers it was the most terrible war the world had known; for civilians the Taiping Rebellion had been worse. Of the 8,500,000 soldiers and sailors who died in the First World War, Germany lost the most, followed by Russia, France, Austria-Hungary and then Britain and its empire. These five powers, along with Italy, which entered the war in 1915, lost nine out of every 10 soldiers killed in the war. In addition more than 20,000,000 soldiers were wounded, and this list of the slain and maimed did not include maybe five million civilians who died as a direct result of the war. Hundreds of thousands of the dead had no known grave. To see at Verdun the war memorial commemorating 130,000 dead French soldiers who have no known grave is to glimpse the grief felt in all those houses and tenements out of whose doors these men had cheerfully stepped away to war. From crowded apartments in Moscow to sheep farms in New Zealand there were millions of mantelpieces on which stood framed black-and-white photographs of earnest or smiling young men, killed in the war which everyone now called the Great War, not realizing that a greater war was barely 20 years ahead.

The Seven Years' War, the Napoleonic Wars and many other wars had redrawn the map, but their imprint was not as pronounced as this war. Without the Great War there would probably have been no Russian Revolution and no victory for communism. But for this war, the activist monarchs in all their splendor would have continued to reign in Vienna, Berlin–Potsdam and St Petersburg, and the sultan would have presided over the Turkish Empire—an empire which also vanished. If there had been no war the name Hitler would probably be unknown, for he arose out of the bitterness of Germany's defeat, just as Mussolini arose as dictator of Italy largely because he played on the deep postwar disillusionment of his people.

In the discussions around the tables of the peace conference at Versailles in 1919, high hopes as well as a desire for revenge were present. Many nationalities seized the chance to set up their own nations. It was a map-makers' picnic. In Europe now stood 31 states and nations where, on the eve of the war, had stood only 20. Some of the new states were tiny, such as Danzig Free City (now Gdansk) on the shores of the Baltic, and some were large, such as Hungary and Poland. Most were republics—though Yugoslavia and Albania were monarchies—and most tried their hand at democracy, not always successfully. Some turned into dictatorships.

The war, much longer than had been expected in 1914, was a jolt to the optimism which had taken root in much of Europe during the relatively peaceful, prosperous and civilized 99 years since the defeat of Napoleon. And yet many Europeans took heart. They dismissed the war as being a result of unusual sores for which they believed they possessed the healing ointment. They believed that the war was a result of the kaiser's and tsar's arrogance, and now they were gone, the one in exile in

Holland and the other murdered. It was argued by others that the war came about because of the greed of the armaments kings—they could surely be curbed. Likewise it was said to be the result of a dearth of diplomacy, of a reluctance to talk and negotiate, and so a permanent round table of diplomacy called the League of Nations was set up at Geneva. A parliament of peace, it was possibly the bravest experiment in the history of all the nations up to that time. The hope of the liberals and idealists of the world, it became just a debating club. While it talked about peace, some of its members prepared for war.

Without the Great War, Britain and Europe would have remained dominant in finance, but during it they had to borrow. So the United States, especially in those war years when it was neutral, became a financier of the war effort. One cause of the approaching world Depression was the new financial power of the United States in the 1920s. Relatively inexperienced as global leader, tolerant of the cycle of boom and setback, and happy to watch the stock exchange in Wall Street acting as a trumpet major, it led an unstable world towards chronic instability. Another cause of the economic downturn visible in 1930 was that Britain tried to restore financially the pre-1914 world and its craving for stable prices. It was like a nostalgic attempt to restore the trench-scarred battlefields of Belgium and France to fertile cornfields and then invite all the prewar workers to return—even from the war cemeteries—and resume their old rural life. But one should not be too critical of these attempts. After the catastrophe of such a war, a determined attempt to piece together the peaceful jigsaw of the lost past was almost inevitable.

From time to time even before 1900, unemployment had become widespread in the industrialized nations. In many nations in the 1920s the unemployment in lean months exceeded 10 per cent. It was partly a result of the dislocations caused by the speed of change. New industrial regions and industries rose and fell, the shift of work from farms to factories continued, but a factory was more likely to suffer from serious slumps than was a farm. On the farm, when prices were low, the farmhands kept on working at much lower wages, or at least they could grow much of their own food. In the car or tire or textile factories, when slumps came, the workers stayed at home and had nothing to live on. Governments and economists, moreover, were not sure how to cope with a depression. The prevailing principle was that they should do nothing and that the economy, after swallowing its medicine in the form of high unemployment and low wages and profits, would quickly cure itself.

The crash of the share market on Wall Street in October 1929 is now seen as the fire-bell. Financial confidence fell, deflation replaced inflation, international trade slipped, and people stopped buying and thereby destroyed more jobs. Unemployment grew, exceeding 30 per cent in some industrial nations in the rock-bottom year of 1932. An economic depression on this scale had no precedent. It was a boost to communism and fascism. It led towards the Second World War, which was really the outcome of what was increasingly seen as an unfinished First World War.

THE GERMAN DICTATOR

Hitler of Germany and Stalin of Russia shaped the coming war. They were the decisive leaders when the war broke out in 1939, a date of their choosing, and briefly they were allies.

Adolf Hitler came from a river-town in Austria where his father was a minor officer in the customs house. A would-be artist, he imbibed some of the anti-Semitism of Vienna and some of the patriotism bubbling over in Munich at the outbreak of the First World War. Enlisting in the German army, he won the Iron Cross for valor on the Western Front. One of the German soldiers who in 1918 were stunned by the collapse of morale at home, when morale was still solid in many parts of the hard-pressed army, he gave vent to his anger and sense of betrayal—on his return to civilian life—by dabbling on the fringes of politics. In 1919 at the age of 30 he became head of a little Bavarian political party, the National Socialist German Workers' Party. His party developed its own private army, which excelled in street fights against the Marxists and other parties of the left. His army was now dressed in brown ties and shirts, these being bargain-price uniforms originally prepared for the German army defending its colony in East Africa. In 1928, on the eve of the world Depression, his party won 3 per cent of the votes at the German national elections.

Hitler knew his Germany. His oratory, magnetic with the aid of astute coaching, warmed the hearts of many Germans who felt their nation and their world had been unjustly torpedoed in 1918. He spoke with such physical and emotional energy that his shirt, after a two-hour speech, would be soaked with sweat. The new outdoor loudspeaker and the radio helped to spread his message. Few party leaders in Europe were quicker to use innovations.

Like many of his leading lieutenants, Hitler was a German romantic. He doted on Richard Wagner's music, knowing much of it by heart, and each August he was to be seen listening intensely in the opera house which Wagner himself had designed on high ground in the Bavarian town of Bayreuth. The highbrow arts are said to be a civilizing and softening influence but they did not soften Hitler and his now-powerful henchmen: Goebbels with his doctorate in aesthetics from Heidelberg University, Speer and Rosenberg with their taste for architecture, and Streicher with his fondness for painting. In stark contrast was another of Hitler's lieutenants, Hermann Göring, who reportedly said, "When I hear the word *culture*, I reach for my revolver." But even he, when the opportunity came, looted and collected works of art on a huge scale.

The world Depression in the early 1930s fostered anxiety and a premonition of chaos. On these fears Hitler thrived. Many Germans saw in Hitler and his Brownshirts the welcome upholders of law and order. Fear of communism won Hitler increasing support from small farmers and shopkeepers. He and his oratory appealed to Germany's pride and exploited the widespread resentment that Germany had been defeated unfairly in a game in which it had long excelled—the game of war.

In the elections of 1930, Hitler's party enlarged its vote. In 1932 it doubled its vote again, becoming the largest German political party. In January of the following year it joined a coalition of smaller right-wing parties, and Hitler was formally appointed chancellor. Soon he became in effect a dictator. The persecution of Jews, suppression of trade unions and crushing of civil liberties were under way. In 1934 the aged president died, and Hitler, by popular consent, took complete control. His enemies were at his mercy.

Believing he could restore Germany's power, Hitler seemed to feel that he was guided by a mysterious force stronger than himself: "I go the way that Providence dictates with the assurance of a sleepwalker." In fact he was ill-prepared for power; he did not like administration or deskwork. Until he came to office his most senior official post had been as a humble corporal in the army. He knew little of Europe; he had not visited Paris or Rome, and he must have been a considerable age before he even set eyes on the sea. He believed ardently that the Germans were the finest race in the whole world, a world of which he had seen little, and that the Jews were the most dangerous race. Why then had this finest of races been defeated in the Great War? Hitler claimed, with scant supporting evidence, that the Jews as well as the socialists in Germany had stabbed the nation's warriors in the back.

A DICTATOR FURTHER EAST

Joseph Stalin was not the real name of the ruler of Russia. An organizer and agitator who had served sentences in Siberian prisons as punishment for his political activities, he took the name of Stalin, meaning "man of steel," soon after the victorious revolution of 1917. As editor of the communist newspaper *Pravda* he was an insider, and increasingly powerful. He became secretary of the central committee of the Communist Party and then head of government, after the death of Lenin in January 1924. He began to eliminate personal and imaginary rivals. He set out to strengthen the armed forces, and for the economy he launched the first of his bold Five Year Plans in 1928. Though the new Soviet Union still suffered from many economic ills and discontents, it experienced no official unemployment, and ensured that virtually all idle hands were put to work. The nation escaped the Depression, and that was a marvellous boost to its prestige.

With clusters of new power stations, factories and mines, Stalin successfully converted Russia into an industrial power. He carried through the most sweeping agricultural change ever attempted by one ruler. Though the peasants after the revolution had simply snatched the land from rich landlords and converted much of it into a chessboard of tiny private farms, the communist plan was that agriculture as well as heavy industry should be nationalized and run by the state. Stalin turned the private farms into collective farms—an astonishing and sweeping change, because more of his people were involved in farming than in any other European nation at any time, and most of them had a peasant's possessiveness towards their own land and an abhorrence of Stalin's collective farms. Peasants who resisted the collectivist policy were deported, starved or killed.

Stalin believed that communism would perish, that he himself might perish, unless he was ruthless. In peacetime his police state ordered or sanctioned the death of his fellow citizens on a grand scale. In 1937 alone his instructions led to the killing of close to one million Russians. Perhaps twice that number died in his prison camps in the same year. His army generals were not immune. The life of his closest colleagues was not safe. He showed less personal loyalty to his comrades than did Hitler. And yet national patriotism was higher under Stalin's rule than under the tsars' rule. The stamina and bravery of the Russian soldiers in the Second World War was to be impressive.

Hitler and Stalin had much in common, including the fact that each came to power as an outsider, Hitler being an Austrian and Stalin a Georgian. Likewise that other mighty European conqueror of recent centuries, Napoleon Bonaparte of France, was of Italian descent. Stalin and Hitler were alike in that they were virtually unknown and powerless at the age of 35 but 10 years later they were becoming powerful. Being men of little education and no experience in international diplomacy, they were hopelessly underestimated by their opponents. Hitler's rearming of Germany in the 1930s took France and Britain by surprise, as did Stalin's rearming of Russia. Both leaders had success in imposing an internal order and a rigid unity that was not easily foreseen because in literate and increasingly liberalized Europe at the start of the century, the era of the authoritarian ruler had seemingly gone forever. Both Stalin and Hitler cultivated an aptitude for telling plausible lies to their people and to the world. They were the field marshals of propaganda in an era when its influence was magnified by radio and film.

Stalin, Hitler and the Italian dictator Benito Mussolini, who seized power in 1922, shared a strong determination to rewrite the results of the First World War and if necessary to resume that war. The fighting that began in 1939 was their tailor-made, long-awaited opportunity.

THE STEPS TO WAR

Traditionally in Europe a long and major war usually led to a long period of peace. By setting up a clear pecking order amongst major nations, a decisive war enabled many problems to be settled by diplomacy. Moreover, in the first decades of peace the realities and terrible human losses of war were usually remembered only too sharply: diplomacy was therefore preferred to war as a way of solving disputes between nations. Just as the decisive victory in the long Napoleonic Wars ushered in a long period of relative peace in Europe's far-flung world, so the end of the First World

War—optimistically viewed as the war to end all wars—was expected to usher in an even rosier period of peace. The tragedy of this war was that in retrospect it was utterly pointless. The victory was soon lost, and another war was in the making.

Why was the victory so brief? Unfortunately for the victors, and for the peace of the world, the massed might that won the First World War was soon dissipated. The United States, whose industrial might was vital even before its first soldiers sailed away in 1917 to fight, mentally retreated soon after the war was over. It quarantined itself, closing its eyes and ears to Europe. Japan, whose sea power had helped during the early months of the war, also retreated. Thus two major powers, with a strong interest in upholding the victory they had helped to win, ceased to use their weight against the defeated powers. This had rarely, if ever, happened in the aftermath of a major war. In addition Italy, also on the winning side, was disillusioned because it was not given the German colonies in Africa and other spoils it had been promised by the Allies when it was persuaded in 1915 to join the Anglo-French-Russian alliance. Italy became the third victorious nation to undermine the hard-won peace treaty.

Russia too was in a strange position. It was on the winning side until March 1918 when, exhausted and revolutionized, it withdrew from its war with Germany. Alone of the original members on the winning side, Russia was eventually a heavy loser. As a result of the war it lost or surrendered a vast territory including Latvia, Estonia and Lithuania. It therefore had an incentive to overthrow the new Europe that came into being in 1919.

Of the powerful nations which were on the winning side in 1918, only Britain and France were left with a strong incentive to uphold the peace treaty and to disarm Germany and keep it disarmed. Here was an incredible erosion of a wartime victory.

Then came the Depression, and a sense of helplessness was felt by many of the industrial nations which had fought in the war. The Depression handed power to Hitler, who was determined to overthrow the peace treaty. On the other hand the Depression weakened the fighting determination of Britain and France, who were absorbed in their own unemployment.

At first Hitler did not seem to threaten Europe, for his Germany was largely unarmed. In March 1935 he formally disowned those clauses in the Versailles treaty which prevented Germany from rearming. When he began to rearm, the League of Nations was too weak and divided to intervene. In March 1936 Hitler thumbed his nose again at the treaty by occupying the Rhineland. If France and Britain together had acted promptly, Hitler's soldiers might have marched out again.

Hitler continued to rearm. The building of the autobahns or motor highways and the recovery of the automobile industry did almost as much as rearmament to abolish unemployment in Germany. German morale and self-respect soared. In March 1938 Hitler's troops entered Austria. In October he suddenly occupied the German-speaking part of Czechoslovakia. France and Britain did not rush to help the 15 million Czechs, and this inertia emboldened Hitler peacefully to occupy the remainder of their country. Bluff and bravado were as much his weapons as were armed forces. Page by page, he had torn up the Versailles treaty. The main loser of the First World War had recovered most of its territorial losses inside Europe.

In explaining why the treaty signed at Versailles in 1919 eventually failed, it is often argued that it was unjust, and being unjust it had fallen apart. But the history of the world does not offer persuasive evidence that an unjust treaty is normally reversed. A war is won primarily by military means: the victorious peace is likewise maintained by threat and implied force. Without doubt the punishment imposed on Germany in 1919 was harsh by European standards, but far less harsh than the peace terms that were to be imposed in 1945. By and large the Versailles treaty was undermined not primarily because it was unfair but because the victors lacked the unanimity and strength to uphold and enforce it.

The new war began in 1939 with Hitler's invasion of Poland. The Soviet Union joined in the invasion. Poland was crushed before France and Britain could give it the aid they had promised. In the years 1940 and 1941, Hitler captured nearly all of central and western Europe except for Italy and Romania, who were allies, and Spain, Portugal, Turkey, Sweden and Switzerland, who were neutral. He caught Stalin by surprise and invaded Russia, and late in 1941 his advance guard reached the outskirts of Moscow. But the further the Germans advanced, the more their supply lines were vulnerable. Hitler's invasion of Russia proved to be the slow turning point in a war which hitherto had favored him.

The Second World War consisted of two distinct wars, one fought mainly in Europe and the other fought mainly in eastern Asia. The Asian war was earlier. It began when Japan invaded Manchuria in 1932, and became more intense in 1937 when Japan and China began to fight on the plains of northern China. Within a year Japan held the eastern half of China and had hope of capturing the remainder, but supply lines became longer and more vulnerable. Hitler's astonishing victory in western Europe in 1940 exposed the weakness of the British, Dutch and French colonies in South-East Asia, and the American bases in the former Spanish Philippines. Japan seized on their weakness. In December 1941 it suddenly attacked territories and bases extending from Burma and Hong Kong to Pearl Harbor.

At once the two wars—the European war and the Asian war—were welded into one, with Germany and Japan fighting on one side and the United States, Britain, China and most of the other nations of the world on the other. This was a world war, whereas the First World War had been primarily a European conflict with ragged edges.

No previous event, in peace or war, had mirrored so much the shrinking of the world. Aircraft and radio jumped across continents. The Pacific Ocean was now as easily crossed as the Mediterranean in the era of the galleys. It was a sign of the new era of mechanical warfare that during the decisive Battle of the Coral Sea, fought close to eastern Australia in May 1942, the fighting Japanese and American fleets did not see one another. They simply launched the aircraft that bombed the warships and determined the victory.

By the last months of 1944, after more than five years of war, the end of the fighting was in sight. Germany and Japan faced total defeat. But it was difficult to forecast whether the defeat would come in six or 36 months. Few human events are as unpredictable as the outbreak of peace.

30

THE BOMB AND THE MOON

EARLY in the 20th century, physics was perhaps the most commanding of the sciences. Busily unlocking and inspecting the long-hidden physical world, it gained glamour. Part of its fame, however, comes with hindsight. If no atomic bomb had been invented, physics might not be viewed with such awe.

For long the atom had been proclaimed as the ultimate building block. An atom was so tiny that if 10,000 million atoms were placed side by side they would just span 1 meter. In 1704 in *Opticks* Sir Isaac Newton wrote that the atom was so hard and so basic that it could never be broken into pieces, "no ordinary Power being able to divide what God himself made one in the first Creation." An even tinier and more complex unit, named the nucleus, was discovered later. The enormous power of the atom and the nucleus to create energy and inflict destruction was not foreseen at the start of the First World War. Only after research by the emigrant New Zealander Ernest Rutherford, Niels Bohr of Denmark and physicists of other western nations was its power clearly glimpsed.

As Germany was to the fore in physics, it could be expected to be energetic in harnessing that science to war. Germany placed racial purity, however, above the search for knowledge. Many of its stars in physics were Jews, and in the 1930s they sensibly found refuge across the seas. In 1939 and 1940, in the English city of Birmingham, several of these refugees did atomic research. At that time atomic research was regarded by Britain as less important than research on radar; and so these aliens—the loyalty of aliens is always doubted during a major war—concentrated on atoms.

THE BIRTH OF THE ATOMIC BOMB

The United States entered the war and soon became the spearhead of nuclear research. In December 1942 it achieved nuclear fission in a controlled way but there was still a long path of experiment and research to be followed. Americans were driven by the fear—it was mistaken—that German scientists were travelling the same road of research and were not far behind. In fact Germany was busily developing the V-2 rocket bomb which ultimately led, by a series of steps, to the first landing on the moon more than a quarter of a century later.

Germany was finally conquered in May 1945, before America was ready to test its first atomic bomb. But America pressed on with its research, for Japan still had to be defeated. Perhaps Japan would surrender if atomic bombs were dropped on its cities. On 16 July 1945 the first bomb was tested in the desert in New Mexico. The explosion generated such heat that the surface of the desert for a radius of nearly 1 kilometer was fused into glass. Here was the most extraordinary weapon in the history of warfare. To the question "Should it be used against the Japanese forces?" there was no easy answer; and the chosen answer has been fiercely debated to this day. Amongst American political leaders was a desire to avenge Pearl Harbor. In the minds of the nuclear scientists was an understandable resolve to test the effectiveness of a weapon for which they had worked so hard. In the minds of American generals was the fear that Japan would fight to the very end, and that perhaps half a million American lives would be lost before Japan was finally defeated.

Even in July 1945 about five million Japanese soldiers were ready to defend most of their earlier conquests, including much of China, the Indonesian archipelago, the Malay Peninsula, Taiwan and the present Vietnam. The munitions arsenals inside Japan were still highly productive. Japan held more than 5,000 Kamikaze aircraft, with brave pilots ready to sacrifice their lives by crashing into enemy aircraft carriers and air bases. Japan was not yet willing to admit defeat. Therefore its enemies predicted that just one atomic bomb and its devastation and terror would finally convince Japan how high and painful would be the price of continuing to fight.

Today many historians denounce the American decision to drop atomic bombs on Japan as another step in human infamy. They point out that the bomb inaugurated a new era of slaughtering civilians. And yet perhaps the new era had already arrived. Air raids on German and Japanese cities with conventional bombs were already deadly. Thus one raid on Tokyo in the previous May had killed 82,000 civilians—or four-tenths of the number of Japanese who were to be killed by the first atomic bomb. And if the war went on and on and only high-explosive bombs were used, hundreds of thousands of Japanese civilians would be killed by air raids and bombardments and perhaps by the ultimate invasion of Japan's islands.

These arguments were broadly accepted by President Truman in Washington. One crucial factor, however, was overlooked. The atomic bomb, when exploded, would do what no normal bomb could do: its radiation would create genetic damage and so punish unborn children for the failures and sins of the wartime generation of Japanese. But even if radiation had been fully understood by the scientists, they might still have come to the same conclusion—that the atomic bomb must be used against the Japanese. For nearly six years the terrible all-out war had been waged. Victory must not be postponed. This argument is always more persuasive to those on the spot than to those viewing it decades later.

The American command of the air and sea near Japan was still so fragile that President Truman could not yet feel sure that his forces would actually drop the atomic bomb accurately on Hiroshima, the chosen target. Nor could he feel sure that the bomb would be as devastating as his scientific advisers hoped. Moreover its key components had first to be shipped from San Francisco to the new American runways on the volcanic island of Tinian in the Marianas group, far south of Japan. The heavy cruiser *Indianapolis*, carrying her tiny but vital cargo, crossed hazardous seas before she reached the island. On that voyage she could easily have been sunk. Indeed three days later, on 29 July, she had fulfilled her mission and was again at sea when she was sighted in the moonlight by a Japanese submarine and was sunk, with heavy loss of life.

On 6 August 1945 a heavy American bomber flew from the Marianas to Japan and dropped the bomb. Much of Hiroshima became almost a blast furnace, and close to 90,000 Japanese were killed. In nearby Tokyo

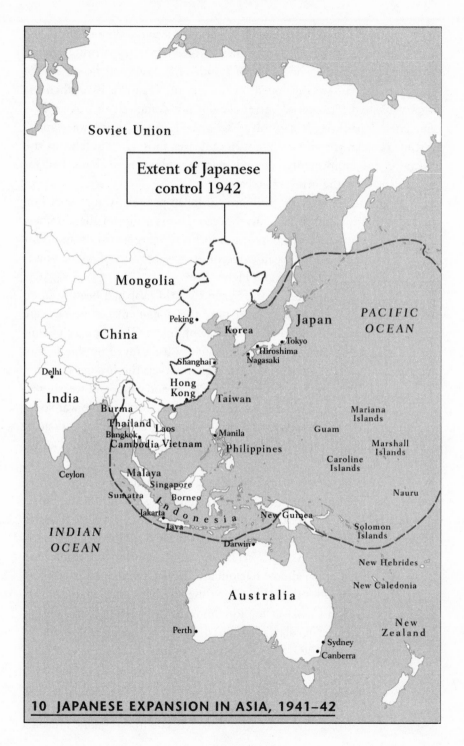

Soviet Union

Extent of Japanese
control 1942

Mongolia

China

Peking •

Korea

Japan

PACIFIC
OCEAN

• Tokyo
• Hiroshima
Nagasaki •

Shanghai •

Delhi •

India

Hong
Kong

Taiwan

Burma

Thailand   Laos

Bangkok •

Cambodia Vietnam

• Manila

Philippines

Mariana
Islands

Guam

Marshall
Islands

Caroline
Islands

Ceylon

Malaya

Singapore

Sumatra

Borneo

Nauru

Jakarta •

I n d o n e s i a

New Guinea

Java •

INDIAN
OCEAN

Darwin •

Solomon
Islands

New Hebrides

New Caledonia

Australia

New
Zealand

Perth •

• Sydney
Canberra

10 JAPANESE EXPANSION IN ASIA, 1941–42

there was no willingness to surrender. Indeed a fierce opposition to the very thought of surrender was quietly voiced in ultrapatriotic circles. Three days later a second atomic bomb—the last such bomb in the American arsenal—was dropped on the city of Nagasaki. Even then the eagerly awaited message of surrender did not come out of Tokyo. Five days later, Japan's leaders resolved to give in. So effective was Japan's wartime propaganda and so high its morale that most citizens felt surprise and deep disappointment that their nation, unknown to them, had for months stood on the brink of defeat.

On 15 August 1945 the Emperor of Japan personally announced on the radio that his nation had surrendered. It was a sign of the aloofness and majesty of the emperor that his voice was being heard on radio for the very first time. Here was an emperor exercising relics of divine power in an era shaped by Marconi and Henry Ford.

The first formal shots of the Second World War had been fired on the northern European plain, and now the documents of peace were signed in a battleship anchored in the Bay of Tokyo. There on 2 September the Allied officers—not the politicians—were arrayed on the deck of the *Missouri*, while the chief Japanese signatory was the foreign minister. Dressed in European style with hat and gloves and cane, and wearing an artificial leg, he signed the document ending the most terrible war so far waged. On shore at sunset that evening could be faintly heard, floating over the water, a brass band playing the hymn "The Day Thou Gavest, Lord, Is Ended."

Not a day but a whole era had ended. More than 107 million people had been enlisted in the armed forces, including 22 million in the Soviet Union, whose forces were the main sufferers. Perhaps 11 million Russian soldiers were killed—a toll larger than that of the total forces fighting on both sides in the First World War. Deaths in the combined German and Japanese forces reached almost five million. Civilian deaths dwarfed those of the previous world war, and in China they perhaps numbered as many as 20 million and in Russia 11 million. Some of the small nations—for instance Poland and Yugoslavia—suffered more civilian deaths than did Germany or Britain, the USA or Japan or even heavily bombed Germany.

The Jews, whose prewar population in all of Europe was small compared to the population of Germany, had suffered more deaths in total than did the German armed forces and the German civilians living in the bombed cities. Ironically, many Jews once felt safe in Germany. Indeed a host of German Jews had held honored positions in the law, universities and medicine. Some had travelled in hope to Germany from troubled lands, and many rejected the opportunity to emigrate to the growing Jewish settlements in Palestine: the state of Israel had not yet been born. Even when in 1938 a major war had seemed likely, most of the Jewish leaders, while living in fear, had had no reason to think that an attempt would be made to eradicate their race. But by 1942, if not earlier, the German leaders had resolved, in all the lands they ruled, to exterminate the Jews.

Jewish families had been rounded up and sent mostly in freight trains to concentration camps, where they were killed either by firearms or in gas chambers built for efficient killing. The Nazis had exterminated perhaps two-thirds of the Jews in Europe when the war ended. The toll would have been higher but for advance Russian troops reaching the big Auschwitz death camp in Poland in January 1945 and other death camps in the following four months. Of the Jewish population in European nations, those cut down the most ruthlessly had been in Poland and western Russia, Hungary, Romania and Lithuania: at least five million were killed.

To this project of liquidation some Nazi leaders gave the name "The Final Solution of the Jewish Question." Later "the Holocaust" became the simple description. In savagery and hatred this event was not unique. Human history, over the centuries, is peppered with acts of large-scale savagery as well as of generosity and goodwill. But the Holocaust was chilling because of the scale of the slaughter, the abattoir-like way in which it was conducted, and the refusal to exempt the very old and the very young. It was a shock to the idea of human progress, for it had been designed and executed by a nation which was seen by many impartial eyes, at the start of the century, as the most civilized and cultured in the world.

The existence of nuclear weapons was also a shock to the idea of human progress. Most people of the world would have felt safe if the United States alone had owned this weapon that was so superior to all other weapons. But the Soviet Union did not feel safe. It had to own a similar weapon. At last in 1949 the Russians secretly tested their first atomic bomb.

President Truman now faced the decision whether his nation should build an even more powerful weapon, the hydrogen bomb. He was influenced not only by the Russian tests but by other events that happened almost simultaneously: the victory of the communists in China in 1949 and the discovery that a leading Allied nuclear scientist was successfully spying for Russia. The new bomb was first tested over the Pacific Ocean in May 1951. Meanwhile war had broken out in Korea, with Russia and China on one side and the United States and member states of the new United Nations fighting on the other side. There was fear that the devastating new bomb might soon be used in Korea. That it was not used in warfare during the remainder of the century was a windfall which few observers positively predicted.

GLUING THE GLOBE TOGETHER AGAIN

After 1945 Europe was divided into two. Democracies dominated the western half. The Soviet Union controlled the eastern half, including part of Germany. Two other communist nations, Yugoslavia and Albania, formed an isolated pocket in the western half. The tension between communism and democratic capitalism was now called the Cold War, though in retrospect it contained far more peace than war.

Germany, occupied by the victors, had lost most of its power. Even Britain and France and Holland were less powerful than they had been in 1939. Wartime damage was on a large scale, and they had run up heavy debts or sold foreign assets in order to finance the war. Moreover their overseas colonies, which were a source of pride and of potential income more than present income, seemed likely to seek or snatch independence.

Most leaders refused to face the fact that their nation was now considerably weaker in influence. Europe had followed in the footprints of earlier centers of power which, in their confident heyday, had quarrelled internally. The Greek city-states had fought self-defeating wars with each other and collectively they had lost supremacy. Rome's empire had been weakened by internal conflict and civil war. Islam and Christianity too had been weakened by schisms. China and the South American empire of the Incas, just when their own self-confidence was high, had been torn by internal disputes. The postwar clash between communism in Russia and capitalism further to the west was another phase in the long history of European disputes. And yet Europe was saved from decline by a growing unity.

This unity began simply as a proposal for a small free-trade zone embracing the coal and iron and steel industries of the traditional enemies West Germany and France. When the zone was launched in 1952 it had six member nations. Following the signing of the Treaty of Rome five years later it became the European Economic Community, and within its wide borders it abolished import duties on all commodities. By the 1970s, with Britain and other new members, it was the biggest common market in history, involving more people and commerce than that older common market, the United States of America. In 1993, when it became a political as well as an economic union, it embraced 15 nations extending, with only two gaps, from Portugal and Ireland in the west to Greece and Finland in the east. Known as the European Union, it now constituted virtually a new nation. If it was to go one step further and become a firm military alliance, it would rival the United States for the overall title of the world's most influential state.

THE COLONIES BREAK FREE

Europe revived even though it lost nearly all its overseas colonies. In some ways the colonies were a burden, though they had not usually been seen as such during the four and a half centuries when, one by one, they had been acquired. Even in 1945 the possession of overseas colonies carried prestige. They were not easily surrendered.

In 1900 Europeans had ruled most of the world. In Africa the only self-governing lands had been Ethiopia and Liberia. In Asia, only Japan and Thailand and Turkey were really independent. Much of China was only half-independent: most of its seaports were controlled by European powers, and even Germany planted a colony in northeastern China.

At the outbreak of the Second World War about one-third of the world's peoples still lived under European colonial rule. The ups and downs of the war, especially the military plight of France, Holland and Britain in 1940 and 1941, shook the European grip. The fighting showed that Europe's colonial powers were not invincible. In many colonies, resistance fighters seized their opportunity. The morality of nations owning colonies was challenged in the British and several other European parliaments where, after the war, the parties of the left were stronger than previously.

The first large colony to be liberated was India. Its chief liberationist was Mahatma Gandhi, one of the most remarkable politicians of the century. His surname means "grocer," for his family belonged to the Hindu subcaste of merchants. In 1891, in his early twenties, Gandhi became a barrister in London and dressed fashionably and learned dancing and elocution. By the end of the decade he was a prosperous lawyer in South Africa but was beginning to live an ascetic life, making his own clothes, and undergoing periods of fasting—a habit learned from his mother. In 1907 the Transvaal parliament compelled Asian residents to carry registration cards, and Gandhi applied his formula of "passive resistance" for the first time: as a result he spent a total of 249 nights in jail. Returning to India in 1915, he shaped the campaign for Indian independence with a strategy of civil disobedience towards the ruling British. Wearing his white shawl, white loincloth and sandals, and often flashing his toothless smile to news photographers, he became the most famous of all Indians in the eyes of the outside world. He tried more than anybody to unite a land which could not be united.

When India gained independence in 1947 it was divided into two separate nations, a Hindu India and an Islamic Pakistan; later Bangladesh became a third nation. In the upheavals surrounding the division of 1947, about 15 million people fled as refugees so that they could live safely in the India of their choice. Gandhi himself was a victim of the first stormy year of independence: he was killed by a militant Hindu.

India held its first national elections in 1952 with a vote available to virtually every adult, literate or illiterate. Here was one of the astonishing events in the history of politics. The second most populous nation in the world was implementing a system of government first devised for small democratic assemblies in ancient Greek cities at a time when the entire world held fewer people than democratic India held in this year of its first elections.

China also liberated itself. While it had never lost its independence completely, it had been too weak, during the last 100 years, to fend off the Russians, British, French, Germans and especially the Japanese, to each of whom it made concessions or surrendered territory. It was also weakened by its own civil war. Mao Zedong, who brilliantly led the communists during a long guerrilla war, was finally victorious in 1949, leaving his opponents only the island of Taiwan.

The new People's Republic of China, as the world's most populous nation, was expected slowly to regain the authority it had held some five centuries ago. But the relationship between population and power has often been precarious and complicated. Instead of becoming a major power, communist China for a time was an economic dunce. The countryside was in poverty, and economic progress was more a chanted slogan than a fact.

China's liberating leader, known now as "Our Great Helmsman," believed that the minds of his people were fortunately "blank" and that he could inscribe on them an indelible message. In 1966 his nation was the vast setting of a cultural revolution or morality play staged on a huge scale, with death, imprisonment or rural exile imposed on those opinion leaders who were judged to be politically immoral and incorrect. The nation which, five centuries before, probably led the world in utilizing its people's talents, now deliberately consigned hundreds of thousands of its teachers, artists and intellectuals to the humdrum tasks of minding pigs, reaping crops by hand and lifting irrigation water on the treadmill. Not until the 1980s did China begin, with a new sense of purpose, to make that great leap forward which had been the boast of its party propaganda three decades earlier.

Indonesia was another of the extraordinary nations that emerged in the decade after the Second World War. In 1940 the Indonesian islands held about 70 million people, only three million fewer than Japan. Just over half a century later Indonesia held almost double the population of Japan, and with nearly 200 million people it was exceeded only by China, India and the United States. It was also the most populous Islamic nation in the world.

A dynamic leader was the hallmark of many of the infant nations. President Sukarno made the nation of Indonesia and then almost unmade it. Born of a Balinese Hindu mother and a Javanese Muslim father, he developed a gift for words and languages. Eventually he spoke Dutch—in which language he received much of his education—and English, French, German, Japanese, Javanese, Balinese and Sundanese. Of course he learned Arabic too so that he could study the Koran. At the same time he was more conversant with technology than most of those who were to lead new nations, and in 1925 he graduated in engineering from Bandung University in Java.

Confident, exuberant, a magical maker of speeches, Sukarno protested against the rule of the Dutch at a time when colonial uprisings in the world were not frequent. For 13 years he was either in jail or exiled from his native Java. When the Japanese occupied the Dutch East Indies in 1942, Sukarno welcomed them and became their special adviser as well as a leader of his people. After Japan was defeated he resumed his fight against the Dutch, winning independence for his nation in 1949. He allowed a parliamentary election in 1955 and, not liking the indecisive result, eventually chose what he called "Guided Democracy," with himself as guide and with democracy not all that visible. Ruling a chain of tropical islands peopled by many proud ethnic groups, he tried with much noise in the early 1960s to humble the new nation of Malaysia. He peacefully took control of the old Dutch New Guinea; and when the Portuguese empire fell apart, his successor sent troops to snatch East Timor. Like many of the founders of new nations he was eventually toppled from his perch: he died in 1970, three years after being deposed by General Suharto. The nation was not yet cohesive. It was really the island empire of the Javanese.

Between 1945 and 1960, colonies holding a quarter of the world's people gained freedom. By 1980 few colonies remained, and most were tiny. Meanwhile the procession of former colonies in Asia, Africa, Polynesia and the West Indies tried to make their independent way in the world. Independence was glorious. It was also frustrating. Most of the leaders of new nations had no experience of governing. Their bureaucracy was untrained. Their eagerness to borrow money far exceeded their ability to repay it. Some of the new nations, because of the boundaries bequeathed to them by European colonizers, were populated by tribes or groups which had little in common except a shared enmity. Various of the ill-suited boundaries could have been altered by the merging of tiny nations, but the tiniest nations had no wish to merge. Wars against neighbors, or preparations for war, absorbed money that might have built railways, dams, hospitals, schools and cities.

The idea, preached often by European socialists and liberals, that all the natural resources of the newly independent land would pour wealth into their people's waiting hands once the colonial overlord had gone, usually proved optimistic. In every nation the exploiting of natural resources depends as much on the enterprise and skill of those who develop them as on the richness of the soil, grasslands or mineral deposits. Few skilled entrepreneurs were available to develop natural resources in the infant nations.

The Third World—the name was coined in France to describe the poor and unaligned new nations—was third on the list in everything, whether average income or level of literacy. In one facet it was first. Its

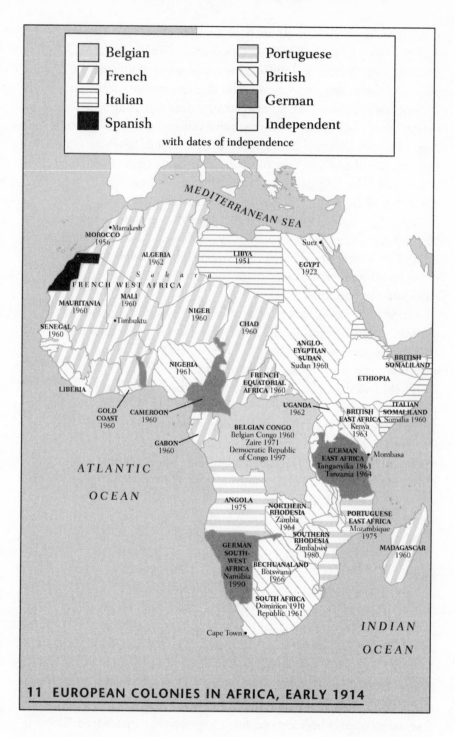

Belgian
French
Italian
Spanish
Portuguese
British
German
Independent

with dates of independence

MEDITERRANEAN SEA

•Marrakesh
MOROCCO
1956

ALGERIA
1962

LIBYA
1951

Suez•

EGYPT
1922

S a h a r a

FRENCH WEST AFRICA

MAURITANIA
1960

MALI
1960

•Timbuktu

NIGER
1960

CHAD
1960

SENEGAL
1960

ANGLO-
EYGPTIAN
SUDAN
Sudan 1960

BRITISH
SOMALILAND

NIGERIA
1961

FRENCH
EQUATORIAL
AFRICA 1960

ETHIOPIA

LIBERIA

UGANDA
1962

BRITISH
EAST AFRICA
Kenya
1963

ITALIAN
SOMALILAND
Somalia 1960

GOLD
COAST
1960

CAMEROON
1960

BELGIAN CONGO
Belgian Congo 1960
Zaire 1971
Democratic Republic
of Congo 1997

GABON
1960

GERMAN
EAST AFRICA
Tanganyika 1961
Tanzania 1964

•Mombasa

ATLANTIC

OCEAN

ANGOLA
1975

NORTHERN
RHODESIA
Zambia
1964

SOUTHERN
RHODESIA
Zimbabwe
1980

PORTUGUESE
EAST AFRICA
Mozambique
1975

GERMAN
SOUTH-
WEST
AFRICA
Namibia
1990

BECHUANALAND
Botswana
1966

MADAGASCAR
1960

SOUTH AFRICA
Dominion 1910
Republic 1961

Cape Town •

INDIAN

OCEAN

11 EUROPEAN COLONIES IN AFRICA, EARLY 1914

population grew at a speed such as no nation had experienced in the known history of the world. The spread of medical knowledge, the presence of more doctors and nurses, the vaccination of infants, the crusade against malaria, and improved public hygiene cut the death rate, while the birthrate remained high. Between 1950 and 1980, during a time when new attitudes and the new contraceptive pill curbed the birthrate in Europe, the population of Africa more than doubled. Likewise China, Indonesia, Brazil and a variety of other poor lands virtually doubled their population. The main task—as formidable as that experienced in possibly any other phase of human history—was simply how to feed their fast-multiplying people. The so-called green revolution with its new breeds of rice and other food-plants was initially a lifesaver; but the population still multiplied. China already held close to one billion people when, in one of the most unusual experiments in global history, it tried to restrict each of its families to one child.

Africa, the busiest arena of decolonization, soon possessed too many nations, too many presidential palaces, and too many ambassadors living in luxury in foreign cities. By 1982 there were 54 nations in Africa—more than twice as many as in the whole of Asia. A dozen of the African nations each held fewer than one.million people. In no African nation did higher education receive a high priority, and the whole of Africa in 1980 had fewer universities than did the American state of Ohio. Black Africa was impaired by tribalism, and even the white settlers in South Africa devised their own form of tribalism called apartheid. The economic stagnation of most rural regions was disappointing, especially to those older Africans who had once felt sure that independence would be the gateway to wealth. In a typical decade the standard of living of most African nations stood still. In the 1970s oil-rich Nigeria, the most populous of African nations, could certainly hold its head high—so long as the price of oil was high.

Outside Europe and North America and the other lands mainly settled by Europeans, economic achievements in the postwar period fell short of initial hopes. Eastern Asia was the spectacular exception. Japan displayed an economic success exceeded by no European nation between 1945 and 1990; but admittedly Japan's economy had been vigorous even before the Second World War. Singapore, Malaysia and Thailand, Hong Kong, South Korea and Taiwan, most of which had a large sector of Chinese ancestry, also began to perform impressively. In contrast China itself, by depriving people of economic incentives, barely hobbled along in the space of three decades. In postwar history a remarkable contrast lay in the sluggishness of China itself compared to the systematic energy of the relatively few millions of ethnic Chinese who lived in capitalist lands just across the sea.

In military affairs, Asia could no longer be discounted. In 1900 the confrontations and collisions with earth-shaking potential had mostly centered on Europe or inside European spheres of influence. At the end of the century, however, most of the grave confrontations were in Asia, and most of the powers facing each other possessed nuclear weapons or an intense desire to manufacture them. No neutral scientists had foreseen, back in 1945, that China and India would test their own nuclear weapons within a quarter of a century, or that nations as small as Iraq and North Korea would pursue nuclear ambitions or that Pakistan would possess its own bomb at the end of the century.

TO THE MOON

The Second World War had spurred a need for new ways of propulsion. In 1944–45 in occupied France the Germans used powerful rockets to launch missiles which flew straight across the sea to London. In peacetime these same rockets offered a way of launching radio transmitters which, from on high, could beam amplified signals to every corner of the earth.

On 10 July 1962, a day as momentous as any in the 20th century, a satellite transmitted television pictures and phone conversations between Europe and the USA. A new Telstar satellite was launched 10 months later and it operated for two years. Satellites soon spanned the world. They became vital for the world's communications, and for tasks as diverse as forecasting the weather, searching for minerals, and enabling ships and aircraft to plot their position. In the Persian Gulf in 1991 the United States used satellites to guide weapons to their distant targets, some of which stood on the site of those early valley civilizations that flourished several thousand years ago.

With the new rockets, outer space could be explored. The main explorers, the Soviet Union and the United States, were even more competitive than were Spain and Portugal in the era of Columbus and Vasco da Gama. In the race to explore this newest world, the Soviets gained an early lead. In October 1957 they launched their first spacecraft, and it orbited the earth. There was no pilot aboard, for the craft itself was small and weighed no more than a large man. In the following year the Russians sent two dogs into orbit in Sputnik III where they rode in cramped glory, 500 kilometers above the earth.

In the expensive contest to send the first person into space the Russians won by 23 days, sending Yuri Gagarin and his space capsule on an impressive orbit of the earth on 12 April 1961. One of the remarkable days in the history of the human race, no subsequent feat in space could surpass it. The brave dream of placing a person on the moon was achieved by the United States on 20 July 1969 when, in front of a huge television audience, Neil Armstrong and "Buzz" Aldrin, wearing cumbersome suits, stepped from their craft and walked on the moon. In 1976 an unmanned American spacecraft landed on Mars. As Mars was 1,000 times further away from the earth than was the moon, this was the equivalent of Vasco da Gama's ship finally reaching India instead of Gibraltar.

In 1986 the Russians, who had poured massive funds into space exploration, launched a space station which became in effect an inhabited port in orbit, with docks for visiting spacecraft. Meanwhile the Americans, following a different approach, had seemingly perfected "space shuttles" which were capable of serving as space ferries and making voyage after voyage. But in 1986 seven astronauts died when the shuttle *Challenger* was destroyed, moments after its launching.

In the United States in 1986 the National Commission on Space foresaw the time when there would be permanent settlements on distant planets. The latest technology, it proclaimed, had "freed humankind to move outward from Earth as a species destined to expand to other worlds." Beyond Mars, it argued, was a belt of at least 3,200 asteroids or small planets which possessed the raw materials to support a population dwarfing that now living on earth. Presumably those raw materials would be exported to earth—if the cost of carrying them was payable. The leading nations of Europe had learned, since 1492, to transport goods efficiently by air and sea to the remote corners of the globe. To transport them from remote planets to the earth would be more difficult.

The exploring of space was a triumph for the Russians as well as the Americans. But in the end the ailing Russian economy could not finance the nation's high military and scientific goals. The cost of the latest missiles, huge armed forces and the space race, and the dint to national morale by a frustrating war in Afghanistan, combined to weaken the Soviet Union. An inefficient economy could not afford these luxuries; and so the standard of living in the Soviet Union lagged far behind that of western Europe. Meanwhile, citizens in Poland—spurred by a strike in the shipyards in 1980—and in Czechoslovakia began to rebel against communism. From Moscow there came no effective retaliation such as that received by Hungary in 1956 and Czechoslovakia in 1968.

The nations of eastern Europe were ready, in the late 1980s, to break away from the Soviet Union and from communism. Even the states that comprised the union were permitted to secede. In December 1991 the Soviet Union itself ceased to exist. Its collapse was another step, though belated and unpredicted, in the process of decolonization. In one swoop, Russia lost its overland empire just as Britain, Holland, France and Portugal, in the period from 1945 to 1975, had lost their overseas empires.

When the Soviet Union was riding high, it seemed possible that Russian would become the chief international language. It was already the diplomatic language of the second-largest power bloc in the world. In the 1950s it was the main foreign language taught in China. Seen as the language of the future, it was studied eagerly by young socialists in Africa. By the end of the century, however, the Russian language had fallen far.

Instead, English was confirmed as the language of international discourse. This Germanic dialect had entered England about AD 450, as the tongue of all those people emigrating from the western European coast. Even in AD 1100, in England itself, this language now known as Old English held only third place behind Latin and French as the official language. By the year 2000, however, English was dominant amongst the world's bridging languages. It was the language of the Internet. Eight of every 10 pages stored in the world's computers were in English.

English initially became a leading language because of the spreading power of the British Empire. After 1945 the power of that language owed more to the global influence of the United States. At one time it was possible that French might become the dominant language of North America, and indeed some of the vivid words in American English—for instance "prairie" and "the rapids"—were French in origin. But after France in 1763 conceded defeat to England in the Seven Years' War, and after it sold its vast land west of the Mississippi some 40 years later, the only strong American base of the French language was in the province of Quebec.

AN AMERICAN CENTURY

The popularity of English as a global language was only one sign of America's increasing influence during the 20th century. During the first 40 years of the century, however, America's influence on the world was smaller than its size and potential power would suggest. Its economy was self-contained and so it was not the dominant trading nation. In foreign policy it tended to be isolationist, and its late entry in 1917 into the First World War was followed two years later by its virtual withdrawal from world affairs. As the American politician Wendell Wilkie truthfully recalled in his best-selling book *One World*: "We washed our hands of the continent of Europe and displayed no interest in its fate while Germany rearmed."

The 1940s and 1950s were the first decades in which the United States exercised both a continuing and profound influence on the world. They could equally be called Russia's decades, for that nation played the larger part in defeating Hitler, in helping communism to win in China, and in winning for itself an early lead in the space race. Thereafter the United States dominated the century. Even the British Empire, when it held colonies in every continent and on nearly every crucial sea lane, did not exert an influence quite comparable to the present power of the United States in economic, military, political and cultural matters.

The power of the United States depended heavily on its pale empire of ideas, attitudes and innovations. Its ideas alighted effortlessly on foreign ground, irrespective of who owned the ground. Much of its influence came from such innovations as the telephone, electricity, aircraft and the cheap car, nuclear weapons and spacecraft, computers and the Internet. Its influence came through jazz, cartoons, Hollywood, television and popular culture. Its influence came from an excitement about technology and economic change, and a belief in incentives and individual enterprise. It was also the most ardent missionary for the creed of democracy. While military and economic might was vital to the success of the United States, the power of its pale empire of ideas was probably even more pervasive.

The global role of the United States is perhaps the ultimate chapter in that long period of European expansion which had begun in western Europe, and especially on the Atlantic seaboard, during the 15th century. Europe slowly had outgrown its homeland. Its cultural empire eventually formed a long band traversing most of the Northern Hemisphere and dipping far into the Southern. The modern hub of the peoples and ideas of European origin is now New York as much as Paris, or Los Angeles as much as London. In the history of European peoples the city of Washington is perhaps what Constantinople—the infant city of Emperor Constantine—was to the last phase of the Roman Empire; for it is unlikely that Europeans, a century hence, will continue to stamp the world so decisively with their ideas and inventions.

31

NO FRUITS, NO BIRDS

ONE PROFOUND CHANGE in human history is so obvious that it is rarely commented upon: the slow blurring of distinctions which had once been all-important. The seasons were blurred; the differences between night and day, and summer and winter, were blurred. As the night sky became less important, the moon waned in its influence on human activities. Work and leisure, city and country ceased to have the same relationship.

In the vast time span of the hunters and gatherers the seasons had been all-important. Summer and winter, spring and autumn determined what people ate, the ceremonies they performed and the comforts or hardships of their daily life. The domesticating of plants and animals lessened the impact of the seasons. Villagers could hoard food, and so seasonal gluts and scarcities had less effect on their diet. Their permanent houses, far superior to those of nomads, fended off the extreme effects of summer and winter. But most human beings, even in AD 1800, were still farmers and keepers of herds and so were deeply affected by the changing of the seasons. Thus in winter, eggs and fruit and meat—unless it was salted—were luxuries. The summer of plenty gave way to a winter of belt-tightening. It was Thomas Hood, the English poet, who wrote:

No fruits, no flowers, no leaves, no birds,—
November!

THE IRON RULE OF THE SEASONS

Religious manuscripts prepared 1,000 years ago emphasized how distinctive was each season. For each month they painted a scene or task; and that task flavored a month in a way in which no work-task can now mark out a typical month.

Today a typical task of the month, if there is such a task, is likely to be a leisure pursuit: the erecting of a Christmas tree or the attending of a football final. In contrast, a Byzantine manuscript of the year 1100 singled out the workday tasks in the Balkans and Asia Minor. In April the shepherd was depicted preparing to take his flock from the barn, where in winter it had lived on stored hay, to the fresh grass of the hills. May was symbolized by the carrying of flowers. June depicted a man cutting lush grass in readiness for the making of hay. By October the summer was ebbing, and a bird-catcher or fowler held on his wrist a small bird which he used to decoy and thereby capture big edible birds before they emigrated. In November the ploughman prepared the land for the sowing of next year's crop, his decision to plough being prompted by "the rising of the Pleiades"—the cluster of stars now visible low in the sky. And so, in orderly procession, the working year was dictated by the seasons, though the actual tasks varied from region to region. In France an illuminated prayer book of about 1475 showed a pig being fed with acorns to symbolise the month of November; and in December the poor pig was killed.

In South-East Asia the farming calendar had its own special deadlines. In the northern highlands of Borneo, the arrival of migratory birds served as a rural clock. One month was designated as the time when the yellow wagtails arrived, having escaped the cold of Siberia and northern Europe in order to feed in the wet rice fields. October and November were the season of the brown shrike, and the last time when rice could be planted. The following month was named after the Japanese sparrowhawk.

Even the fighting of wars was affected by the seasons. In the Northern Hemisphere international wars usually broke out in spring or summer. In the years between 1840 and 1938 a total of 44 wars were fought in those northern lands where winter and summer were clearly contrasted. Of those wars only three were commenced in the winter months but 26 began during the warmer months from April to July. The coming of spring offered a chance to attack and defeat an enemy, for rivers were forded more easily, rural roads were less obstructed by mud and ice, days were longer and advancing armies could steal or buy food in the blooming countryside. In China the traditional time for fighting a quick war was the autumn, for crops had just been harvested, rivers were more passable and dry land enabled troops to march quickly to the locality chosen for their first attack.

Travel was always regulated by the seasons. In Asia the start or end of the annual monsoon signalled the departure of the merchant fleets, whether Arab dhows or Malay praus. In Europe most journeys were postponed until winter storms had passed. On the Mediterranean Sea the Romans had tended to lay up their ships from October to March. Thus in the 16th century most German pilgrims set sail from Venice to the Holy Land in June or July, having left Germany as soon as the snow in the Alps had melted.

In Europe the first day of May honored that boundary between cold and warmth, between hunger and plenty. Midnight on the eve of May Day was greeted by the beating of drums and the blasts of cow-horns. On this day of rejoicing, green boughs were carried into villages and placed in front of houses, with perhaps a branch of the white-flowering hawthorn tree tied to a door or corner post. There was dancing around the maypole—sometimes with such sexual frolickings that the day was denounced by preachers at the time of the religious Reformation.

Suddenly milk and cream were plentiful. In parts of England a highlight of May Day was to milk cows directly above a bucket containing sherry or port, so that the squirts of warm creamy milk enriched the drink. The Venerable Bede noticed how the English in the eighth century gave to the month of May the name of "Three-Milkings," because each day in that month the cows were milked an extra time to relieve their udders of the bulge of milk that had been absent in the lean winter.

The celebration of the first of May extended to the swelling cities. In London in the 18th century the milkmaids made the day their own. A century later it belonged to the army of chimney sweeps who, with the arrival of warmer nights, systematically brushed away the layers of soot which had accumulated in house chimneys over winter. In continental Europe the socialists and trade unionists were to commandeer May Day. Their choice was natural, for it had long been a day of hope and renewal. A day which for centuries was celebrated by the gathering of flowers and green boughs in the countryside, a day of innocent wonderment in nature, was later celebrated in Stalin's Moscow by a parade of military might.

In those regions of China where winter was harsh, the sight of fresh flowers in city markets served as the equivalent of May Day. The early peony was the favorite, and even in the eighth century it commanded the high price of "five bits of silk." When in spring the first buds appeared on the peonies in Henan province, three or four specimens would be packed delicately in small bamboo crates, each flower being cushioned with cabbage leaves so that it could survive the bumps and shakes of the long journey on horseback from the old city of Loyang to the city of Kaifeng, which in the 11th century was the capital of China. The journey occupied a day and a night, and relays of fresh horses were ready along the road so that the plants would be flowering just when they reached the emperor's city. There the arrival of the season's first yellow peonies was as exciting as the arrival in Europe, centuries later, of the new season's teas from China.

The coming of May and its flood of milk, meat, eggs, butter and flowers was rendered less exciting by such innovations as the steamship, railway, canning factory and refrigerating machine. To Europe in the second half of the 19th century came a flow of foods from distant lands. As early as 1850, one-quarter of the bread eaten in England came from grain grown in the USA and Ukraine. At the same time, canned food was shipped across the Atlantic to Europe—tins of beef, mutton and fish to be followed by tins of vegetables, fruits and jam. By 1880 refrigerated beef and lamb were being shipped to Europe from as far away as Buenos Aires and Sydney. Soon, chilled butter in thousands of wooden boxes was reaching European grocery shops from Melbourne and Dunedin, and cheddar cheese was arriving from the United States and Canada.

In prosperous cities in the year 2000, every large department store displays roses, out of season but flown from afar, and strawberries and pineapples too. But in previous centuries, whether along the Yellow River or the Avon, it was pointless to ask for a flower which was out of season, as Shakespeare observed:

At Christmas I no more desire a rose
Than wish a snow in May's new-fangled mirth.

THE BLURRING OF NIGHT AND DAY

For most of human history the contrast between day and night was as acute as the contrast between summer and winter. Darkness kept people inside their cave, bark shelter, hut or farmhouse. Fear of wild animals was also an incentive to stay inside or near the protective light of a blazing fire. Night was linked to the sinister. The devil was said to conduct orgies, and witches rode on their broomsticks in the middle of night. At least two of the major religions saw night as a time when in the silence and darkness God might speak to them. Mohammed received much of the Koran from on high late one night. Early Christians saw virtue in praying in the night because then they could pray in silence. Moreover, as St Ambrose pointed out, demons were busy at night and must be countered by prayer. In those years when the return of Christ to this world was widely believed to be imminent, midnight was the special time for vigils. Many expected Christ to return at the hour of midnight.

As towns and cities became important, darkness lost a little of its terror. But even in the time of Columbus and Luther the main streets of cities were only lit faintly after dark. Inside the typical house in Europe the light was almost too dim for the reading of a book; in any case, most households did not possess a book.

In many European towns at a certain hour of the evening the law decreed that the household fire should be extinguished or covered. Before the family went to bed, the fire had to be made safe. This simple rule helped to save many towns, where wooden houses were jammed together, from catching alight. In England William the Conqueror, fresh from France, ordered the ringing of a curfew bell at 8 p.m., after which all fires were curbed. In Venice the rule applied to all houses except those of surgeons, who might be summoned in the middle of the night. The word "curfew" comes from an old French phrase meaning "to cover a fire." For most of the world's history the advent of night was like the closing of a door. Few occupations were carried on at night. To be a nightwatchman was to follow a lonely occupation.

During the 19th century an extraordinary change reached some cities in Europe, Australia, North America and Asia: the night ceased to contrast sharply with the day. Inside a house, for the first time in history, the artificial light at night was often clearer than the natural light of day—thanks to the abundance of whale oil, the new kerosene extracted from underground oilfields, and the invention of gas and electricity. Many daytime activities could, if necessary, be continued during the early hours of the night. Moreover by 1900 the streets of large cities were lit by electricity and knitted together by trams and trains, and so people could travel a short distance to pursue social activities in the evening.

The new ways of providing light also supplied heat for winter. Houses could become as warm as in summer. Wool had been the main raw material of warm clothes and blankets, but by the end of the 20th century the heating of houses and offices was so widespread—and synthetic fibers so cheap—that wool was no longer in strong demand for winter clothes.

The blurring of night and day was aided in an unexpected way by new electronic communications. They provided instant contact, and so somebody experiencing daylight could talk to somebody who, far away, was already in the night. It was the Italian engineer Guglielmo Marconi who discovered a way of transmitting messages by electromagnetic waves; and he sent an invisible message across the narrow Bristol Channel in 1897. Experiment slowly improved the radius of the message. Four years later Marconi was in Newfoundland when he received, from a Cornish radio transmitter on the far side of the Atlantic, a faint message. It was a procession of sounds more than a clear message, but it was exciting. Known first as wireless telegraphy, the invention caught the ears of the world in a dramatic way in July 1910. In London, Dr H.H. Crippen, after his wife mysteriously died, quietly caught a ship to Canada in company with his girlfriend, who chose to disguise herself as a boy. He was suspected of murdering his wife, his whereabouts was traced, and an urgent radio message crossed the Atlantic requesting that he be apprehended aboard the ship. Arrested at the mouth of the St Lawrence River, he was escorted back to England where he was convicted and hanged.

While the old-time telegraph did not carry the human voice, the radio could carry the voice a short distance. The first radio or wireless station for the public was founded by amateurs in Pittsburgh in 1920. Many Americans purchased or assembled their own "wireless" sets and listened, for the radio soon fulfilled an additional function—the playing of recorded music on a gramophone. Rarely is a modern invention born with its wings flapping, and in the 1920s the gramophone transmitted a sound that was eerie and sometimes scratchy. Radio transmission improved, and by 1939 those listening to the radio in New Zealand at night could hear, not always clearly, that morning's news being broadcast from London. Likewise the gramophone became a household item, and a music lover could listen in the daytime to a concert recorded the previous night—indeed a concert recorded 2,000 nights ago.

Meanwhile in 1926 an inventive Scot, John Logie Baird, transmitted the first television image, in black and white, from a room in inner London. His invention, while dramatic, was in a sense a dead end. For another quarter of a century few people outside Britain and the United States saw a televised picture. By the 1960s in most of the prosperous nations the television—with the aid of the satellite—was beginning to blur night and day. A viewer in Australia, at night, could watch the Olympic Games being contested in broad daylight on the far side of the world. So night and day changed places.

THE FADING OF MOON AND STARS

The moon for long had a special significance. Seen as a god or goddess by countless tribes and peoples in different corners of the earth, it determined most of the early calendars; and indeed the Latin language derived the words for "moon" and "month" from the same root. In Assyria the crescent moon was the symbol of the king as early as the ninth century BC. Israel based its calendar on the moon. The date of the celebrations of Easter and Ramadan were determined by the full moon. The crescent moon became the sign of Islam, and now appears on the flags of Pakistan, Turkey and most of the Islamic nations.

As the night was a prison, the full moon unlocked the gate, allowing important activities to take place. Some crops could be harvested in the light of the full moon. In ancient Athens and other cities, religious ceremonies could be held in the light of the moon. The timing of important military and naval engagements was sometimes influenced by the knowledge that the moon would be bright. In ancient Australia ceremonial dances were usually held under the full moon. In living memory in rural South Africa and Canada, farmers would hold formal dances and Masonic services on the night of the full moon; and then the participants, guided by the moon, could ride or walk home along unmade roads. In that era, rural households possessed an annual printed almanac that told them when the moon would be full.

The dome of the night sky, which seemed to be so near, held an intimacy for generations of people. In a variety of tribes and nations, many of the stars were given the names of familiar creatures—bird, wolf, cow or hen and chickens. The stars foretold the future of individuals and nations. For centuries, farmers planted crops according to the stars as well as the moon. On 4 January 1948 the nation of Burma fixed the hour of birth of its republic, and its independence from Britain, after receiving advice from astrologers that 4.20 a.m. was an auspicious time.

During the last four centuries, the telescope and radio have dispelled some of this mystery and wonder. Sir James Jeans, in his book of 1930, *The Mysterious Universe*, outlined how a multitude of stars were larger than the earth; indeed many stars could each accommodate hundreds of thousands of earths. The total of the stars in the universe probably exceeded the grains of sand on the beaches of the world. "Such," he wrote, "is the littleness of our home in space." For some this revelation of vastness was exciting: for others it was a disappointment to learn that the earth was a drop of water in an ocean of space.

The electricity which enabled day to be prolonged in the big city served also to weaken the majesty of the stars. For countless ages the night sky had been a familiar temple and shrine in the eyes of tens of millions of people scattered across the face of the earth. But in the 20th century, for the first time in human history, the artificial light cocooning a large city dimmed the brilliance of the stars above, diminishing what one balladist called "the wondrous glory of the everlasting stars." Those who scanned the sky for the sight of the Pleiades or Southern Cross had to look twice. Indeed, if a prehistoric hunting family could be resurrected and set down in Tokyo on a clear night, they would first be astonished by the tall buildings and the crowds of people and then they would observe with equal puzzlement that the night sky was no longer brilliant.

The day was also transformed. The work of the day followed a new path in prosperous western nations. Even a century ago the hard work needed to produce food, shelter and clothing was a lifelong task for most adults and many children; and the penalty for idleness or misfortune was hunger or even death. But the machine and new techniques of production transformed most jobs. Hours of work were shorter, holidays increased, and fewer jobs required the lifting of heavy weights or the unremitting use of arms and legs. Moreover a decreasing minority of workers were needed to produce the necessities of life. The typical unemployed couple living in a western land now had a much higher standard of living than that of their great-grandparents who labored 60 hours a week in New Orleans or Salonika at the start of the 20th century.

The increase in leisure, especially for those with money to spare, was now a dynamo of economic life. Many of the booming industries were centered on tourism, sport, recreation, the performing arts or other leisure pursuits. In Europe in AD 1000 the popular heroes were soldiers and saints. In AD 2000 they were more likely, in many parts of the world, to be athletes, actors, singers, artists or other heroes of leisure time.

BIG CROWDS, BIG CITIES

The revival and spread of spectator sport in the western world was a mirror of the rearranging of work and leisure, night and day, winter and summer. The cult of sport also reflected the shrinking of the world. International sport was difficult to organize in the era when the sailing ship and horse vehicle were the fastest means of travel, and so the ancient Olympic Games mostly embraced Greek port-cities linked by galleys sailing along a narrow stretch of the Mediterranean. The new popularity of international sport reflected not only the rise of air transport but also the relative international peace that reigned after 1945.

England and Australia were the first to be obsessed with spectator sport. This obsession first arose more in the cities than in the countryside: more in the Birminghams and Melbournes than in the farming villages. It reflected the increased wealth produced in fewer hours of work, thus facilitating the awarding of a half-day holiday on Saturday or Wednesday in commercial and industrial cities.

At first the rise of spectator sport reflected old patterns. It was not played on Sunday, for such activity was banned on the Sabbath day in those Protestant countries which were the first homes of modern spectator sport. Amongst the players themselves were clear distinctions between professionals and amateurs, or between working-class and upper-class participants. The strict seasons allocated to each popular sport mirrored the age-old contrast between summer and winter; and so football was allocated the winter, whereas cricket, tennis, baseball, athletics, bowls and rowing were given the warmer months.

Late in the 20th century, spectator sport was able to discard some of the conditions originally imposed on it by the seasons, the calendar, the Sabbath and nightfall. With the advent of powerful electric light, the distinction between night and day was eased. What was traditionally a daylight contest could become a night game. With the rise of roofed stadiums the contrast between summer and winter was blurred. With the decline of Protestantism, Sunday became secular and was available for sport as well as for shopping. Moreover with the ease of international travel and the spread of sporting culture, professional players could play the same game throughout the year, moving from country to country and hemisphere to hemisphere in order to catch the change in the seasons.

It is a mirror of the extraordinary spread of leisure that spectator sport is almost becoming the international language. Whereas in 1900 there were few sporting contests that aroused international enthusiasm—the revived Olympic Games was still a minor carnival—now international sporting fixtures stretch from January to December and show tentative signs of becoming a focus for some of the national pride and aggression that was traditionally poured into warfare.

Throughout human history, nearly all people were close to the soil. Therefore their lives were profoundly affected by the alternation of winter and summer, by the coming and going of the full moon, and by the pattern of rain and drought and the annual harvest. Steadily the ever-expanding city displaced the countryside as the home of most of the world's people; and the big cities now dwarfed the biggest city of several hundred years earlier. In 1995 at least 25 cities each held more than seven million inhabitants. Only four of these—London, Paris, Moscow and Istanbul—stood in Europe. In contrast 13 of the greatest cities were in Asia, and another seven were in the Americas, including four in Latin America. Africa had only one, Cairo, on the Nile. Whereas not one nation in Europe possessed a trio of great cities, China and Japan, India and the United States each possessed three of the top 25.

The large cities of the world in 2000 BC had been founded on wide inland rivers but today most of their successors are seaports. These large cities, with a few exceptions, were probably not even villages at the time of Christ. In 2000 years' time, how many of these cities will remain great? The city of skyscrapers seems the most lasting of creations—the skyscraper is almost the sphinx and pyramid of our age—but in some distant era most of these tall cities will presumably go the way of Nineveh and Carthage.

The cities reflect the soaring population of the world. Observers in the 20th century, more than in any previous century, spoke fearfully of global overpopulation, whereas in 1800 even a scholar as learned as Robert Malthus, the population expert, had few means of estimating with any accuracy the population of the world. In his day, much of the world was still sparsely explored and its peoples were uncounted.

As far as is known, the whole world at the time of Christ did not hold a population exceeding 300 million. In essence the population then was about the same as that of today's United States. By the year 1750, the world held perhaps 800 million people—far less than the present population of China. Then came the dramatic increase. The population of the world passed one billion in about 1800 and then doubled in the next 125 years. The most remarkable increase came between 1927 and 1974, when it doubled in the space of less than half a century, to about four billion people. In the quarter of a century after 1974, another two billion were added. More people were added to the population of the world in just the 1990s than in all of history stretching from the origins of humans to the birth of the industrial revolution in England.

Population, aided by technology, was so multiplied that, in the eyes of some observers, it seemed to imperil civilization. The fear that the globe was becoming warmer, and that the warmth would have adverse effects, was little discussed in 1980 but widely monitored and discussed in 2000. A hole in the ozone layer was increasingly measured, and speculated upon, from the 1980s. The fear of famine and of a grave scarcity of minerals and other raw materials—a fear strongly expressed by a circle of scientists around 1970—had waned; but fear of famine rose from time to time as the world's population continued to grow.

Nature was now seen as an old and even a dear ally, to be protected against a soaring population and a powerful technology, but it had long been regarded as an enemy as well as a friend. Since the human race first existed, nature and its extremes of flood and drought, wild beasts, invisible microbes, storms, dark forests and temperamental oceans had often been feared. Nature was capable of inflicting, in just one blow, more damage than humankind inflicted through war and other forms of self-inflicted wound in the course of an entire year. The Black Death killed more Europeans than did the First World War six centuries later. In some centuries, millions of lives were wiped out by cyclones, tidal waves, earthquakes and the erupting of volcanoes. In China alone one famine killed 10 million people in the late 1870s and in Ethiopia famine killed

1,500,000 in the early 1970s. In modern decades, however, human technology was often seen as more devastating than aberrant nature.

THE REORDERING OF THE SACRED

Religion tended to flourish most vigorously when daily life was perilous and often painful. Religion flourished when floods, droughts and other catastrophes of nature were more destructive, when starvation lay around the corner and an early death was the expectation of most people. Religion flourished when people lived on the land and knew how easily a long-awaited harvest could be thwarted by pests, drought, soil exhaustion or storms. For most of history, human life was perilous. The appeal to gods was partly a reflection of the feeling of personal helplessness. Religion provided answers to the inexplicable events in the life of a state or a family or a region. Satisfying a deep and sometimes inexplicable yearning, it was also a source of strength and inspiration.

Religion was the cement of numerous societies which otherwise might have crumbled. Powerful monarchs gained by upholding it. The official religion enabled them to proclaim that they ruled by divine right or were even descended from the gods. Therefore, to disobey the king was indirectly to disobey the gods. The revolutions in France in 1789, Russia in 1917 and China in 1949 set out to overthrow the old religions because they were a prop of the old order.

In the 20th century, religion faced new difficulties in some nations. With increased prosperity and a longer life, part of the appeal of religion was weakened. In Europe and some regions of the United States, especially Protestant regions, churchgoing declined rapidly, as did acceptance of whole moral and sexual codes preached by the churches. After the Second World War the same decline was observed in many Catholic lands.

And yet in the world as a whole, religion remained powerful. Islam was vigorous in all its traditional lands and, through the emigration of believers, expanded into European lands where it had won no converts a century earlier. Evangelical Christianity was strong amongst many peoples on whom its influence once was unknown. Both Christianity and Islam claimed far more adherents than a century earlier, and their meeting houses traced a dotted line across the whole earth. Buddhism, no longer so powerful in China where it had been superseded by what was in effect the state religion of communism, retained vitality in some lands and even in corners of China. In India the Hindus and Jains, Parsees and Sikhs were far from invisible. Judaism was alive and thankful to be alive. In Africa more people ardently practiced religion than had probably ever practiced it in Europe at any one time. What was happening to churches and temples and mosques was complex; but religion was alive. Indeed the very churches which refused to make a truce with rising secular trends—and continued to assert their belief in the importance of the next world—tended to be the most vigorous.

Millions of educated people in the western world had no time for miracles, and distanced themselves from those gods to whom, when young, they had been taught to pray. Part of their self-reliance came from the achievements of science and technology. Science itself was a new rational god and for decades was hailed as all-knowing, all-wise and capable of producing materialist miracles. Marxism for a time was a powerful alternative religion: Karl Marx preached that he was the first to find the scientific laws of human history and that those laws would ultimately produce a heaven, even though the heaven would be on earth. While science and communism claimed to dispense with the gods, they almost enthroned the human race, and its potential, into a god. This utopian attitude, even more than traditional religion, was in decline at the end of the 20th century, with the collapse of communism in Russia and eastern Europe. But it might well appear again in new garments.

Science, hailed in the previous century as the benefactor of the human race, was now condemned by many western critics as the wrecker. A vigorous environmental crusade singled out technology and science as the enemy which was polluting sky, earth and sea. Pollution became an all-purpose word of disapproval. This was the first century in which pollution was seen as a global force. The widespread hostility towards science and technology came when their triumphs were still far more pervasive than their imminent disasters and threats.

EPILOGUE

THE RECENT HISTORY of the human race is like an amazing rebirth. Most parts of the body have acquired a substitute.

Two thousand years ago human legs were indispensable. There was no substitute except a horse or a sailing ship. Elsewhere legs carried people when they worked, when they strolled. People stood on their legs for most of their waking hours, except in a tiny proportion of sit-down jobs. The moneylender and scholar could perhaps sit down while they worked: the rest stood, whether to sow crops or to reap, whether to be a preacher, soldier or cook. Even the act of writing was often performed while standing at a tall desk. But now the aircraft and train, car and motorbike and bus are substitutes for legs.

Likewise, 2,000 years ago, arms and their muscles were essential in most tasks. At sea the wind gave help but arms were necessary to hoist the heavy sails or to row the ship in still weather. The strength of the oxen was vital in ploughing but the strength of human arms was necessary to steer the plough. In fighting and hunting the arm was helped a little by the bow and arrow and by the spear-thrower, which was really a clever elongation of the arm. The arm muscles and fingers were vital for producing food and shelter and security.

Then arrived a chain of dramatic changes, with the human arm and hand being helped or replaced by the waterwheel and steam engine, by the wheelbarrow, gunpowder and dynamite, by countless manufacturing machines, the hydraulic crane, jackhammer, bulldozer, rivet machine, washing machine and vacuum cleaner, by sewing machine, grinding and mixing machines, fruit-picking machines, hole-digging machines, computer keyboards and countless other substitutes. The human arm and fingers have been transformed even more than the legs. The arm and fingers can even send nuclear missiles from one continent to another.

To the human head have also come unimaginable changes. The eyes have been enhanced by the telescope, the microscope, television, radar, spectacles, the printing press. The ears hear more, the mouth speaks more clearly and the voice travels far through radio, microphone, telephone, and music cassette. The creativity of the human brain has been aided and mirrored by the computer. Sexual activities have been altered by the Pill. The efficacy of teeth has been prolonged not only by dentistry and the artificial tooth but by changes in diet and in the processing of foods: an old person with ground-down or useless teeth was a sad sight in prehistoric times. The knowledge of the human body has been further enlarged by the study of genes.

Likewise the human memory, especially the collective memory, has been enlarged by libraries and archives. Curiously this enlarging of the human memory was significant long before the rise of the Roman Empire thanks to the innovation of counting, the devising of the calendar, the rise of the art of writing, and that ingenious aid to a retentive memory, skill in rhyming. In contrast most of the startling gains in the efficiency of legs and arms, mouth and teeth, eyes and ears and memory, and the diagnosing of human illness, came after the 15th century.

None of these profound changes altered the human will, human restlessness, the human desire either for freedom or for conformity. So many of the triumphs of science and technology were skin-deep. It was easier, in this era of mass production in the countryside and city, to satisfy the stomach than the mind. It was easier to tame diseases than to tame human behavior and put an end to warfare.

ALMOST ONE WORLD

The advances in technology magnified the potential power of one particular leader or group. Ten thousand years ago, a leader of a tribe was rarely able to wield influence more than 100 kilometers from home. The world was like a pond with space for thousands of small ripples, each ripple reflecting the tiny sphere of influence of one tribe. The radius of ripples became larger after the emerging of bigger empires—the Chinese and Indian, the Hellenistic, Roman and Aztec.

The sphere of influence of each of these empires was still small. Such was the prevailing technology of war and transport that there was virtually no way of achieving central control of a civilian population spread far and wide. Two thousand years ago, no empire could extend far. Rome in its heyday could have conquered and ruled parts of India and even China but its reign would have been brief. There was no avenue through which even Spain or Portugal could have controlled effectively most of the remote ports of the New World. Hitler, if he had been victorious, probably could not have controlled the whole world. The technology of war, communications and censorship did not allow it.

Today, as never before, it is possible for one strong nation to control the whole world. Within the next two centuries, as the world shrinks and its distances are diminished, an attempt could well be made, by consent or by force, to set up a world government. Whether it will last for long is an open question. In human history, almost nothing is preordained.

SELECTED SOURCES

IN A SHORT HISTORY, where economies of space are constantly sought, the following notes are almost a luxury. They cover only a small part of the sources consulted or read. Most hinge on questions that are more likely to be in dispute, on evidence and matters that are little known, or interpretations borrowed from other historians.

In some sections of the book the events briefly described are well known, and I have not listed sources. Some of the concepts have long been in my head, going back 30 or even 40 years, and I now have no idea who placed them there or how much I have rearranged them. Chapter 28, "A Globe Unwrapped," is such a mosaic.

Many of the places fleetingly described or half-evoked are the result of visits, whether to the carved Buddha in Luoyang in China, the harbor of Zanzibar, the Robert Louis Stevenson house in Western Samoa, the Roman bridge at Rimini in Italy, or the old spa town of Carlsbad in the Czech Republic. Likewise, the objects described in museums are the result of personal visits.

In thinking about and working on a book of this kind, one frequently has a need to consult quickly a reliable reference work on some minor matter: is this year or town named accurately—especially when rival sources disagree—or is that the correct spelling of a name? I have often consulted, with gain, various editions of the *Encyclopaedia Britannica*, especially the 1910–11 and 1989 printings, and various Oxford dictionaries, including those covering the Christian church, quotations, and ships and the sea. For biographical queries I have sometimes consulted the English *Dictionary of National Biography* and another valuable work, Barry Jones's *Dictionary of World Biography* (3rd edn, Information Australia, Melbourne, 1998).

Each entry is preceded by the relevant page number. To save space I have not always cited in full the title of a learned article if it is very long or marginal.

1 FROM AFRICA

6 Predatory animals: Barbara Ehrenreich, *Blood Rites: Origins and History of the Passions of War*, Metropolitan Books, New York, 1997, pp. 43–4.

7 Discovery on island of Flores: *La Trobe Bulletin*, April 1997, p. 3; supplemented by personal information from Dr P. O'Sullivan, University of Melbourne.

8 Homo erectus: displays in the Museum of Natural History, London, 1995; *Yearbook of Science and the Future, 1998*, Encyclopaedia Britannica, Chicago, pp. 241–2.

8–9 Evolution of human brain: Vernon B. Mountcastle, "Brain Science at the Century's Ebb," *Daedalus*, Spring 1998, esp. pp. 9–10.

8–9 Fatty acid in meat: Frank D. Mann, "Animal Fat and Cholesterol . . . ," *Perspectives in Biology and Medicine*, Spring 1998, pp. 417–18.

9 Human speech: Steven Mithen, *The Prehistory of the Mind: The Cognitive Origins of Art, Religion and Science*, Phoenix, London, 1996, pp. 158–61.

9–10 Primitive art: ibid., pp. 21, 177, 199.

11 Elephant in Germany: Philip G. Chase in Harold L. Dibble, ed., *Upper Pleistocene Prehistory of Western Eurasia*, University of Pennsylvania Museum, Philadelphia, 1988, p. 230. For the German village, see Gerhard Bosinski in Dibble, ibid., p. 382.

12–14 Spread of human race: Jared Diamond, *Guns, Germs and Steel: A Short History of Everybody for the Last 13,000 Years*, Vintage, London, 1998, pp. 37–42.

14–15 First settling of New Guinea–Australia: John Mulvaney & Johan Kamminga, *Prehistory of Australia*, Allen & Unwin, St Leonards, N.S.W., 1999, ch. 9.

2 WHEN THE SEAS WERE RISING

16–17 Ice in the Americas: displays and models in the National Museum of Natural History, Washington D.C., 1998.

18–19 Fluctuations in sea level: R.W. Fairbridge in A.B. Pittock et al., eds., *Climatic Change and Variability: A Southern Perspective*, Cambridge University Press, Cambridge, 1978, pp. 201–2.

19 Southern Africa: Lyn Wadley, "The Pleistocene Later Stone Age South of the Limpopo River," *Journal of World Prehistory*, vol. 7, 1993, pp. 281, 285, 290.

19 Sahara lakes: Ray Inskeep, "The Final Days of Hunting and Gathering in Africa," in Andrew Sherratt, ed., *The Cambridge Encyclopedia of Archaeology*, Crown, New York, 1980, p. 175.

22 New Guinea's retreating snowline and rising tree line: Richard Schodde & W.B. Hitchcock in Peter Ryan, ed., *Encyclopaedia of Papua and New Guinea*, vol. 1, Melbourne University Press, Carlton, 1972, p. 80.

23 Tasmanians' hair: Mulvaney & Kamminga, *Prehistory of Australia*, op. cit., pp.

339–40; Geoffrey Blainey, *Triumph of the Nomads: A History of Ancient Australia*, Macmillan, South Melbourne, 1975, pp. 45–6.

25 Early pottery along Amazon: John W. Hoopes, "Ford Revisited: . . . the Earliest Ceramic Complexes in the New World, 6000–1500 B.C.," *Journal of World Prehistory*, vol. 8, 1994, p. 41.

25 Riverbank settlements: J. Scott Raymond, "A View from the Tropical Forest," in Richard W. Keatinge, ed., *Peruvian Prehistory: An Overview of Inca and Pre-Inca Society*, Cambridge University Press, New York, 1988, pp. 297–8.

26 Ecological diversity of the Amazon: Eduardo V. de Castro, "Images of Nature and Society in Amazonian Ethnology," *Annual Review of Anthropology*, vol. 23, 1996, pp. 179ff.

26 Humans reach Japan: H. Kazure in Richard J. Pearson, ed., *Windows on the Japanese Past: Studies in Archaeology and Prehistory*, University of Michigan, Ann Arbor, 1986, pp. 80–3.

27 Japan in the Jomon period: J.E. Kidder, "The Earliest Societies in Japan," in John W. Hall et al., eds., *The Cambridge History of Japan*, vol. 1 (ed. Delmer M. Brown), 1988–99, ch. 2.

29–30 Assessment of nomadic societies: a warning of the danger of generalization about nomadic or forager societies is given by Michael Shott, "On Recent Trends in the Anthropology of Foragers," *Man* (new series), vol. 27, 1992, pp. 843ff. My reading of such societies in Australia (*Triumph of the Nomads*, op. cit.) is that they were relatively well-off, but Shott might not share such a conclusion.

3 THE FIRST GREEN REVOLUTION

31–2 Suberde and early villages: Dexter Perkins Jr & Patricia Daly, "The Beginning of Food Production in the Near East," in Robert Stigler, ed., *The Old World: Early Man to the Development of Agriculture*, Thames & Hudson, London, 1974, pp. 90–1.

32–3 Warm climate and wild grains: Naomi F. Miller, "Seed Eaters of the Ancient Near East: Human or Herbivore?" *Current Anthropology*, vol. 37, 1996, p. 521.

32–3 Coexistence of foraging and farming: A.W.R. Whittle, *Europe in the Neolithic: The Creation of New Worlds*, Cambridge University Press, Cambridge, 1996, esp. pp. 3, 361–70.

34 Obsidian and other trades in the western Mediterranean: Colin Renfrew, *The Emergence of Civilisation: The Cyclades and the Aegean in the Third Millennium B.C.*, Methuen, London, 1972, p. 354 (for long ships, see p. 357); Robin Skeates, "Copper Age Settlement and Economy in Marche, Central Italy," *Journal of Medieval Archaeology*, vol. 10, 1997, p. 54.

34 Spread of farming: Whittle, *Europe in the Neolithic*, op. cit., pp. 1–3; *Science and the Future*, Encyclopaedia Britannica, Chicago, 1995, p. 212, illustrates how dates are pushed back in time as excavations proceed.

35 African domestication: C. Thurstan Shaw, "Agricultural Origins in Africa," *Cambridge Encyclopedia of Archaeology*, op. cit., pp. 179–83.

35–6 Tilling the soil: F. Raum, "The Culture and Historical Significance of the Xhosa Spade," *Tools & Tillage*, vol. 3, 1977, pp. 104; Axel Steensberg, *Man the Manipulator: An Ethno-Archaeological Basis for Reconstructing the Past*, National Museum of Denmark, Copenhagen, 1986, esp. pp. 20, 33–4.

36 Oil and wine: Renfrew, *The Emergence of Civilisation*, op. cit., pp. 282–6, 481–5.

36 Grain pits: Barry Cunliffe, *Iron Age Communities in Britain: An Account of En-*

gland, Scotland and Wales from the Seventh Century BC *until the Roman Conquest*, Routledge & Kegan Paul, London, 1974, pp. 167–8.

37 Diseases from animals: Diamond, *Guns, Germs and Steel*, op. cit., pp. 205–7.

37 Rise of chiefs and kings: W.G. Runciman, *A Treatise on Social Theory*, vol. 2, Cambridge University Press, Cambridge, 1989, esp. pp. 151–5.

37 Farming districts and monuments: Mircea Eliade, *A History of Religious Ideas: From the Stone Age to the Eleusinian Mysteries*, vol. 1, Collins, 1979, pp. 115, 121; for harvest and worship, see Renfrew, *The Emergence of Civilisation*, op. cit., pp. 417–18.

39–40 Danish burials: P.V. Glob, *The Bog People: Iron-Age Man Preserved*, Paladin, London, 1971, esp. ch. 3.

40–1 New Guinea gardens: Thomas M. Marecek, "Shifting Cultivation among the Duna of Papua New Guinea," *Tools & Tillage*, vol. 3, 1977, pp. 67–78.

40–1 Why New Guinea lagged after bright start: Steensberg, *Man the Manipulator*, op. cit., p. 20; Diamond, *Guns, Germs and Steel*, op. cit., pp. 147–9.

41 Cannibalism: Diamond, ibid., p. 149.

41–2 Later Asia–America links: Olive P. Dickason, *Canada's First Nations: A History of Founding Peoples from Earliest Times*, Oxford University Press, Toronto, 1992, esp. pp. 53, 58–9.

42–3 Uses of pottery in Africa: "Smashing Pots," an exhibition at the Museum of Mankind, London, August 1995.

43 First copper: Beno Rothenberg & J. Merkel, "Chalcolithic, 5th Millennium BC: Copper Smelting at Timna," *IAMS Journal*, no. 20, 1998, pp. 1–3.

44 Tyrolean iceman: Whittle, *Europe in the Neolithic*, op. cit., pp. 315–16. Further research (James D. Wilde in *Yearbook of Science and the Future*, 1996, Encyclopaedia Britannica, Chicago, p. 313) suggested that the traveller was very poorly equipped, had left in a hurry on his alpine journey, and perhaps was escaping. The date of his death is assigned to about 3120 BC.

4 THE DOME OF NIGHT

45–6 Tasmanians and sky fears: N.J.B. Plomley, ed., *Friendly Mission: The Tasmanian Journals and Papers of George Augustus Robinson, 1829–1834*, Tasmanian Historical Research Association, Hobart, 1966, pp. 186, 300, 404–6.

46–7 Meteorites: displays in the South Australian Museum, Adelaide.

47 Shooting stars as evil: Baldwin Spencer, *Native Tribes of the Northern Territory of Australia*, Macmillan, London, 1914, p. 106; Plomley, *Friendly Mission*, op. cit., p. 300.

47 Tasmanians on stars: Plomley, ibid., pp. 300, 861.

47 New South Wales Aborigines and stars: R. Brough Smyth, *The Aborigines of Victoria: With Notes Relating to the Habits of the Natives of Other Parts of Australia and Tasmania*, vol. 2, Government Printer, Melbourne, 1878, p. 286.

47 Milky Way as river: T.G.H. Strehlow, *Songs of Central Australia*, Angus & Robertson, Sydney, 1971, p. 618.

47 Babylon eclipse: Sir Frank Dyson, "Eclipses," *Chambers's Encyclopedia*, vol. 4, Chambers, London, 1924, p. 187.

48 Full moon: Neil & Rod Phillips, *Rogaining: Cross-Country Navigators*, Outdoor Recreation in Australia, Melbourne, 2000, p. 104.

48 Moon and religion: Mircea Eliade, *Patterns in Comparative Religion*, Sheed & Ward, London, 1958, pp. 154–72.

49 Paradise in the sky: Strehlow, *Songs of Central Australia*, op. cit., pp. 371, 618.

49 Aboriginal theory of creation: Rhys Jones, "Landscape of the Mind," in D.J. Mulvaney, ed., *The Humanities and the Australian Environment: Papers from the Australian Academy of the Humanities Symposium*, 1990, Australian Academy of the Humanities, Canberra, 1991, pp. 35–7.

50 Hallmark of early religions: Mircea Eliade, *The Quest: History and Meaning in Religion*, University of Chicago Press, Chicago, 1969, pp. 527–8; Eliade, *Patterns in Comparative Religion*, op. cit., p. 111.

51–2 Astrology: Charles H. Haskins, *The Renaissance of the Twelfth Century*, Meridian, Cleveland, 1968, pp. 317–18.

5 CITIES OF THE VALLEYS

55–6 Nile floods: Fekri A. Hassan, "The Dynamics of a Riverine Civilization: A Geoarchaeological Perspective on the Nile Valley, Egypt," *World Archaeology*, vol. 29, 1997, esp. pp. 53–63.

56 Temple-granaries: Richard Alston in Helen M. Parkins, ed., *Roman Urbanism: Beyond the Consumer City*, London, Routledge, 1997, pp. 148–9.

57 Medicine: Warren R. Dawson, "Medicine," in S.R.K. Glanville, ed., *The Legacy of Egypt*, Clarendon Press, Oxford, 1942.

58 Egypt's continuity: Erik Hornung in Sergio Donadoni, ed., *The Egyptians*, University of Chicago Press, Chicago, 1997, pp. 312–13.

59 Sumer's 18 cities : Charles K. Maisels, "Models of Social Evolution," *Man*, 1987, pp. 340–4.

59–60 Writing: J.T. Hooker et al., *Reading the Past: Ancient Writing from Cuneiform to the Alphabet*, British Museum, London, 1993, esp. ch. 2 by C.B.F. Walker; Carsten Peter Thiede & Matthew d'Ancona, *The Jesus Papyrus*, Weidenfeld & Nicolson, London, 1996, passim.

60 Ur burials: display in British Museum, September 1997.

61 Assyrian murals: exhibited as part of "Treasures from Assyria in the British Museum," National Gallery of Victoria, March 1997.

62 Nineveh aqueduct: H.W.F. Saggs, *The Greatness That Was Babylon: A Survey of the Ancient Civilization of the Tigris-Euphrates Valley*, Sidgwick & Jackson, London, 1962, pp. 122–3, 181, for contradictory estimates of number of cut stones.

63 Slaves and women: A.K. Grayson, "Assyrian Civilization," *The Cambridge Ancient History*, 2nd edn, vol. 3, part 2, Cambridge University Press, Cambridge, 1991, p. 207.

63 Erosion: Edwin S. Hills, "History of the World's Arid Lands," in R.O. Slatyer & R.A. Perry, eds., *Arid Lands of Australia*, ANU Press, Canberra, 1969, p. 5.

64 Population decline: J.A. Brinkman, "Babylonia in the Shadow of Assyria," *Cambridge Ancient History*, op. cit., pp. 1–4.

64 Soldiers' slings: John Curtis & J.E. Reade, *Art and Empire: Treasures from Assyria in the British Museum*, British Museum, London, 1995, p. 67.

64 Babylon ransacked: Joan Oates, "The Fall of Assyria," *Cambridge Ancient History*, op. cit., pp. 179–91.

65–6 Indus cities: S.S. Shashi, ed., *Encyclopaedia Indica*, vol. 2, Anmal, New Delhi, 1996, pp. 177–8.

66 Indus floods and erosion: Brian M. Fagan, *People of the Earth: An Introduction to World Prehistory*, HarperCollins, London, 1992, p. 485.

6 AMAZING SEA

69 Hugging the coast: Fernand Braudel, *The Mediterranean and the Mediterranean World in the Age of Philip II*, vol. 1, Collins, London, 1972, pp. 106–7.

69, 71 Galleys at sea: John Coates & John Morrison, "The Sea Trials of the Reconstructed Trireme *Olympias,*" *The Mariner's Mirror*, vol. 79, 1993, passim.

71–2 Sails and winds: Eve Black & David Samuel, "What Were Sails Made of?" *The Mariner's Mirror*, vol. 77, 1991, pp. 217–26. On the winds see Peter Fenton, ibid., vol. 79, 1993.

72–3 Iron: Ian Morris, "Circulation, Deposition and the Formation of the Greek Iron Age," Man, vol. 24, 1989, passim; Roger Sworder, *Mining, Metallurgy and the Meaning of Life: A Book of Stories*, Quakers Hill Press, Quakers Hill, N.S.W., 1995, pp. 24–6, 36.

73 Sukhumi's submerged ruins: visit to Sukhumi, then in the USSR, in 1970.

74–5 Athens festivals: Noel Robertson, "Athena's Shrines and Festivals," in Jenifer Neils, ed., *Worshipping Athena: Panathenaia and Parthenon*, University of Wisconsin Press, Madison, 1996, pp. 27–8, 52.

75 Significance of Greek art: E.H. Gombrich, *The Story of Art*, 12th edn, Phaidon, London, 1972, pp. 48–53, 65.

75–6 Greek food: Andrew Dalby, *Siren Feasts: A History of Food and Gastronomy in Greece*, Routledge, London, 1996, passim.

76 Nudity: Donald G. Kyle, "Gifts and Glory," in Neils, *Worshipping Athena*, op. cit., ch. 5.

76–7 City of Croton: ibid., pp. 116, 131n.

77–9 On democracy: Benjamin Jowett, trans., *The Politics of Aristotle*, Colonial Press, New York, 1899, esp. pp. 44, 156, 112.

77 Pericles as general: A.R. Burn, *Pericles and Athens*, Hodder & Stoughton, London, 1948, pp. 48–61, 130.

78–9 Demosthenes' speech: reprinted in William Safire, ed., *Lend Me Your Ears: Great Speeches in History*, rev. edn, Norton, New York, 1997, p. 783.

78 Slaves: *The World of Athens: An Introduction to Classical Athenian Culture*, Cambridge University Press, Cambridge, 1984, p. 157.

80 Greek attitude to technology: Peter Green, *Alexander to Actium: The Historical Evolution of the Hellenistic Age*, University of California Press, Berkeley, 1990, pp. 458, 469–70, 477–8 (siege engine).

80 Greek innovations: M.J.T. Lewis, "The Origins of the Wheelbarrow," *Technology and Culture*, vol. 35, 1994, esp. pp. 468–75; A.G. Drachmann in Melvin Kranzberg & C.W. Pursell Jr, eds., *Technology in Western Civilization*, vol. 1, Oxford University Press, New York, 1967, pp. 49–55.

82 Pharos lighthouse: Honor Frost, "New Light from the Pharos of Alexandria," *The Mariner's Mirror*, vol. 82, 1996, pp. 203–6; *Grosser Atlas zur Weltgeschichte*, Georg Westermann, Braunschweig, 1972, p. 26; John & Elizabeth Romer, *The Seven Wonders of the World: A History of the Modern Imagination*, Henry Holt & Co., New York, 1955, esp. p. 55. The earthquake was in 1375.

82–3 Incest in Egypt: Brent D. Shaw, "Explaining Incest: Brother–Sister Marriage in Graeco-Roman Egypt," Man, vol. 27, 1992.

83–4 Hellenistic influence: Claudio Véliz, *The New World of the Gothic Fox: Culture and Economy in English and Spanish America*, University of California Press, Berkeley, 1994, pp. 115–16.

7 LORD OF THE YELLOW, KING OF THE GANGES

85–6 Horses on the steppe: W.H. McNeill, "The History of the Eurasian Steppe," *Encyclopaedia Britannica*, vol. 28, 1992, esp. pp. 240–6; Marek Zvelebil, "The Rise of the Nomads in Central Asia," *Cambridge Encyclopedia of Archaeology*, op. cit., p. 255.

88–9 Confucius: Tu Wei-ming, "The Confucian Tradition in Chinese History," in Paul S. Ropp, ed., *Heritage of China: Contemporary Perspectives on Chinese Civilization*, University of California Press, Berkeley, 1990, esp. pp. 112–15.

89–90 Great Wall of China: Joseph Needham, *Science and Civilisation in China*, vol. 4, part 3, Cambridge University Press, Cambridge, 1971, pp. 47–55.

91 China more populous than Europe: Albert Feuerwerker, "Chinese Economic History in Comparative Perspective," in Ropp, *Heritage of China*, op. cit., p. 231.

92 Bride of Yellow River: Herbert Franke & Denis Twitchett, eds., *The Cambridge History of China*, vol. 1, Cambridge University Press, Cambridge, 1994, p. 35.

92–3 Fighting the Yellow floods: Needham, *Science and Civilisation in China*, op. cit., vol. 4, part 3, pp. 232–41.

94 Chinese roads and fire beacons: ibid., vol. 4, part 3, pp. 35–7.

96 Silt in Ganges and Yellow rivers: J.J. Holeman, "The Sediment Yield of Major Rivers of the World," *Encyclopaedia Britannica*, vol. 26, 1989, p. 905.

97 Plough with 24 oxen: Marvin Harris, *Cultural Materialism: The Struggle for a Science of Culture*, Random House, New York, 1979, p. 251.

97–8 Indian caste system: K.M. Munshi, ed., *The History and Culture of the Indian People*, 4th edn, vol. 2, Bharatiya Vidya Bhavan, Bombay, 1968, pp. 548, 557.

98–100 Birth of Buddhism: Mircea Eliade & Ioan P. Couliano, *The Eliade Guide to World Religions*, Harper, San Francisco, 1991, pp. 26–37.

100 Empire of Funan: F.J. Moorhead, *A History of Malaya and Her Neighbours*, vol. 1, Longman, London, 1957, ch. 5.

8 THE RISE OF ROME

102–3 Roman engineering: O.A.T. Gimesy, *Building Our World: A History of Building Construction*, Victoria University of Technology, Melbourne, 1994, pp. 89ff.

105 Size of Roman ships: Deutsches Museum, Munich (which, incidentally, understates Columbus's flagship).

105 Winds and ships: Peter Throckmorton in George F. Bass, ed., *A History of Seafaring Based on Underwater Archaeology*, Thames & Hudson, London, 1972, ch. 3.

106 Virgil on farming: C. Day Lewis, *The Eclogues, Georgics and Aeneid of Virgil*, Oxford University Press, Oxford, 1966, esp. pp. 60–1, 64.

106 Livy on the Battle of Cannae: Michael Grant, ed., *Roman Readings:Translations from the Latin Prose and Poetry*, Penguin, Harmondsworth, 1958, pp. 238ff.

106–7 Mithridates: Michael Crawford, *The Roman Republic*, Fontana, n.p., 1978, p. 145.

107 Consuls at Rome: Christian Meier, *Caesar*, HarperCollins, London, 1995, p. 204.

108 Child slave: carving in Getty Museum, Malibu Beach, 1995.

109 To Cicero from Athens: letter reprinted in Grant, *Roman Readings*, op. cit., p. 56.

110 Silk route and "the Seres": *Cambridge History of China*, op. cit., vol. 1, p. 579.

111–12 Oranges from China: Needham, *Science and Civilisation in China*, op. cit., vol. 6, part 1, pp. 365–7.

9 ISRAEL AND THE ANOINTED ONE

Many passages cited in this chapter are from the Bible's Old and New Testaments. An ms. commentary on Hebrew history by John Levi, Senior Rabbi of the Melbourne Liberal Jewish Community, proved valuable.

114–5 Palestine's geography: L.H. Grollenberg, *The Penguin Shorter Atlas of the Bible*, Allen Lane, London, 1978, pp. 15–21.

115 Changing level of Red Sea: D.J. Baker in *Yearbook of Science and the Future, 1994*, Encyclopaedia Britannica, Chicago, p. 330.

115–6 Judaism takes shape: Paul Johnson, *A History of the Jews*, Weidenfeld & Nicolson, London, 1987, esp. pp. 54–6.

118 Minor rules of conduct: see Exodus and Leviticus in the Old Testament.

119 Jesus' social background: David Fiensy, "Leaders of Mass Movements and the Leader of the Jesus Movement," *Journal for the Study of the New Testament*, issue 74, 1999, pp. 15–17.

119 Literacy of Jesus: Thiede & d'Ancona, *The Jesus Papyrus*, op. cit., pp. 129–30.

119 John the Baptist: Cecil John Cadoux, *The Life of Jesus*, Penguin, West Drayton, Middlesex, 1948, pp. 44–5.

121 Birth of Christian religion: John Riches, "The Birth of Christianity," in Ian Hazlett, ed., *Early Christianity: Origins and Evolution to AD 600*, SPCK, London, 1991, ch. 3.

121–2 Background to Jesus' death: Johnson, *A History of the Jews*, op. cit., esp. pp. 127–9.

122–3 Resurrection concept: Eliade, *A History of Religious Ideas*, op. cit., vol. 1, p. 337.

10 AFTER CHRIST

124 Jews in Roman census: Chaim Raphael, *The Road from Babylon: The Story of the Sephardi and Oriental Jews*, Harper & Row, New York, 1985, p. 33.

124 Jews equal 9 per cent of people of Roman Empire: Horbury, op. cit., p. 40.

125 Synagogues in Sardis and Alexandria: William Horbury in Hazlett, *Early Christianity*, op. cit., p. 43.

126 Antioch today: William Dalrymple, *From the Holy Mountain: A Journey in the Shadow of Byzantium*, HarperCollins, London, 1997, pp. 53–5.

126–7 Gentiles and Jews in Antioch: Knut Schäferdiek, "Christian Mission and Expansion," in Hazlett, *Early Christianity*, op. cit., pp. 65–6.

128–9 Dates fixed for Christmas and Easter: F.L. Cross, ed., *The Oxford Dictionary of the Christian Church*, 2nd edn, Oxford University Press, Oxford, 1974, pp. 1037, 1150.

129, 130 St Helena and St Anne: D.H. Farmer, *The Oxford Dictionary of Saints*, Clarendon Press, Oxford, 1979, pp. 17, 188.

130 Salt and religion: *Oxford Dictionary of the Christian Church*, op. cit., p. 1230.

133 Grand church buildings: Gombrich, *Story of Art*, op. cit., pp. 94–5.

134 Roman persecution of Jews in AD fourth century: Johnson, *A History of the Jews*, op. cit., pp. 164–5.

135–6 Rome's legacy: William Chase Greene, *The Achievement of Rome: A Chapter in Civilization*, Cooper Square, n.p., 1973, pp. xi, 512; Philip Ayres, *Classical Culture* *and the Idea of Rome in Eighteenth-Century England*, Cambridge University Press, Cambridge, 1997, ch. 1.

138–9 Dispute about icons: Jaroslav Pelikan, *The Christian Tradition: A History of the Development of Doctrine*, vol. 2, University of Chicago Press, Chicago, 1974, pp. 132, 142, 145.

11 THE SIGN OF THE CRESCENT

141 Religion and politics in Arabia: Ira M. Lapidus, "State and Religion in Islamic Societies," *Past & Present*, 1996, p. 8.

145–7 Geography and the rise of Mohammed: P.M. Holt et al., eds., *The Cambridge History of Islam*, vol. 1, Cambridge University Press, Cambridge, 1970, esp. early chapters by Irfan Shahid and W.M. Watt.

147–8 Islam and Jews: Yahya Armajani, Middle East: Past and Present, Prentice-Hall, Englewood Cliffs, N.J., 1970, pp. 35–6; Raphael, *The Road from Babylon*, op. cit., pp. 44, 58, 64, 131.

148–9 Spread of Islam in Africa: Timothy Insoll, "Islam in Sub-Saharan Africa," *Journal of World Prehistory*, vol. 10, 1996, pp. 442ff.

149 Muslims not enslaved: ibid., p. 492.

12 THE WILD GEESE CROSS THE MOUNTAINS

152 The nature-poet: J.D. Frodsham, *The Murmuring Stream: The Life and Works of the Chinese Nature Poet Hsieh Ling-Yün*, vol. 1, University of Malaya Press, Kuala Lumpur, 1967, esp. chapters 1–3.

152 Chinese poets precede English lake poets: ibid., p. 95.

152–3 Cliff-face Buddha at Luoshan: inspected in October 1981.

154 Conversion of Japanese emperor: Sonoda Koyu & O.M. Brown, "Early Buddha Worship," *Cambridge History of Japan*, op. cit., vol. 1, pp. 397–8.

154 Worship of kami: Matsumae Takeshi, "Early Kami Worship," ibid., pp. 336, 356.

155 Variable statues of Buddha: H.H.E. Loofs, "Biographies in Stone," in Wang Gungwu, ed., *Self and Biography: Essays on the Individual and Society in Asia*, Sydney University Press, Sydney, 1976, pp. 9ff.

13 TOWARDS POLYNESIA

159–60 Austronesian emigrations: Diamond, *Guns, Germs and Steel*, op. cit., pp. 338, 341.

161 Tupaia the interpreter: J.C. Beaglehole, ed., *The Endeavour Journal of Joseph Banks: 1768–1771*, vol. 1, Angus & Robertson, Sydney, 1962, p. 401.

162 Polynesia's canoes and seafaring skills: Douglas Oliver, *Return to Tahiti: Bligh's Second Breadfruit Voyage*, Melbourne University Press, Carlton, 1988, p. 71, plate 9.

162 Tupaia the navigator: J.C. Beaglehole, ed., *The Journals of Captain James Cook*, vol. 1, Cambridge University Press, Cambridge, 1968, p. 169.

162 Puzzle of Easter Island: Diamond, *Guns, Germs and Steel*, op. cit., pp. 65, 224, 230–1.

163 Breadfruit trees: Oliver, *Return to Tahiti*, op. cit., p. 168; O.H.K. Spate, *Paradise Found and Lost*, ANU Press, Sydney, 1988, p. 35.

163 "Love is the Chief Occupation": Beaglehole, *The Endeavour Journal of Joseph Banks*, op. cit., vol. 2, p. 330.

163–4 Discovery of Madagascar: Robert E. Dewar & Henry T. Wright, "The Culture History of Madagascar," *Journal of World Prehistory*, vol. 7, 1993, esp. pp. 418–19.
164 Coastal scenery of Madagascar: personal visits in 1970 and 1990.
164–5 New Zealand fortified places: inspection of models in Auckland Museum; Spate, *Paradise Found and Lost*, op. cit., p. 17.
166–7 Maori gardening, birding and hunting: inspections of displays in museums in Wellington, Auckland and Christchurch, 1987, 1998–99.
167 Contempt of pain: Oliver, *Return to Tahiti*, op. cit., pp. 71–2.

14 THE MONGOLS

176 Mongolian winter-grazing: Gerard M. Friters, *Outer Mongolia and Its International Position*, Allen & Unwin, London, 1951, p. 12.
177–8 Tactics of Mongol armies: Thomas Allsen in *Cambridge History of China*, op. cit., vol. 6, esp. pp. 345, 356.
178 China's huge army: Mark Elvin, *The Pattern of the Chinese Past*, Stanford University Press, Stanford, 1973, p. 84.
178 Mandarins and the military: Runciman, *A Treatise on Social Theory*, op. cit., vol. 2, pp. 225, 229; John K. Fairbank, The United States & China, 4th edn, Harvard University Press, Cambridge, Mass., 1979, p. 69.
181 Gold-bearing maiden on the silk road: C.G.F. Simkin, *The Traditional Trade of Asia*, Oxford University Press, London, 1968, p. 135.
182–4 China's advanced technology: Needham, *Science and Civilisation in China*, op. cit., vol. 6, part 1, pp. 474–8, 551.
182 Frogs and locusts: Needham, *Science and Civilisation in China*, op. cit., vol. 6, part 1, pp. 547, 551.
182 Chinese handbook of agriculture: Elvin, *The Pattern of the Chinese Past*, op. cit., p. 180.
183 Gunpowder: Fang-Toh Sun, "Gunpowder-Rocket Technology in Ancient China . . . ," in Cheng-Yih Chen, ed., *Science and Technology in Chinese Civilization*, World Scientific, Singapore, 1987, esp. pp. 268–71.
184 Slaves and criminals: *Cambridge History of China*, op. cit., vol. 6, pp. 286–9.
185 Why China despatched no Columbus: Song Zhenghai & Chen Chuankang, "Why did Zheng He's Sea Voyage Fail to Lead the Chinese . . ." in Fan Dainian & Robert S. Cohen, eds, *Chinese Studies in the History and Philosophy of Science and Technology*, Kluwer, Dordrecht, 1996, esp. pp. 308–12; David S. Landes, "What Room for Accident in History?" *Economic History Review*, vol. 47, 1994, pp. 640–1.
185 Chinese voyages of Zheng He (Chen Ho): Ma Huan, *The Overall Survey of the Ocean's Shores*, Hakluyt Society, Cambridge, 1970, pp. 5–33.

15 PERILS OF CLIMATE AND DISEASE

187 Discovery of Greenland: commentary by Jorgen Meldgaard, curator at National Museum of Denmark, 1987; Johannes Brondsted, *The Vikings*, Penguin, Harmondsworth, 1965, pp. 86–7.
187 Greenland farms: Knud J. Krogh, *Viking Greenland*, National Museum Copenhagen, 1967, pp. 52ff; Jacqueline Simpson, *Everyday Life in the Viking Age*, Batsford, London, 1967, p. 41.
188 Procession of poverty in 1315: Emmanuel Le Roy Ladurie, *Times of Feast*,

Times of Famine: A History of Climate Since the Year 1000, Noonday Press, New York, 1988, p. 47.

188 French famines: Harry A. Miskimin, *The Economy of Early Renaissance Europe, 1300–1460*, Prentice-Hall, Englewood Cliffs, N.J., 1969, pp. 26–7.

188–9 Cold Dakotas: Douglas B. Bamforth, "Indigenous People, Indigenous Violence: Pre Contact Warfare on the North American Great Plains," *Man*, vol. 29, 1994, pp. 106–10.

190 Herrings in the Sound: C. Verlinden & A.B. Hibbert in M.M. Postan & H.J. Habakkuk, eds., *The Cambridge Economic History of Europe*, Cambridge University Press, Cambridge, 1966–77 (2nd edn, vol. 3, pp. 147–9, 208), offer alternative explanations for the decline of the Scania herring fair, including the possibility that the Reformation lessened northern Europe's demand for salted fish.

190 Climate and decline of herring: Robert Claiborne, *Climate, Man and History*, Angus & Robertson, London, 1973, pp. 375–7.

190 Population: Julian L. Simon, "Demographic Causes and Consequences of the Industrial Revolution," *Journal of European Economic History*, Spring 1994, p. 155.

191–2 Black Death: William H. McNeill, *Plagues and Peoples*, Anchor Press, Garden City, N.Y., 1976, pp. 166–9; Kenneth F. Kiple, ed., *The Cambridge World History of Human Disease*, Cambridge University Press, Cambridge, 1993, pp. 626–30.

191 Lepers in Norway: R.C. Hastings, "Leprosy at Century's End," in *1998 Britannica Medical & Health Annual*, Encyclopaedia Britannica, Chicago, 1997, pp. 283–7.

192 Deserted villages: Miskimin, *The Economy of Early Renaissance Europe*, op. cit., p. 57.

192 Attack on Jews at Basle and Worms: Barbara W. Tuchman, *A Distant Mirror: The Calamitous 14th Century*, Macmillan, London, 1979, pp. 113, 115.

192 Church as place of drinking and dancing: Peter Burke, *Popular Culture in Early Modern Europe*, Temple Smith, London, 1978, p. 51.

193 Julian of Norwich: Clifton Wolters, ed., *Julian of Norwich: Revelations of Divine Love*, Penguin Books, Harmondsworth, 1982, esp. pp. 33, 65, 101.

194 Prized relics in Italian churches: Michelin guidebooks still list these relics as high points of tourism.

194–5 Inward-looking spirit of Middle Ages: Johan Galtung et al. in *The New Cambridge Modern History*, vol. 13, Cambridge University Press, Cambridge, 1979, p. 343.

16 NEW MESSENGERS

197 "Learn to speak slow": cited in G.J. Holyoake, *Public Speaking and Debate*, E.W. Cole, Melbourne, n.d., p. 34.

197–8 Open-air audience in Philadelphia: Benjamin Franklin, *Autobiography and Other Writings*, Oxford University Press, Oxford, 1993, p. 111.

199 Strasbourg and Augsburg clocks: Carlo M. Cipolla, *Clocks and Culture, 1300–1700*, Collins, London, 1967, pp. 44, 53.

200 Paper mills at Fabriano: Jean Gimpel, *The Medieval Machine: The Industrial Revolution of the Middle Ages*, Futura, London, 1979, p. 27.

200–1 Gutenberg's press and type: equipment displays and reconstructions inspected at Deutsches Museum in Munich, June 1998.

201 Spread of printing to Cracow, etc.: Norman Davies, *Europe: A History*, Pimlico, London, 1997, p. 445.

201 Mainz bibles of 1453, 1455: inspected at Library of Congress, Washington D.C., in May 1977.

203 Ottoman expansion in Europe: J.H. Parry, *The Age of Reconnaissance*, Weidenfeld & Nicolson, London, 1963, pp. 23–7; Paul Coles, *The Ottoman Impact on Europe*, Thames & Hudson, London, 1968, ch. 1.

204 Italian cities and Turkish sultan: J.R. Hale, "International Relations in the West," in *New Cambridge Modern History*, op. cit., vol. 1, p. 265.

17 BIRDCAGE

208 Geneva painted: Gombrich, *The Story of Art*, op. cit., p. 161.

211 Ptolemy's error on width of seas: Samuel Eliot Morison, *The European Discovery of America*, vol. 1, Oxford University Press, New York, 1971–74, p. 7.

211–2 Columbus's voyage: *The Mariner's Mirror* held a fascinating discussion, partly in the review pages, from February 1992 to August 1993. The reference to China and Swatow is Feb. 1992, pp. 76–9.

214 Cortés and his horses in Mexico: Hugh Thomas, *The Conquest of Mexico*, Hutchinson, London, 1993, pp. 152–3.

216 Human sacrifices: ibid., pp. 24–7.

18 THE INCA AND THE ANDES

219 First coastal settlers: Claude Chauchat, "Early Hunter-Gatherers on the Peruvian Coast," in Keatinge, *Peruvian Prehistory*, op. cit., pp. 43, 59–60.

220 War widespread: John V. Murra in Leslie Bethell, ed., *The Cambridge History of Latin America*, vol. 1, Cambridge University Press, Cambridge, 1984, pp. 73, 75.

220–1 Size of Inca empire: G. Conrad in Jack W. Hopkins, ed., *Latin America: Perspectives on a Region*, Holmes & Meier, New York, 1987, p. 37.

221 Inca roads: Michael A. Malpass, *Daily Life in the Inca Empire*, Greenwood Press, Westport, Conn., 1996, pp. 68–9. For sandals, see p. 84.

221–2 Conscripting of ethnic groups: John V. Murra, "The Expansion of the Inka State," in John V. Murra, Nathan Wachtel & Jacques Revel, *Anthropological History of Andean Politics*, Cambridge University Press, New York, 1986, pp. 52–3.

223–4 Walls around coca crops: Patricia Netherly in Keatinge, *Peruvian Prehistory*, op. cit., pp. 270–2.

224 Moon and Incas: Irene Silverblatt, *Moon, Sun, and Witches: Gender Ideologies and Class in Inca and Colonial Peru*, Princeton University Press, Princeton, 1987, pp. 50–1.

225 Frozen Inca girl: *Yearbook of Science and the Future, 1998*, op. cit., pp. 244–5.

225 Alcohol to stupefy human sacrifices: Malpass, *Daily Life in the Inca Empire*, op. cit., p. 108.

225 Inca surgery and antiseptics: Kiple, ed., *Cambridge World History of Human Disease*, op. cit., pp. 307–8.

225 Blood groups in Italy and Peru: "Blood Transfusion," *Encyclopaedia Britannica* (1989), vol. 2, p. 292.

228–30 Spread of disease in Americas: McNeill, *Plagues and Peoples*, op. cit., ch. 5.

19 REFORMATION

232–3 Luther, as painted by Cranach: seen at Burghley House, Stamford, England, September 1997.

233-4 Printing boom in Germany 1500–24: A.G. Dickens, *The German Nation and Martin Luther*, Fontana, n.p., 1976, pp. 102–5, 110–13.

235 Christian names in Geneva: W.G. Naphy, "Baptisms, Church Riots and Social Unrest in Calvin's Geneva," *The Sixteenth Century Journal*, vol. 26, 1995, p. 89.

237 Preacher on the hilltop: Alistair Duke, Gillian Lewis & Andrew Pettegree, *Calvinism in Europe 1540–1610: A Collection of Documents*, Manchester University Press, Manchester, 1992, p. 145.

239 Anabaptist "strippers": Ernest A. Payne, "The Swiss Reformers and the Sects," *New Cambridge Modern History*, op. cit., vol. 2, p. 127.

240 Itinerant career of Ochino: *Dictionary of National Biography*, vol. 14, Oxford University Press, London, pp. 795–7.

241 Calvinists' attitude to music: Albert Dunning, "Calvin," in Stanley Sadie, ed., *The New Grove Dictionary of Music and Musicians*, vol. 3, Macmillan, London, 1995, pp. 630–1.

241 Bach's cantatas: ibid., vol. 1, p. 805.

243 Swedish bells: N.K. Andersen, "The Reformation in Scandinavia and the Baltic," *New Cambridge Modern History*, op. cit., vol. 2, p. 147.

244 Female literacy in Europe: Olwen Hufton, *The Prospect Before Her: A History of Women in Western Europe*, vol. 1, Fontana, London, 1997, pp. 417, 424.

244 Literacy in Norwich: Hilda L. Smith, *Reason's Disciples*, University of Illinois Press, Urbana, 1982, p. 25.

245 Literacy and the Bible in Russia: Geoffrey Hosking, *Russia: People and Empire 1552–1917*, Harvard University Press, Cambridge, Mass., 1997, pp. 139–42, 231–4.

246 Witches, accusers and neighbors: Robin Briggs, *Witches & Neighbors: The Social and Cultural Context of European Witchcraft*, Fontana, London, 1997, passim.

247 Witches in areas of religious rivalry: Hufton, *The Prospect Before Her*, op. cit., vol. 1, p. 340.

20 VOYAGE TO INDIA

248ff. Voyages of Portuguese to India and Japan: C.R. Boxer, *Fidalgos in the Far East, 1550–1770*, Oxford University Press, Hong Kong, 1968, ch. 2.

249 Milton on the sea route: John Milton, *Paradise Lost*, Book 4, lines 159–63.

252-3 Protestants slow to be missionaries: Alec R. Vidler, *The Church in an Age of Revolution: 1789 to the Present Day*, Penguin, Harmondsworth, 1961, pp. 248–9.

254 Internal rivalry in Indonesian islands: Simkin, *The Traditional Trade of Asia*, op. cit., pp. 225ff.

256 Zanzibar and the Sultan of Oman: Gerald S. Graham, *Great Britain in the Indian Ocean: A Study of Maritime Enterprise, 1810–1850*, Clarendon Press, Oxford, 1967, pp. 174–6.

256 Ottoman victories: Bernard Lewis, "Some Reflections on the Decline of the Ottoman Empire," in Carlo M. Cipolla, ed., *The Economic Decline of Empires*, Methuen, London, 1970, pp. 218–21.

21 THE NEW WORLD BEARS GIFTS

258 Maize and potato: G.B. Masefield, "Crops and Livestock," *Cambridge Economic History of Europe*, op. cit., vol. 4, pp. 276–8.

259 Turkey, turkey cock, turkey corn and Turk's cap (tulip): see entries in C.T.

Onions, ed., *The Shorter Oxford English Dictionary on Historical Principles*, 3rd edn, Clarendon Press, Oxford, 1956.

260 Nose gnawed by syphilis: Hufton, *The Prospect Before Her*, op. cit., vol. 1, p. 11.

260 Spread of syphilis: Bruce M. Rothschild & Christine Rothschild, "Trepanemal Disease in the New World," *Current Anthropology*, vol. 37, 1996, pp. 555ff.

262–3 Scarlet and indigo: A. Rupert Hall, "Scientific Method and the Progress of Techniques," in *Cambridge Economic History of Europe*, op. cit., vol. 4, p. 132.

263 Harvesting indigo: Robert Hunt, ed., *Ure's Dictionary of Arts, Manufactures and Mines*, vol. 2, Longman, London, 1861, pp. 498ff.

263 French army wears blue: François Boucher, *20,000 Years of Fashion: The History of Costume and Personal Adornment*, Abrams, New York, n.d., p. 283.

264 Brazilwood and ox gall: *Ure's Dictionary of Arts*, op. cit., vol. 1, pp. 397–400.

264 French settlement in Rio: H.B. Johnson, "The Portuguese Settlement of Brazil, 1500–1580," in *Cambridge History of Latin America*, op. cit., vol. 2, p. 276.

264 Musk and its merchandising: *Ure's Dictionary of Arts*, vol. 3, p. 211.

265 Quinine or Jesuit's bark: Albert S. Lyons & Joseph R. Petrucelli II, *Medicine: An Illustrated History*, Abrams, New York, 1978, p. 454.

265 Cloves and pepper: Braudel, *The Mediterranean*, op. cit., vol. 1, pp. 547ff.; E.E. Rich, "Colonial Settlement and its Labour Problems," *Cambridge Economic History of Europe*, op. cit., vol. 4, pp. 367–72.

22 THE GLASS EYE OF SCIENCE

269 Discoveries of the 1540s: Neville Williams, *Chronology of the Expanding World: 1492–1762*, Barrie & Rockliff, London, 1969, pp. 103–21.

270 Dissecting room and fallopian tubes: Gerald Messadié, *The Wordsworth Dictionary of Inventions*, Wordsworth, Ware, 1995, pp. 178–9.

271 Newton's eyes and teeth: *Dictionary of National Biography*, op. cit., vol. 14, p. 392.

271–2 Science is more than "applied common sense": Professor Sir Hans Kornberg, "The Unnatural Nature of Natural Knowledge," guest lecture at La Trobe University, 10 July 1997.

272 New instruments: Silvio A. Bedini & Derek J. de Solla Price in M. Kranzberg, *Technology in Western Civilization*, op. cit., vol. 1, pp. 168ff.

272–3 Manufacture of glass: visits to glass collections in Deutsches Museum, Munich.

273 Venetian breeches: Edward H. Sugden, *A Topographical Dictionary to the Works of Shakespeare and His Fellow Dramatists*, Manchester University Press, Manchester, 1925, p. 543, col. 2.

273 Galileo and his telescope: J. Bronowski, *The Ascent of Man*, British Broadcasting Corporation, London, 1973, pp. 204–6.

275 Slow adoption of new calendar: *Encyclopaedia Britannica*, 11th edn, 1910–11, p. 999.

275–6 Chaos in "miles": George Landmann, *A Universal Gazetteer*, Longman et al., London, 1840, pp. iii–iv.

277 Transit of Venus: G.M. Badger, ed., *Captain Cook, Navigator and Scientist*, ANU Press, Canberra, 1970, esp. chapters 3 and 7.

278 Cook and sailors' jackets: Beaglehole, ed., *The Journals of Captain James Cook*, op. cit., vol. 2, pp. 61–4.

279   Cook and scurvy: Francis E. Cuppage, *James Cook and the Conquest of Scurvy*, Greenwood Press, Westport, Conn., 1994, passim.

23 DETHRONING THE HARVEST

282   Meals for farm laborers: Alice Clark, *Working Life of Women in the Seventeenth Century*, Routledge, London, 1982, p. 61.

282   Bread and gruel: Fernand Braudel, *Capitalism and Material Life, 1400–1800*, Harper & Row, New York, 1974, pp. 93–4.

282   "Nine grits and a gallon of water": *The Oxford Dictionary of English Proverbs*, 3rd edn, Clarendon Press, Oxford, 1970, p. 331.

283   Opinion of cats: "Felis," *Encylopaedia Britannica*, 1st edn, Edinburgh, 1771, p. 586; E.L. McAdam Jr & George Milne, eds, *Johnson's Dictionary: A Modern Selection*, Pantheon Books, New York, 1963, p. 114.

284   Salt traffic booms: Robert Henri Bautier, *The Economic Development of Medieval Europe*, Thames & Hudson, London, 1971, pp. 218–20.

286   Advance of Alpine glaciers: Ladurie, *Times of Feast, Times of Famine*, op. cit., esp. pp. 147, 171–3.

287–8   Linen: J.R. McCulloch, *A Dictionary, Practical, Theoretical, and Historical, of Commerce and Commercial Navigation*, Longman, London, 1854, pp. 817ff.

288   The bleaching fields of Haarlem, c. 1651: Albert Blankert, *Rembrandt: A Genius and His Impact*, National Gallery of Victoria, Melbourne, 1997, pp. 364–5.

288   The intricate process of bleaching: *Encylopaedia Britannica*, 1st edn, vol. 1, op. cit., pp. 561–7.

288   Children scavenge wool: Clark, *Working Life of Women*, op. cit., p. 66.

288   Cotton in China: Elvin, *The Pattern of the Chinese Past*, op. cit., pp. 212–14.

289   Second-hand clothes: Hufton, *The Prospect Before Her*, op. cit., vol. 1, pp. 169ff.

289   Johnson on Scottish isle: James Boswell, *The Journal of a Tour to the Hebrides with Samuel Johnson*, Everyman, London, 1948, pp. 234–54.

291   Agricola on mining fuel: Georgius Agricola, *De Re Metallica*, Dover, New York, 1950, p. 31.

292–3   Cities and farms: R.M. Hartwell, "Economic Change in England and Europe 1780–1830," in *New Cambridge Modern History*, op. cit., vol. 9, pp. 31–2.

292   Rice versus wheat: Paul Bairoch, in Ad van der Woude, Akira Hayami & Jan de Vries, *Urbanization in History: A Process of Dynamic Interactions*, Clarendon Press, Oxford, 1990, ch. 9.

293   Holland and peat: van der Woude et al., ibid., pp. 8–11.

293   Oil wells in Burma: John Crawfurd, *Journal of an Embassy from the Governor General of India to the Court of Ava*, 2nd edn, vol. 1, Colburn, London, 1834, pp. 95–8.

24 THE FALL OF A PACK OF CARDS

300   Colonists' taxes: R.R. Palmer in *New Cambridge Modern History*, op. cit., vol. 8, p. 438.

302   British prefer Gibraltar to Florida: D.W. Meinig, *The Shaping of America: A Geographical Perspective on 500 Years of History*, vol. 1, Yale University Press, New Haven, 1986, p. 333.

304   French priests deported: William B. Cohen, *The French Encounter with Africans: White Response to Blacks, 1530–1880*, Indiana University Press, Bloomington, 1980, p. 170.

305 Economic growth of the United States after 1760: Paul Kennedy, *The Rise and Fall of the Great Powers: Economic Change and Military Conflict from 1500 to 2000*, Random House, New York, 1989, pp. 93–4.
306 Proclamation Line: Meinig, *The Shaping of America*, op. cit., vol. 1, pp. 284–7.
307 Haiti: *The Annual Register . . . for the Year 1811*, London, 1812, p. 164.
307 Slavery in Brazil: Leslie Bethell, "The Decline and Fall of Slavery in Nineteenth Century Brazil," *Transactions of the Royal Historical Society*, 6th series, 1991, pp. 73–5.
310 Das Voltas Bay: Alan Frost, *Convicts and Empire: A Naval Question, 1776–1811*, Oxford University Press, Melbourne, 1980, pp. 33, 115.
310–1 Norfolk Island: Geoffrey Blainey, *The Tyranny of Distance: How Distance Shaped Australian History*, Macmillan, Melbourne, 1983, pp. 29–34.
312 Ghosts of Aborigines: Geoffrey Blainey, *A Land Half Won*, Macmillan, South Melbourne, 1980, pp. 64–7.

25 BEYOND THE SAHARA

315 Dürer in Venice: Eberhard Ruhmer, "Dürer," in *Encyclopaedia Britannica*, vol. 4, 1989, p. 290.
316 Excitement to see a white man: letter by A.G. Laing, 3 Dec. 1825, in E.W. Bovill, ed., *Missions to the Niger*, vol. 1, Hakluyt Society, Cambridge, 1964, p. 276.
316 Timbuktu the "far-famed capital": Bovill, ibid., vol. 1, p. 168.
316 Virgins to Marrakesh: ibid., vol. 1, p. 170.
317 Rivers of Africa: Thomas Sowell, *Conquests and Cultures: An International History*, Basic Books, New York, 1998, pp. 102–4.
317–8 Tsetse fly: J.D.M. Mhlanga, "Sleeping Sickness," in *Science Progress*, vol. 79, part 1, 1996, pp. 185–6.
318 West African metallurgy: E.J. Alagoa, "African Bronze or Brass Sculpture," in G.M.D. Howat, ed., *Dictionary of World History*, Nelson, London, 1973, p. 22.
319 Slavery in ancient China: Fernand Braudel, *A History of Civilizations*, Allen Lane, London, 1994, pp. 193–4.
321 Slave ships: P.E.H. Hair, "The Experience of the Sixteenth-Century English Voyages to Guinea," *The Mariner's Mirror*, vol. 83, 1997, pp. 3–13.
321 Runaway slaves in the Americas: Eugene D. Genovese, *Roll, Jordan, Roll: The World the Slaves Made*, Andre Deutsch, London, 1975, pp. 650–2. See pp. 525–7 for housing.
321–2 Regions of African slaves in Brazil: Braudel, *A History of Civilizations*, op. cit., map p. 430.
322 Millions of African slaves: Sowell, *Conquests and Cultures*, op. cit., p. 111.

26 NOBLE STEAM

323 Barbarous and "ungrateful" tribes: *The Annual Register . . . for the Year 1800*, London, 1801, p. 222.
324 Swiss travellers' guidebook: John Murray, publisher, *Handbook for Travellers in Switzerland*, 1838, Leicester University Press, Leicester, 1970. See p. 158 for road across Simplon Pass.
325 Spa of Carlsbad, now in Czech Republic: information gleaned at Carlsbad in August 1994.

325 American visits Yorkshire mill: Joseph Ballard, *England in 1815*, reprinted in Henry Steele Commager, ed., *Britain Through American Eyes*, McGraw-Hill, New York, 1974, pp. 100–1.

326 Wordsworth in London: the poem was composed not on 3 September, as the title claims, but on 31 July 1802, which was close to midsummer. Thomas Hutchinson, ed., *The Poems of Wordsworth with Introduction and Notes*, Oxford University Press, London, 1926, p. 269.

326 Early steam engines: William Pryce, *Mineralogia Cornubiensis: A Treatise on Minerals, Mines, and Mining*, J. Phillips, London, 1778, esp. pp. 153–4.

326–7 Evolution of steam engine: David S. Landes, "What Room for Accident in History?" *Economic History Review*, vol. 47, 1994, pp. 649, 651.

329 Thackeray on railways: "Roundabout Papers," quoted in Mario Praz, *The Hero in Eclipse in Victorian Fiction*, Oxford University Press, London, 1969, p. 240.

330 Dickens crosses Atlantic: Edgar Johnson, *Charles Dickens: His Tragedy and Triumph*, vol. 1, Victor Gollancz, London, 1953, pp. 362–3.

330–1 Jules Verne: possibly influenced by G.F. Train, who in 1870 almost rounded the world in 80 days; Stephen Kern, *The Culture of Time and Space 1880–1918*, Weidenfeld, London, 1983, p. 212.

334 Maine–Texas telegraph: Henry David Thoreau, *Walden*, Peebles Press, New York, n.d., p. 45.

335–6 Fewer workers in agriculture: R.M. Hartwell in *New Cambridge Modern History*, op. cit., vol. 9, pp. 31–2.

336 Europe's fast population growth from 1750: Julian L. Simon, "Demographic Causes and Consequences of the Industrial Revolution," *Journal of European Economic History*, vol. 23, Spring 1994, pp. 142–5.

337 Crowded houses in Vienna and Breslau: Arthur Shadwell, "Housing," *Encyclopaedia Britannica*, 11th edn, 1910, pp. 824–5.

337–8 Hygiene and water: Hufton, *The Prospect Before Her*, op. cit., vol. 1, pp. 13, 80–1, 172.

338 Malaria: S.R. Christophers, "Sir Robert Ross," in L.G. Wickham Legg, ed., *Dictionary of National Biography, 1931–1940*, Oxford University Press, Oxford, pp. 752–3.

338–9 Composer and cholera: Alexander Poznansky, *Tchaikovsky: The Quest for the Inner Man*, Lime Tree, London, 1993, pp. 575ff.

27 WILL ALL BE EQUAL?

340ff. Lincoln and slavery: David Herbert Donald, *Lincoln*, Simon & Schuster, New York, 1995, passim.

343 Lincoln's words at Gettysburg: reprinted in Safire, *Lend Me Your Ears*, op. cit., pp. 49–51.

344 End of Brazilian slavery: Bethell, "The Decline and Fall of Slavery in Nineteenth Century Brazil," op. cit., esp. pp. 71–6, 87–8.

345 Origins of Taiping Rebellion: Immanuel C.Y. Hsu, *The Rise of Modern China*, Oxford University Press, New York, 1995, esp. pp. 221–9; Braudel, *A History of Civilizations*, op. cit., p. 202.

345 Taiping female soldiers: Hsu, *The Rise of Modern China*, ibid., p. 236.

346 Porcelain tower known in English nurseries: "Chronicle," *The Annual Register . . . for the Year 1857*, London, 1858, p. 23.

346–7 Equality in Greek and Roman empires: Henry Phelps Brown, *Egalitarianism and the Generation of Inequality*, Clarendon Press, Oxford, 1988, pp. 24–5, 259–60.

347–8 Marx and Engels on technology: Geoffrey Blainey, *The Great Seesaw: A New View of the Western World, 1750–2000*, Macmillan, South Melbourne, 1988, pp. 41–2; Frank E. Manuel & Fritzie P. Manuel, *Utopian Thought in the Western World*, Belknap Press, Cambridge, Mass., 1979, pp. 715–16.

349 Pioneer female voters in the USA: Richard J. Evans, *The Feminists: Women's Emancipation Movements in Europe, America and Australasia, 1840–1920*, Croom Helm, London, 1977, p. 214.

349–50 Dr Elizabeth Blackwell: Edward T. James, ed., *Notable American Women 1607–1950: A Biographical Dictionary*, vol. 1, Belknap Press, Cambridge, Mass., 1971, pp. 165ff.

350 Career of Marie Curie: Adrienne R. Weill, "Curie," in Charles Coulston Gillispie, ed., *Dictionary of Scientific Biography*, vol. 3, Scribner, New York, 1970.

350–1 Frugal way of life in York: Runciman, *A Treatise on Social Theory*, op. cit., vol. 3, pp. 46–51.

353–4 Geography of Jews in Europe: *New Cambridge Modern History*, op. cit., vol. 14 (Atlas), p. 187.

354 Anti-Semitism after 1873 crash: Fritz Stern, *The Failure of Illiberalism: Essays on the Political Culture of Modern Germany*, University of Chicago Press, Chicago, 1975, pp. 45–6.

354–5 Marriage of Hannah de Rothschild: Robert Rhodes James, *Rosebery*, Phoenix, London, 1995, pp. 79–83.

28 A GLOBE UNWRAPPED

357 Wallace the collector: H.W.C. Davis & J.R.H. Weaver, eds., *Dictionary of National Biography 1912–1921*, Oxford University Press, London, 1927, p. 546.

358 Atlantic "telegraph plateau": M.F. Maury, *The Physical Geography of the Sea*, Sampson Low, London, 1856, p. 253.

359 "Supernatural" terraces at Rotorua, New Zealand: James Anthony Froude, *Oceana, or, England and Her Colonies*, Longmans, Green, London, 1886, ch. 16 and esp. p. 291.

360 Samoan "boatman sings": Robert Louis Stevenson, *A Footnote to History: Eight Years of Trouble in Samoa*, Cassell, London, 1892, p. 11.

360 Filming Aboriginal dance: Baldwin Spencer & F.J. Gillen, *Across Australia*, Macmillan, London, 1912, pp. 218–20; D.J. Mulvaney & J.H. Calaby, *So Much That Is New: Baldwin Spencer, 1860–1929*, Melbourne University Press, Carlton, 1985, pp. 197–9.

364 Flow of ideas from Africa and Asia: Blainey, *The Great Seesaw*, op. cit., ch. 6.

367 Trains and Mecca pilgrims: T.E. Lawrence, intro. to Charles M. Doughty, *Travels in Arabia Deserta*, Jonathan Cape, London, 1926, p. xxv.

29 THE WORLD WARS

An expanded version of the interpretation of these two wars is scattered through Geoffrey Blainey, *The Causes of War*, Macmillan, London, 1973, 1976, 1988.

373 Rise of air power: Geoffrey Blainey, "Power in the Air," in Alan Stephens, ed., *Smaller but Larger: Conventional Air Power into the 21st Century*, AGPS, Canberra, 1991, pp. 165–7.

377–8 Hitler as orator: John Toland, *Adolf Hitler*, Doubleday, Garden City, N.Y., 1976, pp. 130, 218.

378 Hitler's power: ibid.; Alan Bullock, *Hitler: A Study in Tyranny*, Penguin, Harmondsworth, 1962; Michael Howard, *Studies in War and Peace*, Temple Smith, London, 1970, pp. 110–21.

379 Rise of Stalin: Roy A. Medvedev, *Let History Judge: The Origins and Consequences of Stalinism*, Macmillan, London, 1972, esp. ch. 1.

380 Stalin and Hitler as outsiders: lecture by Sir Alan Bullock, Boston University Conversazione, 8 May 1997.

382 Harshness of the Versailles treaty: a compromise view is Robert Skidelsky, John Maynard Keynes, vol. 1, Macmillan, London, 1983, p. 398 ("Too harsh to conciliate, it was not harsh enough to secure compliance").

30 THE BOMB AND THE MOON

385 First atomic bombs: Margaret Gowing, *Britain and Atomic Energy 1936–1945*, Macmillan, London, 1964, passim; Sir John Wheeler-Bennett & Anthony Nicholls, *The Semblance of Peace: The Political Settlement After the Second World War*, Macmillan, London, 1972, pp. 384–90.

385 Japanese Kamikaze planes: Samuel Eliot Morison, *History of United States Naval Operations in World War II*, vol. 14, Little, Brown, Boston, 1960, p. 352.

388 Surrender in Tokyo, 1945: ibid., vol. 14, pp. 362–9.

392 Young Gandhi in London and Natal: Francis Wylie, "Gandhi," in L.G. Wickham Legg & E.T. Williams, eds., *Dictionary of National Biography, 1941–1950*, Oxford University Press, London, 1959, pp. 282–3.

396 Fewer universities in Africa than Ohio: Emmanuel A. Ayandele, "Africa: The Challenge of Higher Education" in "Black Africa: A Generation after Independence," *Daedalus*, Spring 1982, p. 168.

398 Resources of outer space: *Pioneering the Space Frontier: Report of the National Commission on Space*, Bantam, New York, c. 1986.

399 French words in American English: C.J. Kay & Lee Pederson in *Encarta World English Dictionary*, Pan Macmillan, Sydney, 1999, p. xxvi.

31 NO FRUITS, NO BIRDS

403 Byzantine calendar and seasons: Margaret M. Manion & Vera F. Vines, *Medieval and Renaissance Illuminated Manuscripts in Australian Collections*, Thames & Hudson, Melbourne, 1984, pp. 24ff. See also p. 188 for French manuscripts.

403 French prayer book depicting pigs: Margaret Manion, ed., *The Wharncliffe Hours: A Fifteenth-Century Illuminated Prayerbook in the Collection of the National Gallery of Victoria, Australia*, Thames & Hudson, London, 1981, pp. 44–7.

403 Borneo's rice birds: John Mackinnon & Karen Phillips, *A Field Guide to the Birds of Borneo, Sumatra, Java, and Bali*, Oxford University Press, New York, 1993, pp. 13, 36, 366.

403 Months when European wars begin: Blainey, *The Causes of War*, op. cit., pp. 97–101.

404 Season for war in China: C.P. FitzGerald, *Why China? Recollections of China, 1923–1950*, Melbourne University Press, Carlton, 1985, pp. 56–7.

404 Exodus of German pilgrims: Braudel, *The Mediterranean*, op. cit., vol. 1, p. 264.

404 May Day: Charles Pythian-Adams, "Milk and Soot," in Derek Fraser & Anthony Sutcliffe, eds., *The Pursuit of Urban History*, Edward Arnold, London, 1983, esp. pp. 84–9.

405 Chinese peony: Needham, *Science and Civilisation in China*, op. cit., vol. 6, part 1, pp. 395–402.

406 Midnight and Christ's expected return: information from Professor Eric Osborn, Professorial Fellow, University of Melbourne.

409 Multitude of stars: Sir James Jeans, reprinted in A. Norman Jeffares & M. Bryn Davies, eds., *The Scientific Background: A Prose Anthology*, Pitman, London, 1958, p. 164.

410–1 Rise of spectator sport: Geoffrey Blainey, "Heroes of the Arena," in Claudio Véliz, ed., *Monuments for an Age without Heroes*, Boston University Professors, 1996, pp. 78–80; Véliz, *The New World of the Gothic Fox*, op. cit., ch. 7; and books by Raymond Flower including *Motor Sports: A Pictorial History*, Collins, Glasgow, 1975; and *The Story of Skiing and Other Winter Sports*, Angus & Robertson, London, 1976.

411 Big cities multiply in Third World: calculated from *Britannica Book of the Year, 1996*, Encyclopaedia Britannica, Chicago, 1997, p. 279.

412 Natural disasters in China: E.L. Jones, *The European Miracle: Environments, Economies, and Geopolitics in the History of Europe and Asia*, Cambridge University Press, Cambridge, 1981, p. 28.

413–4 Religion in decline: Peter L. Berger, "The Decline of Secularism," *The National Interest*, Winter 1996–97, pp. 3ff.

INDEX

Abacuses, 183
Abyssinia, 141
Achin, 254
Acorns, 28
Acropolis, 74, 75
Adelaide, 332
Aegina, 75
Aeschines, 78
Afghanistan, 399
Africa: barriers to outside powers, 314–318; climate changes following the glacial era, 19; contemporary economic conditions, 396; diversity of languages in, 317; early agricultural methods, 35–36; European colonial empires and, 363; gold and, 316; hominids in, 3–4; independence movements and independent nations, 391, 396; influence of Asia on, 318–319; influence on European civilization, 364; Islam and, 148–149; metallurgy in, 318; millet and, 284; modern missionaries in, 362; population growth, 396; Portuguese explorations, 209; pottery of, 42; religions in the twentieth century, 414; rivers of, 316–317; Roman colonization, 314; Sahara Desert, 19, 314–316; slavery within, 320; tsetse fly and sleeping sickness, 317–318. *See also* East Africa; Egypt; North Africa; South Africa; West Africa.
African-Americans, 244, 321, 322

African slavery and slave trade, 149, 209, 319, 320–322, 340
Agathocles, 79
Agra, 253
Agricola, Georgius, 269, 291
Agriculture: in the Americas, 41; of the Aztecs, 217; cats and, 283; in China, 94, 182, 284; decline in workforce needed to produce food, 335–336; in early Japan, 28, 29; early tools and methods, 35–36; global interchange of plants and animals, 258–260, 261, 263, 266–267; grain harvests, 36, 282–283; grain yields, 283–284; in Greece, 34, 36; Incan, 226–227; Indus civilization, 66; of the Maoris, 165–166; in Mesopotamia, 59; in New Guinea, 40–41; origins in the Middle East, 31–34; population growth and, 37, 287; radiation out of the Middle East, 34–35; Roman, 106; seasonality and, 403; Soviet collectivization, 379; steam engines and, 336; use of sewage as fertilizer, 285–286. *See also* Cereal grains; Farming societies; Gardens; Livestock; Maize; Rice cultivation; Rural life.
Air raids, 386
Airak, 176
Aircraft, 373
Alabaster, 104
Alaska, 23, 24, 308, 363
Albania, 375, 390

Nationalism, 243, 352
Native Americans: Dakotas, 188–189;
  Louisiana Purchase and, 305–306
Natural law, 346
Natural resources: Third World and, 394
Nature: contemporary views of, 412
Nature-poets: Chinese, 152
Nautilus (ship), 310
Navigators (European), 206, 207; Vasco da
  Gama, 212–213; voyages to reach Asia,
  209. *See also* Columbus, Christopher;
  Exploration.
Nazareth, 119
Nazca people, 219–220
Neanderthals, 9
Neapolitan disease, 260
Nero Claudius, 127
Nestorianism, 150
Netherlands: American colonies, 257–258;
  colonial empire in Asia, 254–255; grain
  yields, 283; Indonesia and, 265, 279,
  393–394; literacy and, 244; peat bogs
  and, 293; Protestant Reformation and,
  239, 244; Second World War, 390; trade
  with India, 254; trade with Japan, 255
New Babylonian empire, 116
New Britain, 14
New Caledonia, 161, 363
New Guinea: cannibalism and, 41;
  development of human culture in, 23;
  early agriculture in, 40–41; Germany
  and, 363; human migrations and, 13–15,
  161; rising of the seas and, 22, 23
New Ireland, 14
New Kingdom (Egypt), 58
New Orleans, 302
New Testament, 130
New York, 258
New York City, 301, 337
New Zealand: British control of, 309;
  James Cook and, 279; democracy and,
  349; First World War, 372; migrations
  of Polynesian peoples and, 161;
  telegraph lines and, 332; travelers to,
  359; welfare state and, 350; wool and,
  288. *See also* Maoris.
New Zealand eagles, 166
Newcomen, Thomas, 327
Newcomen-Savery steam engine, 327
Newfoundland, 187–188, 257
Newman, John Henry, 69
Newspapers: steam printing presses, 329
Newton, Sir Isaac, 270–271, 384
Niagara Falls, 24
Nicomedia, 132–133
Niger River, 316

Nigeria, 42, 318, 396
Night and day: blurring of, 406–408
Night sky: decline in significance of,
  408–409; religions and, 48–49, 51–52;
  significance in ancient world, 46–49. *See
  also* Astronomy.
Nightwatchmen, 406
Nile River, 316, 317; changes following the
  glacial era, 19; early evidence of
  agriculture, 34; early sails, 71; Egyptian
  civilization and, 55
Nineveh, 50, 62, 64–65
Nirvana, 98–99
Noah's Ark, 276–277
Nomadic societies: dispossession in the
  modern world, 360–361; fear of storms
  and meteorological events, 45–46; health
  and, 37; night sky and, 46, 47, 51; power
  in, 38. *See also* Hunters and hunting.
Norfolk Island, 310–311
North Africa: climate changes following
  the glacial era, 19; early presence of
  agriculture in, 35; marble and, 104;
  Roman control of, 102
North America: climate change and,
  188–189; early European colonization,
  257–258; first human inhabitants, 23–24;
  glacial era, 16–17; impact of
  Protestantism on, 243–244; land bridge
  to Siberia, 23, 24; melting of the
  glaciers, 24–25; Viking settlers, 187–188.
  See also American colonies; Canada;
  United States.
North Korea, 397
North Sea, 190, 362
"North-west" passage, 279
Northwestern Europe: ascent of, 367,
  368–369
Norway, 189–190, 191
Norwich, 244
Nova Scotia, 300
Novgorod, 186
Nubia, 148
Nuclear weapons: in Asian countries, 397;
  atomic bomb, 384–386, 388; hydrogen
  bomb, 389–390
Numeral systems: Babylonian, 60
Nuremberg, 240, 273

Oats, 284
Ocean levels: during the glacial era, 17–18;
  rising of, 18–19, 22–23, 24, 25, 26, 29
Oceans: empire building and, 180–181;
  scientific studies, 357–358
Ochino, Bernardino, 239, 240
Odessa, 354

A NOTE ON THE AUTHOR

Geoffrey Blainey, one of Australia's most prominent historians, held a chair at Harvard University in the early 1980s and taught for many years at the University of Melbourne. He is the recipient of Australia's highest honor, Companion in the Order of Australia. *A Short History of the World* was judged by the Fellowship of Australian Writers in 2000 as the best book of the year. Mr. Blainey lives near Melbourne.